In Paris We

Chris say
men are
more fiddles
customers because
are less patient
as customers. Long
hair means get out
less offe. Shirt
hair no diffe. And in
the 90s men wore it
period & shaved heads, men's
came it at all 'OK' so come
because to

Accout less
diverted to
career, have
well -
more. But
that her style as
well.

She came into
the West End
was different was
fixed in a shop

back.
stay in work as a mobile.
Dealer Austr. all lower

Further that ...
don't care give
(need) to set up
shop because
can earn good) so
way (already) so
don't need it.

Adolp 14,   1c.
                2.10
                3.00
                3.45

In Paris We Sang

A Memoir

Rose Cannan

Ashgrove Publishing
London

This book is dedicated to my parents

Contents

Prologue

In July 1939, I came to England from Germany with the now much celebrated *Kindertransport*. I was seventeen years old and couldn't speak one word of English. With Hitler's Germany behind me, I was in two minds about being Jewish; living in Germany had split me in half. Eight weeks after my arrival, England was at war with Germany. Speaking the enemy's language was uncomfortable and I stopped speaking German altogether. I avoided meeting other Jewish refugees who flocked to their meeting place, the Cosmo Café in Golders Green, London. Most of them seemed not to have left Germany; the air was thick with accented English mixed with German. At home we spoke Yiddish, but the need to speak English became paramount.

I can't remember what language my dreams were in, although, significantly, a memorable one is where my jaw was stuck with my mouth wide open in a long, silent yawn; I was struck dumb, unable to speak in any language.

New language, old questions: to eat kosher, or not; to cook milk and meat dishes separately, or not; and, on a more spiritual level, to go to synagogue, or not; to fast or not on Yom Kippur. The strongest memories I had at that time were of graffiti on the walls in Ludwigshafen, my hometown, and of my personal brushes with a Gestapo official. All Nazi experiences, I stored in layers of negative thinking. From time to time, a layer flashed to the surface, and being afraid of what I was, I denied its power.

But the past caught up with me. Forty years later, I met my neighbour Mrs Boxer on the front steps of our flats behind Baker Street in London. She was dressed in shocking pink with a hat to match, its brim stiff and up-turned like a sail. 'Going to a wedding?' I asked. Reproachfully, she said, 'No, I've just come from the synagogue, it's Yom Kippur!' It was mid-day and I was on my way to the supermarket across the road. I had been 'married out' for fifteen years and had blinded myself to anything Jewish. On this, the holiest day in the Jewish calendar, I went shopping for food – probably, among other things, bacon. Like Bloom senior in *Ulysses* pricking the conscience of his son Leopold, Mrs Boxer certainly pricked mine: I too was hiding the metaphorical pigs' trotters behind my back. I was surprised by guilt. It was like a punch in the face. Eating bacon wouldn't kill me, but staying ignorant of why the Jews were hated, would.

On Sunday mornings, when sewing or cooking, I listened to church sermons on the radio. Nothing seemed to disturb my peace, except for hymns and choral music – apparently the key to my soul, as far as I knew what a soul was. Surprisingly, on the rare occasions I heard it on the radio, I was ambushed by the cry of *Kol Nidre*, usually sung at the start of Yom Kippur Eve. An altogether different commotion began in my throat, tears welled up in my eyes, and I saw a prayer-room full of men, the cantor lamenting his way through the cry to his God, taking the congregation along with him to admit their wrong-doing, and to atone. I was eleven years old at the time and sitting with my mother in the women's section.

Listening to church sermons became a habit – so, like some undercover detective, I hoped to solve the crime perpetrated against us. Who, I wanted to know, was this man on the cross that the Jews denied and Christians called 'Our Lord?'

On another Sunday, my foot froze on the pedal of my sewing machine during a sermon in which Jews were portrayed as the most obdurate of people, the moral lesson put over with such ease, I remember thinking: 'They are talking about us as though we no longer existed.' I began to read, mostly pre-war discourses written by Christian theologians elaborating that Jews had thought of nothing new, that Judaism was a fossil, and that Jesus had made the ultimate sacrifice. *The Treatise on the Gods*, written by the illustrious American journalist H.L. Mencken, is a potent reminder of how the Jews were esteemed and hated simultaneously. He says:

But in one respect at least, Christianity is vastly superior to every other religion in being today, and indeed, to all we have any record of in the past: it is full of lush and lovely poetry. The Bible is unquestionably the most beautiful book in the world. Allow everything you please for the barbaric history in the Old Testament and the decadent Little Bethel theology in the New, and there remains a series of poems so overwhelmingly voluptuous and disarming that no other literature, old or new, can offer a match for it. Nearly all comes from the Jews, and their making of it constitutes one of the most outstanding phenomena in human history. For there is little in their character as the modern world knows them to suggest a talent for noble thinking.

Even Renan, who was friendly with them, once sneered at '*sémitiques*' as '*sans étendue, sans diversité*, and *sans philosophie*.' One might go still further. The Jews could be put down very plausibly as the most unpleasant race ever heard of. As commonly encountered, they lack many qualities that mark the civilised man: courage, dignity, incorruptibility, ease and confidence. They have vanity without pride, voluptuousness without taste, and learning without wisdom. Their fortitude, such as it is, is wasted upon puerile object, and their charity is only a form of display. Yet, these same Jews, from time immemorial, have been the chief dreamers of the human Race, beyond comparison its greatest poets. It was Jews who wrote the magnificent *Psalms*, the Song of Solomon, and the books of *Ruth* and *Job*; it was Jews who gave us the Beatitudes, the Sermon on the Mount, the incomparable Christ Child, and the twelfth chapter of *Romans*. I incline to believe that the scene recounted in *John viii, 3-11*, is the most poignant drama ever written in the world, as the Song of Solomon unquestionably is the most moving love song, and the twenty-third *Psalm* the greatest of hymns. All these transcendent riches Christianity inherits from the little tribe of sedentary Bedouins, so obscure and unimportant that secular history scarcely knows them. No heritage of modern man is richer and none has made a more brilliant mark upon human thought, not even the Greeks.

As I read this, my heart pounded, the way it might if I were told that I had only weeks to live. I read it again and again and each time I found new ways of saying the same thing. The paper in the margins wore thin with all my different versions having been rubbed out. My relationship with this piece deepened until one day I rubbed out what I had written for the last time, ashamed that whoever might read this book after me would wonder about my sanity. But what did stay in my mind was the devastating thought of how well the way to the Holocaust had been prepared.

PART ONE

Chapter One

In Germany – A Dream Come True

In 1919, my parents scrambled illegally from Poland into Germany – a country that had just lost the war, was humiliated by defeat, and whose economy was in turmoil with hyper-inflation hard on its heels They couldn't have chosen a more turbulent time to better their lives. Their destination was Worms on the Rhine, where Jews had lived since the 10th century and where three of my mother's siblings had already lived since before World War I: Lotte, Chaskel and Adolph in Worms, and Pessa in Ludwighafen, also on the Rhine. In the beginning, my parents' existence in Germany was not that different from how they had lived in Lodz. Their hope was that life would be better in Germany which was considered to be more civilised than Poland with its endemic anti-Semitism.

I was born in 1922, in an attic in 7 Kieffhaüser Straße in Worms. My food ration card doubled up as my birth certificate. For most of my life I didn't question how this came to be; most likely it was part of post-war chaos, added to by language difficulties with new immigrants. On my ration card my first name is Rosa; probably a misunderstanding between the official and my parents' faltering voices – colourful anecdotes on this subject abound amongst Jewish immigrants from Eastern Europe. Rosa eventually turned into Rosel, its German version. My mother called me Ruchel, the Yiddish for Rachel, and Uhele, a special endearment.

An early memory of Kieffhaüser Straße is of my father repairing shoes; a cluster of nails in his mouth, he'd push them out with his tongue one-by-one as needed, and then he'd hammer them rhythmically into the sole of a shoe, gloved on a cobbler's last: a dull metallic sound. Other memories are just fragments, and some are as flimsy as dreams.

In our attic, the arrangement of furniture always remained the same. My cot was in the nook under a dormer window, and my father's workbench consisted of a chair for his tools and a low stool to sit on. Both were placed on the same side as my cot, slightly askew to catch more light coming from the window. Under the window was a small table with a gas ring on top. To the right of it was a washstand with a bright blue and white floral china jug and bowl on top, – the most cheerful objects in our room. On the wall opposite the workbench were my parents' two beds that took up most of the room. Of our two chairs, one always had folded washing on the seat, and underneath both of them were cardboard boxes filled with shoes waiting for repair. Finished work was on a shelf behind the workbench. Gangways? None to speak of except for the exit from the side of my parents' beds to the door. The branches of the tree outside our window made shadows on the wall opposite the beds, moving according to the pace of the wind. Sometimes, the night was dark and still and nothing moved.

The landing was our dressing room, where Mother always dressed me. On one occasion, she sat on a chair with me lazily leaning between her knees. She had just slipped a new dress over my head; the dress was made of thick, brushed wool with a soft low belt in the fashion of the 'Twenties. The dress on, she started to fiddle with a white bow she had knotted into the centre of my hair and still fiddling with the bow, she mumbled, 'The dress is too big for you… though never mind, you'll grow into it.' The sleeves of the dress had wide cuffs and dangled heavily round my hands. Every time Mother turned them up, they fell down again. It was a special day and I was having my picture taken. When we were walking to the photographer, Mother said, 'The dress you are wearing is for best,'

The worst smell in the world must be of burnt milk and in our room it boiled over a lot; Mother calmed down Father's dyspepsia with porridge. The sink not being in the room made clearing up the mess an awful chore. Curses flew from my mother's lips as she fetched bowl after bowl of fresh water to rid the table of the slimy porridge mess. The pan she tackled in the sink. She was flustered, not knowing what to do first. Finally, she threw open the window and yelled, '*Pfui*, what a *Stinkerei*!' It was a cold day. Father protested and pulled his cap over his ears, and waving his arms about he yelled back, 'Marie, shut the window! Enough fresh air already!'

The landlady's stipulation for letting her attic to my parents had been that they promised not to have children. 'No children?' I once heard my father say to a friend, 'Better said than done – we were just married!' What did that mean? The landlady's name was Mrs Totzauer. All I could manage was 'Totzel'.

Kieffhäußer Straße was more of a lane than a street: though it had detached houses, their gardens and 'front' doors were to the side of them and with lots of big trees dotted round about. When the moon was out and the wind was gentle, the branches of the tree outside our window swayed every which-way making shadows on the wall opposite my parents' beds: my very own 'mobile'. Opposite our house was a green slope, an avenue of mature trees along the top. The slope was opposite Totzel's kitchen window: she could see me, and I could see her: I liked that. Sitting on that slope, I saw people coming and going, and when I turned my head to the right, I could see the Rhine Bridge just a hundred yards away, and when the trees shed their leaves I could see the river as well as the bridge.

One night, fires sprayed down from the sky, lighting up the bridge, the trees and faces in the crowd. 'Fireworks!' people cried, looking up, their mouths open. Every time there was an-other burst, I jumped. My parents and I were looking out of our window; then Father said, 'Come, let's go down into the street!' I remember crying and my parents laughing at me, Mother wiping the tears from my cheeks. My parents always laughed when I was frightened; maybe their laughter was meant to reassure me that nothing really frightening was going on. Father took me firmly by the hand and led me down the stairs and into the street. I pulled at his hand to go back home. Everyone but me said 'Ooh!' and 'Aah!' at every explosion and clapped, but I buried my head in Father's neck when he picked me up to comfort me. To encourage me, he stretched out his arm, right into the fire, it seemed. He loosened my grip around his neck and pushing me slightly backwards, he smiled at me, and Mother smiled too. With hindsight, the fireworks must have been for New Year.

When I started school, the playground in the Kindergarten was a mysterious place. I watched boys wrestling, tumbling over each other like puppies, girls linking arms, talking a while then separating and running away, and then chasing each other, screeching. Children often bumped into me, and being in the way, I was pushed from pillar to post. It took me years to work out why I didn't join them: before I went to school I probably spoke a mix of Yiddish and Totzel's low German which is similar to Yiddish. All that was sorted out eventually as I learnt to understand both.

In Lodz, Father had been trained as a furrier. Worms had only one fur shop. Furriers seeking work exceeded work available as furriers came aplenty from Eastern Europe. With hardly any time to think of his fallen status as a craftsman, Father did what other immigrants had done before him: peddling soap was a start. Then, a *Landsmann* (compatriot) and a wholesaler in new shoes, told Father that selling soap was a dead end. 'Selling new shoes,' Inger said, 'will be better because the farmers buy them on tick, and I can be your supplier.' Inger had been in Germany since before World War I, and apart from being a wholesaler, he had a retail shop in Ludwigshafen with living accommodation above. Inger and Father worked well together, but sometimes Father grumbled – more out of frustration than anything else: his ambition was to be established like his *Landsmann*. Nevertheless, he took up Inger's suggestion. My parents' conversations about this were my bedtime stories.

It wasn't long before my mother and father left home every morning, rucksacks on their backs filled to the brim with new shoes, toecaps peeping out at the top. They walked to the train station and boarded stopping trains to the villages: Gernsheim, Oppenheim, Viernheim. These names often cropped up in their conversation. 'Good business at Oppenheim,' they assured each other when they got home. My first geography lessons were naming these villages. As my parents' reputation grew, other village names were added. One day, I heard my mother say to my father, 'The fresh air is better for your stomach, better than squashing yourself up sitting on a low stool!' Good though this work was on fine days, on rainy days it was not. They came home soaked to the skin. They hung their wet clothes on a string on the landing where the warmth rose up from Totzel's kitchen. Their rucksacks were hung on two nails on the wall, side by side. I remember Mother saying, 'Max, leave a gap between the wet and dry clothes.' I touched them once: stiff and soggy. I can't remember which rainy day it was when my mother sneezed a lot and my father said '*Gesundheit*' after every sneeze. When she didn't stop sneezing, he started to laugh: 'One more sneeze and your head will come off!' When both of them laughed, I stopped fretting. Then Father said something they didn't laugh about: 'The whole of life is a trudge.'

After World War I, Germany had plenty of peddlers of its own. Men broken in limb and spirit, and some blind, stood on street corners selling matches from trays that hung from their necks. The more able went from door to door, offering dusters and dishcloths from baskets. I never heard Father mention other peddlers. Maybe knowing the ropes meant waiting your turn as buskers do performing to cinema queues; a code of conduct of sorts.

Granting credit to customers meant more work for my parents, and they began to talk about book-keeping: who better to do that than Mother's brother Adolph. He became a partner in my parents' set-up – convenient too because he lived just two streets away from us. His job was to collect outstanding bills from customers. 'Adolph is good with figures,' Mother said. But soon enough, he took more than his share for himself. Mother was sure his wife put him up to it. A phrase frequently repeated in our house was *Handelschaft ist nicht Brüderschaft* (business is not about brotherhood). Their partnership ended abruptly, but it was by no means a clean break. But, despite my uncle's dishonesty, good times were ahead.

My parents weren't all that law-abiding themselves, trading as they did without a licence. Happily, the village policeman turned a blind eye to the goings-on; he even teased them, shaking his finger at them: 'Don't let me catch you again!' At home, Father imitated the policeman wagging his finger, suggesting his trading was a cat-and-mouse business. To my father, the policeman was a good-natured man, and he imagined that he and the policeman were buddies. 'I know him!' he'd say, as if they had slid down the banisters together as boys.

Apparently, my mother had taken Mrs Totzauer seriously: 'No children!' meant just that. When I was older, my father told me, 'You weren't our first, you know! When your mother was pregnant, she threw herself down the stairs, and she aborted. A few months later, she was pregnant again with you. What a time she had having you! Days of pain. Eventually you were pulled out of her like an onion from the earth – with forceps! I've never heard such screams! What could the landlady do? You were here. And then, when you were nine months old, you nearly died – double pneumonia the doctor said it was. Both of us feared consumption and, fearing the worst, your mother fell at the doctor's feet, "Save my child, save her!" she cried. We had just bought you a new dress and when you were taken to hospital, we laid it in your cot, and our tears fell on it.' I've lost count of how many times I asked to be told this tale. I needed their grief. How hard it must have been for them in those early days in Germany.

Chapter Two

Totzel, Christmas, and Karl

Despite Totzel's ban on children, she looked after me when my parents were out earning a living. Better a working tenant than an unemployed one? Who knows? Perhaps my parents paid her; after all, payment is more reliable than favours. That was ever my parents' way. Looking back, I know Totzel liked me, pay or not.

One cold, sunny, winter morning, my parents and I stood together in Totzel's unheated bedroom. A big pine tree was standing in the corner by the window, decorated with silver and gold baubles, and small coloured candles in holders were clipped onto the branches. The sun streaming through the window made the glitter on the tree swirl in colours of the rainbow. The fairy on top of the tree held my attention; I looked and looked, absorbed. We seemed to be waiting for something to happen.

The knock on the door made me jump. When Father said, 'Come in!' the door creaked open. A stooping figure appeared, covered in a white sheet from head to toe. A small protrusion moved down the sheet, and lifting up a corner, a bony finger popped out, and a croaky voice declared, 'I am an angel… promise me that you will beeeee aaa gooooood giiirlll, Rosel.'

When the figure stepped forward holding out its finger for me to hold, I stepped back, bumping into my parents. Father pushed me forward, saying, 'Go on, take the angel's finger.' 'No, I don't want to hold the finger,' I whimpered. My parents reproached me for making a fuss; 'How can you cry when Totzel is so good to you?' they said in Yiddish. If they knew it was Totzel, why did they pretend she was an angel?

The 'figure' then disappeared and Totzel came back as herself. When she and my parents were talking, white breath puffed from their mouths. The early morning sun did not make the ice-cold room any warmer. Shivering, I cried. Now my breath puffed out white too.

Totzel's bed stood against the wall, the plump duvet rolled over broadside like an omelette. The bed-linen was embroidered, and broad, coarse-lace inlets revealed blood-red ticking beneath. I loved stroking the silky little bumps of embroidery, but the inlets I followed with my finger were rough. Totzel's bed was where I imagined the wolf in *Little Red Riding Hood* to be, dressed as a Grandma. Even now, I can see him under Totzel's mountainous duvet, his long, pointed nose peeping out from under a frilly cap. Totzel must have told me that story.

My days with Totzel were mostly spent in her kitchen. She gave me things to do, like darning my stockings. Using my knee as a darning egg, I pulled the hole tightly together until none of my flesh showed – nothing like the way Totzel darned. The moment I walked, the hole split open again bigger than before. Of course I failed, being just four years old! Totzel then stroked my head, took off my stocking and put it into her mending basket and, pulling out a clean and mended one for me to wear, she said, 'Don't worry, Röslein, I'll do it tomorrow'. To be with her, I had to climb down the open staircase from our attic, and although it was perilous, I did it by bumping down one stair at a time on my bum; Totzel's anxious voice calling out, 'Be careful!'

When my parents arrived home from work, I remember embracing my mother and asking her what I could do. When she said, '*Scloog Kop in Wand*' (bang your head against the wall – a grim sort of jest), I knew it wasn't serious because she was hugging me a lot and laughing. Totzel was busy at the stove, smiling. Mother's rucksack leaned against the wall, empty. Moments later, Father walked into the kitchen and put his empty rucksack next to Mother's. 'Good day, sold out!' he said, smiling.

One day, when I was alone with Totzel in the kitchen, a storm tore the heavens apart; thunder and lightening came in quick succession. Standing in front of the open window, my head level with the sill, the rain splattered on my face. The rain shone like Totzel's darning needles. I cupped my hands to try and catch the downpour, the way Totzel held water in her hands when she washed her face over the kitchen sink, the water running down to her elbows. I seemed not to mind the lightning but the thunder made me leap back into the kitchen.

Totzel called to me from the stove, 'Come, Rosel, watch me cook the bacon.' Wearily, I rested against the rail on the stove. 'Not too close, you'll get burnt from the fat spitting,' Totzel cautioned. The pan was big and black, and heavy. When the bacon was done, Totzel wiped the pan clean with newspaper and wiped the fat left on her hands onto my curly hair. 'There, that's better, that'll make it stay down!' she said.

Totzel's hair was dark with grey at the temples. The moment she got up in the morning, she took a wide-toothed comb off the shelf next to the kitchen sink, and combing her hair through, she pulled it back into a knot at the nape of her neck, securing it with two large pins. Any hair lost in that tussle, she rolled over her finger, opened a lid of the range and dropped the ring of hair into the fire where it sizzled and smelled wondrous. Young women at that time wore dresses above their knees but Totzel's were still long, reaching to the floor. There wasn't a Mr Totzauer. When I was four, the war had been over seven years. Perhaps she was a war widow, I thought years later.

The only other adult in the house was Totzel's nephew, Karl. Whether he was visiting his aunt or living with her I don't remember. One day, I was standing by the stove in the kitchen with a ball in my hands – Totzel had gone to the yard to hang up the washing and fetch some coal – when Karl came rushing towards me, and picking me up under my arms, he laid me flat on the kitchen table, and then, taking off my knickers, he opened my legs wide and fumbled clumsily in my crotch, all the while looking down on me, smirking. I went rigid. I was holding my ball close to me. Frightened, I lost control of it and it rolled along the floor. At that moment, Totzel called up from downstairs, 'Karl, will you come and take the bucket of coal upstairs!' Hardly had Totzel finished her request when Karl grabbed hold of me and put me back on the floor next to my knickers. Then he ran off, clattering down the stairs. When Totzel came into the kitchen, she looked from me to my knickers, frowning.

On another day, Karl and a girl much older than me were standing in Totzel's bedroom by the window where the Christmas tree had stood. Karl's hands were up her skirt which was now high above her thighs and Karl's hand was even higher. Karl was smirking, the way he did at me. When she saw me, the girl pushed Karl's hand away and smoothed down her dress. Totzel was busy in the garden, snipping things.

Another time, a different man. I had been bedded down in the middle of my parents' beds. When I woke up the light was on. Beside me lay a man, fully dressed, wearing a trilby hat. The point of his elbow rested on the bed, his cupped hand supporting his head. The flies of his trousers were open, and outside his fly lay his limp penis. As he looked down at me, his penis grew bigger. How long he had been there I don't know, but suddenly my mother called up from the street, 'Ztupack! What on earth are you doing up there?' Like an arrow, the man my mother called Ztupack shot off the bed, bundled his penis back into his trousers, switched off the light, and, as had Karl, he clattered down the wooden stairs. The moon was out and the branches of the tree outside our window made shadows on the wall opposite my parents' beds; my 'mobile' was swaying gently. Ztupack, I later learned, was the husband of my mother's sister, Lotte.

When I was five, we moved to 27 Römer Straße, into a flat fronted by a shop. At the back of the shop, a few steps went up to an attic. Behind those open stairs, a door led to a kitchen, and another door led into our big bedroom. Compared to the attic we had lived in, the space we now had was palatial: one room large enough for two beds and a wardrobe with a long mirror in the centre. The furniture was white, trimmed with black wooden beading. A round wicker table with matching armchairs was arranged in front of the window and white cross-over voile curtains with deep frills gave the room a touch of luxury. Mother dipped the curtains in tea – 'Makes them look softer', she said, 'less ghostly.' No sooner were the curtains up, or so it seemed to me, they came down again for washing; Father up the ladder and Mother supervising from below. Our ottoman, against the wall opposite my parents' beds, was covered with an Oriental plush throw. In the gangway between, a linoleum runner, patterned like the throw helped to brighten up the dark, painted floorboards. I remember my cousin Bertel looking up at my knickers when we were jumping around on our ottoman. Play ended suddenly when he came too close to where Karl's fingers had been – a place that for me was now a forbidden area. Touched on any part below my navel, I heard voices of alarm: my mother's coming from the street... Totzel's from the yard... men running away, leaving me blinking.

The kitchen window looked out over a courtyard with three small houses either side of ours making a T-shape. From there, the courtyard narrowed into a straight, country lane. At the end, a huge tree blocked the view to the sky. When a wind was up and the sun was out, the tree lit up erratically. One of the houses to our left had an iron staircase leading up to a flat on the landing where a man who wore hobnail boots lived. Going to work and coming home, his boots clonked. My mother declared, 'We don't need an alarm clock, the man's boots are our clock!' I didn't find out anymore about that man except that my Aunt Pessa had a problem with him. When she was visiting, she shouted up at him from the yard. This annoyed my mother, 'Trust our Pessa to pick a quarrel with someone when she doesn't even live here!' I watched my aunt from our kitchen window, pacing back and forth in the yard, her face screwed up with anger.

The ground-floor kitchen windows of the other houses were low, like ours, without curtains. I loved looking into the kitchens to see what was going on. In one, a woman was frying a snake-shaped fish in a pan, pushing and poking it about. I told Mother the fish wriggled. 'Eels,' she said, 'they're not kosher,' and with a furrowed brow, she asked, 'Are you sure the fish wriggled?' What was kosher?

My parents were now selling new shoes in their shop, and in our attic Cornelius was employed to do the shoe-repairs. I used to watch him work for what seemed like a long time. And all at once it was too long, and his hand was under my skirt. I ran away. 'Where is Papa?' I asked my mother when she came in from the yard. 'In Ludwigshafen buying shoes from Inger,' she said.

I remember constant talk of money in our house which I later learned had been about the inflation after WW I. Talking to a new immigrant about it some years later, my mother recalled, 'We were handling fistsful of notes just to buy a loaf of bread,' and, showing the immigrant my doll, she added, 'She cost millions and millions of Marks!'

However precious the doll was, she was far too big for me but, despite her size, we were inseparable. To see her eyes open and shut I had to sit down and put her on my lap. Her clothes were white and soft with lace trim. One dull day, I was standing on the iron landing with her in the yard next door to ours. Looking down, I saw a boy and a girl going into the outside lavatory, shutting the door firmly behind them. Why were they pushing against each other going through the door? Totally absorbed in what they were doing, my doll slipped from my grasp and bumped down, stair by stair, until she landed on soft ground. I followed her down. She was smashed to bits inside her clothes; even her head lay shattered under her frilly bonnet. Her eyes were open, gazing at me. All that money she cost! I don't remember playing with any toys after my doll broke. Did I get a hiding? I can't remember.

Playing hide-and-seek one day, I was crouching behind some stacked tree trunks in a garden behind the house across the street from ours when a dog came running towards me barking very loudly. Baring his teeth, he knocked me over, tore off part of my dress with his teeth and bit me below my left nipple. I howled all the way home. Horrified, my mother took me to the doctor whose practice was on the corner of our street. As she was telling him what had happened, he was cutting off a white muslin bandage from a fat roll with a pair of scissors. Then he picked up wads of cotton wool with tweezers from a dish on a trolley and dabbed the blood from my wound, and dipping a fresh wad into mauve liquid with tweezers, he dabbed the wound some more. I yelled, 'loud enough,' the doctor said, 'for the whole of Worms to hear!' To pacify me, he nodded his head sagely, saying, 'The dog bit you because her puppies were hidden behind the stacked tree trunks, and when she saw you sitting near them, she jumped on you to protect her children.' The expression on my mother's face, her lips clenched together, suggested that she had been bitten herself. The doctor gave the dog a breed: Alsatian.

Was it after the dog bit me that I became an observer on the playground? The links between events are hazy, but what stands out is the memory of other children having fun – talking, shouting, pushing, running, linking arms, playing pat-a-cake, reciting age-old ditties, slapping each other's hands together, keeping time and rhyme, boys in mock combat, girls whispering into each other's ears, and then shrieking with delight, sharing, sulking, walking away in a huff. How can you say, 'Play with me?' What if they said no? Standing apart from the children gave rise to feelings I didn't understand. The playground being a mysterious place; adults now supplied my needs: their voices and noises and weighty remarks.

But life in Römer Straße was good. Mother had a range to cook on now, and there were fewer smells of burnt milk; even if there were, the kitchen sink was close to the range. There were new tastes too: such as toast. Mother made it by sitting on a stool in front of the range, her face and the grid glowing, a slice of bread spiked on a long fork. Both sides toasted, she rubbed a whole clove of garlic on the hot toast until all but the tip had dissolved, and still hot, she broke off a corner for me to taste, the taste of garlic so strong, it stung my tongue!

For Mother, joy was having a washing line in the yard; coming into the kitchen, a dry bale of washing over her arm, she would bury her nose in it, sniffing loudly and then, holding it under my nose, she would cry, 'Smell!' I knew our life was better financially too; every time my mother clanked open the cash register and tucked yet another note under the clip, her face was wreathed in smiles, and then for the hell of it, she scooped up the change and let it drop from her fingers piece by piece counting, 'This week,' she said, 'we can afford a chicken for *Shabbes*.'

My parents were on the way up. Mother had clothes made for me: my favourites were small-checked, cotton blouses that buttoned onto a pleated skirt. On a more practical level, there were two black overalls with white detachable collars, convenient for washing. Trying them on me, she said, 'These are for work.' Soon, I was to know what that meant.

Chapter Three

Life's Getting Better

One day, after school, Mother changed my clothes and dressed me in the overall she had made for me, giving me instructions as she did up the buttons: I was to greet customers with a smile and ask them to take a seat, and then call her. Mother was always in the kitchen, just through a door at the back of the shop. It was a small shop; just two chairs and stools. The customer seated, I would call out to Mother. Having established the shoe number, she would call out grandly: 'Number forty!' I remember how hard it was for me to align the three-step ladder along the shelves to where the shoebox with that number was. Men's and women's shoes were on separate shelves. Pulling the box from the shelf wasn't easy. Mother would watch me, smiling encouragingly. When I had chosen the right number, her smile broadened, and sometimes, when the box threatened to fall from my hands, she stood by to prevent an accident. There never was one. Customer gone, she'd embrace me, murmuring 'Uhele' into my ear. Mother's praise warmed me. 'Earning your living is a serious business,' she said at suppertime.

My mother wore stylish hats. Her hair was thick and curly, cut into a *Bubikopf*, (bobbed), regularly Marcel-waved. 'I am going to the *Frisseur* to have my hair *onduliert*,' she would call out, in a mix of German, French and Yiddish. I remember French soldiers in Worms and French words mingling with German; when Hitler came to power, he rid the German language of foreign influences.

When Mother had come back from the hairdresser, shopping over her arm, the smell of singed hair filled our kitchen.

No time to lose: cross-over apron on, she nimbly lifted the shopping bag onto the table, and holding the two bottom corners high, a fish slithered out and jumped across the table. Seeing my eyes pop, Mother explained, 'The fish was just swimming in a tank moment ago.' Mother pursued the fish round the table but, every time she grabbled hold of it, out it slipped from her fingers. Exasperated, she took our wooden potato masher from the drawer of the kitchen table, and giving her last command to the fish, weapon at the ready, she said, 'Come here, you!' One bang on the head did the trick. The fish and Mother were now eye to eye: yes, it was dead. Then, sharpening a pointed knife on the kitchen doorstep, she plunged it into the fish's belly all the way up to its head. After clawing out guts and gills with her fingers, she used the knife to scrape the thin black lining from the fish's belly. Then, her hands cupped, she shoved the innards straight into a bucket below the table, and the surface now cleared, she rinsed the fish and cut it into sections and placed them side by side into a large wide pan of water, with a good pinch of salt and a little sugar for seasoning – and lastly, rings of onions and carrots on top. The simmering fish smelled heavenly but, what a collision of smells: singed hair and simmering fish.

In our big room, a small square table and two chairs that served as a token dining area were arranged against the footboards of my parents' beds. It was there that my mother's youngest sister, Chana, looked into Oskar Pollack's eyes as if into a crystal ball. She was my mother's last sister to leave Poland. Oskar Pollack showed himself to be a willing husband for her. That was the first time I heard the word *Shidduch* (arranged marriage).

On the morning of my Aunt Chana's engagement party, all the family had come to Aunt Pessa's flat in Ludwigshafen. It was a dull day and naked light bulbs were on in every room. I can't remember the train journey from Worms to Ludwigshafen, but there I was, seemingly older – about ten – than I was when Chana and her intended first gazed into each other's eyes.

Curious, I left the adults and their chatter to look round the flat. Passing my Cousin Bertel's bedroom, a flash of colour made me stop and look. Chana was wearing a cream satin slip, beige stockings and silver-coloured shoes, their straps hooked into diamanté buttons. Why was Chana trembling – it wasn't cold! The 'flash' was Chana's dress for her engagement party, I gathered. It was made of peach-coloured chiffon, so delicate and so light, Chana was able to gather it together between her hands and put over her head. When her arms were through the armholes, the dress rippled down her body, ending just below the knees. One last thing to check: standing in front of the long mirror outside the wardrobe door, she flicked her fingers back and forth over her hips to make sure the dress *did* move easily. 'Just right,' said her smile. Still absorbed with herself, walking up and down the room to test the comfort of her shoes, someone called from the kitchen: 'Are you ready Chana?' Startled, she patted her short, waved hair with open fingers, and sighing deeply, she turned on the ball of one foot and walked past me into the corridor, her lips in a pout, an anxious frown between her eyes. Chana was the sister who most resembled my mother.

I remember nothing of the engagement party, or their wedding. Chana and Oskar seemed to have disappeared from my view like a pair of party balloons. The next thing I remember hearing was that Chana and Oskar were in Argentina – which town they lived in is now lost to family history. Later I heard my father read out a letter from her to us that said Chana's life with Oskar was not a happy one, and some years later still, another letter said that she had died of cancer. Children were never mentioned and it was assumed there were none.

In October 1927, my brother Heinie was born. Lots of people came to celebrate. Eight days later, our big room was full of men, their clothes reeking of mothballs. I darted between them, pushing hither and thither. Now and then, a man patted me on the head. Prayers were recited and blessings sung while my brother was held aloft on a cushion. Suddenly, he let out a sharp yell, to which the grown-ups responded with a resounding *Mazel tov*! Heinie had been circumcised. I have never forgotten that yell: how my baby brother's chin quivered, his little being so vulnerable and helpless, and so abandoned to his fate. I knew that circumcision without anaesthetic would always be an issue for me.

At the end of my mother's pregnancy I had apparently tried to put my arms around her swollen belly saying, 'What a lot of potatoes you have eaten today.' Laughingly they repeated this to their friends, as all parents do, thinking that just about anything their children say is amusing. But what I didn't find amusing was when they told me that the stork brought Heinie to my mother and bit her leg.

I sulked a lot after Heinie was born. A slab of chocolate given to me did not cheer me up. Had it been less sweet, the bribe might have worked, but I had unusually sophisticated tastes for my age. More enjoyable was to rub through the silver paper over the embossed chocolate, revealing a scene of the sun, its rays striding over hills and dales, sprigs of foliage in the foreground. I rubbed until every last blade of grass emerged and glittered on the silver paper, though I still wondered about the bite on my mother's leg.

Mother's confinement lasted for a week. She was propped up in bed like a queen, her baby beside her in a cot. Aunt Pessa cooked for us and generally bustled about, so there was no hardship. 'Isn't he lovely?' everyone cooed over my baby brother. Aunt Pessa surprised me by giving me a gold snake bracelet with ruby-red eyes, but her present didn't please me at all. It was far too big for me. I dimly remember sitting on a kerb with a girl, our feet in the gutter, bartering with it; I have no memory of what she gave me in exchange. Aunt Pessa was furious: 'I will never buy you anything of value again!' The bracelet must have been real gold and its eye was probably a ruby. Why else would Aunt Pessa have been so angry?

My parents delighted in their son. A few months later, going for a walk on Sundays became a family affair. Before anything pleasurable happened, Mother cleaned my brother's glossy mauve-coloured pram, deep like a boat. She cleaned and polished, aired pillows, and vigorously shook out sheets and covers; everything was scrutinized for stains, and crumbs in crevices inside the pram, her head getting lost in the depths of the pram as she sniffed for smells. Finally satisfied, she took Heinie from Father's arms; both had been waiting and watching. Heinie, anticipating 'walkies', jumped up and down in Father's arms, ready and dressed in a white piquet jumpsuit. At last he was lowered into his pram, and Father, teasing Mother, said, 'The way you've gone on with your cleaning hasn't left much time for us in the sun.' But he wouldn't have had it any other way: proud as a peacock, my father was. The moments spent walking out with us were golden; his step was relaxed and his head was high, and now and then, he'd look at us as if to say, 'This is mine, all mine.' I was supposed to help Mother to push the pram. I had other ideas: I wanted to link arms with my father, and that is what I did, trying to keep in step with him.

In our newfound comfort, I became a problem eater. Fed up with me refusing to eat, Mother engaged a nursemaid to be banished with me to our big room for mealtimes. I overheard her telling Father, 'I was looking through the keyhole to see what was going on – too quiet for my Ruchel, I thought – and guess what? The nursemaid was eating Ruchel's food! Max, what shall I do?'

Now at primary school, my eating problem became public. On my way to school, I opened the flap door of the cellar below the window of our big room facing the street and threw down the immaculately packed food parcels Mother had prepared for me. A neighbour told on me. My parents checked, and there they were, tied with string like parcels for the post. But unexpectedly my eating problem was solved. At milk-break, trays of *Schneckenudels* (Danish pastries curled like snakes) arrived on wooden trays, smelling like nothing I'd ever smelled before. When I told Mother about the pastries, she came to school and said to the baker, 'Give her as many as she wants! I'll pay!' I was standing next to her, thrilled. How long I ate the pastries, I don't remember, but however long it was, my hostility to Mother's food was broken because, now having a range instead of one ring to cook on, she could make all manner of delicious things.

One problem solved, another arose. The male teacher didn't like me. Except for the singing before the lessons started, I felt I wasn't really part of the classroom. I was too busy thinking of the stories of my parents' troubles, especially the story of my aunt Pessa who was shot at on the Polish border when she was trying to smuggle herself into Germany. And then, there was my mother's brother Adolph who was stealing from her. All of it I heard – their woes were my woes – but they vanished when we sang. My favourite was Brahms's *Wiegenlied*, '…to slip under a cover embroidered with pinks and roses… that sleep would be sweet, and next morning, God willing, you will wake up again…'

Most days, the teacher's wife would tap on the classroom window. Excitedly, he'd rush to open the window and they would kiss. Some children giggled and a few clapped their hands. After his wife left, the teacher's face was full of laughter. The singing over, lessons began: suddenly, mental arithmetic. The teacher's arm shot through the air, pointing at children whose arms were bending and stretching, impatient to answer. 'You,' he said, looking at me, waiting. I remained dumb; the children turned to look at me. I went into hiding, head down, eyes closed. Then I heard a thump. Looking up, the teacher had stepped off the dais and was rushing down the aisle. He stopped beside me, and my eyes now open, I saw his arm high above my head – and down came his hand on my cheek: a carpet beater. Pinks and roses scattered.

The bell rang for milk-break. Mother was outside. 'Who?' she asked, looking at my scarlet cheek. Helpless, her own face now flushed, she did what she'd come to do: she brought me, she fed me, a soft, boiled egg.

Chapter Four

Sepia Photographs

Father was now busy with the shop and Mother, not having
to climb stairs anymore, made their life less of a drudge. One
fine spring day, Heinie and me dressed in new white linen out-
fits and Mother in her best clothes, the three of us – Heinie in
his pram – walked to the photographer in the High Street.
Why not Father? The obvious reason was that he was working.
Come to think of it, the only pictures I have of him in his
younger days are with Mother on their wedding day and some
casual snapshots later on. But even without him, there was a
sense of occasion.

Mother and Heinie were first. Mother sat on a stool with
ornate grips on each side. Heinie, not yet walking, sat nude on
her lap looking straight ahead. Mother's dress was made of
soft black fabric, a mottled black-and-white velvet collar
plunging down to her waist. A black satin chemise restored
decorum. When the photographer went under the black cloth
to focus the camera, Heinie became restless on Mother's lap
and as he stood up, she grabbed hold of him round the waist.
Now face to face with her, he turned back to the camera and
then Mother's lap became his trampoline: treading, gurgling
and laughing out loud, he addressed the photographer with
outstretched arms. Mother, in profile, looked up at her son;
both were radiant. Before the final buzz of the camera, Heinie
appeared to be walking off her lap, and when the photographer disappeared under the black cloth again and requested
the last 'watch the birdie', Mother, her smile now fixed,
popped Heinie's circumcised penis between his thighs. In the
blink of the camera's eye, Mother made her son into a teddy

bear. From time to time when I look through our family album and find the picture of Heinie standing on Mother's lap, I say to the person looking with me, 'Wasn't my brother a beautiful baby?' I only ever see his face. What the person looking with me thinks, I don't know, but for me the image of my mother making her son into a teddy bear has never left me. Why did she do this? What was she hiding? I remember reading many years later about an incident from the Nazi era when a Jew in hiding was caught. He was asked to drop his trousers and because he was circumcised, he was shot. Was that why my mother did it, out of inborn fear?

The next photograph was of Heinie and me, my legs crossed on a small French sofa, looking grand with a big, white bow that Mother had tussled with to keep upright on the side of my head, a bow every bit as good as any of the rich children had in the picture of my Kindergarten.

Looking at pictures of those times reminds me how happy my mother was with her life, helping my father run the shop, the customers in and out, the door bell tinkling. But alongside her happiness were less uplifting things. I remember hearing snippets of conversation my parents had with newly arrived immigrants from Poland, referring to each other as *Landsleute* (country people). Names ended with '-ski' and '-kov', so different from our own name Lerner (the German word for 'a learner'). All of it was so strange, and not understanding much, I puzzled over what they laughed – and sometimes cried – about.

One day, home from school, I rushed into our big room and saw an old man sleeping in one of my parents' beds, his beard arranged on the counterpane. I ran crying to my mother. Laughing, she said, 'What are you crying for? It is your *Zaide*!' Seeing my grandfather for the first time held no excitement for me because no one had prepared me for this visitor from Poland. I sat on his lap only once; kisses from an old man with a long, white beard were not agreeable. Sliding off his lap I sensed that my mother wanted me to respond to his affection in kind. Grandfather, it seemed to me, went back to Poland as suddenly as he had arrived. That was the last time any of his children saw him. He died before the Second World War started, 'What a blessing he didn't die in a death camp,' my mother said, lighting a memorial candle for her father after World War II.

My grandfather Herschel had come to see if he could live with one of his children, but it wasn't possible for any of them; all had two children, and like us, they didn't have enough room. My grandmother, his second wife, had died and he was now living alone.

My father's family remained in Poland – all except some cousins who came to England and a niece who went to live in Paris. Mother's family migrated to the West, their quarrels remained quarrels throughout their lives, nothing was ever healed. When I was about four or five, I saw my mother cutting a picture of my cousin Jacob and myself in half. Mine she kept, but Jacob's she let fall into a bucket of rubbish; a vivid illustration of how my mother avenged her brother's wrongdoing, though I doubt whether my mother remembered that passionate moment, accompanied by angry words. But time seemed to lessen her vengeful tone. Years later, Uncle Adolph died in Palestine. World War II was raging and overtook the grudges she once harboured, but I remember my mother's anger: it seems her reality was spewed-up from ancestral experiences like fires from under the sea, and wrongs done to her wrapped themselves round her life. Some way into my own life I felt myself going the way of my mother, brooding for days on end, trying to unravel the knots of a quarrel. Glimpsing my father's vivacity, the way he challenged life with an on/off switch for laughter and for tears. In those moments of recognition, I would choose to be like him. At other moments, I preferred my mother's ways, thinking her to be more thoughtful. And so, back and forth, Mother or Father? Choice ensnared me, and, none the wiser, I left what was meant to be to the fancy of fate.

Of another's fate, my mother told me of when I was about thirteen. She was dicing carrots when, casually, she said, 'There was a pogrom in Lodz and people were sheltering in the cellar while Cossacks on horses were charging around upstairs in the house, and there was a woman with her baby, and when it started to cry, she pressed it to her breast so as not to endanger the rest of the people in the shelter. When the sound of horses' hooves died down, the full horror became clear: the woman had suffocated her baby.' 'Who was this woman?' I asked. 'A woman from the neighbourhood,' Mother replied, absentmindedly cutting up carrots between her thumb and forefinger. Her story finished, there was blood all over the carrots, which left me wondering why Mother was not her usual sure self with the knife that day. In our house, stories were never told when we were sitting down comfortably round a table – no, they came casually, handed out in passing like newspapers through a letterbox.

To prod my memories, I turn the pages of my family album. I look at myself in a school photograph taken when I was six years old. I am in yet another dress for 'best' with an A-shaped embroidered inlet, and standing next to the teacher who once had hit me. Turning more pages, there is another school photograph, and it is me who is the shabby one. I am standing alone on a stone disk beside steps curving up to a double door behind us; the playground fanning out before us. I am wearing boys' boots cut down; the raw, white edges don't show in the picture, but when I looked down at them on my way to school, the edges showed and I felt ashamed. Did everyone see what I saw? In that picture nearly all the class are wearing fancy dress. I was the only Jewish girl in that class. It was *Fastnacht* (Carnival). Improvising a fancy dress must have been the last thing on my mother's mind – the year was 1935, by which time the

Nüremberg race laws had been established. Quickly, I turn back the pages to times when my mother was happy with her son, when I watched her playing with him, throwing him up in the air, both of them laughing at each other.

It was around that time I disappeared 'for a whole day' my parents said, 'we nearly asked the police to look for you!' But it was my parents who found me, my head cupped in my hands, elbows resting on the low sill of a toyshop window, my nose pressed hard against the glass. I was severely beaten by my father on my legs and my behind. Afterwards, I fell asleep in our wicker chair in front of a round wicker table, my head resting in the crook of my elbow, my feet dangling above the floor. 'When will you ever be sensible?' my mother asked. Blank-minded, I put the question aside. I didn't yet realise that 'when' meant there and then, or at the latest, the next day. I remember her asking that question again when I broke my doll, but this time she added something else, '… how impossible it is to put an old head on young shoulders.' Father nodded in agreement.

Mother's appeals for me to be more grown-up never fitted my feelings. Her words were often hot and angry, then steely and cold which made me feel unwanted in her life. I longed for the caress of tender words, the way my father comforted my mother when she was upset about her family. Verbal injury always preceded physical punishment, always instigated by my mother. Sharp words scratched my hurt more. When Mother was upset, she, like other women I knew, uttered bitter curses. I often wondered why Father never used curses. Years later, I thought my mother's curses might have originated in frustration about sex. I remembered as a child having witnessed my parents having sex, my mother passive; she allowed – rather than participated.

My father was the only one of his siblings who migrated to Germany. That was most likely the reason he gladly attached himself to Mother's family. Her woes became his woes. Most of my mother's siblings were illegal immigrants like my parents, which made their stay in Germany insecure. I happened to be in my uncle Chaskel's house in Worms when his deportation papers arrived. Unfolding the letter, he read out its contents in stumbling German, and as the contents of the letter became clear, his children, Sally and Heinz, hung onto their mother Hella's skirt, wailing. Hella embraced her children, head bowed. I watched this scene as if it were from a silent movie, and that is how it has remained in my mind, the gestures they made, clinging to each other, their faces tearful. Uncle Chaskel's deportation was a blow to family confidence. Who would be next was the question often asked. Uncle Chaskel and his family left for Poland at the appointed date, several years before Hitler came to power. Chaskel was the only one of the siblings to see their father again. What a pitiful fate Chaskel and his family suffered when the Nazis caught up with them.

Our early time in Worms was full of promise but, no sooner had we had our photographs taken, my mother began to suffer from violent mood-swings: the slightest demands on her were too much. I remember my father telling me that I should 'leave her be' because 'her nerves are weak'. Knowing what we know now, she must have had post-natal depression. To make matters worse, she had lost all her teeth when she was just thirty-five years old: 'Gum disease when she was pregnant,' Father explained to me years later.

When another grievance against her brother Adolph was uncovered, she broke down altogether. It appeared that he had, encouraged by his wife, laid claim to a gold watch-and-chain my grandfather had given my father as a wedding present when Mother and he left Poland. In their wedding photograph, Father is wearing the watch. They talked about this blessed watch for years, and each time they did, they referred to

Adolph as a *Ganav*, a thief. So deeply was my mother affected by the quarrel with her brother that, when Heinie and I had a squabble, Mother prophesied, 'Siblings,' she cried, 'are torn apart… what will happen to you two when each is in a different corner of the world and neither wants to know about the other?' Mother wasn't speculating; she seemed to 'know' these things. Heinie and I were nurtured on such stuff.

The next time the doctor visited, he recommended that Mother should take up knitting; with her hands occupied, her mind could rest. My memory of what the doctor said is sharp, because when he left my father said to my mother, confirming the doctor's suggestion, 'It's a good idea; it will rest your nerves.' What were nerves? I imagined something active, twitching about inside her body, and when she cried, they were washed away.

Knitting was, as the doctor predicted, the start of my mother's recovery. She knitted yards of stuff without patterns: two-ply, three-ply, thick needles, thin needles, undoing, starting again. In the end, she achieved expertise of a kind, making dresses for herself quite well, and jumpers for me and Heinie, and socks, for which a neighbour helped her to work out the heels. However well knitted they were, they itched unbearably. To start decreasing for armholes, Mother used two fingers broadside under her arm: 'Two more fingers and I can start casting off.' From then on, my mother and her knitting were never parted. The doctor's more radical suggestion was for us to move to another town. The best idea yet.

Chapter Five

Ludwigshafen

In 1932, we moved to 40 Wrede Straße in Ludwigshafen into a block of flats on the ground-floor, with two bedrooms and a large kitchen. I was twelve years old and Heinie was six. Mother had her sister Pessa to comfort her, and Heinie and I got two more cousins, Bertel and Rosl, unfortunately too old for us to play with: Rosl was seventeen and Bertel, fifteen.

The move was a downward step for my father; the kiosk-sized shop he found was not big enough for selling new shoes, and so back he went to shoe repairing. Being next to Schreiber's – a large grocery store – was an advantage: easy shopping for mother and passing trade for Father. Wrede Straße ended at the banks of the Rhine just a couple of hundred yards from our shop. The church opposite towered over its forecourt, where the sun was always absent. Moss grew between the flagstones as thick as cushions and it was great fun to hop from one to the other. Turning left by the church, Ludwigshafen's main shopping street began, a busy thoroughfare with trams going down the centre, ending at the railway station. I spent a lot of time in Ludwig Straße. Here shops sold luxury goods – fine china, furniture, elegant women's clothes and hats – and pressed between the big shops was a small narrow one, selling brassieres and corsets. When I was twelve, I bought my first brassiere there, a luxury I paid for by scrubbing a floor. Mother said I didn't need a brassiere yet, but being armed with my own money made me feel powerful. Now that was a daring thing to do for those times because, as a rule, my money was family money.

The furniture we had in Worms came with us; the white

bedroom suite and the ottoman with its rich throw was placed in the room which became my bedroom, glamorous with its deep-maroon damask wallpaper, its pattern defined with bunches of grapes, lush and ripe, not forgetting Mother's cross-over curtain. Luxury was a small oblong table alongside the ottoman which doubled up as a dining area for Mother, Heinie and me, a treat for the three of us when Father was working in his shop. Heinie slept in a separate bed in our parents' room and I had a room of my own. Another new beginning.

Our flat was part of a bigger one. Across the corridor from our kitchen was a large room, its door permanently closed. The room had a separate entrance in the block at right angles from ours. Mr and Mrs Kuss lived in that room, its window facing a brick wall. A naked lightbulb burned all day long. 'Kuss' means 'kiss' in German, though my father doubted that much kissing went on between them. Every weekend, Kuss staggered home from the *Kneipe* – pub, 'Aha!' my father said, 'we're off!' Invariably, Kuss announced his arrival with abusive language, 'Slut, whore… it is no use you hiding, I'll get you wherever you are!' The moment their door was shut, furniture flew from one side of the room to the other, and somewhere in between was Mrs Kuss. The next morning, she would pass by our kitchen window: a plain woman, her eyes black-and-blue, her head down.

It was around that time that my father cautioned me about *Goyim*: 'Never marry one; either he gets drunk or he's an anti-Semite, or both.' Those words were branded on my mind. Was this the eleventh commandment? It must have been, because Father had such a solemn look on his face.

Amazingly, Kuss could speak Yiddish. Kuss speaking Yiddish wasn't as miraculous as it seemed: Yiddish is mostly *Niederdeutsch* scattered with slave and Hebrew words. This language was used by the Jews for trading, picked up by them as they wandered up from the Middle East through Germany

centuries ago on their way to Eastern Europe and elsewhere
in the West. They took Yiddish to wherever they happened to
go, adopting the languages of the lands they stumbled into,
leaving Hebrew to be their holy tongue. Many decades later, I
read *Mother Courage* by Brecht in German, and to my pleasure, I realized that Yiddish was the peasants' language. Maybe,
without knowing, Kuss was reclaiming his ancestral tongue
back from the Jews, and maybe that was why he was having
such fun when he placed himself in front of two Jewish women
in the forecourt of the church, and being nearby, I heard him
let forth a stream of 'Yiddish'. Taken aback, the two women
hurried away and Kuss ran in the other direction, shaking with
laughter. He was a small, skinny man with concave shoulders,
a fag end, damp and yellow, always dangling from his lips, his
eyes narrowing from the rising smoke. The thought 'You
pinched my language' may or may not have occurred to him.
Back in our shop, I asked my father, 'Did you know Kuss
speaks Yiddish?' 'No,' he said, though I doubt if my father
knew he himself was speaking medieval German. For that
kind of knowledge, you had to be a German Jew who thought
Yiddish was a barbarous tongue. The two women Kuss accosted were German Jews, and for one on them, I scrubbed
floors.

Another one of our rooms was rented out to an old man. It
was at a right angle to our corridor and opposite the second
door of our kitchen – which was permanently shut. I don't remember how the old man got in and out of our flat, our front
door being the only entrance. Much as I try, he doesn't come
to mind except for the unpleasant smells coming from his
room: smoke from burning grease, the profane stench of
bacon and *Bratwurst* oozing from under his door mixed with
urine odours, all of them stagnating in our corridor. Mother
improved the situation by hanging an old blanket across the
corridor. That trapped the smell to some extent. What a mud-

dle my memory is about this man! Did he climb in and out of his window, away from, or back into his room?

The old man apart, life was pleasant enough. Heinie went to the *Ludwigsschule* and I to the *Rhineschule*. Father was very busy in his shop and talked of getting a bigger one to sell new shoes again. Although Mother and Pessa had each other, it seemed not to have been an equal relationship. Mother said to Father, 'Pessa needs looking after; her husband is a bad earner.' How could that be when he always had a smell of paint and turpentine about him? He must have been busy decorating someone's house and been paid for it! When he came to us straight from work to meet Pessa, he'd put down his workbag inside our door, metal stencils clinking. The tins of paint, he hung on the handlebars of his bike.

Uncle Avrum, working or not, didn't stop Mother from buying extra apples for her sister. She'd wash them, cut out the bad bits, and put the rest into a colander. 'Be quick,' she'd say, 'before they go brown; hurry.' And hurry I did, the colander dripping all the way to Aunt Pessa's who lived a five-minute run from us. By the time I got to her, the bits of apples were very brown indeed.

'Come, I'll teach you to ride a bike,' Uncle Avrum said to me one day. His bike was leaning against the wall under our kitchen window as usual. I jumped with excitement, running ahead of him. In no time, I was on the saddle with Uncle Avrum holding onto it to keep me steady, back and forth from our flats to the *Bierstube* (beer hall) on the corner of our street and back again with Uncle Avrum running beside the bike. Soon, I could ride alone. On my last lesson, I announced, 'I want a bike of my own, a lady's bike, without that nasty bar across its middle – and balloon tyres!' 'Have you lost your mind?' my mother said, throwing her brother-in-law a menacing look.

That was the only time my mother gave me a choice. 'You

can have a white costume edged with navy blue, or a bicycle,'
she said, playing on my vanity. Being eleven at the time, I
wasn't all that bothered about clothes except for my cut-down
boys' boots, but that was different, that was about making do
in difficult times. I had the feeling Mother regretted the de-
parture from more reliable ways, a sharp 'yes' or 'no' cutting
short my demands. Mostly, lack of money was the best arbiter.

I have no memory of why I stayed a night with Aunt Pessa.
Mother sometimes sent me with things other than apples,
sometimes a cake or a *challa* (a braided loaf) she'd baked herself. Maybe I asked to stay, maybe Pessa invited me. Why not?
I liked my cousin Rosl, I looked up to her: she played in a
Mandolin orchestra in Mannheim and had elegant long hands
and legs and huge, blue eyes. There was a touch of glamour
about her, though less becoming was the long bony nose she
inherited from her father.

Who organized the sleeping arrangements the night I slept
over, I don't know, but there was nothing strange about them;
the poor often shared beds; adults and children together, often
head to foot, like sardines. I remember my parents much later
laughing at such arrangements, evoking the bad old days.
Knowing this, I didn't find anything extraordinary in two single beds pushed together, sleeping four, Uncle Avrum and I
next to each other where the beds met, and cousin Rosl and
Aunt Pessa either side of us.

In the middle of the night I awoke with Uncle Avrum's
rapid breath on my face, reeking of tobacco, and moments
later, my body convulsed with a feeling so strong, that I rose
from the pillows, my elbows supporting my body. I was surrendering to what I didn't then know was an orgasm and simultaneously a liquid was running between my legs, sticky to
the touch. When it was over, I knew that what had happened
had to be kept a secret – and instantly, I felt responsible, afraid
that the liquid might go on the sheet. I disentangled myself

from the bedclothes, and from Uncle Avrum's arms holding on to my thighs. Carefully, I crawled down the bed so as not to wake my aunt and my cousin, and as quietly as I could, I tiptoed to the lavatory, leaving the door ajar – shutting it might wake someone. Standing legs astride the pan, I wiped myself clean with newspaper squares hanging on a nail in the wall, easing off square after square with my fingers in case ripping would be too noisy, and I didn't pull the chain either. More worries: why so much paper, someone might ask?

Then a thought struck me. Maybe Uncle Avrum had made a mistake and meant to do what he did to me with his wife. Holding on to that thought, a memory came of when we were still living in the Römer Straße in Worms and I was six years old. Uncle Avrum had been on a visit and stayed the night. In the morning, my mother and father and Uncle Avrum were laughing and joking together, all of them still in bed, two single beds side-by-side. I was running across the beds in my night-dress joining in the fun. Suddenly, what seemed for no reason at all, Uncle Avrum had smacked my bare bum, a significant smile on his face, and I knew even then that his slap was not innocent or playful. Something became indelibly inscribed on my memory; something so strong that the moment the orgasm was over, I knew that the two events were linked. And I was stuck to guilt like an insect to flypaper.

Back in bed, Uncle Avrum was snoring, his mouth open wide. Dawn was breaking. I didn't know which way to turn to avoid his bad breath. Breathing restlessly myself, I stretched out on my back, looking at the ceiling. Something momentous had happened; that much I knew. Aunt Pessa and cousin Rosl seemed to have been asleep throughout the goings on beside them. I have wondered about this all my life. What silenced us?

Cousin Rosl once told me that her father was the only boy among nine sisters. Was it because he had so many females around him that he behaved like a cockerel in a chicken run? That analogy came to me later when I was living in the country in England and we kept chickens – one cockerel among twelve hens.

I was now bound to my uncle with a secret so huge, it overwhelmed my knowing right from wrong. One lunchtime, I was playing marbles; when I stooped to pick up my winnings, I saw the turn-ups of a pair of trousers: looking up, I saw my uncle standing above me, silent. I knew at once what that meant: he wanted to do 'it' again. I sprang to attention; felt I was obliged to follow him. He was tall and thin, and legs long enough for two people and his trilby shaded his bony nose. A few steps on, I practically had to run to keep up with him: my uncle was in a hurry. I held onto my marbles, tightening my fingers round them. In his flat, he pushed me along the corridor into their bedroom. Stretching out his arm towards the ottoman, he bade me to lie down. Then he lay next to me and turned me onto my side, facing the wall. Having spat into his hand, he pulled down my knickers, and with his other hand, he took out his penis and covered it with the spittle; seconds later, he put his penis high between my thighs and instantly he shoved it backward and forward and, when he pushed it upward, my body went rigid, and rigid it stayed throughout this procedure and as the shoving got quicker – so quick, his liquid exploded into his cupped hand. His last push made one of my marbles clatter onto the wooden floor.

At that very moment, I wondered: if he had been that noisy when I was asleep, my cousin and Aunt would surely have woken up. Would I ever know? – Of course not!

There had been no pleasurable feelings for me this time. When my uncle had calmed down, he jumped off the sofa and, careful not to spill the liquid in his hand, went to the kitchen sink about five long paces away, and running after him, I saw him rinse a milky liquid down the sink. Then he washed and dried his hands and put his penis back into his trousers and buttoned up his flies. My knickers up to my waist again, he made sure that I picked up my marbles. I crawled under the bed to get the one that had rolled there. Looking up from under the bed like a cat might, the turn-ups of his trousers came into my view again, and this time, one of his feet impatiently tapped the floor. Then, with his voice trembling, he said, *schnell schnell*!' The missing marble reclaimed, I got to my feet, and then, he put his hand between my shoulder blades and propelled me to the front door.

Had my mother called me for lunch from our window wondering where I was? Where would I say I had been? Moment by moment, my life was becoming more complicated. In the street, he pressed a few pennies into my hand and hurried away. I bought chocolates with the money. I ate them all before I got home, licking off every bit from my teeth until the taste had gone.

Through the years I was sure he had a plan: he must have heard me pleading with my mother to buy me a bike, and he would teach me to ride it – that was his bait! I was sure of it. The orgasm I had experienced with him bound me to him – like thunder to lightning.

There was Gipsy camp on a dirt piece of land adjacent to the block where Uncle Avrum and Aunt Pessa lived. Whenever I had passed by on foot, the gate to the yard was shut, but through the slivers of the broken fence I snatched some details. Now looking down at the camp from the flat, I could see it as if onto a stage. What was going on in the yard was new and I didn't bother to watch Uncle Avrum rinsing the stuff off his hands this time. Below the steps of a vividly painted caravan, a man was playing a violin with his eyes closed, his body swaying to the sounds coming from the instrument, his sleek black hair glossy like polished boots. Some children sat on the steps of the caravan, and others ran about in the yard, playing hide and seek among iron scrap heaps. Uncle Avrum brought me back with a jolt: 'Stop dreaming, *Mach Schnell!*'

Once, when all the family were together in our flat, I remember sitting on Uncle Avrum's knee. The family were talking and laughing and singing Yiddish songs from Daheim (the homeland), each choosing their favourite. My father's was about a rabbi's passionate way of praying, and joyously he sang the last line: '...oh how he prayed... the way you crack a whip... that's how he prayed.' The room was filled with his passion for the subject. Uncle Avrum sang an altogether different song; his was about a Jewish girl having *Chain* (charm), and while singing he looked at me with raised eyebrows, barely able to disguise his flirtatious smile. I flinched, not knowing how to respond, vaguely smiling with my mouth closed. My uncle hardly had to swear me to silence. It was what he didn't say that made me his accomplice; like a damp handshake might indicate a weak person, I complied, and as the family chatter continued apace that afternoon, I heard the word Jentz (sex). All at once, I knew the word was linked to what my uncle did to me, and still sitting on his knees, I was overcome with panic. Soon enough, my life was blighted with wetting the bed nightly. Mother's despair was hard on me. Launderettes might have made the difference to the degree of her despair, or a rubber under-sheet.

From the time of my involvement with my uncle made going to my aunt Pessa's not exactly spontaneous. I must have shown reluctance when my mother asked me to go and see them.

'It ought to be natural for you to want to see your relations without being told to go!' she said. Ought... ought... ought...

But go I did, a tide of feelings falling over each other as I walked with apples dripping and, as usual, getting brown. She was alone in the flat and in the process of curling her hair with tongs heated on the open flame of the gas stove. When they were hot, she clamped them onto newspaper until the paper stopped scorching. Then, and only then, did she use them on her hair. All through this procedure, she smiled at me as if to say, 'So you enjoyed it.' My heart was in my mouth. So she did wake up! But then again, why was Aunt Pessa so pleased if my thoughts *were* right? Did her husband do 'that' with his daughter when I wasn't there? But why did these thoughts come to my mind at all? And believing I was weak and wicked, I vowed never to allow myself to have these feelings again. Physically, I seemed to have been ready for pleasure but, the older I got, the more I knew that adult sex was not right for an eleven year old.

What happened next was an event that changed the world and the fate of European Jewry. On 30th January 1933, Hitler became the Chancellor of the country my parents had chosen to live in for a better future. My mother and father, Aunt Pessa and I, were in our kitchen when the election results came through over the radio. The cheers seemed to crash through the fabric of the loudspeaker, over and over, '*Sieg Heil! Sieg Heil!*' Mother was cooking lunch. Kitchen noises seemed to intensify: the water running from the tap was like hailstones beating into the kitchen sink; the cutlery Mother put on the centre of the table sounded like iron chains falling into a heap; saucepan lids placed on pots clashed like cymbals; the plates she put out on the table turned like tops before they settled. The electrical machine Aunt Pessa used to help her rheumatism was buzzing monotonously like a swarm of bees; then, abruptly, it began to crackle louder, the blue, electric current flashing even more alarmingly in the glass bar as it made contact with Aunt Pessa's hands. Had she turned up the knob? As a rule, my mother and her sister chattered through this treatment, but this morning Pessa turned off the apparatus with an impatient flick of her wrist. 'Enough, enough!' she said, winding the cord neatly over her hand, putting it back into the indents of the box. Then, folding her hands in her lap, she looked into space, her brow twitching. As more salvoes burst through our loudspeaker, Aunt Pessa's agitation increased. Father had had enough too and switched off the radio. 'Well, we'll see.' he said.

All was quiet except for the rumbling of my stomach. Food now on my plate, I shovelled it down, and even before I had finished, I asked for another helping. The braised meat was delicious. 'You can have more potatoes but no more meat,' my Mother said more firmly than in her usual regrettable tone. Finally sated, I asked Father, 'What will we see?' 'I don't know,' he said carefully. But I knew that something dangerous for Jews was happening when Aunt Pessa said, 'They'll be after us…'

In the following days and weeks, my father went to his shop as usual. But now, with Hitler in power, there was no longer an air of optimism in the family. Graffiti was now everywhere and the messages on walls mirrored the things said about us on the radio. The message to the German people was clear: *Germans, open your eyes, never trust Jews, they're traitors.*

Columns of the SA (brownshirts) sang as they marched through the streets. Once, walking on the pavement beside them, I heard them sing the Horst Wessel song, a line from it cutting through me, '…*wenn das Judenblut vom Messer spritzt…* (…when Jewish blood spurts from the knife…).' Yet, the singers' enthusiasm aroused me powerfully. Then I did not consciously know what had moved me; I only knew the word 'power' the way my mother described a wilful person: 'He' – it was always a he – 'is strong as iron,' and clenching her fist, she'd gesture the way footballers now do after scoring.

Days dawned and dimmed as before, but red, morning skies were as nothing before the sight of the brash red of the Nazi flags, an altogether different red. Hanging from masts and from private dwellings, the symbol of the black *Hakenkreuz* ensconced in its white domain were seen more every day. And God, being ever-present, followed me everywhere: when I picked my nose, when I thought of the feelings Uncle Avrum gave me, when I wet the bed. No matter how I tried to conceive myself, the weight of guilt was the house my Uncle built, the house a snail carries and hides in.

Then without warning my 'income' dried up. Uncle Avrum, Aunt Pessa and cousin Bertel were emigrating to Palestine. I never heard them talk about this; perhaps in my feelings I was too confused to hear. On a fine sunny day, they came to say goodbye. We had coffee and cake in the communal yard below our kitchen window, our round wicker table brought out for the occasion. After we had eaten our fill of my mother's home-made cake, Uncle Avrum went and sat on the third step going up to our flat, his long legs stretching over the two stairs below, his feet flat on the ground. I flew over to him and asked for pennies. 'I don't have any,' he said, a low harsh sound coming from his throat. Not believing him, I ransacked his waistcoat pockets and all the pockets of his jacket. I looked up at his face; beads of sweat were on his forehead and his eyes were all over the place. 'Don't pester Uncle Avrum,' my mother said. How like the time she came to school to feed me the boiled egg, the proof of the teacher's five fingers on my cheek and how easily she could have given the teacher what for! Although there was no 'proof' today, I wanted her to 'know', and yank open the door to my secret. And thinking of these things, I could weep for both of us.

Being Jewish in Nazi times was bad enough, but having to add Uncle Avrum to the list of my fears was a worry too far. If the Nazis knew what I let him do to me, we would be arrested. We were 'dirty Jews', they said. My thoughts bypassed the family's hugs and kisses and their never-ending goodbyes. I fled to the washhouse in the yard where I could watch them through the window. I waited until they had finally finished saying their goodbyes and Aunt Pessa, Uncle Avrum and Bertel had waved as they walked through the big gate of our flat with their backs to us. That was the moment I emerged from the washhouse, a limp hand waving. No harm in that.

Chapter Six

German Neighbours

The Hermann family lived on the ground floor in the block at right angles to our flat. Mrs Hermann and my mother became friends, and her daughter Liesel became mine. Hitler being in power didn't stop Mrs Hermann coming to our flat most days, Friday sundown especially. She loved my mother's noodle soup: 'Just the smell of it, Mrs Lerner – that has to be for angels.' And sometimes she'd pour out her heart to my mother. 'My husband is grateful to Hitler – too grateful – for having a job, the first since the end of the war; I hate it when he raises his arm in the Nazi salute, when not so long ago he was a communist; whichever way the wind blows. Mrs Lerner, I wouldn't mind a modest gesture, after all, wages are wages – but he goes over the top shouting *Heil Hitler* to anyone who comes his way.' Sighing she went on, 'My husband has become a damned Nazi. How dare he think Hitler is our saviour!' Passionate in her argument on saviours – Jesus was hers – the plate of soup she was holding in her hands nearly spilled over. Tearfully, she confirmed her views, '*Die Nazis sind unser Unglück,*' paraphrasing Hitler: *Die Juden sind unser Unglück* (The Jews are our misfortune). And my misfortune was that I didn't know what they were talking about.

One bright summer morning, before Uncle Avrum, Aunt Pessa and Bertel went to Palestine, Mrs Hermann and my mother cajoled me onto the kitchen table, pulled down my knickers, and forced my legs open. 'What can it be?' they said, looking at each other from either side of me. I screamed so loud they stepped back, and with them out of the way, I jumped off the table and ran out into the street. It has taken me a lifetime to figure out what they were wondering about. Uncle Avrum's stuff must have dribbled onto my knickers and my mother must have thought it was a discharge coming from me.

Mother never set foot into Mrs Hermann's flat, but I did. Eating the forbidden sausages and bacon with Liesel was a treat guiltily consumed. Another attraction was the sweet sticky flypaper hanging over Mrs Hermann's kitchen table. As the flies died, I became absorbed in their fight for life, their legs in the air, moving furiously. I detached a dead one from the paper and took it to a spider's web under the coal flap below my parents' bedroom window and threw it into the web to watch the deftness of the spider parcelling up her next meal. To further my research, I caught a fly with a net, and pulling off one of its wings, I kept it in the hollow of my hand and hurried to my 'laboratory'. Flies dead or alive, the results were the same.

Mrs Hermann's flat was an escape for me, for I could not do my experiments at home, just as Mrs Hermann couldn't talk the way she did with my mother in her home. As for Mr Hermann and my father talking to each other, they never even exchanged the time of day, never mind setting foot in each other's homes. Mrs Hermann's association with us was reported to the Gestapo. With hindsight, I have wondered if her husband had something to do with it. Perhaps he gossiped in the pub about her being too attached to Jews. The State encouraged individuals to inform on family. Whoever it was that reported her to the Gestapo, she was summoned. When she returned from the Gestapo, she came straight to our kitchen. 'I tell you, Mrs Lerner,' she said, with more satire than she knew, 'The Nazis' 'rooves' are damaged.' Handing my mother the letter she got from them was not the trusting deed she may have thought it was. My mother's face flushed with fright. She couldn't read, but seeing the swastika on the letter heading was enough. Mrs Hermann was oblivious of the danger she brought into our life – and hers. Having given her opinion on the matter, she didn't tell my mother what *they* said, only what she was *against*. We'd heard it all before. Going to Mass every morning seemed to be enough for Mrs Hermann, and despite having had a warning from the Gestapo, she remained friends with my mother, as her daughter, Liesel, did with me.

Many Jews started to leave Germany. I was then still at school, and one day coming home for lunch, I burst in on a family scene. My mother's brother Adolph and his wife had come to say goodbye before leaving for Palestine. The siblings hadn't seen each other for years, in fact, not since her brother cheated my parents.

This was the wrong moment for me to say, 'I'm starving!' Words catapulted about in our kitchen and tears lay on my mother's cheeks. Everybody was looking at her, waiting. Why? What did they want from her? She was leaning against the wall, her face full of grief. When Father tried to comfort her, she shrank from his touch. I guessed that it was about that watch they'd quarrelled about. Mother seemed to be sliding back to her bad, old self, red-eyed and crying.

My uncle and aunt left without anyone saying anything conciliatory. A sorry scene, bowed heads all round. Hardly had they gone, my mother said to my father, 'I can't forgive him.' Father tried to comfort her again.

I didn't understand everything, but some words stuck out, the same ones she used when she urged me to go to see our relations: 'should' and 'could', 'if' and 'ought'. And here was my mother, stuttering out words she couldn't put into practice, fresh tears running down her cheeks. If I had the words to say what I thought, it might have stopped her from crying: my mother was, on the whole, quite reasonable. 'Perhaps you're right,' I often heard her say in arguments, though seldom when she argued with my father.

But at this moment, my father was the realistic one: 'Hoping for too much can turn out to be disappointing.' 'But if we don't admit our wrong, how will things get better?' Mother said feverishly. And then, with eyes dried, she said, 'families are all right until the strangers come!' The stranger, I guessed, was her brother's wife. Over the years I thought about my mother's views on 'strangers' and I decided that this must have been the legacy of an extinguished tribe.

All that my mother now had left near to her of her family was Pessa's daughter, Rosl, who had married Natan Goldberg before her mother, father and brother left for Palestine. I don't remember being at their wedding, but looking through my photo album, I stare at Rosl's wedding picture, and see the intensity in her eyes. This makes me wonder if that look was connected to what my mother and Mrs Hermann talked about so long ago: that Rosl had been a 'wild girl' – that she had had an affair with a German man. 'Oih…' my mother said, and Mrs Hermann said 'Ach…', and on they talked about abortions and knitting needles, and death; none of which I understood. What was abortion? And holding fast to that word, I remembered a girl telling me at school that when girls start to bleed, they can have children. Baffling. Bleed from where?

In a carefree mood one lunchtime, my mother said, 'Today, we are going to buy your bicycle, the one with the balloon tyres.' I shook with excitement: 'Where?' 'The shop opposite the baker where you have been looking through the window for ages,' she said. So, she'd been watching me. But never mind what she did; today she was the best mother in the world.

'Be careful!' she said, when she saw me wobbling on my new bike. It took a few goes before I could ride away smoothly, and when I did, my mother was all smiles, she even waved me off. When more practiced, I freewheeled joyously down hills, arms spread wide. This, I would never tell my mother! She might put my bike in chains, or worse, sell it!

Then, one summer evening, my bike being in for repair, I

walked to Mannheim and back after having spent the evening with my friends. Night had fallen. Halfway down Wrede Straβe, I noticed a car crawling next to the curb. It stopped beside me; the driver wound down the window, looked up at me and said, 'Which way are you going?' 'Number 40, Wrede Straße,' I replied.

The man opened the car door and said, 'Jump in, I'm going your way!' 'Thank you,' I said, getting into the car next to him. I felt rich. It was like in films. The only thing missing was not being wrapped in furs! If dreams are endless, the journey could have gone on forever. Sadly, the lift the man offered me turned out to be just that – a lift. He stopped at the corner of our street and stretching past me opened the door for me to get out. My dreams faded on the pavement. But the excitement of the drive made me tell my mother; breathless, I said, 'Mamma, Mamma, guess what? A man gave me a ride in a car!' My mother's face reddened and she flung her hand across my face. I knew I'd crossed a line. But what would she do to me if she knew what her brother-in-law had done to me? No! I would never tell her that!

Having been initiated, I noticed every mention of sex. Why and in what context was my father talking about prostitutes? 'They sell themselves for money,' he said. How much money? I thought, comparing it to the amount Uncle Avrum had given me. What made me speculate about such things? And how come my father knew about prostitutes earning money? And topping my thoughts, he added, 'One of the Daphners' daughters is a prostitute.' He didn't have to say which of the six daughters, because I instantly knew the one he referred to. Going to Mannheim one day, she had been walking across the road from me. Her bleached, orange hair matched with the lipstick and the floral-patterned dress of nasturtium yellow blooms, luminous on the black background, and her small waist was made smaller with a black patent leather belt. Her black patent leather shoes, with the highest heels I had ever seen, made her hips sway as she walked. I trailed her past the *Pfalzbau* – a new picture palace – on the road to the Rhine leading to Mannheim. On the busy footpath, she walked a few metres in front of me. Fearing to lose her, I then ran well in front of her and lent over the railing of the bridge, pretending to look back at Ludwigshafen. Taking a look at her face, I found another clue to her 'trade': very thin, dark eyebrows, and under them, the tell-tale of a shadow, like a man in need of a shave. I let her pass me and brooded on her swaying hips – a well-known feature of a prostitute, a friend had told me. I speculated on how hard she had to work to achieve for that look.

My father took a dim view about the Daphners living across the railway line, isolated from the Jewish community, and worse was that they lived in a wooden bungalow, that he called a 'shack'. The memory came flooding back: I had been to that 'shack', for what reason I don't remember, but what I do remember fits my father's description. The Daphners' priorities, in contrast to my parents' attitudes to housekeeping, were poles apart. The shack's wooden floor was grubby and the range was caked with grease, clothes hung over the back of chairs, and clutter was everywhere. My mother's opinion on clutter was that it 'creates arguments in a family, everyone shouting where is my this or my that.' Despite the reasons for disliking the Daphners' 'shack', it was surrounded by tall, majestic trees.

Well away from Lodz and strict dietary traditions, Mother had changed some rules. She stopped observing the use of separate pots and pans for milk and meat, and different bowls for doing the washing up, though she continued koshering meat and poultry. I remember her arguing with Father: 'If a pot is washed clean, it is clean, whatever was cooked in it!' On the whole, Father let her have her way, but then he was still humorous and full of contradiction himself, as when the time I won a bottle of fizzy drink at a fair. Excited, I ran to our shop, demanding that my father open the treat: 'Now!' I remember such an uneasy smile on his face as we drank. Since *Pesach* (Passover) lasted eight days, and I had won the prize on the workdays between the holy days, *Kosher El Pesach* food was still the rule and I had made Father stray from the rules. But at the time I am speaking of, he still laughed with us, and often he would say, looking heavenwards as if to ask God's advice, 'What can I do? Sadly, I live with two Gentile women.' Father lumping Mother and I together surprised me. Perhaps I had nodded in agreement when Mother broke yet another rule.

Laughing with us was good, but levity stopped when Father was praying. Eyes to heaven, his index finger over his mouth, he'd stop us from talking. Now was 'holy time'. That finger could also win an argument with Mother: 'Stop talking, Marie.' I know my mother didn't feel threatened by him. She merely saw his gesture bringing to mind the divine feminine perception Jewish women must have uttered for centuries: 'To live with a man is to study a page from the *Gemara*.'

Our religion was a mystery to me. Father assumed I knew all about it; he supposed that children automatically knew the principles, modes and manners to observe. 'Why do Christians pray with their palms together?' I asked my father. 'We pray with our hands holding each other as we do for washing them; we wear skull caps and they don't. Anything they do, we don't,' Father said dismissively. But that wasn't saying much; it was more a skilful avoidance than giving me something more to think about. Another time, he told me something interesting: 'We have an invisible God and they have a man-god, forbidden by our God.' That kept me busy for a long time because it didn't connect with what Dr Jacobs told us in one of my rare visits to religion class: 'God sits in the heavens and the earth is His footstool.' And there He was in my thoughts, sitting on an enormous padded chair, a long, black skirt covering His knees, His hands folded in His lap and His eyes up-turned, just like my mother's when she was annoyed with my father. But then again, how could He be invisible when Father said, 'he didn't grab hold of God's feet' which I later understood to mean that he wasn't excessively pious. I reflected on God's shape and practised catching air with my hands.

Even more puzzling was when Jews were linked to capitalism. Liesel told me what her father said: 'Karl Marx invented communism and was against capitalism, and Jews belonged to both, and Marx was a Jew and Hitler didn't like anything that Jews were, and worst of all, they were rich and took money from Germans.' That couldn't be right because we weren't rich and we often had to borrow money to buy food. Liesel was as perplexed as I was on that subject.

Another time, I asked my father, 'Why do Christians know us better than we know them?' That question, I had heard when I was listening to someone else talking about religion in the *Habonim* (Young Builders, a Jewish youth club). Some people I knew talked about such things, but nothing my father said gave me anything to think about. He just knew how to pray in Hebrew so fast the words melted into each other. Another time I heard somebody airing his views in our kitchen: 'We are like splinters under their skin which fester around Easter time, and somehow, we make them angry.' In our house, being Jewish was knowing about pogroms, Cossacks on horses, getting away from fires and going to other countries to earn more money.

I had no one close to me to share and discuss my thoughts with: Heinie was too young to understand these matters. I saw my life as being squeezed between ultimatums. Nothing was about being happy, in a way a cat or a dog could be, leaping and running, lazing in the sun, contented and carefree like the children in my class when we had been on a picnic in a meadow above the Rhine. They ran about playing hide-and-seek behind rocks and shrubs, shrieking when there was a 'find'; I sat alone, leaning against a tree as if shackled, brooding and squinting into the sun. It was a hot day and thunder was in the air. I seemed to be tied up like my gym shoes in a cotton bag gathered at the top with a drawstring. For the picnic, Mother had tried to make me happy by making sugared lemon-tea, pouring it carefully into a bottle with a snap-top opener, she cooled it under the cold tap. After wiping it dry, she wrapped it in several layers of newspaper, and done, she said, 'Don't break the bottle, you know we get a *pfennig* when we return it to the shop.'

Hitler had been in power only two years. People around us were changing. Helmut had changed. He was a year older than me and he lived in the flat above ours with his family. He wasn't my friend, but I knew him because he took my brother Heinie to school on his shoulders every morning; they both went to the same school. Heinie was six when we moved to Ludwigshafen. My school was in the opposite direction to theirs and it seemed natural that Heinie should go with Helmut. I'd see him swinging my brother onto his shoulders, Helmut the horse and Heinie the rider. 'Gee up, gee up!' Helmut called out, galloping along the pavement, Heinie's laughter ringing through the air, his curls flying.

And then one day, Helmut appeared, strutting, in the Hitler Youth uniform. Like a blast of wind shutting a door, Helmut's association with us stopped. When next he and I passed each other in the street, he looked at me from under his lashes. And from then on, I did the same. 'Why has Helmut stopped taking me to school?' Heinie asked. My mother bit her lip and remained silent.

German schools were now closed to Jewish children. Heinie was moved to a Jewish school. For me, going back to school seemed pointless. I was thirteen years old and ready to go to work. At least the money would be helpful, especially as

Mother was forever going on about the lack of it. 'If you worked as a domestic, you'd be fed as well,' she said. Having found a solution, she said, more joyously than I liked, 'One less mouth to feed!' Necessity silenced much.

My only regret about leaving school was missing my teacher, Fräulein Karsch. She was different than the other teachers. *Grüß Gott* was no longer the commonplace greeting it had once been. Avoiding greeting her colleagues in the Nazi salute showed her dislike for the regime. *Heil Hitler*, the official greeting now, distressed her; warily, she'd walk along the corridor holding a folder under one arm, and with her other hand she'd reach over to hold on to the folder by its corner. With both hands busy, and her eyes down, she could avoid greetings altogether, but inevitably keen party members accosted her enthusiastically. '*Heil Hitler,*' they shouted as if she were deaf. Cornered, she'd let go of the file to free the 'greeting' arm, and articulating speedily from the elbow she seemed to be swatting a fly, her eyelids hooding her eyes like secrets under a roll-top desk.

Fraulein Karsch was tall and slender, dark-skinned and dark-haired; her plump turned-up nose was, I thought, too large for her face. When she stood on the dais teaching, gathering her thoughts, her head held high, I could see up her nostrils, as into dark caves.

One day in class, Fraulein Karsch stood at the edge of the dais holding a book open towards us. She had asked us to gather in front of her. We looked up at the pages held open where a black-and-white picture of a painting faced us: female nudes, rotund like my mother. I watched the other children, their hands covering their mouths, their shoulders shaking with laughter.

Another time, Fraulein Karsch was standing on the dais beside the window, the light on her face, when she solemnly said,

'The next war will create new boundaries in human behaviour and there will be brutalities hitherto unimagined.' I didn't know what this meant, but I knew at once that what she had said was dangerous, not so much with my head but by the banging in my chest. That morning, I was full of fears; fear of the Nazis, fear for Fraulein Karsch and fear of my mother. Before I had gone to school that morning, my mother was distraught: I had wet the bed again. On leaving for school, she called after me, 'I will come to school and tell everybody!' I believed her and was waiting for her to knock on the classroom door. She didn't come. Another time, another threat: 'I'll wrap the wet sheet around you and make you go to school in it!' Again, I believed her. I have often thought of Fräulein Karsch since. How did she cope in the war?

Talking to me might have changed my bed-wetting habit more than Mother's threats. When the subject was brought up we were always grouped the same: me sitting at a corner of our kitchen table with my parents either side of me. They talked alternately; elbows resting on the table left their hands free to illustrate. 'Be good!' they begged, waving their hands about, opening and closing them like flowers, 'If only you were good.' There were other appeals, none of which I remember. But what I do remember is the way their words followed each other so smoothly: how did they do this? 'I promise' were just two words and I couldn't even manage them. 'Say something!' Father said, beside himself with frustration. When nothing emerged from my mouth, my parents fell silent too. But then Father in his usual way cleared his throat, gave a little laugh, and putting his fist on my back he turned it as if he were cranking a car, round and round, starting and stopping with grinding noises coming from his throat. This always made me laugh. I loved this self that needed winding up. We laughed together.

Father's jests were also good. I think it was on a similar occasion, after one of their 'talks' that I put my arms around my mother's waist and asked, 'Do you love me? I mean, really love me?' Looking up at her, I saw her eyes go cold, and with a voice to match, she said, 'Only if you're good!' By then, I knew perfectly well what this meant: don't wet the bed. I would have given anything not to, but how was I to stop the flood from flowing out of me when I was sleeping?

Years later, when we were in England, my mother, around seventy then, saw a programme on television on bedwetting. The next time I came to see my parents, she said to me, 'I have done it all wronk for you, darlink.' I fell about her neck crying. She then said, 'I know for why you are cryink, because I understand.'

Astoundingly, my school days ended with a flourish. I won a prize for geography, a book of poetry. Some poems were signed 'Anon'. Someone told me they were by Heinrich Heine. I learned he was a Jewish poet – a Jewish poet?

Chapter Seven

Boycott: Wrecked Hopes

In 1934, throughout Germany, Jewish shops had the Star of
David daubed on their windows and 'Jew' written in the middle
with the command below: *Kauft nicht bei Juden*! (Do not trade
with Jews!) I learned a new word: boycott. Worms was in the
past. Any hope we had of building up our lives again was shattered. Father's small shop in Wrede Straße was closed down
and his workbench was moved to under the bay window in our
kitchen. Our flat had the only private entrance facing the courtyard. Chance had it that tenants living in the block at right angles to ours, and those living above us, had to pass our kitchen
window where they could see Father working. 'Passing trade!'
he said, surprised. He even dared to fix a coloured enamel sign
on our front door showing a pair of trousered legs from the
knee down, the trousers neatly pressed, their turn-ups ending
above gleaming toe-caps. The prohibited service Father gave
tempted our German neighbours, but not for long. When trade
from them dried up, our customers came exclusively from the
Jewish community. By the end of 1938, their numbers had
dwindled too: customer emigration.

Our kitchen was now a noisy place. What with the hammering and clattering of pots and pans, I needed to be a contor-
tionist to hear the radio which stood on a triangular shelf in a
corner above a day bed in the kitchen. With my upper body
straining towards the soft cloth of the speaker, and my index
finger pressed down on the gristly bit on my other ear, I could
hear perfectly. We only had one wavelength in the Third Reich.
Politics apart, we had lots of music: Lehar, Strauss, Mozart,
Beethoven, Wagner. Listening one late afternoon, a news item

announced that Hitler was expected in Bayreuth. Curious, I continued listening. The commentator spoke in hushed tones, 'The *Führer* has arrived… the *Führer* is sitting down… the *Führer* worships Wagner….' After several moments of total silence came the national anthem, *Deutschland über Alles*. Then Mother touched my shoulder and said, 'You have to do some shopping for me.' That was the end of Wagner for that afternoon.

Listening another time, I heard Wagner's *Tristan and Isolde*, its *Liebestot* so overwhelming I asked myself how I could be so moved by something Hitler worshipped. And another time, a programme in a more frivolous mood came from the Scandinavian film actress Zarah Leander singing about human folly, *Ich hab heute Nacht, eine große Dummheit gemacht* (I was very foolish last night). I pondered on the notion of folly. Many years later, looking into the history of the Nazi era to compare it with my experiences, I realised that Goebbels, the propaganda minister, saw to it that the German people had bewitching creatures to admire. Glamour mingling with national zeal made tyranny more palatable, I deduced.

One lunchtime, my mother announced that I was going to a Mrs Dreifuß in Mutterstadt as a full-time maid. When was this arranged? Things were always being arranged for me without my participation.

It was spring 1935. On my first night with Mrs Dreifuß, I slept until the sun opened my eyes. The apple tree outside my bedroom window was in full bloom. I jumped out of bed and opening the window, a branch full with blossoms nudged its way into my room like a horse nodding over a stable door. Pulling the blossoms to me, I breathed in deeply and went back to bed. The walls of my room were covered with a patterned wallpaper of fruits and greenery. Staring at the sun-drenched wall, the fruits changed into faces with red noses and the greenery turned into hillsides and mountains with castles on top. When the sun inched away, my pictures faded. Jumping out of bed a second time, I become conscious that I had something to celebrate: a dry bed. And dry it remained for the time I was with Mrs Dreifuß.

Mrs Dreifuß had no children. She was tall and broad, and gaiety, like her body, spilled over abundantly. Her laughter was a series of loud chuckles that made her chin wobble. From her I learned things I have never forgotten, of how to clean and nourish wooden floors: first pour on turpentine, a square foot at a time; scrub with a hard brush and wipe with a dry cloth; when dry, rub in milk; let dry and apply beeswax; let dry, buff with soft cloths, but 'only when the cloth can run over the surface without catching,' Mrs Dreifuß advised. Done, I saw myself reflected in the floor, an opaque self. I never saw the room used. The living was done in the room behind their shop where rustic-patterned cotton was sold, stiff with dressing.

Mrs Dreifuß had dresses made for me with material from the shop she and her husband owned. 'This one and this one… and… this…' she said, taking the bales of fabric off the sloping shelves. My measurements taken, she wrote down the yardage needed for each dress, and looking from me to the fabric, she made her choices. One by one, she cut each length with a huge pair of scissors, cutting through the fabric on the wooden counter: clonk, clonk, clonk. When she had finished, she put the fabric in a paper bag and went off to the seamstress in the village, measurements held tight between her fingers.

A few days later, I knew the dresses were ready before she even came into the house. 'Rosel,' she called out, 'leave what you're doing to try on your dresses.' When Mrs Dreifuß pulled the two sides of the bodice together to button up the dress, they popped open again when I breathed. Again, Mrs Dreifuß tried, again and again, until I said, 'Ouch, it hurts!' Only then, did she give in: 'You must have grown since I measured you.' But, despite her conclusion, she continued pulling, pinning, mumbling, her chin wobbling with disappointment. No use, my breasts were growing. Defeated by nature, she said, '*Ach*, I'll take them back, and hopefully there is enough material in the seams to let out.' There was. A sigh of relief ensued. A few days later, the altered dresses were ready. At last, they fitted. Mrs Dreifuß was satisfied. But I wasn't. Their shop was stocked with worthy fabrics suitable for country folk, so inferior to what I had in mind. But how dare I look a gift horse in the mouth! Who did I think I was?

Whatever I may have thought about my new dresses didn't affect the way I felt about Mrs Dreifuß. She cooked, and I loved what she cooked; all the food was so different from ours at home. She even instigated a competition between me and her nephew, who was visiting, for who could eat the most dumplings. Thirteen was my limit. I grew plump in the six months I was with her and, disappointingly for her, the dresses she had taken so much trouble over became too tight.

Her nephew's name escapes me, but his image persists: the way his black curly hair stuck out above his ears, matching the black stubble round his chin, the pearls of sweat above his upper lip and his unruly movements, flexing his biceps against his chest. When the cat had kittens he picked up the unwanted ones (first making sure I was watching) and threw them against the back wall of the cesspool with smacking sounds. Seeing my eyes pop, he said, 'Everybody does it, it's a country custom!' Soon after that event, he asked me to come pillion riding on his motorbike, and when he put his hand under my skirt, I wasn't really surprised: this wasn't just a country custom, sex happens every where!

On yet another day, the cat playing with a mouse on the mat outside the kitchen door treated me to a live spectacle of nature at work: the delicacy with which she lifted her prey between her paws, pushing it, tossing it up in the air, claws retracted – and then, like a bell going off, she pounced, claws extended. Only the tail was left on the mat.

Washday was hard work. White linen was boiled in a copper, and when cooled down, it was rubbed on a washboard. Mrs Dreifuß did most of it. My arms didn't have the range. The stool I had to stand on became unstable from all the moving around I had to do. Mrs Dreifuß made light of that task, with her great height and large hands. There was masses of water for rinsing, and then the washing was put through the mangle and onto the washing line behind the vegetable garden. Hand-embroidered linen was ironed on the underside, slightly moist, which enhanced the glory of the craft; white on white was the most splendid. Beds were changed once a month. Linen was used in strict rotation, each new batch tied with pink ribbon and always placed at the bottom of the pile. Pink ribbons and Mrs Dreifuß's bulk struck a wrong note. She could easily reach the top shelf of the linen cupboard which looked taller than it really was, because the ceiling was low. Even I, standing on a stool, could get to the cobwebs.

Being with Mrs Dreifuß was more like being with a friend. I loved the routine of the household and the different smells, the chops and sausages we never had at home, and there was no lack of whole eggs – wonderful! Although, sometimes they were laid in odd places. Mrs Dreifuß encouraged me to find them.

In the front garden of a house across the way a pig squealed for ages. Mrs Dreifuß explained, 'It's the same every year, their knife must be blunt or something, kosher killing is better – but worse is that they make *Blutwurst* from the blood.' A few days later, passing the garden where the pig's life had ended, a woman rushed towards me with a chunk of what Mrs Dreifuß said was *Blutwurst*. I shrank in horror. Eating blood? Disgusting! And that was how 'kosher' made sense to me then, (but less so as I grew older). Steak slightly pink in the middle – delicious! All the same, eating blood still gave me doubts. How come my mother sucked my finger until it stopped bleeding after an accident I had with a knife?

The Easter I was in Mutterstatt it snowed hard. I don't know what I thought would happen, but whatever it was, Mrs Dreifuß saw me looking anxiously at the flurrying snow, and rocking with laughter she patted my cheek, her chin wobbling as usual. I wasn't afraid when I was with her.

Mr Dreifuß was slender and fawn-like. His eyes turned up like ticks and were the softest grey imaginable. His skin was delicate and creamy, and his sleek, silver tinged hair was swept back from his brow. The gold chain draped across his waistcoat led to a gold watch, and taking it from its pocket, he clicked it open to check the hour, his hands moving up and down as if to weigh time, and sighing, his eyebrows arched and his eyes closed, lids stretched thin. Watch back in its place, he walked through the lace-curtained glass door separating the shop from the living room. Standing behind the counter, he re-aligned the bales of fabric. Pattern and notebook on the counter, his finger ran down the list, pencil poised, ready. I was laying the table for lunch in the living room. Mrs Dreifuß called out, '*Mittagessen*,' (lunch). A few hundred yards from the Dreifuß's house lived Heinz, a Jewish boy. We had not been introduced, but we'd noticed each other when I was passing his house. Once, when he was on the porch, he extended his arms up to a rail and stretched them back and forth, his head inclining my way from under his arms. Pretending not to see me, he looked up and down, then back at me as I walked from his view. Heinz was blond, good looking and sturdily built, fifteen perhaps. I don't know why I remember his name. Maybe Mrs Dreifuß talked about him because she wanted us to meet.

Then one fine day, she said, 'No work today, Röslein,' (the German diminutive for Rosel), 'we're going to Spyer to see my relations.' A couple of memories remain from that visit: a white, chipped enamel bowl standing in a corner on a high stool outside the kitchen door; soaking in the bowl were ribbed tricot cotton pads stained with blood, the water marbling the same way as when my mother koshered meat. Again the blood issue confronted me. Then, looking up at Spyer Cathedral, I thought it was not as big as Worms Cathedral.

Late that summer, Mrs Dreifuß's niece visited with her fiancée. She was about twenty, the age of my cousin Rosl. Coming into the house, holding a bowl of plums she'd picked from the tree in the small orchard at the back of the house, she said importantly, '*Tante*, I only eat fruit and vegetables, it's better for the skin.' Her skin certainly had the hue of the plum in her hand, but my mother's skin was like hers, and she ate meat – puzzling. This was the first time I heard the word 'vegetarian'.

Although I loved being with Mrs Dreifuß, my feelings were in a muddle. I had no way of telling her about her nephew's hands threatening to paw me. Torn between Mrs Dreifuβ's goodness and her nephew's wandering hands, I was relieved when she assumed I was homesick. She appeared to be sorry that she had suggested this, and contradicting her suggestion, she said, 'But why? Everything you need is here!' Other things bothered me too: why did the Dreifußes still have their shop in 1935? How come they were still trading, the boycott having come and stayed? Perhaps someone in that household wasn't Jewish, but then, how come Mrs Dreifuß knew about kosher killing when I never saw any meat being koshered in her house? And no Sabbath candles?

In 1936, now back home, I joined the Jewish youth club *Habonim*. Mixing with Aryans was now rare. 'Jews, go back to Palestine!' was now scrawled on walls. In Habonim, we took this very seriously; we certainly were preparing ourselves to go there. But quotas for Palestine were limited, and what with Aunt Pessa writing, 'Don't send her here, we have trouble with the Arabs,' where could we go? From one crisis to another, it seemed. Meanwhile, I went from door-to-door to our Jewish customers collecting money for Palestine, rattling the blue-and-white box we called the Pischke. If anyone refused to give,

I put my foot in the door. Jews refusing to give? How dare they! *Habonim* was a solace. I turned into a fervent Zionist – if putting your foot in a door is proof of this.

We read no newspapers at home. Information came from the Jewish community and from the Reich's only radio station, so hope hung around a little longer. Streicher's rabid anti-Semitic newspaper *Der Stürmer*, displayed on stands in the street, killed hope stone dead. Grotesque caricatures of Jews gleefully pouring the blood of Christian children into a bowl full of matzo dough; I saw, but I never stopped to read; the corners of my eyes were good enough spies. Blood in matzo – perhaps it was those brown blisters on the flat surface? And why Christian children? Mrs Hermann said the Nazis weren't lovers of Christians; then why use them in that way to create hatred? It was the first time I saw us portrayed in this light. I wanted to be invisible. Before I even had a chance to know what being Jewish meant, really meant, it was destroyed for me by those images; they were so ugly. Another headline screamed: 'Death penalty for *Rassenschande*' – marriage or sexual relations between 'Aryans' and 'non-Aryans', a crime under the Third Reich – 'German women, open your eyes, Beware of the Jew!' A caricature of a hook-nosed man was drawn in bold black outlines and next to him was a woman's face, drawn with soft outlines, suggesting whiteness and purity. The headlines were in thick, black capital letters. Who needed details when the picture told the story only too well? We were outcasts. Streicher proclaimed that the Jews were the nastiest people in the world. Every day more 'proof' was found to confirm the Nazis' view of us. The father of a friend of mine was accused of *Rassenschande*. He was arrested. That was the last we saw of him. Even in our kitchen, we believed there was no smoke without fire, and reminding me, my father said, 'You see, this is what happens when you get involved with *Goyim*.'

Lots of Jews in Germany married-out or had Gentile girl

friends, and soon we were identified as people who 'polluted German people'. Moreover, anything the Jews had written was burned on bonfires. I saw this in a newsreel, book on book thrown into the flames. What Jews had written was bad. How could I judge, not having read any books? I began to see us as *they* saw us. Yes, I knew Jews who were ugly and I chose the ugliest among us to prove the Nazis right. And testing my own prejudice, I looked into German faces and saw pigskins. It was the bacon they ate, wasn't it? And the sweat on their faces was because they got drunk. But why then did I eat bacon? I couldn't reconcile my thoughts and beliefs with my actions. At home, fear of Nazi round-ups was common. Father's face was set, solemn. High-ranking politicians who were against Hitler just disappeared. 'Who will be next?' Father said, while tidying up his tools. My life was too small and the events around me too enormous to understand. And then some momentous news: Hitler was coming to Ludwigshafen. The year was 1936. I was fourteen years old. There was a lot of hammering in our market place, a podium and terraced seating was built, masses of flags were hung from private homes and offices and bunting and banners were drawn across streets all over town. Usually I saw such decorations in newsreels with Hitler's arm stretched forward in a solemn salute, more like a blessing.

I wanted to see what was going on. Father was alarmed, 'What do you think this is, *Simchas Torah*?' (a party for our Torah?), he asked. I felt envious: their celebrations, their Christmas, their New Year, their Easter – *our* nothing, I thought angrily. Where was the glory in being Jewish? I wanted to feel glorious, the way Germans did.

Despite Father's worry, I slipped out of the house. I walked along the pavement, my head bowed, close to the houses, 'creeping along the ghetto walls' as the phrase for Jewish misery is commonly known. And I did see, did hear, did envy; and feeling like this depressed me. Was I God's vomit? In woeful moments my father used to say, 'I am a sinful man!' Was I sinful? Was I being tested because I defied Him constantly, riding on trams on the Sabbath, slipping into cinemas, challenging His authority? Would He strike me dead, this moment? My bed-wetting made my mother angry, and what with Nazi threats against us, more every day, and God seeing everything, how then could I sort out my worries? Even when my father asked me to be sorry for my sins on Yom Kippur, his hands flat on my head, his tears raining down on my hair; my heart was rioting. I didn't know which sin to be sorry for first, and enraged, I cried. Did Father know why I cried? I didn't think so. Didn't I wish my sheet to be dry when I woke up? Didn't I long not to see those crooked black crosses when looking up at buildings? And if it is true that God knows and sees everything, couldn't He make Mother less harsh towards me and ask the Nazis not to say those dreadful things about us? And here I was, going to the market place to hear more dreadful things said about us.

A trickle of people walked beside me. Getting nearer the market place, the trickle turned into a flood, and slinking beside them, I hoped not to be noticed. I relied a lot on my turned-up nose; despite it not being hooked as Jewish noses were generally believed to be, I decided not to go too close to their celebrations: I would watch from behind the crowds lining the streets. I saw only the backs of heads and profiles, their mouths open expectantly. I knew the moment Hitler had arrived. Necks stretched upward and cheers burst from mouths. Women swayed like garlands in a breeze, their arms aloft, cheering. Small children sat on the shoulders of grown-ups, waving little flags. '*Sieg Heil, Sieg Heil,*' they roared. Was God deaf? No need for me to be afraid any longer, the crowd was exultant. Listening to them, I feared something new: their passion. It was the first time I realized that anti-Jewish propaganda and slogans written on walls were endorsed by the cheering crowds in front of me. Something happened in my head, I wasn't quite sure what.

One night, after Hitler's visit to Ludwigshafen, Mother got very ill. Her temperature was so high, she was delirious. Father rushed out to get Doctor Gottlieb. 'Kidney infection,' he said, 'very dangerous, she must go to hospital at once!' In no time the ambulance arrived and I worried, would she come back home? Would they let her die? Walking anxiously beside the stretcher on its way to the ambulance, I asked my delirious mother what I should do about the blood oozing from between my legs. My body was bleeding. 'Now you are a woman,' my cousin Rosl said. Later that day, she handed me a packet of disposable sanitary towels. By the way she looked at me I knew my bleeding was something universal to women.

Mother was in the hospital a long time; at least that is how it seemed to me. I did the housework and helped to cook. Rosl was heavily pregnant and did as much as she could. 'And yes,' she said when I concentrated on her vast stomach, 'you can have children now!' It was all too much for me, being Jewish, politics mixed with blood, and being a woman – no, I am still a child, I protested silently.

Mother came home feeling much better. Then I got ill. A few days before, Mother had decided I had not washed myself properly, and taking charge of my neck, she scrubbed it with a brush, the softer of the two we had, saying all the while, 'Where has all this *Schmutz* (dirt) come from?' 'Ouch,' I cried, 'it hurts!' but Mother scrubbed until my neck felt sore. 'That's better,' she said, judging the result. I don't know how she could tell, because when I looked in the mirror my neck was as red as borscht. Then I noticed that the whites of my eyes had turned yellow. Mother had been so busy scrubbing my neck she didn't notice my eyes. Better not tell her, else she'd take them out and scrub them too! I had, in fact, jaundice. 'Six weeks in bed will cure it as long as you don't eat fatty food,'

Dr Gottlieb said. The illness began with me being sick over my favourite food: noodles topped with dried stewed fruit and a knob of butter on top. The moment I smelled the melted butter I spewed all over my food, and over our lovely plush throw on the ottoman. Heinie and Mother sat facing me, our special treat being to eat away from the noise in the kitchen.

The thought of having to stay in bed for six weeks, as Doctor Gottlieb prescribed, was daunting. Time passed slowly. I spent a lot of the time looking at my eyes, then one day the yellow had gone. On the doctor's next visit, I greeted him jubilantly: 'The yellow has gone, the yellow has gone!' 'Good,' he said, 'you can get up now.' Doctor Gottlieb barely gone, I jumped out of bed, so suddenly, my legs gave way under me. On his last visit, I had tackled him about my fat knees. Could he do something about them? He smiled and stroked my hair. Doctor Gottlieb's hair was golden like my father's. When I was better, I became ill again. Doctor Gottlieb said I had diphtheria, but it was Mother who also said it, remembering such dangers in her youth. But Doctor Gottlieb confirmed that I must go to hospital. I implored him, 'Please don't make me go, please!' Despite Mother's safe return from hospital, I was afraid, partly of wetting the bed and what they would do to me if I did. My throat hurt, even when I whispered. Doctor Gottlieb decided, 'All right, you can stay at home as long as you take your medicine regularly.' But why, if I didn't have diphtheria, was our flat fumigated a few days later? Three possibilities: diphtheria scare, bed bugs, or us being Jews.

Swallowing the medicine was painful, quite apart from all sorts of vile-smelling poultices put round my throat. Eventually I did get better,.

Now fully recovered, I went camping with *Habonim*. We stayed in an old mill in the Odenwald. The winter that year was very hard, lots of snow. We would be there over Christmas and New Year, sleeping on straw sacks on the floor in outhouses. The more substantial building across the yard was our living area: a room warmed by a cylindrical stove. We spent the evenings sitting around that stove singing Yiddish and Hebrew songs. Our days were spent rambling over the snow-covered hills. A few boys from our group got lost in a snowstorm. Search parties went out to find them: a thunderous lecture followed by one of the group leaders. 'I've told you a million times not to go too far!' The heads of the boys hung sheepishly, red cheeks above soft fluffy beards.

All was well again until one night a scream pierced through the otherwise silent night in the sleeping quarters. Come dawn, there were whispers of misconduct. The culprit was sent home in disgrace. Male? Female? I didn't know. I had problems of my own: bed wetting – more accurately named, sack wetting. It stank to high heaven, my shame so deep the only enjoyment left to me was sitting round the stove, singing, a kettle humming on top. Then, on New Year's Eve, cosy and warm around the stove, a car screeched to a halt outside, two of its doors slamming shut in quick succession. Then, thumping footsteps dulled by the deep snow stopped outside our door. We looked at each other, our eyes conferring: who could this be? Suddenly a violent thump opened our door. Our group leader was in the middle of saying 'enter' when two SS men, revolvers in holsters on their hips, swayed into our room. The gusto of our singing stopped. Then, the two men tottered to the empty wall behind us, and having got there, groaned as they tried to straighten up, and failing, they slid down to the floor like rag dolls, each in a pose of his own. One fell sideways against the wall and, unstable, his whole body dropped to the floor, one arm at right-angles its hand curled like a ladle while his other hand, lay limp over his fly, and his mouth wide open. His companion remained in a sitting position against the wall, his head resting on one shoulder, wrists crossed floppily in his lap. Apart from their snoring, they could be thought of as dead. We spoke to each other only with our eyes, and singing very quietly we filed out of the room. To our relief, the next morning the men had gone.

Although some of the camping was fun, I was glad to be home again to eat Mother's cooking: good plain food. My favourite was borscht, potatoes and meatballs, served together in a soup plate, eaten with a spoon and fork, the roughly squashed potatoes packed tightly to one side like a cliff, and next to them the borscht hovering like a red sea. The meatballs were placed like boulders on top of the potatoes, and to finish, a couple of spoons of 'short' gravy over the meat. 'Who could top *de Mamme*'s cooking?' Father said, as he started to eat. We all agreed: 'No one!' Mother glowed with pride. By contrast, Mother's baking was inconsistent, sometimes it worked and sometimes it didn't, though her *Challas* worked every time.

Sometimes Mother bought live chickens, always boilers. They were full of fat, which she rendered down and stored in a jar to use for cooking and spreading on bread as a savoury, sprinkled with salt. The shrivelled bits of fat were a treat that Heinie and I shared between us, though not always equally. I was greedy and he let me have more than my share without quarrelling, just as he did with the pennies he saved. 'You have them!' he'd say. He was such a little father.

It was me who took the live chicken to the local *Shokhet* (ritual slaughterer). The bird sat quietly in the straw bag, its feet tied together with string. The rite was performed in the Shokhet's kitchen. Sharpening his knife on a stone, he ran his thumb tenderly along the edge of the blade to check its sharpness, and satisfied that it was, he started to say a blessing. Barely had the last words left his lips, the knife slid across the bird's extended neck, blood now running abundantly into a bucket below. On the way home, I touched the still twitching bird: warm. The chicken was for Passover, the last we were to observe in Germany. Older now, I burned with awareness. I helped Mother prepare for *Seder* (Passover meal). Being Jewish had meaning after all; holy moments, holy optimism.

I always called the clean-up before Passover the yearly 'spring clean'. The smell in our home, fresh and airy, old things made new with boiling soda water poured over kitchen utensils, and wooden surfaces scrubbed until they gleamed and then rinsed with fresh water, the table clad in white, laid with the white gold-rimmed plates Mother had saved money for in a jam jar, the white pillowcase folded three ways for the ceremonial three matzo, the candle light, the aroma of food coming from the stove – all of it done to rid the house of leavened bread. Father looked festive in his white Jacket. Leaning back in our straw armchair, a white crisp pillow behind him as if he were a king, and like a king, he prefaced the *Seder* as usual, only this time I understood more. 'Tonight we celebrate freedom: I am a King and Mother is my Queen, and we remember that we were slaves in Egypt!' What was I to do? Suspend reality? Egypt? We were oppressed now! Again, Father luxuriated against the pillow, leaning one way and then another. This was indeed a dream, so poignant that we all had tears in our eyes.

Then Father lifted his eyes and signalled to his Queen, ready to start the ceremonials. In turn, his Queen nodded to me: time for the blessing. My task was to bring a bowl and a full jug of water to the table from which I had to pour equal amounts over the King's hands, each in turn, every last drop. Then the King took the towel from over my arm and dried his hands reciting the blessing, and we all said Amen. The Exodus began: in no time we were at the stage when our tradition was passed from one generation to the next, usually by the youngest boy in the family. My brother Heinie asked in Hebrew, 'Why is this night different from all other nights?' That Hebrew question I knew because Father translated its meaning over the years. But for the rest of the story, Hebrew was the norm in our house without any translations. For each event in the Exodus, Father passed round little heaps of food on small pieces of Matzo in memory of how hard life was in slavery: the bitter herbs, the sweet mince for a sweeter life after liberation, and lastly, hard-boiled eggs served in saltwater for new life and new tears. Freedom, that universal dream, concealed in ritual and song, the Exodus remembered from our distant past. Had I been able to read Hebrew and have it translated into German, there could have been a debate round our table. Instead, as in other years, I was disappointed. I experienced our religion like emotional thumps in a mix of disgrace and fear, heaped on us by forces outside.

Chapter Eight

The Weilers

I was now fifteen and a wage earner. I worked part-time as a domestic for Mr and Mrs Weiler for five marks a week. They lived a few streets away from us. On the way to their flat, I had to pass the Gypsy camp next to where Aunt Pessa and Uncle Avrum had lived – a daily reminder of what happened there.

Mrs Weiler's cooking was more sophisticated and more varied than Mrs Dreifuß's, but she wasn't as merry and not as generous of spirit. Her gait was full of purpose: suddenly she'd be beside me, changing the way I'd done something. Her face was serenely colourless, and her bloodless lips, when parted in a smile, showed teeth like aged ivory. But her eyes burned like embers in grey ashes. I never saw her dressed in anything but black, and with a black hat to match when she was going out: she was a carbon copy of a Mediterranean widow. When going out with her husband, she wore the hat that had a bunch of plastic red-cheeked cherries above the brim which wobbled as she walked. Going to the market, she'd plonk on the hat without an ornament, and clawing it with her hand she'd secure it with a long pin with a jet bead at the end. When she bought asparagus, I salivated, already thinking of eating those thick, white tender stalks 'grown locally', so Mrs Weiler said. She served them with lashings of homemade mayonnaise speckled with chopped chives and we ate them holding the ends with a clamp on a short handle. We never had asparagus at home, I doubt my mother knew that asparagus existed!

Going to market with my mother was very different. To save money, we went just before closing time when traders sold off their produce for next to nothing. Mother spoke German muddled up with Yiddish. My heart pumped with the fear that traders would notice her Yiddish and, it being largely low German, would be understood except for the words in Polish and Hebrew. I had no such worries concerning Mrs Weiler, her German was perfect. She didn't look anything like a Jewish woman, and I doubted her Jewishness because she didn't cook borscht or poached carp, neither did she buy kosher meat. All my doubts were confirmed by the way she cooked soup using freshly shelled peas mixed with milk and butter, followed with braised meat: divine! Many of Mrs Weiler's dishes made me forget things kosher. I would cook like her one day, and to blazes with over-boiled chickens.

Nosy, I searched through Mrs Weiler's dressing table drawers. The search yielded only two interesting items: a pouch of Palmolive dry shampoo, and a black and white Art Deco clasp for her hair, for special occasions I supposed. Of no interest at all were a few bent pins and a fine hairnet tucked into a soap-box. Every other day, Mrs Weiler patted her grey hair with the dry shampoo. The clouds of pleasant smelling dust that floated about her made her hair look dull. I tried it on mine; the result was nothing like the way the glamorous actress Lil Dagovar's hair looked on street hoardings – apparently having used that product, *her* hair was smooth and glossy. It never occurred to me that Mrs Weiler might smell her shampoo on me.

Mrs Weiler was every bit as good as Mrs Dreifuß at making jam and bottled fruit, and like her she weighed fruit and sugar, then boiled the mixture until it stopped being too runny. And then the fun began: I was allowed to fill the Kilner jars with a lipped, long-handled spoon. That done, Mrs Weiler wrote dates and contents on the labels with a fountain pen, and passing the jars on to me she'd say, 'Take care you put them on straight!' – so unlike my mother, who turned the jar against the light to identify the fruit. That Mother made jam at all was surprising; she measured and weighed nothing, so it was mostly guesswork. Pectin? I am sure my Mother didn't know about that! As with her knitting, she learned by trial and error. Luck mixed with experience often got good results.

One morning the Weilers were going out, and as usual Mrs Weiler looked up at me from under her hat – the one with the cherries – to brief me just in case I'd forgotten what was to be done. 'Make sure you use the shammy for the glass doors of the bookcase and not dusters, because, as you know, they smear the glass... and, make sure you polish the dining table and chairs, and be sure to use a clean cloth which is in the third drawer of the kitchen dresser!'

Doing the glass doors of the bookcase, I noticed a title on the spine of a book: *La Bohème*. I had learned to sing all the arias by ear from the radio and from a film made of the opera. I found the words difficult to understand when sung in high notes but here they were written down in the book between the score – in German! Book in hand, I sang to my heart's content being Mimi and Rudolpho alternately, and lost in pleasure, I was startled when I heard the front door shut. The Weilers had come back. I picked up the leather and continued where I'd left off. There was no mention of my singing, or the time I had wasted.

Arriving at the Weilers' one morning, a newspaper lay unfolded on the kitchen table, the front page showing a large picture of a townscape dense with black fog. Buildings, street and car headlights, all had fuzzy outlines. The caption read: 'London under fog.' How miserable, I thought, I won't go there! Our fogs were white, like steam from a boiling kettle; I was briefly proud of where I lived.

Between negative thoughts of London and the torment of my nocturnal problems, Mother helped me to be an ordinary perverse teenager. She knew the day and time of the week I cleaned the windows, and there she'd stand on the corner opposite the Weilers' flat, watching me, one foot off the sill and the other swinging free. Her lips and brows drawn together, my mother waited in silence until I had finished. I loved her being there: cleaning windows appears to have been my act of defiance.

Weiler had been the owner of a large store of men's clothes, four storeys high, in the main shopping street in Ludwigshafen. After the boycott, his store was confiscated. Nevertheless, a former German employee still made shirts for him – dangerous for both of them. Laws against Jews were shaming for us, and frightening, a little more every day.

One morning, a heavy envelope came thudding through the Weiler's letterbox. When they'd read the contents of the forms, they repeated out loud what they'd just read, 'All valuables must be ready...', date and collection time underlined, a warning added that withholding anything would be punished with imprisonment. They looked at each other, their eyes locked in disbelief. From then on, Mr Weiler grew more silent every day. We had the same forms as the Weilers – all Jews did. Someone who could read German and understand its meaning read out what I already knew. Although my parents were illiterate in German, they understood what was going on. 'What will become of us?' Mother cried out, 'we have nothing, not even a *Menorah* for *Chanukah*!' My parents planned to have a silver *Menorah* (seven-branched ceremonial candle) when times were better. For now, father fixed the candles on a flat piece of oblong wood with wax from another candle. One candle was lit for each day of the week to re-enact the undefiled oil, which apparently burned miraculously for eight days. Father never sang the traditional *Chanukah* song *Moazur*; I learned that in *Habonim*. But whatever our individual responses to anti-Jewish legislation, times were changing fast, and it seemed that any progress we had made as Diaspora Jews, shrivelled back as speedily as an umbilical cord.

Why was Weiler not acknowledging what was going on around him, when his son was going to America after having been thrown out of Heidelberg University? Perhaps to convince himself as he once said to a visitor in my presence,

'Hitler only means to torment the uncultivated *Ost-Juden* (Eastern Europe Jews) and as for the Yiddish they speak, the way they've barbarised the German tongue – no wonder Hitler is after them! That I was present when he said this seemed not to bother him. Surely, Mr Weiler must have talked about the situation we were all in with his friends? Was Mr Weiler too upset to 'see' that, when his son was forced to leave Heidelberg University? Did he think he would be excluded from the Nazi plan?

Only a few weeks before his son was to leave Germany for America, I was helping Mr & Mrs Weiler pack for him. Mr Weiler's movements were robotic when he ironed his son's new shirts on the kitchen table, and having folded them, he passed them on to me. It was my job to roll up ten mark notes and ease them into the shirt collars in place of the whale-bone strips. This deception was exceptional, because the amount of money Jews were allowed to take out of Germany was a derisory ten marks. Had Weiler's son been caught, the punishment would have been disproportionate to the crime.

Weiler ironed shirts well enough to be displayed in the windows of his shop – had he still been the master of it. I watched him carefully, and being aware of me watching, he let me have a go. A few words of instructions sufficed, more like grunts than words.

As the date for packing up the goods to be confiscated by the Nazis neared, I helped the Weilers: hampers and boxes were filled with silver, tankards, crystal bowls and vases, precious china and jewellery. Mrs Weiler complied in every particular except for one gold chain. 'Would you send it to my son if you go to England?' she said, holding the chain midway between us. Her eyes fixed on me, assessing my honesty and then, having considered, she withdrew her hand and let the chain fall into the padded jewellery box already in the hamper. It occurred to me later that she may have imagined me being searched at the border. Maybe.

My father was more realistic about our situation. As long as he could still earn a living, we would manage. When things got rough, he dismissed the goings-on with a shrug of his shoulders, 'Yes, they are clobbering the Jews again!' This was not nearly as strong as my friend Eva's father's words, 'This time round this tyrant Hitler will tell the Jews a real story.' His friends laughed at him; laugh or not, Eva's father secured a visa for Palestine, and the people who laughed were trapped.

When I was free in the afternoons, I went to the cinema. One film I saw implied that Jews were rats, scuttling in and out of slum houses. Then, Jews were changed from clean-shaven to bearded. The former, the film showed, were as the world tolerated them: cultured, straddling two worlds, converts to Christianity. Those faces dissolved and were transformed into Jews as commonly perceived: scruffy characters with hooked noses, sly, deceptive smiles on their faces, tricksters and traitors; evoking Judas. The point was made several times from one image to the other with pauses to feed the subconscious, driving home the point that *all* Jews must now be seen as scruffy and deceitful. In the film, euthanasia was justified for the mentally ill who, like the Jews, were depicted as freaks of nature. The cinema was packed. Walking home, I saw some justification for euthanasia; I had briefly been a nursemaid to a boy who was born with Spina bifida, and one day when I was out with him, he fell out onto the pavement, arms and legs dangling every which way. Stupidly, I hadn't strapped him into his buggy. Had I caught the Nazi sickness?

I was sure my father's complacency came from the fact that he was happier in Germany than in Poland. My parents never learned Polish. As for any studying they did, learning the Talmud was enough, though the mark of real learning was if you could translate Hebrew into Yiddish. Although Father was fluent in Hebrew, he was not a good translator. The teaching of girls was rarely an issue in my day.

Discredited as the Star of David had already been, observance of *Rosh Hashanah* and *Yom Kippur* affirmed how seriously my father was affected by Nazi politics. The four of us were walking to *Shul*; Father was holding his Talith bag embroidered with a Star of David in gold, under his arm, inward to his body. Father was anxious – we all were: anxiety is catching. My private thoughts were: If I smiled, it could be read as an often-heard phrase, 'Let's cut down those brazen Jews.' I didn't want to be at the mercy of anyone's mood that day, or any other day for that matter. Had I been as good in mathematical calculations as I was in finding reasons to avoid German people's eyes, I could have gone far.

To this day, I carry the remnants of that time. Taking a taxi to a synagogue, I always ask to be dropped off at the corner before. But should I have the temerity to ask to be taken to the door, I first look at the driver's face, as nowadays I fear it might be a Muslim with a grudge. 'The corner will do' is my rule.

Ost-Juden living in Germany had yet to catch up with their German-Jewish brethren. Depressingly, Eastern European Jews, like circus performers, had walked on eggshells for centuries to avoid religious anti-Semitism.

Vilifying Jews in the political context started around 1875; the *Herrenvolk* practised Hitler's religion, and if not yet clear enough why they should hate the Jews, they had but to remember going to church, sitting next to their Granny listening to condemnatory words said about Jews coming from the pulpit. Swearing loyalty to Hitler was simple, the subliminal religious content in Hitler's speeches was a gift to them from on high.

Licensed prejudice fired even the most withdrawn individuals, and they didn't have to be members of the Nazi party. Once, I was having fun with a girl by unwinding cotton reels and stretching the threads across the road to each other's windows on the ground floor. What this was supposed to achieve I don't remember, and stupid as this game was, it had rather unfortunate consequences. The flimsy threads went across a neighbour's throat as she passed our window, and looking up, she saw me. I thought no more about it, until I heard Mrs Hermann tell my mother that the woman had reported me to the Gestapo. Her claim was that I tried to kill her. My mother, as ever, reacted wildly, clutching her chest. Mrs Hermann calmed her by saying that the woman's story was pathetic; adding, 'I am sure she needed to believe that Rosel wanted to kill her. Our block is riddled with stupid Nazis like her. And you don't have to raise your arm in the Nazi salute to be one either!'

A few weeks later, my accuser died. In the antechamber of the burial ground, I looked down at her in an open coffin. It was the first time I had been at a cemetery or seen a dead person. I was relieved she was dead. I couldn't stop looking at her laying there, her grey hair neatly combed back, exactly as it was when she'd passed our kitchen window. shopping basket over her arm, not a hair out of place. Her face seemed to get smaller as I looked at her. I was startled when men came and put the lid on her coffin to take to the grave. The sound of clods of earth falling on her coffin boomed up at me. Liesel touched my arm: 'Come on, Rosel, let's go home!'

On another day, Liesel asked me to come with her to her father's allotment. I hated being near him. Liesel reassured me that she too didn't like 'the Nazi in him', and jollying me along she said, 'Don't be a donkey, come with me, the gooseberries are ripe.' When we got there, she wandered off to another allotment, leaving me alone with her father. Uneasy, I waited by the gate. Soon, Liesel returned, and pushing open the gate, she pulled me into the gooseberry bush laden with plump ripe berries. Between popping them into her mouth, she said, breathlessly, 'There is a boy on the allotment I went to…' and pulling me closer she went on, her voice low, 'He made me touch him. It was hard.' Her face reddened. Maybe *I* could tell her that I knew about such things but my throat closed and my heart ticked apace. Picturing Liesel with that boy, I saw Uncle Avrum's penis. Dirty business.

Disagreements between Germans and Jews, however commonplace in the past, now took on fresh meanings. 'What can you expect from Jews?' was one among many once 'harmless' prejudiced asides, hand-me-downs from before Hitler's time. Germans now had a choice of accusations, not just that of killing the Christian God. *Die Juden und das Kapitalismus* (Jews and Capitalism) were linked in Hitler's speeches: Jews were rich and were crooks and robbed Germany of its wealth. That meant me as well. But I wasn't rich. I tried to make sense of this. Injustice weighed heavy. In my head, I was already living elsewhere, but my body was still in Ludwigshafen, and to me it was a dump. Its sister town, Mannheim, was elegant: it offered a *Schloss* (palace) surrounded by a park. I loved walking over the Rhine Bridge away from Ludwigshafen. The moment I saw the *Schloss* my mood changed. Walking the other way, the chimneys of the *I.G. Farben Fabrik* (a dye factory) prodded the sky. A few blocks from the *Schloss* was the National Theatre. I remember going there with my cousin Rosl and Natan, risky even in the early Hitler years. Gigli, rotund and short, sang of love and loss, and the more moving the song, the more his eyebrows sloped downwards.

Rosl and Natan were at that time expecting their visas for Palestine. Natan had been reading mathematics at Heidelberg University, and having been thrown out in his third year, had time on his hands. Living with us, except for sleeping, they rented a furnished room in the good part of town. Jeanette, their daughter, was born there. My mother was now surrogate grandmother and great-aunt to Jeanette. She gave her all, we all did; we adored her. Jeanette was our star. Heinie and she were inseparable; she followed him everywhere and called him 'Nihei'. Father minded her when we were out, but he grumbled when she rummaged around among his sharp tools, the knife for cutting leather especially. What she really enjoyed was banging the hammer on his cobbler's last: 'Bang, bang, bang,' she said, in rhythm with the sound she made. She lit up our lives; even her eating the weekly ration of our two ounces of butter, her face shining, amused us.

Natan spoke good English. 'The,' he would say, trying to teach me, 'No! Put your tongue between your teeth!' He illustrated, and like a parrot I repeated, 'the, the, the…' though I could have sworn Natan said, 'zee' as I continued walking around the flat repeating, 'the, the, the' until he protested, 'Enough, Rosel!' When Rosl and Natan's visa came through, the wrench of parting from them was profound. It was 1936 and we weren't going anywhere yet. Rosl took photographs of us all before they left.

When they were in Palestine, pictures of them came regularly, but they never had the warmth of the cuddles we had with Jeanette. Our separation from them struck deeper than I understood at the time. I would never be able to check whether Rosl knew about how her father was connected with me. Had she been asleep or not?

'Jeanette's classmates have changed her name to Carmella,' Rosl wrote. Ever more pictures of her arrived, her fair curly hair now darker and straighter, parted at the side, a slide holding back a heavy lump of hair, and she was smiling shyly at the camera. Later pictures of her would show she had inherited her mother's teeth set low in her upper gum; later came a picture of her aged fourteen dressed up for the festival of Purim, looking sensuously at the camera.

Why were we still in Germany? Contented – of course not! On a bitterly cold Friday, the year the Rhine froze, it was my turn to deliver the repaired shoes. Father was putting the last touches to them before the darkness and the Sabbath arrived: huffing and puffing, his hand poised, a stick of wax to the flame, and when it softened he steered it round between the ledge of the sole and the uppers, followed by a zigzag metal wheel before the wax hardened: a beautiful finish. As the afternoon waned, Father's rear danced around on his stool. Cranky, he said, 'How hard it is to be a Jew!' Mother continued with things still to do: the extra coal for the stove to heat the water for our weekly baths in a zinc tub; Heinie and I shared one tub of water and my parents shared another. The sheet hanging over the string stretching across the kitchen was to hide their nakedness when they bathed; Father's clean underwear near-to-hand by the tub, the fragrance of winter apples in the air, stored on slatted shelves in our wardrobe; and sometimes, the sound of Mother's spittle sizzled on the iron as she tested the heat for a last minute press of collar: the thumping of the iron on the table. our clamouring questions, where was this, or that? Lack of time never diminished intimate moments with our mother. When Heinie and I bathed, it was a time for leniency and licence, much splashing and giggling, the pursuit of lost soap, the luxury of hot water, and time enough to notice Mother's rosy cheeks as we had fun, instigated by her. It was heaven to dry ourselves in front of our roaring fire, the nearest we got to being by the seaside. Finally, pots of food back on the stove. And as sundown loomed, Father got ever more agitated still having thing to do: the sweeping, the tidying of tools, sorting them for the next working day, the bucket of water in which the leather had been soaking to be emptied in the yard. The shadows of sundown now everywhere, Father made his workbench 'disappear' by throwing a white sheet over it, momentarily aloft like a tent.

Mother then lit the Sabbath candles: making three circular movements with her hands over the flames she gathered up the spiritual value to her face, mumbling the blessing for lights, her Hebrew not altogether accurate. A sharp sigh from Father ended the week and by the time he said the blessing over the Challa and wine, he was in praise of how good it was to be a Jew. He had fulfilled the obligation to welcome in the Sabbath.

Well, are you ready?' Father said, bringing me back to the present. Sure I was! The smell of melting wax was my signal. Mother was doing up the buttons on my coat right up to my neck, and pulling off a scarf hanging over the back of a chair, she wound it round my neck – twice! 'No!' I protested, but Mother, knowing my ways, said, 'Don't you dare undo the buttons on your coat – not today!' Continuing to bundle me up, she thundered, 'I know you. And don't lose the money!' Defeated, I gave in, but I wanted to brave the weather, the way my friends did at *Habonim*.

Mother was right about the money; I had lost it once. This, I was given to believe, was a financial meltdown for the Lerner family. When was my mother not anxious? According to her, I was going to die prematurely of something; if not from the cold, or the Nazis, it would be from drinking water from the tap. '*Oih*,' she'd cry to Father, 'Look how she's gulping down the water!' Her reaction was most likely prompted by memories of typhoid from impure water in her past.

At last, I was on my way, and there was to be no dawdling. Passing an old, disused marketplace, I heard children's laughter and shrieks of delight. The merriment arose from people three to four rows deep in a moss-stitch pattern. Criss-crossed above their heads hung naked, electric light bulbs cheering the cold gloomy afternoon. The ring of laughter drew me. Mother's warnings dimmed as I pushed my way to the front. A space was roped off like a boxing ring. On the ground lay thick, frozen ice, the edges frilled and fringed – a skating rink! Children were skating; some did it well, others hung onto the ropes, and those without skates slid on a run of ice burnished from continuous use. The dull thud of stomping feet and gloved hands banging together was a commentary on the biting cold. Children fell on their behinds sliding along the ice, legs in the air. Some onlookers called out encouragement, and others teased; rolling laughter and billowing breaths rose and ebbed away.

I had never skated before. Watching these children gave me confidence. But how was I to get a pair of skates? Money was short. I'd earn it, the way I did for my first bra, by scrubbing floors. This was more reliable and practical than hoping to find money or giving broader smiles to customers to get tips. I rarely got any. Full of plans, the string bag suddenly heavy on my arm, I looked up at the sky. It was pitch-dark. Father would be home from prayers and he'd be furious! I'd tell Mother, she'd understand. And with that comforting thought, I pushed out of the crowd.

No longer surrounded by human warmth, the icy wind lashed against me. What made me look back was a thin, rhythmic rattle. A rough-edged piece of tin, hammered flat, was strapped to a post with hairy string, pushed through holes punched out on the top two corners, which left the bottom half free to flap. The wisps of string quivered in the wind. A bulb above the post lit up the sign written in chalk: 'Jews are not allowed here!' On the way home, I thought of my last Christmas at school.

The whole class had been busy trying on costumes for the nativity play. I was the only Jewish girl in the class – wasn't I always? I wasn't given a part to play but was allowed to stay and watch the rehearsals. Aryan children were dressed as ancient Israelites, like those illustrated in drawings I had seen in rarely attended religion classes. I was thinking hard about my origins: I came from the Israelites… I would think more about that some other time… but then, who did these children think I was? A Jew, of course! But who did the children think *they* were, dressed up like Israelites? What was the difference between being a Jew and an Israelite? Meanwhile, Mothers sewed costumes, ripped open seams, adjusting, pinning, unpinning; there were cries when a needle pricked flesh. The teacher's desk was piled high with glitter and tinsel, gold braids and cords, and beside the desk on the dais was the stage. A light beamed down on the golden-haired Mary, on her lap baby Jesus, a doll whose eyes were closed, straight lashes round the lids. All of them spoke their lines in German. But Israelites spoke Hebrew. Don't they know this, I thought out of the blue. I felt sore and raw and gouged out. Empty, I walked home. And empty were the sheets of paper where my essays should have been. But then, even if they'd let me take part, Father wouldn't. And on went the muddle in my head.

As the Thirties neared their end, the Nazi plan for us unfolded ever more worryingly. Jews left in droves. Departures were often abrupt and goodbyes weren't always managed. We didn't think people bad mannered; telephones and cars were not widely owned. If someone didn't turn up a couple of times at the club we said, 'He or she must have left.' Now fewer in numbers, we still met but in smaller premises, a whitewashed room in a basement. A picture of Theodore Herzl with his imposing black beard hung on the wall in three-quarter profile, the standard picture of him seen on the walls of most Jewish institutions at that time. I was swept along by ideas not fully understood. What became clearer as each day passed was that Germany could no longer be our home.

I left the club one night pushing my bike through the park of the *Schloss*. Halfway through, I saw a dark-haired youth pushing his bike too. He stopped next to me, and in no time, we fell into conversation, both of us holding our handlebars. We exchanged names; his was Kurt. I must have been brave enough to tell him that I was going to England in a few weeks time 'I envy you,' he said, 'I wish I could go with you!' He went on to tell me how he disliked Hitler's Germany and how he lived in dread of a knock at the door because he had defected from the Hitler Youth. He seemed to know that war was being prepared for, and said, 'I don't want to take part.' I held my breath; I saw traps everywhere. I knew that the word for such reluctance as Kurt's was traitor, but then, only Jews were traitors! Could Germans be traitors? I was afraid to talk to him about it. Say a word and it is evidence; think it and it can still get lost. Run, Rosel, run! That was the first time my senses connected to the name Judas, who, I heard it said, was a traitor, his name written on street walls with the added word, *verrecke*: '*Juda verrecke*!' (Perish, Jew!) Why was I to perish? What did all this mean? Why did it make me feel so wretched? Why did our name carry so much blame? I asked no one in case I would suddenly die from blame. Why tackle those thoughts now? On and on the questions came: why were we thought to be so vile, and so hated?

Kurt's confession was news to me, so new and so hot, my senses burned. But if Kurt is a traitor to Germany, I knew six more Germans who were: Fraulein Karsch, Liesel and her mother, and the two Catholic sisters who lived two floors up from Mrs Hermann. Although I was by no means sure of anything I thought, I didn't want to risk seeing Kurt again, and I decided to cycle round the ring road, the longer way home. Dangers everywhere. If I took chances it might mess up my going to England, but secretly I wished to know more. Perhaps Kurt had told me too much and was afraid like me. That was a much later thought; by then I had made him into a hero and wondered what he did when the war started. Did he lock up his objection to Hitler's Germany in the most secret place in his heart, and storm forward in a battle in some God forsaken place, and die?

Each time I stopped to look into a mirror, no matter how good-looking I thought myself to be, I saw myself as the Nazis saw me: a dirty Jew, reinforced with the black letter 'J' for Jew that now dominated our identity cards, written over other particulars, and no matter what our first names were, from now on, men and women were Israel and Sarah respectively, meant as an insult. No matter who we thought we were, or what we did or dreamed of, Hitler unified the Jews: the rich, the poor, the wise, the simple, the pious and the rogues, atheists, artists, scientists, and all the fools among us. Most poignant of all were those who no longer knew who they were, surprised they were summoned at all, thinking they had detribalized themselves, proud to be free thinkers. And thus stunned and confused, Jews complied with Hitler's conscription laws that swept throughout Europe, observed in the most meticulous way by people without a land of their own – that was part of their tragedy! Hitler had achieved the perfect transference of his hatred. Jews stopped playing their violins, shut the lids of pianos, stopped hammering out words, pushed aside their tools, moved from frenzied life to silent prayers and none, from visibility to invisibility. No time to cook, no time to wash themselves or their dishes; complying, they put a few belongings in a case, and gathering their infants, they attended the Jewish roll call.

On these roll calls, some put their infants into sacks and were able to carry their 'belongings' over their shoulders for journeys named 'resettlements', the euphemism for murder, hoping they'd fool the guards. But they, ever conscientious, tested the wriggling contents with bayonets. And those who hid in cupboards and in secret places were found by dogs or consumed by fire. After the war, the mountains of suitcases, spectacles and hair bore witness to an atrocity few imagined could have taken place in the heart of a country so rich in music and philosophy and, helpless on high, a merciful God.

Chapter Nine

Lost in Hatred

When I was first accused of Deicide, I had no idea how old this blame was. For me, it was as fresh as the day I heard it. I rushed home and told my father. 'You can't kill God,' he said, 'God is a spirit, not a man!' So Father did know the difference between the two religions! I was content – that is until I heard that Jesus was a Jew.

I went to look for him in the church opposite my school. People dipping their fingers into a font and crossing themselves before entering the church reminded me, in part, of Passover, when we dip our little finger into wine, counting the plagues meted out by God to the Egyptians… *dum, sephadea*… With this ritual, I came to understand that religious symbols are similar and that they are used for different reasons evolved from earlier times. The more I compared procedures, the more mysterious they became. I looked at the man hanging on a cross, his bowed head wreathed in thorns. When others knelt, I remained standing. Men didn't wear *Kipot* and women stood next to men. I was sure everybody could hear my heart pounding, yet despite the turmoil inside me, I went again and again. Why did we have an invisible God, and why did Christians have a human God, and why did he hang on a cross? And why was he celebrated as a baby – a baby in a crib being God? Absurd!

In one of my visits to the church, I came face-to-face with a bridal couple. They were leaving to the sounds of a booming organ. In my haste not to be noticed, I almost collided with them but managed to dive into a pew. The bride wore a black satin dress and a white veil fixed to small, stiff flowers round her head; cradled in her arms was a bouquet of red roses, their stems wrapped in a paper doily. Smiles all round. When a congregant said, '*Guten Tag*!' to me, I fled, my footsteps in rhythm with my heart. What if my father knew?

Going to the cinema tested my feelings differently. I bought my ticket under the now ubiquitous sign in public places: 'Jews Are Not Allowed Here'. Bowing my head, I truly believed that no one could see me. I waited for the exact moment the credits rolled and the lights were dimmed. A quick look across the auditorium for an empty seat by the gangway always proved fruitless: middle of the row only. With no choice, I pushed past people already seated, and holding down the free seat, I flopped down, panting. When the film ended, the procedure was the same in reverse, but being in more of a hurry to get out before the lights came on I practically fell over people's feet and into their laps. At last in the gangway, I ran up the aisle and out of the cinema, more noticeable than was safe.

One evening at the cinema, as I sat in the middle of the row one of our neighbours was sitting next to me. The screen was lit up. Our eyes met. Would she tell on me? The film was a light comedy made by UFA starring a young Ingrid Bergman. As far as I know, our neighbour kept her mouth shut.

Despite the strain of this hide-and-seek, I continued to go to the cinema. I loved the time I spent staring at those glamorous pictures displayed outside the cinema of scenes from the film. Of course, actors ate and belched and went to the lavatory, common sense told me, but despite this I wanted to own those pictures. Across the road from the German Jewish synagogue was a shop that sold them. The owner of the shop led me into a back room – 'The best pictures are in here,' he said. On a large table was a mound of pictures to choose from. I felt the few *Pfenige* in my pocket; at most, I could only have two. I chose Greta Garbo and Shirley Temple. The man stood behind me, breathing down my neck. As I was about to turn round to pay, he put his hand up my skirt. Ah, *that* again! So *that* seemed to happen randomly, anywhere! I made connections to my past experience in these situations: my mother slapping me on my cheek after my ride in a car with a strange man, and further back when Totzel looked at my knickers next to my feet, and when Karl and Uncle Ztupack clattered down the stairs, and more recently, the feelings Uncle Avrum gave me, and going with him again… the shame of it all. No, *that* would never happen to me again, I wouldn't let it! Firmly, I took the man's hand off my thigh, and shoving him out of my way I threw my pennies on the table and ran out of the shop, the pictures firmly between my fingers.

I turned the pages of my film star album most days. What was I looking for behind those studied poses? I tried to copy them, the way Garbo looked upward, her lashes perfectly placed against the smooth curve of flesh above her eyes, and Shirley Temple's dimple beside her mouth. I knew that wishing to be a film star was useless. I had long lashes but no dimples, so back to Garbo, but to see myself in her pose, I would need two mirrors. In any case, what was the point? My legs were too fat, and besides, I wasn't yet allowed to use make-up. But stargazing was one of my daily occupations. Adolph Wohlbrück (he became 'Anton' when he left Germany) made my veins tingle, especially in the role of the *Zigeuner Baron*, in the shot where he was sitting on a horse, his beret on one side, enigmatically looking down from a hill, his gaze for me alone.

But along with that enchantment came other films, notably Leni Riefenstahl's *Triumph of the Will*. We see Hitler coming to Nürenberg in an aeroplane droning through dark clouds. On the ground behind the scenes, we see boys from the Hitler Youth enjoying the open air camping, as we did in *Habonim*. We see Nazi troops assemble for the rally, shots of SS and SA grouping according to rank. Hundreds of flags flutter in the breeze and torchlights puncture the darkness. Then introductory speeches by Goebbels and others in high office come from the podium. Finally, Rudolph Hess, Hitler's deputy, reverentially introduces the Führer. Hitler comes to the podium to the accompaniment of rhythmic *Sieg Heils*. The crowd finally falls silent and we hear him say, 'V*olksgenossen…*,' followed by stern, angry complaints of how the world has treated Germany after WWI: 'Never again will Deutschland be treated this way, *niemals!*' Then, praise for workers who are standing in columns with spades over the shoulders. A few of them are chosen and asked to say which part of Germany they are from, and when the camera is on a chosen man, and with his head held high, he gives the name of his homestead. So this is what Mr Hermann feels: pride at being appreciated; and here are the men who are building the Autobahn, some, like Mr Hermann, working for the first time since WWI. The salvoes of *Sieg Heils* are now symphonic with their Führer's passion, and when he speaks of his vision for the Reich, a slick of hair falls loose from his immaculately smooth hair. Passion prolonged, his arms cross over his chest and his eyes are closed and stillness seeps through the scene. He and the people are one. When the camera scans and finds a moistened eye, my eyes are moist. Unified, a chorus of *Sieg Heil* storms the heavens again. The drama deepens: Hitler leaves the podium, a lone figure descending some broad steps, around him his retinue hovering like a bridal veil. Then walking down a broad aisle they stop in front of the first row of standard bearers. An orderly holding a flag now stands beside Hitler. Hitler enfolds his hand with the bearers in the flag, each in turn. Hot tears are now running down my cheeks.

On the way home, I was ashamed to have felt so strongly and I tried to debate with myself: what was the difference between the Hitler Youth and *Habonim*, both enjoying the open air? Why did I think these activities similar in spirit? Why did

I feel as though I had committed a crime in my thoughts, and why were my feelings in harmony with our enemies? Dazed, my senses were trapped. I didn't tell a soul where I'd been, or what I'd seen. Remembering other speeches coming from the mouths of Nazis about Jews, I thought of myself as I was supposed to think: I'm nothing but a dirty Jew. Writing this in old age, I know that Hitler had a way of knowing how to finger people's innermost feelings: he was feeding their fears and starving their conscience. And, inappropriately, he fingered mine.

A few weeks later the thoughts I had of myself were confirmed again. I was in a long queue with other Jews at the Gestapo headquarters. The official had a list of our names and addresses on his desk. After he called out a name and a person answered '*Ja*', the official ticked the name off the list and beckoned the person to come forward. On top of a small table next to his desk was a black inkpad. The person who had come forward had the tip of his index finger rolled on the ink pad, and from there it was rolled onto the document. Those of us still in the queue asked with our eyes: why? My turn came. Although I had seen the procedure, the process suddenly became very personal; the way my finger was pressed down on the pad and rolled, the grip of the official's fingers in control of my fingers. Then the official lifted his eyes and said, 'Next.' 'Ja' was the last word I heard as I left that room. I was sure the Nazis were mind-readers; they knew my crimes, even the ones I nearly did. At home, I washed the ink off my finger with Vim. I don't remember saying anything to my parents, or they to me, but I knew when they were going because my mother cried, leaning her head against my father's shoulder.

My picture-going habit came unexpectedly to an end. I had converted the time spent in *Habonim* into time spent at the pictures. My parents had no idea of the risks I took; disregarding the sign above the ticket office forbidding my entry was only the half of it. I bought the tickets with the money given to me to pay the nuns who, it was hoped, would teach me dressmaking. I went to them for a while but hated fiddling with threads.

Before the boycott, my parents could keep an eye on me: the nuns' workroom was at the end of a stretch of grass behind our shop. The nuns went daily to the church across the road; I saw them hurrying, their habits flying when the wind was up. My parents knew the nuns' routine and this reassured them of my integrity; the nuns would say if I hadn't attended a lesson. After our shop was closed down, my deception was easier as my parents could no longer watch my comings and goings. The lies worked for a while, and then I was found out. How, my parents didn't say, but first things first: punishment. It was the last hiding I had from my father, and this time my mother shouted her instructions: 'Take her to the back room where the neighbours won't hear her scream and make sure you thrash the thief out of her!' My mother firmly believed in 'evil veins' – sure, they could be thrashed out, or cut out, or something like that! Her belief had an effect on me. When she said I was a *Verbrecher* (villain) I was fifteen years old and I had begun to understand right from wrong. This time, I didn't scream nor did I resent the thrashing. My parents went on about their punishment being justified, practically apologizing for what they had to do because I was now such a *groiße moit*, such a big girl. After the physical punishment came the sermon about justice and rules given by God. 'What belongs to someone else you don't take for yourself,' was my mother's solemn pronouncement. My thoughts raced: this was a world away from what we were experiencing living under the Nazis.

For the next moral crisis I was better prepared. I was standing by a counter in our local grocery shop. The shopkeeper went to the back room 'to fetch something', she said. Alone for a few moments, I noticed a small basket full of chocolate eggs on the counter wrapped in variously coloured silver paper.

Tempting. The whole of my future stood before me. If caught, it would be true what the Nazis said about us: 'Another Jewish thief,' words generally used openly by Germans echoing old beliefs down the ages. My head cleared. I would prove them wrong. I paid for the sugar I had come for and left the shop, relieved. I seemed to grow taller on the way home.

I now joined another club, less ideological then *Habonim*. The *Maccabi* was about sport activities and amateur theatricals. Directors and musicians from Berlin, thrown out of their posts there, helped to make *Orpheus and Eurydice* into a reasonably professional enterprise with the bunch of amateurs we were – in fact, the musical director discovered that I had a good singing voice when innocently I sang along with the leading lady. That overlooked, his finger insistent on the high C on the piano with me chirping away up there, he said that I should ask my parents to allow me to train. 'What? In times like these?' they said. I wasn't too upset and, my father warning me about disappointment, I decided that a hairdresser would be a more reliable trade. Going between the two clubs now I no longer wanted to wear the heavy uniform of *Habonim*, once so beloved by me with its black corduroy culottes, bomber-style jacket and coloured neckerchief, its points pushed through a plaited leather ring. When on a particularly hot summer day I came home in a sweat wearing it, my mother said, 'You need a summer dress, maybe I have enough money in my jam jar.' She had. A seamstress made me a dress in pale blue muslin gathered under the yoke, reaching down to my ankles, but being my only summer dress, it needed washing frequently. Many times the dress was still wet from the yoke down when I had to go out. No matter; walking in the sun, the wet hem slapping against my legs didn't last long and soon enough, the dress flowed about me. It felt luxurious.

Going to the *Maccabi* became very exciting. Bruno, a visitor from Italy, looked at me the way no one had before. He was dark and handsome like Valentino, aged twenty-seven to my fifteen. I barely reached to his shoulders. He burned me with his eyes. Apart from him being an Italian Jew, I knew no more about him – except for his kiss. Just thinking of our lips meeting tightened my throat, and I was hardly able to eat. My mother said, 'What is the matter with you, why are you not eating lately?' Then one evening Bruno proposed to meet me outside our flat to go to the club. Halfway to the corner of our street, I heard footsteps behind us and turning round to look – like pop-ups, my parents were there. The evening was cool. Bruno's jacket was round my shoulders, and so was his arm, his fingers near my breast. A strong smell of tarmac rose from a boiler at the curb. Whatever had happened to the promise I made never to allow those feelings in myself? Bruno and I walked on and my parents turned left at the *Bierstube*. No reference to seeing us was ever made by them.

Bruno was so handsome, I ached. Just looking at him, a sweet dread rushed through me. Yet nothing had happened, only in my thoughts, but the legacy of those moments with Uncle Avrum… I was often out of control, tearful and near to fainting. I had sudden bursts of anger, and for once the turmoil inside me had nothing to do with the Nazis or with my cheating, or with those awful men in my past. Yet all these things were muddled up and floating around inside me like feathers, tormenting me – the feelings so strong, so hidden away, and so deep, I pressed down on them with my finger. Then I heard that Bruno had gone back to Italy.

At Christmas time, I compared Gods again. The nativity was staged everywhere: behind the windows of homes, and in shops, lit up with coloured lights. I seemed to be bound to the God story. Now, I knew a little more. Ours was an invisible God whose language I heard but couldn't understand. Theirs was a baby at Christmas and for the rest of the year a grown man hanging on a cross, the one Mrs Hermann talked about, and called her saviour. I began to realize that our religions were linked to each other and to Jewish persecution, and, as I already knew, it was me who killed Jesus. But the Nazis disliked both religions, then why were there scenes of the nativity in windows and shops, and why was *Stille Nacht, Heilige Nacht* sung on the one national radio station? Which Saviour would win, Hitler or Jesus? Was that what Mrs Hermann meant when she talked about Hitler not being her saviour? Maybe that was why I cried when Hitler was swearing in the standard bearers, the way I cried when I heard *Kol Nidre* on *Yom Kippur*. What did *Kol Nidre* mean? Why were there more Christians than Jews, and why were there more Nazis every day? And why did I feel that Hitler was winning despite Mrs Hermann cursing Nazis the way they cursed us? And why, when I saw *Jude verrecke* scrawled over street walls, was I reminded of who I really was, and knew I was in danger, my body stuttered with emotion? And why did tears come into my eyes when I thought about God? Ensnared, I decided that God was mean, and I was calmer for thinking that. But my contests with Him changed from day to day. I was never free. Why couldn't I be something other than a Jew: perhaps a butterfly, giggling about doing nothing but sitting on leaves, sunning itself? And thinking of these things on my way home from the dairy, the milk can half full, and being curious, my grip now firmer on the handle, I started to swing the can over-arm until I was taken over by the athletics – faster and faster the swings came – so fast, they made me giddy. Then balance restored, I wondered why the milk didn't spill.

All that I thought and wondered about came to nought very shortly. But should there be any doubt among us regarding Hitler's plan for the Jews, it was dispelled on the morning of the 10th November 1938. News came through the radio that Herschel Grynspan, a Jew, had shot dead the German diplomat von Rath in Paris. '*Oih weh!*' my father said, 'a Jew with a gun!' At dawn we had heard an explosion. Over breakfast we decided that it must have been the gasworks. Although Heinie was frightened, he went to school, and I, not knowing what I felt, went to work as usual. While I was washing up the breakfast dishes, the doorbell rang: a long, urgent sound. I rushed to the door, drying my hands on my apron. Rabbi Wexler from the German Jewish synagogue stood there, very upset. His agitation spelled alarm. He lived in the flat above the Weilers and they came running down the corridor, their footsteps clattering on the wooden floor. 'What is wrong?' they asked. 'The explosion,' Rabbi Wexler said. 'Yes, we heard it,' the Weilers replied, somewhat too composed. Rabbi Wexler looked to me for help and said, 'Our synagogue has been blown up and is in flames. I urge you to leave Germany as soon as you can.' Choking on his words, he continued, 'How I blame myself for not having left Germany before, but now I know that more terror is to come and that we will never be safe in Germany again.' His voice cracked and tears blistered his eyes, his words fading into a whisper: 'Try… try to get away as fast as you can.' His duty done, he covered his face with his hands, his dignity in disarray.

As Rabbi Wexler was about to go, Weiler said what I had heard him say to other people, 'Calm yourself, the Nazis don't mean the German Jews. After all, we fought for the Fatherland. Surely that must count for something!' Rabbi Wexler looked at Weiler for a long time and saying no more he left, his face alive with sorrow.

Weiler swept past me down the corridor, muttering, 'Pessimism! All this pessimism!' And pushing out his upper lip, the way he always did when he was annoyed, made his black moustache look more like a broom than ever. Mrs Weiler's eyes followed him down the corridor until his office door clicked to.

Weiler's blindness to our situation troubled me. Disheartened, I went back to finish the washing up. Now explosives and fires were being used against us, and still he believed nothing had happened! I took comfort in knowing that my grandfather living in Poland was doing his best to persuade his nephews and nieces in England to get us out of Germany, but thinking of safety, the shattering of glass ended my contentment. I bolted to the front door, again drying my hands on my apron. The facade of the flat went some three metres wide across the landing. The crinkly coloured glass, set in a metre high wooden base, lay shattered on the floor and up the stairs to the next floor. The front door, set in its own frame, was hanging from the wall like an ear.

Four men, dressed as labourers, stood on a sea of glass, each holding an axe, its handle halfway up to their elbows, its iron head hovering just above the floor. The Weilers' footsteps clattered down the corridor a second time. Weiler didn't have a chance to say anything, because one of the men (I assumed he was the ring-leader) yelled, 'I want that Jew Weiler!' Weiler found his voice. Quietly, as if to teach an unruly child manners, he said, 'I am Herr Weiler, what do you want with me?' The ring-leader turned to his men. 'I can't believe I heard this, mates. Did you hear the Jew call himself *Herr*? Ha-ha-ha, *Herr*!' And fixing Weiler with his eyes, he yelled again, 'You listen to me, Jew. You are nothing but a Jew pig – do you hear me? You are nothing, nothing, nothing!' – the last 'nothing' a hysterical shriek. The ring-leader was shorter than Weiler and it seemed that by moving his body from side to side, he could wipe him from his view. Weiler now rigid, the ringleader kept yelling anti-Semitic abuse until the veins in his neck stuck out so bold and blue, I thought they would burst. Then changing his mood he said, 'Come on, Jew, surely you know that you can never be *ein Herr*, so for your own sake, don't ever let me hear you say that you are. Never again, never, never, never!' The last 'never' another hysterical shriek. Then he slapped his hands to his sides, and rolling his eyes he gave Weiler a final command, '*Raus, raus, verfluchter Jude, raus!*' Out, out, you cursed Jew, out!

His men stepped forward as if help was needed to defend their mate. The glass under their heavy boots powdered on *my* highly polished floor. I was pressing hard against the wall behind me, wishing for nothing more fantastic than a revolving door, when I heard Weiler say, 'But I am a German citizen, I fought for the Fatherland!' The ring-leader's face contorted. Beery breath and riotous laughter flew from his mouth. Weiler shut his eyes and turned his head away in distaste. The rest of the men snickered rather than laughed. Evidently they were not prepared for resistance. Waiting for instructions, they stomped awkwardly from one foot to another with their heavy boots, treading more glass to powder.

The ring-leader recovered. Narrowing his eyes, he filled his lungs and yelled even louder than before, 'German citizen you think you are, ha, ha, ha! By the time we're finished with you…' Then, breaking off, he thrust his fist close to Weiler's face, and putting thumb and forefinger together he opened and shut them several times until the space between them was exactly right. Closing one eye, he looked down the length of his arm and concluded, 'We'll have you hopping like a flea!' Now frothing at the mouth, he pushed his shoulders upwards towards Weiler, and lost for words he took a deep breath and blew out more foul air. This time, Weiler did nothing to avoid the stench coming at him. Panting with impatience, the gang leader yelled his last command, 'For God's sake, take this cursed Jew down to the lorry!' Weiler, still reluctant, was helped down the stairs by two of the men who lifted him up from under his arms, which left his feet dangling. Weiler's dangling feet will forever be etched on my mind.

The gang-leader's face was now wreathed in smiles when he said to the ashen-faced Mrs Weiler and me, 'You can now leave your flat in our care for an hour or two and when you come back, there'll be a surprise waiting for you!' Still smiling, he tested the weight of his axe, and satisfied, he flicked his other hand towards the door for us to leave. His men came up the stairs, two at a time. Without further ado, each picked up his axe, leaning against the wall.

I flew past the men. In the street, a lorry was pulling away. Weiler was among other men standing at the back of the lorry. Hurrying on, my legs zigzagged under me like kindling wood. I was pouring with sweat and felt alternately hot and cold and groaning sounds staggered out of me. I seemed to be tethered to a nightmare, but somehow I reached the corner of our street. Drunken laughter came from the *Bierstube*. Outside stood the same kind of lorry I had just seen, empty. Hurry, I said to myself, time to warn my parents. I ran better for the rest of the way. We were the only Jewish family living at the end of our street. Had they forgotten us?

It was now lunchtime. The *Tor* (gate) to our flats was open. The front and back blocks had their blinds down – in November? I went up the three steps to our front door and banged my fist against it until it hurt. Only then did I see that *our* blind was down too. Our kitchen window was set high from the ground, the only window facing the courtyard. On tiptoe, I looked through the gap between the bottom of the blind and the windowsill. All was dark – except for a glimmer of fire in the range, a broken chair and glass on the floor as far as I could see. I was too late. They had been. But where was my mother and brother? Howling, my body folded to the ground, and cross-legged, I cradled my head in my lap, rocking and whimpering. I seemed to have mourned a lifetime, when through the eerie silence I heard a blind being drawn up, 'Frrd, frrd'.

The face looking down at me was one of the two Catholic sisters who lived on the second floor. 'Psst, psst!' she said, crooking her finger for me to come up, and then straightening it, she held it against her lips as a sign for me to be quiet. I ran up the stairs two at a time and outside her front door, her finger still against her lips, she yanked me into her flat with her free hand. The door now safely shut, she led me to the last room at the end of the corridor. My mother, Heinie and I, huddled together; the two sisters stood caringly beside us. None of us could stop crying. My father had already been taken away.

Chapter Ten

The Days After

'Heinie, you must have seen something!' 'No,' he said, 'all I remember is running away from school after the teacher was arrested. "Run home!" the teacher said as men pushed him out of the class room door... pushing, hitting, pushing...' Heinie's eyes were shaking in their sockets. He was dealing with his anguish as I did with mine but this information appeared to be vital to me. 'Did you see Father being taken away? Did you find Mother alone? Did the sisters come down to get you? Did you and Mother go to them?' 'I don't remember,' Heinie said, sobbing. I had asked too much of my young brother – the truth was, our troubles separated us. Mother was connecting what happened today with events in her past: 'So it has happened again, there's been another pogrom. Pogroms, pogroms... where ever we go, pogroms hound us... Russia, Poland, *Deutschland*, where to next?' Try as I might, I can't remember where we slept the night of the 'pogrom'.

I don't remember going back to our flat. Mother must have protected us from seeing it destroyed. Going back to the Weilers, I saw what she protected us from; their home was devastated. My mother's instructions to me were: 'Tomorrow you'll come straight from work to 9 Wrede Straße.' Who had moved us? I never did find out. Although I had witnessed Weiler's arrest, I couldn't quite relate it to my father. Did he resist? Was he pushed? An unbearable thought.

One morning, on my way to the Weilers', the woman who lived in the house next door to them tapped my arm in passing, and stopping briefly, she whispered, 'I put my hands over my ears not to hear the banging.' Then, fighting for breath, she declared, 'I am ashamed to be a German,' and with that said, she hurried away. A few days later, at the same place in the street, she tapped my arm again. Night had fallen. Gripping my arm firmly, she said, 'Meet me tomorrow by the bench above the playground, eight o'clock sharp.' Despite the safety of darkness, she dashed into the night. I knew little about the woman except that we met most days outside the Weilers' flat, me going to work and she coming home from Mass. We only ever exchanged the time of day. I heard the Weilers say she was 'devout'. All the same, both of us lowered our eyes when we met. It was generally safer to do so.

The night was cold. The playground was carved out of the ground like a bowl, and being a moonless night, it looked like a heap of soot. I got used to the dark and placed myself by the bench, now with a sign in black on white bold lettering: 'Jews are not allowed here'. The street lamp was a safe distance away. Not long to wait, I judged, having left home with time to spare. Before long, I heard a dragging sound; seconds later, the woman was in front of me, her chest moving up and down conspicuously, and instantly a suitcase bumped to the ground. When her breathing became more even, she whispered, 'You might need these things.' Then she turned on her heels and walked off into the night. Moments later, I saw her under the street lamp, shoulders hunched, arms swinging beside her, fists clenched, resolute. The case was heavy. Pushing it with my knees was the only way I could get it home. Were there stones in that case? No, lots of men's clothes, and, mysteriously, yellow dusters.

Our new home was shared with three other Jewish families. Each had one room and we shared the kitchen and a lavatory. We were told the house was still Jewish-owned and therefore safe, we assumed. Except for our clothes, everything was strange, though the warmth from the range made it feel like home.

The family on the same floor as ours was called Hoffman. They had three daughters. Considering the situation we were in, the flat was full of laughter. Leah, the oldest (a friend of my cousin Rosl), told us her dreams: 'I want to meet a tall, dark, handsome man,' she'd say, her eyes shining. But what she got was Julius: short, bald, and rotund. She met him at the *Maccabi* sports club. They fell in love. When he came to 'our' flat, their chatter filled the room, and we younger girls shared in their laughter. She kissed his bald head and looking at us playfully, she gave him an affectionate hug. Julius's parents were divorced, and having escaped arrest, he had reason to be happy, and twice as happy because of Leah. But, despite his escape, Julius negotiated feverishly for a guarantor from family he had in America.

We learned our fathers were in Dachau. Visas were now the focus. All of us were waiting for somewhere to go, anywhere. Meanwhile, we took pictures of each other for keepsakes in the foreground of the *Schloss* in front of the fountain, ever the favourite backdrop.

In the days following the pogrom, we checked if our Polish Jewish friends were still living at their old addresses in Mannheim. They were not. Their windows were boarded up and splinters of glass were left in the gangway of the flats. Arriving at one address, a neighbour told us in hushed tones, 'I overheard the police talking among themselves, saying that your friends have been deported to the Polish border.' It was true then, what we had heard. In the next street another witness to a smash-up saw a man in the middle of swinging an axe sit down and weep, 'I can't go on doing this; these people have done me no harm'. How glad we were to know that not all Germans were thugs. We repeated this story again and again.

Less hopeful was the story we heard about a German Jewish man who wandered from room to room in his devastated flat, unable to clean up the mess the thugs had made, and 'worst

of all,' we were told, 'was the smell of burned food'. Unbelievably the splintered mirrors among the broken furniture were
turned to the wall, a custom the demented man used from orthodox mourning. Leah went to see the man. 'He looked
through me with red-rimmed eyes,' she reported back to the
Jewish committee. 'Yes,' a secretary said, 'we know about him,
but however much we try to help him, he escapes to roam the
streets; and more to the point, we don't know how he avoided
arrest.' Thousand's of men throughout Germany were arrested
on the tenth of November 1938.

No time to be lost. Mother set me up with a pen and ink to
write letters to relatives all over the world: North and South
America, Luxembourg, Paris, Palestine, Poland. Most of Father's family still lived in Poland: uncles and aunts and cousins
galore, and most important, my grandfather Chuna Aaron, the
scribe who was already in communication with our family in
England.

Now I was to be a scribe. To the question 'What shall I
write?' Mother said, 'Write from the heart!' I struggled to get
words down on paper but nothing came from my head or from
my heart. Mother, I thought, knew more than she let on. Seeing that I couldn't write anything, she suggested, 'Why don't
you write to your cousin René from Luxembourg? You know,
Tante Lotte's youngest son. He is learning to be a hairdresser.
Remember, when we thought of sending you to them?' Yes, of
course I did. What a crazy idea that was. But what would have
been worse was to have faced Uncle Ztupack. Meeting him
again meant seeing him jump off the bed wearing his trilby
hat. For a split second, Nazis offences were as nothing compared to Ztupack watching me, watching him. Thank goodness
their plan didn't take root.

Writing to René would be easier. He was yet another relation
I had never met and for that matter, neither had my parents.
Aunt Lotte must have gone to Luxembourg with sons born in

Germany. I remember my mother saying, 'So, Lotte has had boy number six!' as my father read out the letter with the news of René's birth, and now, fifteen years later, I was looking at his photograph. Mother, glancing over my shoulder at René's picture, said, 'He has his mother's nose!' and looking at me, she confirmed, 'Yes, it's the family nose!' I felt related. But more to the point, I had dreamt of being a hairdresser too – better than doing housework. That plan cheered me up. I was looking at a future. René didn't have one: Aunt Lotte, Uncle Ztupack and their six sons perished when Hitler marched into Luxembourg. What a muddle everything was, even to find pity for Uncle Ztupack.

Great joy! Heinie's visa came through to go to England with the *Kindertransport*. The exact date I can't remember but it must have been soon after *Kristallnacht* because Father was still in Dachau and Heinie had written a goodbye letter to him – a cherished image of mine is Heinie sitting on cushions to raise him up, his head to one side, his small hand in control of the pen, ink pot above the paper.

When we were packing his things, he asked for a picture of me – 'A big one!' he said. As it happens, someone in *Habonim* was an amateur photographer, and just days before, he had given me the picture he had taken of me which was more than just a snapshot. When we asked Heinie why he wanted 'a big one' he told us of his plan. 'When I get to England, I will show your picture to everybody, and I will tell them that you are my big sister, and that you can cook and sew, and that you are a good cleaner, and look, she's beautiful!' My little brother's cheeks were flushed with excitement, and putting my picture between his clothes in the suitcase he resolutely patted them down with his hands, his lips tight over his teeth. Mother and I laughed out loud. Heinie was eleven years old, for goodness' sake!

On the way to the station, Mother and Heinie clung to each other. Nearing the station, he said to her, 'Promise me that you won't cry, Mamma.' Then, stretching to his full height and she bending down to him, they kissed, to seal the promise, I suppose, and so they remained clinging to each other until we got to the station, their eyes glistening. If the heavens didn't weep, I have a complaint! Our 'little father' ran true to form. Before he got on the train, he pushed the ten marks he was allowed to take out of Germany into Mother's hand, and she accepted, as if from a father. She let him give, and she obeyed: no tears and that meant me too – though our eyes rolled about trying to avert a flood. My mother and I linked arms to walk home, and at home, she said, 'There is a stone in my heart.'

Father didn't get Heinie's letter and Heinie left, believing he had. That was a blessing we counted.

A few weeks later, Mother and I were asked to come to the Jewish Refugee Committee. We panicked. Perhaps Heinie had not succeeded with his plan. In the office we were greeted by smiling faces. Heinie had written to the committee: '… a big thank you for all you have done for me, and now, will you please do the same for my sister!' When his letter was read out, everyone in the office smiled into their chins, banging away on their typewriters.

Heinie's letter was sent from Birmingham. It wasn't long before we heard that a Mr and Mrs Cohen from Dudley had become my guarantors. Heinie's plan had worked. He must have been a pest going on about his sister. The Cohens acted immediately, and a good thing it was too – the age limit for the *Kindertransport* was sixteen. In May 1939 I would have been seventeen, and that would have been too late. What mattered was the date of the application which was before my seventeenth birthday.

Still working for the Weilers, I helped to clear up the mess made of their flat by the thugs. Before going to them, I swept the pavement outside the synagogue. Glass everywhere, on the pavement and in the gutter and the bitter smell from the fire on *Kristallnacht* was still around. Furious, I swept the pavement, consciously intending to get at people with my broom, getting as near as I could, and given the advantage, I swept faster and faster. Women held their shopping baskets against their ribs, tiptoeing over debris, their brows puckered. Across the road, Inger's shop windows had been smashed, and it looked as if his entire stock of shoes was on the pavement; they had fallen from their boxes and from their tissue paper. The strong wind that morning lifted the paper into the air, floating against faces and car windscreens. Passers-by quickly moved on, eyes to the ground.

At the Weilers, there was lots to be done. All the jars of jams, the bottled fruits, the pickled eggs stored on top of the wardrobe – all of it had been smashed and thrown onto ripped featherbeds (duvets). One of Weiler's ties ended up round the flex above a hanging light, its broad end arranged on the shade like a tongue. In the kitchen, shelves and cupboards were cleared of their crockery which was hurled to the floor. A broken cut-glass wine goblet was thrown into the middle of a painting of flowers, a splinter of it sparkling like a drop of water. The painting must have been overlooked when we packed the valuables for the Nazis.

News now flew from mouth to mouth of visas granted, people leaving, people waiting, hoping, smiling bravely. Although our misfortune was collective, not everything was shared. One morning, I was holding a printed card in my hand, postmarked Dachau. It gave the whereabouts and health of my father. The phrase 'well and healthy' struck a sinister note. Our name and address was written by hand in beautiful gothic script. I told Mother what the card said, but not what I thought.

Three months after Father's arrest his visa came through. My grandfather's most fervent wish was granted: his nieces and nephews in England stood as guarantors for their cousin. We expected his release, soon. Time dragged.

One midnight in January 1939, our doorbell rang, long and shrill. I fell out of bed and ran down the stairs. The top half of the street door was glass. The passage was dimly lit. Was the man behind the glass my father? Yes, I could see it was! His head was shaved and he was half his usual size. I tried to open the door but it was locked. I ran upstairs for the key. Where was it? Mother was standing in the kitchen, dazed. Down I ran again rattling the doorknob. The door would not open. I ran back up again searching in drawers and cupboards. Where was the key? I went down again and rattled the doorknob. Breathless, I ran up a third time. Mother was near to tears, though more in touch now with what was going on, she said, 'What is the matter with the door?' I couldn't speak, let alone explain, and down I went again without the key. A chance rattle of the knob…the door had been open all along. Throughout my frantic fumbling, my Father said nothing. The door now open, he walked past me up the stairs, light-footed, silent.

He showed neither gladness nor relief for being at home. He must have been told we had moved, coming as he did to our new address. He just stood in the middle of the room. 'Sit down,' Mother said, to which he replied, 'No, standing still is what I am used to, because that is how I survived… a man could be beaten for nothing more than swinging his arms about to keep warm. Punishment depended on where the guards happened to look. I watched them, *their* routine, and whenever possible, I was where they were not. As for the meeting of eyes… and then, I came face to face with Helmut. Into his eyes I looked – after all, I knew him as a boy – and unbelievably, he dropped his. And for all the time I was in the camp he never touched me. But he touched others; very hard to think I was privileged, watching him beating others. How long would my privilege last? A blessing it was not.' I could not stop my teeth from clattering.

Perhaps Father survived because he was vigilant. Not a good time to think about these things at the moment, though Helmut was on my mind. Maybe his heart had softened because he remembered taking Heinie on his shoulders to school. Was there a right way to think and behave these days? When my father started to talk again, I stopped speculating: wrong was right, and right was lost.

Still standing, Mother said, 'Eat something!' 'No,' Father said, 'I don't want any food, my stomach has shrunk. All the time I was in the camp, I didn't have one stomach upset; the lack of food was good for it, it seems. I'll eat later.' Then, brusquely, he ordered us to switch off the light and draw the curtains. That done, he said, 'Promise me that you will never tell a soul what I am going to tell you – swear it!' We swore. Father shivered as he spoke: 'Before I left the camp I had to sign a form which said that I was treated well. If not, I'd suffer the consequences. Fear, always fear, you could smell it'.

Then Father gathered the three of us together, one arm on Mother's shoulder and the other on mine. And so we stood while he talked. 'The roll calls, the ice and the snow, standing on it for hours every day, dressed in thin striped prisoners' uniforms; the icy winds, the watery soup, the sudden sickness of men… death. I was the only Pole among German Jews. Most of them were doctors, lawyers, musicians, merchants… On arrival, the commandant, his face wreathed in smiles, asked each of us in turn, "And what do you do, Jew?" Those with professions stuck out their chests, proudly saying what they were, and each in turn was battered with a truncheon until their blood ran. I waited my turn. "And what do you do, Jew?" My throat dried and in a mere whisper I said, "I am a shoe-repairer." "Louder!" the commandant shouted, his breath hitting my face. "I am a shoe-repairer," I said, waiting for the blows. None came. Why? Was being a humble work-man a reason to let me live?'

'Hopping', as Mr Weiler was promised by the gang leader, was exactly what Father now described: 'Up and down, the young, the old, the sick, the lame. One man had a rupture and was unable to keep up. A surgeon in our hut tried to comfort him, "*Kindele*, if I could, I would help you, even with a kitchen knife!" On the next roll call, the man with the rupture couldn't stand up straight enough for the guard.' 'Helmut?' I asked. 'No, not Helmut,' Father said, 'But the one on duty that day beat him with a truncheon until he fell dead next to me, his blood seeping through the snow. We already knew not to help inmates. Help and you were dead too. I felt I was no longer a human being, only a calculating machine, each man for himself.' And, as if to himself, Father asked into the air, 'Is wanting to survive being a human being? Everything happened so quickly. *Gott*… A hundred men to a hut in a space which could barely hold a quarter of that. They solved the problem by us having to sit with our legs wide open as each man was thrown between the last man's legs. The guards were practised.' Father then continued in short gasps, 'Having packed us in like sardines, the guard left. I don't know what would have happened to me if he hadn't. I was the second man to be thrown but with the weight of the other men against me, I got cramp in my groin. I cried out in pain. The men lifted me above their heads to the front and I have no idea where I landed. I think I must have fainted because the lifting is the last thing I remember. I think this was how we spent our first night, with me suspended, resting on their shoulders. Whether we slept or not, I don't know either, but suddenly dogs barked, and guards screamed, '*Raus, Raus, alle Juden raus!*' Everything was done on the double… *schnell, schnell*… I thought the hours on roll call would never end… but, thank God, we could get yellow dusters from a canteen of sorts, to put round our necks and ankles to hold in some warmth.

'How come the Weilers' neighbour knew about yellow dusters immediately after *Kristallnacht*? Maybe a Nazi relation told her, boasting how the Jews were suffering, and she, swapping hatred for pity, put some into the case she brought to me. I see her still, under the lamplight, fists clenched…

Father continued, 'On the journey to Munich we were on a passenger train and after that, we were herded onto cattle trucks. When the doors opened again we were in Dachau: *Juden raus, alle Juden raus*! Truncheons flew in all directions, on the old and young alike. "Jump, Jew, jump!" they mocked, commanding us like dogs in a circus, though with less pity. I was still young, I could jump!' Father lifted his chest in a moment of self-esteem. 'But the old…' and remembering, he started to sob. Mother and I looked at each other, helpless.

We seemed to have taken root. The stove needed feeding and Father needed to blow his nose. Mother handed him a handkerchief she had in the pocket of her apron and he had a good blow. All he now wanted was water and sleep. He downed the water in huge gulps. Then he stretched out on the bed with his clothes on. Seconds later he was asleep. The light from the street lamp filtered through the cretonne curtains. The three of us slept in the same room. In the middle of the night, I woke up. Father had risen from his pillow crying, sweat and tears coursing down his face. Now fully awake, I saw Mother wiping him down, and Father still restless, she put her arm round his shoulders and murmured, 'Sleep, Max, sleep, you are at home.' Father slept until early evening that day. While he was sleeping, Mother went round the flat whispering, 'My husband is sleeping.'

I stayed just long enough with the Weilers to see Herr Weiler after his release from Dachau. He walked around his broken home in silence, doing one task after another: sorting papers, pasting together the ones that had been torn and helping his wife salvage clothes not beyond repair. Mrs Weiler's eyes reflected a frozen soul. She often looked at her husband first to sense his mood before she spoke to him. When their eyes met, he looked away, grinding his teeth.

Twenty-five years after the war, the council of Ludwigshafen published a book on the history of Ludwigshafen's Jews, which included those who had perished in the Holocaust. Weiler was on that list. Also noted was number 9 Wrede Straße, the house we were moved to after Kristallnacht. What had happened to Mrs Weiler? Among the pictures in that book was a woman very like her, looking straight at the camera, her white narrow face clenched with fright. The woman wasn't named, and I was not at all sure it was Mrs Weiler. Named or not, in the end it made no difference: the picture of the old woman sitting on her belongings articulates defeat: she was waiting to be transported – to where? It doesn't say. It was brave of the council of Ludwigshafen to publish such a book. Whenever I make mayonnaise or iron shirts, I think of the Weilers; I did so even before I got to know of their fate. Weiler's first name was David. I never knew that. What his wife's name was I never heard. Perhaps he called her Liebchen (darling). No, he couldn't have done, I would have noticed. Thinking of the misunderstandings between us, regret gets at me.

Father went out rarely; when he had to, he told us, he looked over his shoulder. I saw him once through the window of our flat. I was staring out at what exactly I don't know, but then my father came into view on the pavement opposite and I saw an old man, dragging his feet, his back bent. He was then about forty-two years old. Mother begged him, 'Stay a while longer, at least long enough to get your strength back.' 'You haven't seen what I've seen,' he reminded her, 'besides, the sooner I get away to England, the sooner you will get your visa.' Grudgingly, Mother accepted his reasoning. I didn't want him to go either. I was convinced he wanted to abandon us, to get away for himself and not because of Mother's visa. Fear rifled reason. The term 'post-traumatic shock' was not one we knew.

In spring 1939, a few of us from the *Maccabi* met in the garden of the synagogue. We sat on scorched chairs among scorched trees, leftovers from *Kristallnacht*. Someone older than us read poetry. Her shiny black hair was arranged in floppy curls round her head. I don't remember what she read, but I knew something profound was happening in my head. A flare lit up a language I had never heard before, and I knew that words differently arranged could police hatred, change a heart, a mind. Multiple meanings of the word '*ruach*' (spirit), a Hebrew word in Yiddish, took years for me to appreciate: when the fire in the range didn't crackle straight away, my mother would cry out, '*Oih, es geight nicht kein ruach!*' (there is no wind), and furiously, she'd flap a saucepan lid to stimulate a glow. And that was the only meaning of *ruach* I knew until years later when I read Genesis in English, '*...and the spirit of God moved upon the face of the waters...*'

Everyone we knew talked about visas now, and waiting for them was hell. When Father got his, a great sigh flew up from the depths of him. There was a lot to do, but in no time at all, we were walking to the station again carrying suitcases: Father carried two, Mother and I, the smaller ones. On the platform, my parents kissed good-bye. Conditioned as I was by films, I knew that a couple's lips would meet and stay together long and hard, and then a door would close on the scene... fade-out. My parents' kiss was a gentle meeting with closed lips barely touching. Their eyes embraced something I could not possibly imagine at that time. When did they say goodbye? I kept thinking. There seemed to be two of me watching, each seeing different things; one was ashamed of the other. Standing on the steps of the carriage, Father looked down on Mother, '*Schnutele*', he said, 'we will see each other again, soon.' And to me he said, 'Be good to Mother, look after her.' Why didn't Father say anything endearing to me? He seemed only to be concerned with Mother. This wasn't the time to be jealous, I told myself; feelings like that belonged to normal life and what we were living through was not normal, I thought sensibly on our way home. Now empty-handed, Mother summed up her life, 'Everything I have saved for and treasured in my life has been broken and smashed and who knows whether I will ever see my son and your father again.' Leaving flesh and blood out of the equation, I asked, 'Your china dinner service as well?' 'Yes, everything,' Mother said with a wave of her hand, eyes down. How brave my mother was I understood much later in my life, much later…

More families came to live in our new flat and, short of sleeping space, I was farmed out again. I left the Weilers to be the live-in maid for Mr and Mrs Berg in Mannheim. It seemed to me miraculous that they still lived in their own flat. It was huge. My room was in servants' quarters across the landing. Mrs Berg was young, plump and jolly, and not all that particular round the house. The floors in the flat were a vast expanse of red painted composite stone, highly polished; rugs slipped all over the place. Mrs Berg's priorities in the way of cleaning were different from the ones I had been taught. To save time, she demonstrated how to clean electric plugs. 'Spit on the duster, it's just as good!' she said, spitting and rubbing. I was aghast. And where did they buy smoked salmon? I had never eaten it before. The Bergs' two children were talked of but never seen; perhaps they had already gone with the *Kindertransport*, or perhaps the Bergs weren't Jewish. They weren't anxious like other Jews, more like carefree. Yet despite the relaxed atmosphere in the Bergs' household, I wet the bed again. I was distraught.

A few weeks on, my visa came through. Why should I care if the bed was a stinking mess? I'd be going to England soon, never to return! But care I did, hot with shame when I woke up and felt the wet sheet under me. Desperate, I imagined the moment Mrs Berg turned back the featherbed. I had to do something! I found a piece of cloth and sewed it over the wet patch. It wasn't easy with a straight needle on the tight-stretched box mattress. But having done it, I felt worse. There seemed to be no hiding place for me. God was watching, prodding me in the back, making me feel ashamed. Why had Dr Joseph said in religion classes that God was forgiving?

After the war, knowing that Mannheim had been bombed I hoped finally to be rid of my shame. But looming up in front of me still were visions of demolition men pulling out the mattress from the rubble, and I wished they would think that the stink was the deposits of a cat or a dog. Better still would have been a firebomb. No amount of rationalisation has ever obliterated my shame.

Time was running out. Chamberlain, the British Prime Minister, had been and gone without getting the substantial appeasement he wanted. In any case, no one believed what was written on that piece of paper he waved about when he returned to England. If the German papers mocked his visit in cartoons and in newsreels, and if we talked mockingly about Mr Chamberlain in our kitchen, a good laugh must have been had among the top brass in the Nazi party.

A letter from Father suggested I should learn English '… because,' he wrote, 'there are many young cousins to speak to who don't speak Yiddish.' In another letter, he wrote, '… everybody in England is forever saying sorry, seemingly for nothing at all' – that was not something I needed to worry about just then.

English and Hebrew classes sprang up all over the place, any large room sufficed. I enrolled. The teachers were charged with purpose, but I was unchanged from the time I was five years old in the arithmetic lessons; as then, I was tongue-tied. I left both classes. Hebrew would remain more or less unknown to me until quite late in my life, but English, I persuaded myself, I would learn when I got to England. I am not even sure my thoughts were that clear.

Ha'shara, training for Kibbutz life, had more appeal. Heinz, our group leader confirmed, 'It's like camping with work, in readiness for Kibbutz life.' But what would I do about my bed-wetting? And the other thing I heard people say was, '… the things that go on in *Ha'shara*, young people thrown together, practising 'free love'. I knew I couldn't have coped with that, whatever it meant. In the end all my worries melted away; I had my visa and a date for going to England: July 6th. 1939.

I rushed about doing last minute things. I should have been excited but I wasn't; not even the blue-and-red sandals Mother bought me at the smart shop Salamander in the *Planken* cheered me up. The day before, we had received an eviction order from Gestapo headquarters. We were to leave the flat 'at once'. Why were we being evicted if the house we lived in was still owned by Jews? Or was that just what we wanted to believe: foolish thoughts floating about us like confetti.

Walking through the high street doing my errands, who should be a few yards in front of me but the Gestapo official who had taken my fingerprint! Trams clanked, sparking overhead; women with shopping baskets and string bags window-shopped. I ran through the crowd, and passing the official, I faced him wailing, 'How can you do such a thing? Where is my mother to go?' He seemed to know me at once, and shouting he said, 'What the hell has this to do with me? For all I care, your mother can sleep in the lavatory!' I tried again. 'I'm leaving for England tomorrow, please help my mother, she'll be all on her own!' I said pathetically. Then he made a different point altogether, 'What do you think the Poles are doing to us Germans?' Poles persecuting Germans? What has my mother's eviction to do with Poles, and why was he telling me this? His eyes hardened, but I stuck to my point. 'But why, if the house we live in belongs to Jews can't my mother stay there?' 'Ha,' he said, 'don't push me, I'm a busy man, get out of my way!' When I didn't, his head came centimetres from mine and his index finger rotated close to my eyes; sounding a warning he said, 'If you're not careful, I'll have you transported to the Polish border where the rest of your scum is!' Split-second thoughts: he could do it… Weiler was taken away… my father… and my friends are in Poland… Despite the hot day, I was shivering, and regardless of the debate going on in my head, I heard myself repeat my pathetic request only to be met with 'I told you I was a busy man,' and with that he lifted his arm high above his head and down came his hand on my cheek. Directly, he walked into the crowd, leaving me standing there, my hand holding my cheek. Home was a couple of hundred yards away. 'Who?' my mother asked again.

My head ached to bursting. The state my mother was in, I will never know. We packed, unpacked, re-packed. Dawn came without us having had much sleep. Even the fine day couldn't lift our mood. It seemed that we had nothing more to say to each other. Then Mother sighed and said, 'Let's check your case again, may be we have forgotten something.' I complied and we unpacked and packed again.

Late that afternoon, Mother and I walked to the station. Talk was sluggish. Then she said something relevant to me: 'Be sure you learn a trade, the Jewish Committee promised you could! If not one trade, another will do, as long as it is practical you can use it anywhere in the world,' and passing over my deceit she continued, 'Pity you didn't learn sewing with the nuns.' I went over old ground too: 'Are you sure it is right for me to leave without you? If we waited until your visa came, we could go together.' Out of breath, I put my suitcase on the pavement. I sat on one end, and I made Mother sit on the other. After a while we got up and Mother bent down to pick up the case. 'It's my turn,' she said, sighing loudly. I am not sure whether by accident or on purpose, I elbowed her a little. 'No!' I said, 'it's mine.' I wasn't coping well.

I took my case onto the train, looked for a seat by the window, and having found one I returned to my mother on the platform. Having nothing more to say or to plan, it was time to say goodbye, time to board the train. Holding each other, a cry escaped from my mother's throat: 'You go, my child, you're young. I have lived my life!' Her hands were clasped onto my shoulders and it seemed as if she was swallowing rocks. In barely audible tones, she repeated, 'I have lived my life...' Had father told her more of his experiences in Dachau? I got back on the train.

In the compartment were several more girls from our town. Margot Sommer was the one I knew best; she belonged to *Habonim*. With her thick blond plaits and blue eyes she could have been taken for a German *Mädchen* of the type portrayed in posters all over Germany, but here the similarities ended. Margot's eyes looked bruised, matching our times. She was going to Scotland – 'Schottland', we pronounced it. I don't re-member us speaking much. When the train started to move, both of us rushed to the window straining our heads out for a last look; handkerchiefs fluttered and hands waved. My mother, a lone figure, her arms to her side, her lips tight, her face drained of its usual colour, wasn't waving anything, not even her hand. That moment, I longed to embrace all she had been to me, and all she hadn't.

When the platform vanished, I slumped back in the seat and closed my eyes. My mother's image endured. What would she do this evening? Where would she sleep? Where would she be tomorrow? Who would console her? Were the other families evicted too?

Then, with a start, I opened my eyes: my mother's image and all my questions vanished. More children came on the train; some compared labels round their necks; some shrieked rather than talked; Cologne cathedral came into view; factory chimneys looked like pencils on the horizon; the train stopped with a jerk; we were inside Holland; someone was shouting '*Papieren*!' Escorts dashed up and down the corridors in the train; I felt that all the rushing about had nothing to do with me. Next, Hook of Holland; people were on the platform; they held flowers and trays of food. Children ate with gusto. The train left. Next we filed onto a boat; people waved from the quay.

Out at sea my stomach heaved; I hurried to the rails of the boat; I was a gargoyle, spewing; the wind buffeted the boat; sea foamed against the boat; my vomit blew back at me; my legs were frail; death was near; my stomach was empty; I staggered to the rest room below deck; smells of vomit ingrained in the wooden walls; I lay down on a bench integral with the wall; I fell into a bottomless sleep; I woke up; boat rocked gently; I was alone in the rest room; I went back on deck; read name plate; got as far as Ha... the word was meaningless; we boarded a train; wheels gathered speed: da-di-daa da-di-daadaa...

Above left:
*Chuna Aaron Lerner,
my paternal Grandfather.
He died of hunger in the
ghetto in Lodz, Poland.*

Above right:
*Herschel Rotman and his
wife, my maternal grand-
parents, Lodz, 1900. She is
not the only member of the
family whose name I never
knew.*

Left:
*My parents, Mendel Max
Lerner and Manja Ryfka
Rotman, on their wedding
day in Worms, Germany,
1920.*

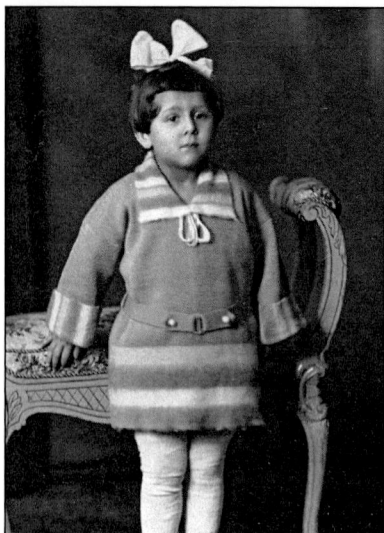

Top left: *Me, Rosel Lerner, 1925.* Top right: *Father, Mother and Aunt Pessa, Worms, 1926.*
Above: *With my brother, Heinie, Worms, 1929.*

Top: *Me, far left at school in Ludwigshaften, 1934.* Above left: *Heinie, aged eleven.*
Above right: *My Mother, Manja, 1926.*

Top: *Me (right) with my friend, Trudel, 1937. She didn't survive the Holocaust.*
Above: *Habonim group, 1937/38. I was on the same* Kindertransport *train to England as Margot (third from left). Her destination was Scotland and we never met again.*

PART TWO

Chapter Eleven

England – Safe at Last

My wits returned. We had disembarked in Harwich. The English countryside was green and lush. Clouds squatted low for miles ahead in different shades of grey and black – in July? I stared ahead, and sometimes into the window beside me reflecting my ghostly image, back and forth, at the clouds and me: not a patch of cheer anywhere. It was raining hard. Margot was no longer in my carriage. I have no memory of us promising to stay together. Had I fallen asleep? Then, the train jolted to a halt. It was still raining hard. I read 'Liverpohl Striet Station' out loud. An escort corrected my pronunciation. I repeated what I heard her say – how well, I can't say. Too much effort for an English lesson at that moment.

Less effort was to see thing around me: I was instantly struck by the smell of dust in the forecourt of the station, the grimy walls, the cursory cleaning, corners by-passed, footsteps, slow and fast hitting the ground, arrivals of trains squealing to a halt, the blow of a whistle piercing the air – and me; a train snaking into the distance exhaling great woofs of smoke; a hollow voice booming from the Tannoy – I was hollow. Outside the station entrance a bus passed two storeys high, its engine growling among cars and a cyclist.

Next, we were taken to a large hall. Narrow stairs led up to a gallery running all round the hall. Clerks hurried in and out of doors with folders under their arms. The hall was packed tight with children and luggage. Escorts held clip-boards in their hands, rushing about between children, checking labels round their necks with a flick of a wrist, matching names with guarantors or relations. Then, raising their arms and stretching their necks, they called out names over the children's heads. The shoving, the pushing, the yelps of joy; the silences. An escort looked at my label again. Soon I was to go on another train journey, she told me. I couldn't see my father anywhere. Looking about me, all became a blur. Mother had told me that he would come to see me before I left London. My label read 'Doodley'. 'Dudley', another escort said, 'u' is 'a' in English.' I had mouthed 'Beermingham' when I was still on the train. No matter how it was pronounced, all I wanted was my father – where was he? More children left, and ever more speedily, escorts ticked off names, everybody's name but mine. The hall was now less crowded; voices echoed more, porters were shouting and pushing luggage trucks.

I stayed rooted to the spot and people bumped into me. I seemed to have no legs to get out of the way with – when suddenly I was grabbed from behind. 'Rosele,' I heard my father say, and simultaneously I heard Yiddish over the din, '*Er 'ot sie, er 'ot sie!*' (He's got her, he's got her!) Father pointed up to two women standing in the gallery. Both were wearing black coats and black hats, those flat things fashionable then. 'These are your *Tantes* Eva and Rosie,' Father said. My new aunts were my father's first cousins. In those days it was disrespectful for a young person to call older people, related or not, by their first names, and to the end of their lives I called Eva and Rosie my aunts. Their full bosoms heaved as they laughed and cried simultaneously, dabbing their eyes and noses with handkerchiefs. Father took me up to meet them, leaving my suitcase in the hall. My aunts were still laughing and crying, and Father was crying too. I don't remember what I did, or felt.

An escort approached, 'Sorry, the train is leaving shortly'. Now I felt something: I didn't want to say good-bye again. My father's and my aunts' lips were pressed together, only their cheeks were smiling. I was urged by another escort to say my goodbyes. I don't remember if Father and I embraced but, a warmth had radiated over me; something had been found, and then lost again. In the commotion, I saw Margot waving frantically from across the now less crowded hall, calling anxiously up to me, 'Rosel!' and I called down to her, 'Margot!' equally anxious. A couple of people were standing close to her. And then she was gone. Worst of all was that we didn't even exchange addresses despite them hanging round our necks. We never saw each other again. When I think of Margot, I see her 'bruised' eyes filled with tears.

On the train, I felt I ought to cry, but much like a lost sneeze, my tears lost their way. The journey to Birmingham was a distraction: rows of houses with gardens back and front, and familiar things, trees and grass and hills. The train passed through sunny patches, washing hung out, boisterously blowing about, the same as in Germany. Only I was different. When we arrived in Birmingham, it was raining. I was puzzled about the changeable English weather; I had assumed that if it rained were I was, it would be raining everywhere. How parochial I was.

A woman about my mother's age met me on the platform. 'Hello' she said. I held out my hand to shake with hers. Stiffly, she stood with her arms down; embarrassed, I put my arm down too. Directly, she put my case in the boot of her car, came round and opened the door for me next to the driving seat. Then she got into the car, switched on the engine, and we drove off.

We passed row upon row of red-brown, flat-fronted houses that I thought needed a good wash. When the car stopped, it was in front of one of those houses. My 'driver' opened the door of the car for me, took my case from the boot, and moments later, the front door of the house opened and a woman greeted me, waving her hand. My driver reversed the car, waved and drove off. I was left alone with Mrs Cohen, my guarantor. She spoke some Yiddish and I learned that my driver was her daughter.

Mrs Cohen was a friendly, kindly woman and although her Yiddish was not fluent it was enough to make me feel more at home – very comforting not to be dumb anymore. Mrs Cohen's two sons didn't speak Yiddish. They were grown men and barely nodded in my direction. I don't remember a Mr Cohen, but when I started work next morning, I realised there must be one because both sides of their bed had been slept in. I've forgotten him like so many things. What I do remember of him is a pair of trousers hanging by its braces on a hook on their bedroom door, the elastic worn and wavy round the edges.

Quite soon after my arrival, Mrs Cohen spoke of Heinie in relation to my coming to England, 'Your brother has charm and he is as sweet as sugar, we couldn't say no to him.' She even attempted to talk about why I was in England. What I said has gone and only a fragment of what Mrs Cohen said is left: that '… our religion is an ancestor religion.' Nothing intelligent could possibly have come out of my mouth, but I had the feeling that her tone was conciliatory. I'd give anything to remember what I stammered on about.

It was still light when Mrs Cohen took me up to the fourth floor of her house, to the room I was to sleep in. My suitcase, already in the room, was placed next to a four-poster bed, its dank-smelling curtain ending just below the mattress. The dank smell was explained by the watermarks I saw when I opened the cupboards beside the chimney breast. Mrs Cohen smiled at me encouragingly and then she left me alone. Sitting on the edge of the bed facing the window, I measured the space to the wall, a leg-stretch wide. All the space around the bed was more or less the same. No jumping out of bed in the middle of the night!

In the morning, looking out of the window, I saw a long narrow garden extending backwards, hemmed in by broken fences. At the far left of the garden, a rickety hut perched on a mound of earth. No shrubs anywhere, just bumpy grass with yellow patches dotted about here and there. A large tree from the next garden shaded the hut.

After breakfast the next morning, the Cohens' sons disappeared into deep low armchairs either side of the fireplace in the dining room. They were holding enormous newspapers open, four fingers visible on the outer pages, their legs in front of them, stiff as broomsticks. Above them, wooden wall-lights with dark red shades gave barely any light. I raked the ashes in the grate next to their feet. Two cups of tea stood on tall narrow side tables next to the fender. I was aware that I was invisible to them, but had they addressed me I would probably have jumped ten feet in the air. The dining room window faced the back garden. Not a blink of sun came into that room in the time I was with the Cohens. The window was half covered with sombre coloured velvet curtains, darker between the folds. It was then I remembered the staircase going to the Weilers' flat. 'The sun has bleached the treads,' Mrs Weiler said to me one day, and as she pointed out one thing, I saw another: the stained glass window above the stairs reflected onto the other side of the wall along the stairwell. The warmth on a sunny day was pleasurable when I was scrubbing the stairs with turps. Satisfying. They were *my* stairs! But nothing would be mine here.

The Cohens' house must have looked cheerful sometimes, but it didn't seem that way to me. The square piece of maroon-patterned linoleum was trodden away under the dining chairs and table. The wooden floor boards around the linoleum were painted black and the brown and beige-patterned wallpaper glowered over the lot. Strangest of all were bottles filled with brown and red sauce left permanently in the middle of the dining table, their contents poured over all food even before it was tasted. Most days, the crumbs from previous meals were left on the table and routinely inspected by flies, making the ornate brass dustpan and brush placed on a triangular shelf on the sideboard a superfluous utensil. Mrs Weiler would have been appalled. *I* was appalled! I practised a good deal of food xenophobia. Although I liked smoked fish I insisted that grilling kippers was completely wrong. 'We ate them raw!' I pontificated, thinking they were the smoked salmon I had at the Bergs.

Part of my duties was to empty the chamber pots that were left under the beds, uncovered. Mrs Weiler and Mrs Dreifuß had china buckets with china lids, a space between the knob and lid for the urine to run away. Even so, they emptied and rinsed them with Dettol themselves.

Doing what we always did at home, I set to cleaning the windows on the top floor, bucket and leather to hand, standing on the window ledge, one foot outside. Mrs Cohen shouted up from the garden in Yiddish, 'Don't do it!' and I shouted back, 'Who does it then?' 'The window cleaner!' she must have said. I didn't stay long enough to see this most extraordinary arrangement; I knew that if I stayed with Mrs Cohen, I wasn't going to learn a trade in England, as the Jewish Refugee Committee had promised. But something incredible did happen; from the day I set foot in England, I never wet the bed again. That was a miracle.

I wrote to my father every day that I missed my mother, my bicycle, my friends, and speaking German, and although I understood Yiddish well, speaking it was always difficult. I couldn't connect with anything or anybody here. Even the routine of household duties didn't oil my life. Regardless of Mrs Cohen's homely charm, I couldn't get used to the cold summer with fires burning in the grate. My letters worked; I was to go to London after having stayed with the Cohens for only a few weeks. Happy in one way, I felt awful in another because I had abused Mrs Cohen's kindness. All the bother she went through to get me here, but I was in a rage at still having to be a domestic.

The end of August approached. I don't remember anything of the day I left Mrs Cohen. Did I pack? Did I say goodbye? Did I say thank you? Was I grateful to her for saving my life? Was I on a train? Which station was I picked up from and by whom? The only certainty that I'd packed at all was that I remember unpacking, sorting through my clothes; which to keep and which to give away. Some were like hot coals in my hands. The hottest was a mackintosh, a cheap copy of a trench coat made popular in Germany by Marlene Dietrich. To wear it would identify me as German, which I didn't think I was anyway. I was born in Germany to Jews who were born in Poland. Without the mac, no one would know who I was – at least not by looking at me – and as long as I didn't open my mouth, I'd be safe. Finding my identity was not what I needed at that moment; the label 'outcast' would take time to disentangle – the Nazis had made sure of that – but despite their efforts to destroy my hope, it was alive and well and getting stronger as my English improved. It was halting maybe, but if anyone listening to me asked my nationality, I learned to say, loud and clear, 'I am a citizen of the world!' Many refugees, I learned a good many years later, made this declaration. Though we went our different ways, our aspirations were the same.

My father's cousins – Eva, Rosie, Blooma, Paul and Jack – had all come to England with their parents after the end of World War I. Bringing my parents to England was a joint effort of all the cousins. It was Jack and his wife Sally who gave me a home when I didn't want to stay in Dudley. They had two daughters: Rene was fourteen and Masha eleven. Jack was a cabinet-maker; his workshop was under the kitchen in their house in Hackney Road. Compared to Eva's house, Jack's was dull, work-a-day, fronted with a shop where furniture – the cheap end – was bought in and then sold. Eva's husband Joe was in the cheap end of the furniture trade too. Paul was the first of his siblings to have a furniture factory in Hackney Road: a three-storey house with a showroom on the ground floor.

Eva and Joe had three teenage children: Ralph, Sadie and Rene – Ralph was eighteen, the oldest. They lived in a Queen Anne house in Hackney Road. The living room on the ground floor had three elegant long windows looking down on a long uncultivated garden. Despite having a full house, Eva made the large room on the first floor available to my parents – my mother was expected any day now. Sally and Jack lived a five-minute walk down Hackney Road from Eva's. They had two daughters: Rene, fourteen and Marie, eleven – she was often called Masha or Mashala, depending on mood. It was to Rene I gave my mac; flushed and delighted she ran to a mirror. Blooma, the youngest of the cousins, lived with Rosie, her husband Rubin and their two sons Ralph, twenty-two, and Alf, eighteen, in Blythe Street, Bethnal Green, a ten minute walk from Hackney Road.

It was Rosie who sat waiting for my parents' papers at Bloomsbury House, the office for refugees from Germany; not a moment was to be wasted in writing letters, Eva told us. It was believed that Rosie's constant presence at Bloomsbury House would spell urgency. Days turned into weeks. Rosie had our respect. We never tired of telling her how wonderful she was to have given up her time for us. On one occasion, our praise went a step too far for her liking; busy at the stove giggling into her chin, she said, 'Don't be silly, it was the slack season!' She and Rubin were section workers in the tailoring trade – the cheap end – lining coats and jackets.

When I had first arrived at Sally and Jack's, Sally was fixing her hair in the kitchen using the mirror hanging above the fire place. She was taking pins from the mantel with her fingers to secure her lush auburn hair into the then fashionable roll, beginning just below the cheekbone. Smiling, her brilliant white teeth were framed with red painted lips which she always dabbed with a handkerchief after application. Turning to the door, she affirmed what must have been arranged before my arrival from Dudley: 'Yes,' she said, 'I told you Rosel can live here, so I'll put another cup of water into the borscht!' Not understanding much, I was alerted to every nuance as my status as a dependent was established, and, appropriately, I felt a mix of humility and gratitude – not a bad thing to have a little of, but as those feelings lingered in the centre of me, virtue slipped away, and still thinking in German the word *Selbständigkeit* (independence) spread itself across my mind. Yes, I agreed with my thoughts, independence is best.

Sally and Jack's kitchen was smaller than ours in Ludwigshafen, but it served the same multi-functional purposes, though it wasn't big enough for a tin tub; an enamel bowl had to do. On a triangular shelf in the corner above the kitchen table was a radio, its lead trailing behind chairs against the wall to a plug by the door. As at the Cohen's house, a fire blazed in the grate. Jack's workshop was a short flight below the kitchen, and next to it, the lavatory. The smell of glue and urine together was extremely unpleasant. Jack cleaned the house every Sunday. Apparently, Sally didn't care one way or the other; the state her stove was in would have made Mrs Weiler faint. I marvelled at Sally's indifference. My fingers itched to peel the grease off the stove, though a knife would have been more suitable.

Sally struck bargains in the shop. One memorable time was when she was standing on a ladder, adding a chair to others on a shelf well above wardrobes and tables, when a woman wandered in from the street. ''ere Missus, 'ow much is that wardrobe over there?' she asked. Sally eyes followed the woman's arm pointing to the opposite side from where she stood. 'Ten Pounds,' Sally said. ''ow much, Missus?' 'Fifteen pounds,' Sally said more loudly. ''at's nice, I'll 'ave it.' As the woman was paying, she said, 'My son will fetch i' wiv' the barrer this evening.' I laughed and Sally laughed too, but we weren't laughing at the same thing. I had begun to understand simple sentences spoken slowly, even Cockney which was heard at every turn in Hackney Road. None of the cousin's children spoke Cockney. I heard Toynbee Hall, a venue for evening classes off Commercial Road, mentioned a lot; which of the cousins went there I don't know.

A third bed had been put into Rene and Mascha's bedroom for me on the second floor of their house. Rene and I soon found ways to talk to each other, exchanging the latest pop songs from our respective cultures. I sang 'Ich liebe dich' as sung in duet by Martha Eggert and Jan Kipura in a film of *La Bohème*, and Rene, in her rich contralto voice imitated Lena Horn singing 'Stormy Weather'. Then I learned 'My Own', reaching for the high notes like Deanna Durbin. On the radio Bing Crosby crooned 'Brother can you spare a dime' and 'When they begin the Beguine'. The radio and our singing filled the house as we each repeated the other's song, line by line, until perfect in tune, lyric and language. Mascha looked on dolefully. Contentment for Mascha was sitting on her father's knee by the kitchen fire, sucking her thumb, her huge blue eyes taking everything in.

Sunday mornings we idled in bed and Rene talked non-stop; understanding little, I looked at her lips as they changed shape with each word. My hearing apart, she spoke too fast, that was until the words 'to buy' came into her monologue and when I still looked blank she repeated those two words 'to buy' several times. As not even a nod of recognition came from me, and she, perhaps thinking she could make me understand by the sheer force of sound, screamed, 'to buy, to buy, to buy, to buy, to buuyyyy!' until Sally flung open the door and explained in Yiddish, '*Keüfen!*'

Fun maybe, but I was worried with each idle day that went by. When would I start to learn my trade? Yitzak, an honorary

uncle and friend of the family, had a barbershop in Well Street, Hackney. He knew of Adolph Cohen, who reputedly had the best hairdressing shop in the Whitechapel Road in London's East End. Yitzak would speak for me. Good news. He struck a bargain with Cohen: would he halve the apprenticeship fee from the usual 50 guineas as a *Mitzva* (good deed), a favour to a refugee? In fact he blackmailed Cohen, going on about my refugee status. Eager to start work, I ignored the favours granted, but favours or not, the fee, however small, had to be borrowed. Debts in my family were mean little ones, constant and oppressive, an anxiety throughout the Hitler years. And now, in England, we would be in debt again.

English instructions in hand, I was on my way to work: left at Shoreditch Church, then left at Bishopsgate, and into Commercial Street. Sally had translated each turn into Yiddish twice for me. Surely her slow pronunciation would stick in my head! Past Shoreditch Church, I was lost. Doubtful of the name on the street sign, I stopped at Bishops Gate, a semi-circular building. Instructions still in my hand, I turned round and round, trying to decipher the name of the next street. A policeman came to my rescue. 'Are you lost?' I must have said 'Vitechepel?' Why else did he throw back his head, laughing? At that time, many immigrants must have amused him. Still smiling, he bent down to my height, and stretching out his arm, he spoke very, very slowly, pointing the way and holding up five fingers: 'Five more minutes and you'll be in Whitechapel Road.' As he spoke slowly, I noticed the different way he pronounced the letter W. Decades later, I read a book about the *Kindertransport*: ...*And the Policeman Smiled: 10, 000 Children Escape from Nazi Europe*. Remembering *my* policeman, *I* smiled.

It was now the end of August. My mother was due in England any day now but alarmingly there was talk of war and of borders being closed. My father's hands shook as he passed on

Mother's papers to Sally, literate in English, to check: 'Yes, it says that she'll be on the train scheduled for the end of August.' 'Why no date?' my father asked. Sally, now in a panic too, searched the papers again, and before she could find anything relevant to my mother's arrival, Alf, Eva's Ralph and Rosie's Ralph – the young second generation British born cousins – had rushed off to Liverpool Street Station to collect her. They came back without her; much wringing of hands and laments in a mix of Yiddish and English. I lost much of what was said, but woe being a universal language, I gathered what had happened. My mother was not on that train. Alf, Ralph and Ralph pacified my father: 'Perhaps there will be another train.' Doubt was not what we needed at that moment. The Yiddish word Greniz (border) came up frequently. Jack was the one who had a phone, which was the reason my father ran up and down Hackney Road from Eva's to Jack's for news of what might be the last train coming from Harwich, the young cousins were told, before Europe's borders were closed. They had promised to phone the moment they knew, but so far there had been no call. Rather than stand still, my father ran up and down Hackney Road again while I waited outside Jack's shop waiting for the phone to ring. He came rushing towards me breathless, his eyebrows raised in anticipation of news, and when there was none he paced back and forth outside the shop, over and over again until, later that evening, the cousins went back to Liverpool Street Station, and this time they came back with my mother.

My parents fell into each other's arms. 'Marie, Manjele,' Father said alternately, stroking her head, both of them in tears. I was powerless to take part in this event, its enormity too great for onlookers to spy on, be it passers-by, Sally and Jack, or me. But all of us would understand when a few days later, on 1st September 1939 Germany invaded Poland, and by September 3rd England had declared war on Germany. Neville Chamberlain, the Prime Minister, solemnly made the announcement on the radio. 'What is he saying?' I asked Sally. 'The *Melchama* has started.' she said. *Melchama*, I knew, was a Hebrew word in Yiddish for war, often used. Instantly I thought of my friends who were now trapped in Germany, holding visas in their hands, rushing about making travel arrangements, packing, what to take and what to leave behind, and now that Europe's borders were closed, how would I know what was happening to them in the place where we grew up and called our home?

After the war, the world saw skeletal bodies being bulldozed into pits. The truth of it shamed me because I imagined my friends shaking their fists at me when I laughed too much, enjoyed too much, shopped too much for things I didn't really need. How many times have we seen the film-clips of Jews being coerced onto cattle trucks? How many times was I stunned by the horror, unable to imagine myself among them? Was I the free animal who freezes when sensing danger and having sensed it, runs? And still running, I cry, 'Should I forget or die, let the winds howl for them, and let the grass under which they lie, bend and sigh'.

Despite my passionate thoughts, I looked forward to Rosie's son Ralph's wedding for which Eva was going to make me a party dress. I imagined myself swirling and dancing to a band playing on a balcony above a great hall, Ruritanian style, the way I had seen in films but, because of the war, the wedding party was cancelled. Disappointingly, only the ceremony took place.

The good thing was that my English got better every day. Knowing the word 'war' cleared something up for me. *War* is the past tense of 'to be' in German, *Krieg* is German for war and one of its meanings is 'to quarrel'. So war is a quarrel, the way my mother quarrelled with her brother? Other revelations about words came when walking with Eva's son Ralph down Hackney Road. Once on our way to their house, I wore the grey swagger coat his mother made me with a new pair of maroon shoes from Dolcis in Whitechapel Road which had cost one guinea. How this guinea was spared didn't for once interest me, but what did was how to say something in a new language: the daily search for words. Another time I must have been using the word 'kind' in the wrong way. 'No,' Ralph said, 'not kind, kindly.' The context in which this word was used, I don't remember, but by the time we got to their house, I had learned how to use an adjective. On a more threatening level, sand bags were being stacked against the house to absorb bomb blasts.

Back at Sally's, gas masks were issued with instructions in how to put them on. I refused to put my head into the rubber bag Jack held open for me. 'No,' I yammered, 'don't make me… don't make me… I will choke, please don't….' In what language I expressed my fear, I don't remember. Years later, at a family gathering, Jack would teasingly come up with his party piece as my complexion changed to red: 'Have I ever told you…?' and there and then he would act out, in tone and facial expression, my hysterical outburst.

The first time the sirens wailed over London no gas attack occurred, and even when none came at all during the whole war, gas masks continued to be a war accessory, although nobody I knew bothered with them. Free from gas and bombs, the lull was named the 'phoney war'. Then the London docks were bombed. On the way back to Germany, the bombs left over from a raid were dropped anywhere. Kreamer Street, off Hackney Road just opposite Sally and Jack's shop, was hit. I learned two new words, 'stray' and 'docks'. Walking over to Kreamer Street, I stared at the hole for a long time. Much worse than the mess the thugs made at the Weilers; here, the whole house was destroyed. Would England bomb Germany? And, like striking a match in the dark, I remembered 1936, my last year at school, when an air raid was simulated. The whole class, earnest faced, had to file out and go to the cellar to the sound of the school bell ringing loud and long. I heard it said that this had to do with the Spanish Civil War, when Hitler wanted to try out his war machines to help General Franco. I saw news-reels of this 'help': planes dropping bombs fat as cigars with fins at one end, swaying drunkenly before whistling to their targets. That must have been the 'guns before butter' policy we heard so much about on the radio which was indeed a reality for the population of Germany: two ounces of butter per week.

Back in Sally's kitchen, Ada, her char from Hoxton, helped to clean the house. Jack wouldn't let her touch his furniture; that he did himself. Ada, thin and scraggy, wore ankle-length dresses and a sack tied round her waist with string as an apron, contrasting with a black velvet hat adorned with two blue fox pompoms above one ear. Whether Ada was dusting, sweeping or scrubbing the doorstep, the hairs of the pompoms moved in time to her rhythm. For her appearance alone, Ada would never have got a job as a cleaner in Germany, the door would have been shut in her face. Although as unsophisticated as me, she was kind of shameless, brave even. All of us were in the kitchen one lunchtime when the news came through on the radio: '… last night German bombers were active over the Thames estuary… Ada, standing by the sink, her head cocked to one side, asked, ''ere Missus, where's the Thames?' I was surprised: Ada was a native of London. By then I knew that the Thames flowed through London, but in heaven's name what was an estuary? It was from Ada I learned there was no shame in asking. Both of us, politically backward and tradi-tionally stuck, stood on thresholds, I thought much later.

A few weeks on, I wasn't just listening; I was taking part in conversations. One morning at work, Frieda, another em-ployee and I were chatting at reception, our hands clasping the top of our broomsticks. Cohen, coming down the stairs from his flat caught us in mid-stream. He shouted, 'Home for the day, both of you!' When he was out of range, Frieda

1939 — 10 years before Sussor

protested, 'He's got a cheek, it isn't even nine o'clock yet!' Frieda went home and never came back. I felt as bad as Frieda but Mother implored me, 'We can't afford for you not to go back!' Amelia, another apprentice at Cohen, had chic more Holly-wood than Whitechapel Road. If the rules for our pay were the same, how come she could afford the clothes she wore when she lived in a dark and neglected house in Wentworth Street off Commercial Road? On my way to work, I had seen her come out from the doorway of this dingy house, sweeping past two barrels of herrings outside the front door of a grocery shop, one each side like potted plants, her swagger coat jauntily moving about her, clutch-bag under her arm.

Sometimes she and I strolled down Whitechapel Road to-gether on our way home after work. Amelia chattered on about the lipstick she could not possibly do without. 'I can only use Louis Phillipe,' she declared. In a more emphatic tone, she let me know that she would only 'marry rich', a statement helped by resolutely folding her coat about her, and with lips tight, she said, 'I mean it!' defiantly tossing back her carbon-copy Joan Crawford hairstyle, bunched curls fluffed out on her fore-head, and more fluffed curls touching her shoulders in their strawberry-blond glory. Having made her point, she let go of her coat revealing a soft wool dress snug against her body. Her slender hands ended with filbert-shaped nails varnished to match her lipstick, her mouth in a pout; she stabbed the air, adding emphasis to what she said. If she went out straight from work, she powdered her nose, re-fluffed her curls with a tail comb, and to finish, she dabbed her favourite scent, extracted from a flat midnight-blue bottle with a glass dip, behind her ears and on her wrists. Breathing in luxuriously, she put the bottle back into the side pocket of her bag with thumb and forefinger, leaving the other three extended like a wing.

I thought Amelia was a cut above the rest of the staff. Her pronunciation for instance wasn't Cockney like theirs. Her voice was high and her laugh an infectious 'hihihi'. Her eyes were hazel, overhung with straight black lashes, and her lids were finely drawn near her eyes. To make my envy an even deeper green, Amelia's legs were so slender she could wind them round each other like rope. I had short legs, short fingers and small nails. Annoyingly, my mother's family had children with legs like carthorses, but it was reassuring that my lashes were long and curled naturally: no clamping needed for them!

Amelia took for granted all manner of everyday things that I didn't even dare think about, for example I had learned never to expect a birthday card. Sending birthday cards seemed not to be a tradition in our family; it was not malice on my parents' part. Neither of them even knew their birthdays. When birth certificates were needed for emigration to England, Polish authorities were contacted. I didn't read them at the time. Years later, when my parents were dead, I found them in the filing system my father had made in a small cardboard box. Translated into German, my mother's birth certificate reads:

> It happened in the town of Lodz...there appeared Herschel Rotman with witnesses and showed us a female child, (eight years in fact), which he said was his own... born to the single Schajka Chana Karpinska...claiming that he was late because of family circumstances... .younger children...

Being illiterate he did not know the date, but he knew the exact time my mother was born: eight o'clock in the evening. Under the date in the document, it says: signature illegible.

I went into shock. My mother illegitimate? All sorts of assumptions I had about my mother's past surfaced: her depression, her sometimes tragic mien. Hastily, I rang my cousin Rosl in Israel. She laughed out loud, 'Silly fool, how could children be legitimate if Jews didn't live under secular law? The rabbi was our law!' What a relief! Rabbi or not, family respectability was restored. My mother was legitimate!

A few weeks into my work, Rene believed I was better than I was and asked me to comb her hair before she went to work. She worked as a sales girl in a fur shop in Oxford Street and as it took a half an hour's bus ride to get there she had to get up earlier than me. To get to my job was a ten-minute walk. If I was to comb her hair, I had to get up when she did. One morning, still half asleep, I heard Sally shouting up the stairs, 'If you want your hair combed, why don't you wake her up?' And this was what Rene did: shake me, wake me, every day. My reluctant hands fiddled about with her hair.

Glad to have an escape from the emotional discomforts I felt at Sally's, I concentrated on my English. What sort of English was determined by the broad vowels spoken around me. Frieda's vowels were very broad. 'Baiby,' she said with her mouth wide open. Miss Page, a client at Cohen's, was appalled at hearing me articulate those sounds, especially as I was 'fresh to English', she said, looking up at me regretfully. Miss Page was on a mission. 'Beiby,' she said, stretching her lips back to her ears as narrowly as possible, again and again, 'Beiby.' After her lesson, I practically walked into everyone's mouth to get pronunciation right. I even 'walked' into Aunt Rosie's, but she, as usual, giggled into her chin and shooing me off affectionately said, 'You will soon speak better than me!'

Miss Page was different from our other clients. I heard Mrs Cohen say that she worked as a secretary at the London Hospital in Whitechapel Road. Cohen didn't do her hair the same as his other clients. Hairdressers know at a glance when a woman knows how to present herself, and clients like these are usually better to work on, more satisfying and more fun, thrilling even, as I found out for myself later on. Watching Cohen do the secretary's blonde hair was exciting as he coaxed it under with his cupped hands into a smooth pageboy style.

Finished, he held the hand mirror aslant for her see the back view. They smiled at each other in the big mirror over the washbasin in mutual appreciation.

Miss Page didn't come to the shop often, but I worked hard on my vowels. The lesson was learned. The truth was that I needed her every day. All of Father's cousins spoke accented English except Blooma, the youngest, who went to school in England. Eva was the funniest and the second most fluent. 'Trompitis,' she would say. Her English born children said, 'No Mum, it's bronchitis!' and she would say, 'Yes, yes, I am saying trompitis!' My world hadn't changed much in this respect; I was still living with comics. Father and Eva together was something to be savoured; it was extraordinary to hear them get at each other in Yiddish. Father having no English, they had to sort out their differences in the ways of the old country: jabber, jabber, loudly.

And that is how I slipped into their lives, learning English orally, and adopting a new pop culture. The Big Band programmes on the radio were part of that life, and sacred moments they were. Rene stopped working up west. She wanted to work with me. My mother was not pleased and although I understood her reasons – she didn't want me to be used. It was hard to see how this could be managed in reality. When Cohen gave Rene a job, the good thing was that anybody could now do her hair, she could even do it herself! Relieved though I was, I never felt at ease. At any moment, some other thing would be expected of me. My mother watched anxiously, saw every frown on my brow regarding Rene's and my relationship. 'Don't worry, Mamma, I will speak up for myself,' I assured her. This never happened.

Whether I liked it or not, Rene and I were thrown together. Being a refugee was demanding; freedom had a price. I hid what I really felt but we did have some fun as well. Home for lunch, we stomped up the stairs to the kitchen just as Geraldo's signature tune faded and the first tune was announced. Out of breath, we flopped down on chairs, banging our hands on the kitchen table to the rhythms coming from the radio. A few moments later, Rene would say, 'I'm starving!' and as if bouncing from a spring she jumped off her chair to prepare her lunch. The first thing to do was to wash and dry a used cup and a plate left on the table from breakfast; then, hunting round for the cleanest tea cloth she could find, she flicked the crumbs that were all over the table off to the nether regions and laid 'her' table. Licking her lips with anticipation she opened a tin of sardines and tapped them out on the plate. Pivoting round on one foot, she grabbed the half used lemon from the kitchen unit behind her and squeezed what juice was left over the sardines, and then sprinkled them with salt and powdered pepper. Standing still for a moment, one hand splayed over her hips, she licked the fingers of her other hand, sighed, and sat down. Then she pulled a slice of bread from its waxy wrapping, and tearing off half, she dipped it into the oil until it was well soaked, and craning back her head, she held the oil-soaked bread above her open mouth, letting droplets of oil descend onto her tongue.

Wonderloaf (wrapped sliced bread) was a new experience for me; bed bugs were not, we had plenty of them in Germany. Out of habit, I made it my task to eradicate them, the way we deluded ourselves we could in Germany with the legs of the bed in a bucket of water heavily laced with carbolic. We were sure this would flush them out, but all our efforts were wasted. Plump from our blood, they lurked behind the wallpaper and in the creases of our hair mattresses, waiting for their next feed. Damned bloodsuckers! Their smell was distinctive. The Weilers didn't have them and my mother was as house-proud as Mrs Weiler, but despite this, cockroaches reigned when all of us were out for the evening and the lights were off. Up they came through the gaps in our kitchen floorboards from the cellar. I hated being the first to switch on the light; seeing them scuttle back under the boards was an assurance of sorts but I couldn't forget the fat, black shiny things I imagined would crawl all over me when I was asleep, partying with the bed bugs. Mother used to scrub the boards, muttering under her breath wishing for an end to her plight. I was never sure whose end she meant, hers or the cockroaches. And here I was in Hackney Road, doing my best, as she had.

Chapter Twelve

Father in the Isle of Man

In May 1940, Father was interned in the Isle of Man. I don't remember where I was when he was taken and didn't dare ask what kind of knock on the door it was – a gentle sound like a visitor's or a loud bang? And what kind of transport was it, a car or an open lorry to ferry the individuals to a collecting place? No, this couldn't happen here, I reflected, this is Hackney Road in London. Mother's face told another story. Again her husband had been taken from her side. There was an air of defeat about her, head and eyes down, lips folded away.

Not long after my father had gone, I had to spend a long time in Commercial Road police station. Ralph took me there but waited outside in the street. When finally I emerged from under the blue lamp, he asked, 'Why so long?' I couldn't tell him how scared I'd been at the sight of so many sheets of paper being scrutinized, handed from one policeman to another – four or five in all – sat in a row behind a narrow table. I wasn't asked to sit down. Then one of the policemen leaned forward and asked me lots of questions, none of which I understood. More out of panic than anything else, I remained silent. They searched through the papers again and turned to each other, whispering. Then one of them leaned forward and spoke to me very slowly, asking if I had sent back the forms they'd sent me to fill out. 'Did you get them?' 'What forms?' I said. That was the first time I heard anything about forms. I said 'No' to everything. They looked at me and I looked at them, and again, they whispered to each other. Then the policeman who had first spoken to me said, 'You can go now.' This I heard clearly; everything else they said came to me as if

spoken into a drum. Cautiously I walked down the long corridor, but halfway along, I began to run.

I couldn't tell Ralph how I feared filling out forms so remi-
niscent of my packing days with the Weilers, and how relieved
I was not to have my fingerprints taken – a dread passed on
from the Hitler years when anything official was frightening.
When there was no follow-up from the police, I stopped wor-
rying and decided that England wasn't Germany.

Decades after the war, I learned that the data on my arrival
in England were kept by the *Responsible Area Committee of the
Kindertransport*. I sent for the particulars. The committee had
followed my progress right through the war and most probably
it was they who were in contact with the police. I had indeed
ignored letters of inquiry about me sent at regular intervals
from January 1940 until August 1945, by which time the war
was over and I was British by marriage. Apparently, concerned
committee ladies called at whichever place I lived. First, a Miss
Smith saw my mother; afraid like me, she probably wrung her
hands in despair at the sight of officialdom. Then a Miss Moore
called and she too drew a blank. Heinie, the memo says, promised to pass on the letter he received from Mrs Noyda to me.
Sixteen calls in all. I have no memory of any letters, or messages.

When Father came back from the Isle of Man, he reported
nothing sinister. On the contrary, he teased me for not having
sent more newsy letters: 'I turned your card from one side to
the other, hoping to find revelations between the lines,' and
jesting some more, he said, 'had you written in larger letters
there would have been even less to read.' I still wrote in the
pointed German Gothic script, and Father's jest was that the
points led nowhere. It was comforting that he knew me so well.
He seemed to be his old self – animated, poking fun. The Isle
of Man had *not* been Dachau; apart from doing some garden-
ing, nothing alarming happened. What occurred to me much

later was the psychological damage he may have had, his head still full of Dachau imagery, fears waiting to be fulfilled.

On a practical level, work was good. Eva and Sally fed me on alternate days and I am certain Ralph ('Sonny' his mother called him sometimes) engineered our meeting for lunch at their house. Exactly when we became kissing cousins I don't remember, but I suspect it must have had something to do with Ralph saving me from an embarrassment. Eva had made a family lunch party a good while after my father came home from the Isle of Man. The meal started with grapefruit, cut in half. I had never eaten grapefruit in any shape or form before. The flesh had not been segmented and it had to be scooped up with a teaspoon. I dug and poked the fruit unsuccessfully. Ralph, sitting next to me, saw me struggling. Deftly he took the saucer with the fruit on it and put it on the floor beside him. I threw him a grateful glance. Perhaps it was after this that we began to kiss.

Routines can create false feelings of belonging. Eva was generous, though her eyes moved shrewdly from Ralph to me, trying to gauge our involvement with each other; I was being vetted, that was clear! One lunchtime, Eva and Ralph were talking (I couldn't understand what about) when suddenly her hand came down hard on his cheek. His eyes flashed at me, shaking with humiliation. 'I'm in charge!' said the slap, to both of us. What a pity, Eva needn't have gone to such length: his kisses were warmer than mine. I was an idol in his hands, lifeless.

One day, my mother walked into the bathroom in Eva's house where Ralph and I were kissing. 'One thing leads to another,' she mumbled, picking up the bowl she'd come for. The 'other' was what Uncle Avrum gave me, and here I was with Ralph who my mother said 'wanted the other', which reminded me of the time my father told me not to 'marry a Goy' and the warning not to let myself be 'used'. Apart from having let myself be 'used' already, I decided on another version of the same thing: Ralph didn't treasure me enough – according to the mores of the time when respectability dictated that you didn't have sex before marriage. I was not equipped to walk into this minefield; it was better to give credence to my father's belief that I was still innocent, which, unwittingly, paralysed my sexual impulses. To manage the present I had to wipe out the past, but I couldn't wipe away guilt. I interrogated myself ruthlessly: why did you go with Avrum? Why did you take the money – even look forward to it? Why did you eat the chocolate so pleasurably, licking your teeth clean before you got home? Why so easily, and why the cunning? Why couldn't you walk away from this, the way you did from your desire to steal the silver-wrapped chocolate eggs? And how did I know the difference between the two wrongs? Because one gave me a sense of achievement and the other accused me daily: you are nothing but a whore! The accusation was so deep, and so logically acceptable to me, that to rise from these depths, I needed to sink the 'whore' tied to a stone. My secret was society's secret too and I felt I was the only one this happened to.

For Ralph, I contrived a prudish stance of respectability. That was where I wanted to stay. That way I had a future, and although I was sexually dead and emotionally blank, the reward was freedom from mental torture. My abuser's deed paled against the smear campaign I led against myself.

Soon after Eva had slapped Ralph, she proclaimed, 'Cousins don't marry!' and not aware that a proposal was offered, I was only too glad a decision had been made. I felt like a cow being paraded in an auction. Other reasons followed swiftly. My mother told me what Sally had whispered in her ear: 'they', not mentioning any names, said that her Ruchel wasn't very bright. Sally didn't get on too well with her in-laws; telling tales to my mother was her way of paying them back. But their opinion of me went deep into my mother's vitals and looking at me, she said, 'What a *Chutzpah*! I think he isn't good enough for you.'

Then she started to cry. Between sobs, she said, 'How much more shame do I have to suffer?' I comforted my mother in the only way I knew would help us. 'Don't worry, Mamma,' (she wasn't Mum yet), 'Soon, I will earn enough for our keep,' and inwardly raging, I vowed, 'I'll show you, I will be good enough,' and it wasn't Ralph I was thinking of.

Although Mother spoke out for me, she was mute in other situations. The days I had lunch with Eva, she didn't emerge from the basement. I heard her opening the back door downstairs, emptying buckets of water in the yard, shaking out mats; it was her way of contributing, being grateful. It had been a long time since I saw my mother laugh, and I wasn't helping by ignoring her.

Our dependence continued. When Father was in the Isle of Man, Mother remained in Eva's room. I didn't know where I belonged, in Eva's house or Sally's. One afternoon, alone in Mother's room, packed to the hilt junk-shop style with furniture, and not having any place to settle, I created a new me with the help of Max Factor makeup. I applied pancake several layers thick. It gave me the ghostly appearance fashionable then. I added eye-black, also several layers thick, and lipstick. I looked more like an accident at birth than the product of God's artistry, though art I thought it was. Well satisfied with the result, I sat myself sideways on a high-backed chair, my chin resting on my hands placed on top of each other on its back, and gazing into space, I struck a pose like an actress in one of the glossy pictures in my album. I imagined an observer being devastated by the effect I created, though if I'd moved a muscle, cracks might have appeared on my face as in a drought. I stayed in that pose until my mother came into the room. On seeing my face, she said, 'You've painted yourself because you were langweilig.' 'What is *Langweile* in English,' I later asked Eva, and she said, 'Ask Ralph.' That is how I learned the word 'boredom'.

Father back from the Isle of man, I remained the breadwinner for us – though my tips couldn't be counted as wages: three pence for doing a shampoo and sometimes a sixpence piece would glitter among the coppers. The rules for an apprentice were no pay for six months, and after that, five shillings a week. I consoled myself that it was better than housework for five marks a month! I was making progress, I comforted myself. Frequently, Mother came to Cohen's shop to collect my tips; 'to buy bread', she said. Bread was a generic term for all kinds of food. I gave her the pennies I had, and as I watched her walk down Whitechapel Road, her head down, my oath to make good felt more urgent than ever.

Then one day she came to the shop with a jar of strawberries and cream. How did she get the money for this luxury? Outside Cohen's shop, Mother tried to feed me as in days gone by: 'Eat, Uhele,' she said to her now seventeen-year-old daughter. A couple of mouthfuls on, I took the spoon from her hand. She let go reluctantly and watched me eating with a look so tender, it made me feel for her. She wasn't feeding me now, Eva was, and Sally. Her declaration not so long ago in our kitchen in Ludwigshafen, 'One less mouth to feed', belonged to the Nazi years; we manoeuvred around those politics as best we could – and that is what we were still doing, manoeuvring.

I still have the letter from the Jewish Refugee Committee, dated 1946, with the confirmation that we lived on charity. Reading the letter years later, I drew comfort from the fact that we were not entirely dependent on family: 'Last week we had a visit from Mrs Hirschkovitsch (Sally) of 156 Hackney Road, E.2 who handed us £20 on your behalf... and promised that in the future you would pay six pounds a month.' In 1946, we still owed £114 17s 3d.

Chapter Thirteen

The Smartest Shop

Cohen's shop, fronted with black Vitrolite and chrome trim, was one of the smartest in Whitechapel Road. Other shop fronts round about were of an older period. Compared to the black Vitrolite, they looked neglected and in need of a lick of paint: Rosy's Millinery, Edith's Dresses, Yarnovsky Corsets (the owner weighed at least eighteen stone), and between the corsets and hats was Strongwaters, the salt beef shop. Mrs Strongwater had her hair done while still wearing her white overall, the imprints of greasy finger marks on both her hips, and what wasn't deposited there was splattered over the rest of her overall: mustard, ketchup – a painting in the making. Her fingers were banana-shaped and her nails varnished an orange red, always chipped. Barehanded, she'd dive into a barrel of cucumbers. Her hair was sunshine yellow, and the moment her black roots showed, she had them re-touched. Orange-coloured lipstick and matching nail varnish clashed with her florid complexion.

Many of our clients similarly lacked taste in my view. They used phrases like 'ged awaiy' and 'I never did' and when not wanting to take life for granted they either pleaded with or thanked God depending on the situation. Among them, Miss Page seemed to be like a stray cat from another region. But I liked the bustle of the shop, the constant chatter and the way women assessed themselves in the mirror, posturing, not seeing themselves – anything but themselves. Like me at times, they just saw the current idols of the times reflected in the mirror. 'I will change that' crossed my mind.

One busy winter day, I lifted up the visor of a dryer to test the dryness of a client's hair. Lice were crawling in and out of it. I stepped back in horror. 'Quick, burn everything!' Cohen ordered. A fire was burning in the grate in the room we used as a staff-room behind the shop, and we burned the client's blouse, skirt, the towel and the gown she had round her. A whole generation of lice had incubated in half an hour under the warmth of the dryer. It was fascinating to see them, crawling helter-skelter through the hair like babies at top speed. The instructions given to the woman of how to get rid of the rest of those 'babies' are a faint memory; my English was too limited, still.

On Saturday afternoons, Whitechapel heaved with the populace. Young people who worked up west in the week were out in force with Mums and Dads, Aunts and Grannies, shopping and gossiping, walking in rows of four and more, and sometimes they clumped together, arguing, and shrieking. Others from further away disgorged from Whitechapel tube station. In the summer, Cohen's shop door was left open; snippets of family histories, wedding arrangements discussed and disputed, could be heard. Girls lumped together looking into shop windows considering and pointing at things, then on impulse one might say, 'Come on, let's go in.' On Sunday mornings, the wide pavement outside Cohen's shop served as an employment exchange. Tailors met and exchanged news of jobs, for section workers mostly. In the slack season, ten men might run after one job, Cohen said, furious about the mess they left behind. Just round the corner was Blackline Yard and bang in its middle was a jewellery shop where most locals bought wedding and engagement rings. Who among the daughters of lower middle-class Jewish families has not inherited a diamond ring bought in Blackline Yard or a wedding picture taken by Boris in Whitechapel Road? His backcloth was a French Art Deco window in front of which the newly-weds posed, a mass of veiling mimicking a cloud formation placed at their feet regardless of how sumptuous the bride's own veil might have been.

I worked and practised till late at night on anyone who'd let me get at their hair. Before Christmas we worked through the night and getting extra tips was very exciting, but more to the point it was helpful to Mother. Tips apart, working all night was like getting a black belt for judo. I grew in confidence, my hands deft and curious. Nothing was phoney about the war now. Bombs started to fall in earnest. London docks were bombed regularly, all within hearing distance of Whitechapel Road. The Cohen's living accommodation above the shop made the building just two storeys high. A good gust of wind could have blown it away, never mind a bomb blast! In the cellar under the shop, women allowed themselves to be wired up to *Eugene Permanent Waving* machines while raids were in progress, their arms folded over their bosoms, relaxed, as if they were safely ensconced in a concrete bunker. The method of doing these perms was risky enough, never mind the possibility of needing easy escape if bombs dropped near. Small sections of hair were soaked in a chemical solution and wound round metal rods, secured with 'crepe hair' and then inserted into rods, electrically heated sheaths, which sizzled slowly to boiling point. If the solution dribbled, it could burn the scalp. I never heard of anyone suing, but remonstrate they did, very loudly: 'It's too hot – I'm burning!' Wireless Permanent Waving came in later; many an ancient hairdressing shop had *Harmless Permanent Waving* written under or over the owner's name, whichever was considered more important, the name or harmless perming. Cohen was late in using new equipment; in any case getting new machinery in the war was on hold for everyone.

Money apart, I was convinced Cohen had nothing more to teach me. I liked my hair wild and ruffled, tossing about in the wind. Cohen, a hairdresser of his day, didn't like the way I failed to represent *his* look which was to torture hair into rows of lop-sided curls, held in the grip of sweet-smelling shellac, its stiffness often lasting until the hair was washed again. It was the apprentice's job to pump the stuff from sprays, which constantly clogged up. To unblock the nozzle it had to be soaked in solvent, not always available during the war. Poking the nozzle with fine wire was a sticky task, and not always satisfactory.

Cohen pestered me to let him cut my hair and before I could say 'scissors', my long tresses lay on the floor. In no time, I felt the cold clippers against my neck above my natural hairline, the sides of my hair left just long enough to twist into those dreadful curls. Seconds later, he was lacquering my hair, and as if to spite me, the spray worked perfectly right up to the last moment when my hair became immovable! 'There, that's how your hair should look!' he said, holding the back mirror for me to see. Cohen, I realised, wasn't going to be dictated to by a 'nobody' like me in his craft, especially as he had taken me in as a favour. Even if he didn't say this, I saw it in his smile: 'That'll teach you!' I was angry; I knew he wouldn't have dared to do that to Amelia.

Eating lunch at Eva's that day: as I came through the door she cried, 'What on earth has happened to you? You look like an old woman!' I was too hungry to say all I thought; though miserable, my appetite hadn't waned. Eva made good egg-and-chips; for 'afters' she made hot stewed apples or plums with custard, and sometimes, for a treat, ice-cream. The contrast of hot with cold held wonders I had never experienced before. I don't ever remember having puddings in Germany, not even at the Weilers.

Halfway able to do a professional job, I counted the perms I now did unsupervised. At fifteen shillings each, and doing at least six a week, I thought I was making Cohen rich. Convinced he didn't appreciate my skills, I asked him for a raise. Mrs Cohen, who was within earshot, yelled down from the top of the stairs, 'She's got a *Chutzpah*, Adolph, tell her to go!' Although I knew that the rules for apprentices' pay were fixed, I stuck to the facts: fully skilled I may not have been, but I wasn't just passing up pins and cleaning lacquer sprays anymore. Father not having a work permit, I had to stay with Cohen. Although the money we received from the Jewish Refugee Committee helped, it had to be paid back.

Chapter Fourteen

To the Country for Safety

After the bomb in Kreamer Street, Sally panicked. She hired a coach to take Jack and their two daughters out of London. My parents and I were outside their shop hoping they'd take us with them. When no offers came, Mother asked, 'Perhaps there's room for us?' And even more agitated, Sally shouted, 'No, there isn't!' Turning to Jack she said, 'Come on, Jack, let's go,' and the four of them boarded the empty coach. Sally made us more scared than we already were. With hindsight, I can see that having refugees tugging at your elbows must have been a nuisance. Remembering no more of this situation, my guess is they came back to London after a ride around the countryside.

The 'phoney war' over, German bombers now droned over London every night. Mother proposed: 'Perhaps we should leave London and go where Heinie is.' For the first time since I came to England I wondered, 'Where *is* Heinie?' With Mother's next statement I began to understand our refugee status, 'Since we don't have a home of our own, or jobs, what difference is it where we are?' Encouraged by her own idea, she turned to me and said, 'You go to where Heinie is.' Then, turning to my father she asked, 'What is the name of the place where he lives?' 'Tylers Green near High Vyckham, in a *galach's* house, a vicarage.' Father struggled to pronounce all the names but this meant nothing to my mother, and turning back to me she said, 'Yes, Ruchel, tomorrow, you go and see what you can find.' So far I only identified with England in a couple of ways: one was to have tea with milk and the other was the endless chatter about the erratic weather pattern; of course I knew about that – coal fires in July?

The next day, I got a train to High Wycombe. Who told me which station to go from, I don't remember. When I arrived at High Wycombe it was dusk. At the bus stop, I asked a woman in the queue behind me which bus went to Tylers Green. 'I live in Tylers Green, come with me,' she said. Still nervous about my English, I didn't say any more. Posters all over the place warned 'Walls have Ears', the implication being that aliens could be anywhere, and I, with my bad English, wouldn't fool anyone. I must have told the woman something about looking for a room, because she said, 'Don't worry, we'll see about that tomorrow.' But where shall I stay tonight? I wondered. Getting off the bus, and seeing how worried I was, the woman took hold of my hand and said again, 'Come with me.' And I did.

Her house stood in its own grounds and had a pebbledash exterior painted a soft white. Shrubs grew up the walls and trees edged a huge garden. The woman led me upstairs to her bathroom and turned on the hot water for a bath. Then she went out to the landing and came back with a fluffy white towel and put it on the gold-and-apple-green-plaited wicker chair. Soon I was enveloped in steam as dense as a sea mist. When she left, she said, 'Have a good soak, and when you have had enough, come down and have supper with us.' Did I smell? No, I reassured myself, this is what well-off people do as a matter of course. I will be able to have a bathroom like this one day, and scented fine soaps and soft dry towels. I had never dried myself with anything like it before, absorbing as it did every last drop of water from my body. Light hearted, I went downstairs, a new self, my head filled with new dreams. The woman patted the chair next to her for me to sit on; I don't remember what we ate.

The house was full of dark furniture and chintz curtains, their vivid flower arrangements on a yellow background, hanging round diamond-shaped leaded windows; the smell of furniture polish, distinct. Two girls about the same age, though much younger than me, sat next to what I assumed was their father, one on each side of him. The woman and I sat facing them. Throughout the meal, the husband remained silent. He had unruly steel-grey hair, and his blank eyes perturbed me. On the long dark dining table, each of us had a place mat with pictures of people wearing bright red jackets and black dome-shaped hats riding horses and jumping over hedges. The silver cutlery with chunky embossed flowers on its handles framed the mats.

The woman's voice was gentle, so different from my family's boisterous sounds. 'You'll feel better after a good night's sleep,' she said, taking me upstairs to a bedroom (thank goodness I no longer wet the bed) and before that thought had time to settle, she tucked me in with that strange English custom: blankets. No matter that I don't remember the woman's name; it was her kindness that stays with me. 'I have found rooms for you in a house in Penn,' she said coming in from the garden in the morning, a basket on her arm filled with string beans. I was to go back to London to fetch my parents. She took me to the station and when the train started to pull out, she said, 'When you're settled in your rooms, come and see me again,' and other words that were lost as the train gathered speed. Leaning out of the window, I waved and she waved back at me, smiling.

In London, my parents were ready and packed. Clearly, they'd assumed I'd find something, and as it turned out, Rene and Mascha were coming to live with us too. The thirty shillings we had from Bloomsbury House would have to be enough for three growing girls and two adults. We all went Green Line to High Wycombe, changing buses for Tylers Green. From there it was just a five minute walk to Penn.

I often walked to the white house, alone. The woman's husband invariably sat at the end of the garden by himself, a blanket over his knees, his back bent. 'He's mental,' our landlady said, rotating her forefinger next to her right eye for me to understand what she meant, and in the same breath she added, 'and her girls go to a posh day school.' What did 'posh' mean?

The landlady's husband was in the army and was expected home on compassionate leave for the birth of their third child. I don't remember much about their other two children except that they were boys, three and four years old perhaps, and very noisy! They quarrelled over whose turn it was to ride their tricycle up and down the concrete paths in the garden, the bell on the handlebars ringing and ringing. The smell of the cooking in that house reminded me of Mrs Hermann's sausages and bacon, and as with her, or Totzel, the black iron pan was always ready, glistening with fat from previous fry-ups. I felt homesick for the secret morsels I had with Liesel. But with my father around, not a chance!

The entire floor of our room was covered with mattresses with just one gangway to the fire and the door. Good at improvising, my mother managed to cook giblets when available from the village butcher; with no stove in our room she'd use the fire in the grate. When it glowed, she raked it flat and put a piece of flattened tin on top. Only then did she start to cook. First, she melted the margarine in a pot. When it sizzled, she placed the giblets next to each other, turning them at regular intervals until every crevice was golden. Staying by the fire, she added tiny amounts of water, and after it had reduced in the cooking she made up the loss, again and again, until the giblets were soft, and then with just a sprinkle of salt, she nurtured a taste that teased the palate. Delicious!

Rene and I went for long walks through woods, along footpaths and across fields. Rene would tell me long stories and when she stopped speaking, I asked, 'What happens next?' and she'd say, 'There isn't any more, I made it all up.' So, storytelling was 'lying'; I did that when I looked into space, only I never told anybody. Maybe that was what Father wanted me to do when he was winding me up.

Walking as we did most days, Rene and I picked up the windfalls from under apple trees. We gorged on them. 'Bring some back,' Mother said when we told her of the treasures lying on the grass. Picking out the best, she stewed them and we ate them with hot rice. When our sugar ration ran out, the apples were still better than nothing. The hot bland rice ameliorated their sour taste.

When Jack and Sally came to visit their children, they brought a tin of sardines as a contribution to their keep. Mother made them her giblet dish, and Sally, demonstrating her appreciation, licked her fingers. Sally seemed to go from generosity to meanness, but, being helplessly indebted to her, my mother said to my father, 'How does Sally think that feeding her two growing girls needs no more than a tin of sardines, quite apart from feeding her and Jack when they come?' Given the circumstances, my mother riled against having to delouse Mascha's hair as she pulled at it with a fine toothcomb, teeth clenched. Mascha winced and whined her way through the merciless tugging. Despite my mother's clumsy handling of Mascha's hair, they were inseparable – an incongruous alliance. Father repaired all our shoes, the landlady's and her children's, in the room next to ours; Father and his *Dreifuß* were never parted for long.

Close to giving birth, the landlady called out to her husband from upstairs, 'Go and fetch the midwife!' When she arrived, I was given the job of carrying pots of hot water upstairs, lots of it. And there were lots of screams too from our landlady when her baby was being born; the noisy boys had a sister. It is remarkable how we all managed in that council house. The good thing was that a big garden opened on to fields, and beyond them woods as far as the eye could see. Birds flocked and took off together in a way I had never noticed before.

The first time I recognized the word 'that' in print was exciting. From then on I recognized other words in the slim volumes of romances I got from the village library. I felt my way through these romances rather than understanding every word. Soon the pages turned as if blown by a wind – would the lovers ever kiss? It was a start; reading war reports in the newspapers was more difficult, but with headlines like 'El Alamain: Rommel routed by Montgomery', it occurred to me that Hitler could lose the war and I would see my friends again.

The house we lived in was one of two sets of four attached houses on the brows of two hills which were separated by a sharp dip. One day we saw a great glow on the horizon. Rene, Mascha and I stood on the edge of a field on the brow of the hill, watching with other villagers. 'That must be London burning,' the vicar said, his arm outstretched towards the fire. We watched for a while until my mother said in a worried voice, 'If that is London burning, will we have to stay here until the war is over?'

I must have told the vicar that I was learning to be a hairdresser, because one fine autumn day he knocked on our door and asked, 'Would you like to practice on my hair?' 'Yes,' I said, uncertain. Wanting to encourage me, he said, 'Practice makes perfect!' His garden became the salon and the kitchen window became the mirror in which I saw the vicar reflected. With his pocket comb and a pair of kitchen scissors, my masterpiece took shape: 'steps' all over his head. The cut could not have been worse! The vicar pretended to be pleased, and looking at his reflection, he said, 'Well done! Just what I wanted!' 'Dreadful!' was what he should have said. No money in that kind of work, I worried.

Doing nothing made time drag. One morning, Mother said, 'Perhaps you could find a job in *dem Stetle* High Vyckcombe?' I didn't need much persuading. The next day, I took a bus to the bustling centre of High Wycombe and, sure enough, there was a hairdresser's much like Cohen's shop, fronted with yards of green Vitrolite. Waiting to see the boss, I watched stylists at work through a gap in the curtains drawn across one of the cubicles. Hair was dragged into waves and held in place with clamps – tramlines they were contemptuously called in the trade, even in Cohen's shop.

'You haven't got enough experience, dear,' the boss said, smiling at me a little too apologetically. I was upset because he didn't even ask me to do a trial. Judging from what I'd seen in his shop, I was more than annoyed with myself for having maligned Cohen's work. 'When are you going to start work?' Mother asked on my return. I bowed my head.

Despite the Blitz being in full swing, my parents decided that we should go back to London. My father was still without a work permit which made me the chief breadwinner for the family. Having come to England as a domestic, I believed I could have any job, after all, hadn't I worked for Cohen? Though, begging him to take me back was not the humble pie I wished to eat. The loan from Bloomsbury House was not humiliating because it was a loan. It was Mother who pointed the way to our independence: 'If we are going back to London, living with family is not what I want to do again, however much I appreciate what they've done for us.' Father agreed. 'Yes, to be independent would be better,' he sighed. I was not in touch with family undercurrents of who said what to whom, nor why we went to Soho in London and didn't take my brother with us. While in Penn, I only saw Heinie once, and that was for his Barmitzvah. What surprised me later on was that I didn't go to see him more often. Did my parents visit him? Was I aware? Not really. Family separations were commonplace in the war, which helped to dilute the Jewishness of our situation. But Heinie was only a ten-minute walk away from us.

Chapter Fifteen

Back to London and the Blitz

Whoever rented a room for us in Berwick Street, Soho, made a good decision. It was in the centre of London. The room was on the first floor of a flat-fronted, redbrick terraced house. The room was dark and cluttered: but it had a basin, a gas ring and a narrow bed, the mattress, worse for wear. Springs worn out, popping up from under the cover – no one could sleep in that bed! The wardrobe's doors shuddered when opened or shut, and the drawers of the chest got stuck on opening. What a mess – even my mother couldn't make it homely. Somehow her life was patterned this way, struggling in small spaces, cooking, boiling water in kettles for doing the washing up, washing ourselves and our clothes. I remember having only breakfast in that room. Cornflakes mostly.

We slept at Lex Garage. The garage was about a hundred yards away from our room. Its massive underground car park was sectioned into large sleeping bays with two-tier bunks, twenty to a bay. Sleeping beneath petrol tanks was undoubtedly playing Russian roulette with our lives, should we, God forbid, 'have a direct hit' as people feared in the shelter. But risk-taking had its rewards: a job came my way very near the shelter.

For the time being, it was good living in Berwick Street, more like living in a village than in the centre of a metropolis. Everything we needed was within easy reach: Rupert Street's fruit and vegetable market, tool and hardware shops in Brewer Street and Soho's French and Italian Restaurants; the aroma coming from them was happily free – West End stores were only to browse through – nothing affordable in them for us! On the entertainment level there was Tea Dancing at the Astoria in Charing Cross Road, and going to the smart cinemas in Leicester Square could only be afforded when tips allowed. To see *Gone With The Wind*, I saved, penny by penny.

Berwick Street was the tail end of the rag-trade area. The house we had a room in had a workroom straddling the top floor, and the one-room lets on the other floors were probably rented out to factory workers before the war. If workers still lived in them, I don't know; I wasn't curious enough to go much further than our front door. Most of the side streets off Bethnal Green Road had houses like that with workrooms across the top floors: light a plenty from skylights facing east and west. Aunt Rosie and her husband Rubin earned their living that way: they were self-employed section workers in the tailoring trade.

The trimming shops in Berwick Street were boarded up against bomb blast, as all shops now were. A glass window about thirty by ten inches was left for a sign in the then familiar bold black print: BUSINESS AS USUAL. Shining my torch into one of those windows revealed old displays of cotton reels and binding, hessian for stiffening lapels, and shiny accessories; sequins sewn onto strips of net and loose beads were piled high in open dishes covered in a film of dust, glinting vaguely.

During the Blitz, sirens sounded every day at dusk. Regulars streamed into the back entrance of the shelter straight from work or whenever they could. ARP wardens helped people to our shelter after the sirens had gone and didn't know their way about. Lovers snogged beside the back entrance of our shelter to scarper down if a bomb whistled down close. In the blackout, it was hard to tell couples apart, their faces and bodies being fused together. 'French letters' – as condoms were called, were discarded carelessly. Was that what was meant by protection? I pondered. 'Busy night' someone said one morning. I jumped to conclusions. Heavy bombing was often referred to as 'a busy night'. How come an innocent girl like me thought such things? An entirely factual observation, said my conscience.

The brightest place in our shelter was the bay next to the canteen where the bunk of a woman called Lina was tucked into the corner. A folding chair leaning against the wall suggested a social life. Her light was always the last to go out. She attracted people like moths, and I was one of those 'moths'. I must have told her about having being thrown out by Cohen. 'Don't worry my dear,' Lina said, 'Mr Luis will give you a job!' Lina was the receptionist at Luis and Woolf, the hairdressers in Quadrant Arcade. off Regent Street, just five minutes' walk from the shelter. She arranged the interview. I got the job for fifteen shillings a week, five shillings more than with Cohen and more tips, Mr Luis assured me. Luis Tedesco and Lina were Italian. I started work the day after my interview. Lina transformed our lives; Mother called her a *Malach*, the Hebrew word for angel.

Lina was about five-feet tall and almost as broad, but despite her size she moved with the grace of a dancer, her knife-pleated skirt swinging. On her face grew a robust beard which she carried off with a smile as if to say, 'What beard?' A man in the shelter said, 'She must shave at least three times a week else she'd have a five o'clock shadow by Sunday!' I saw the joke. English was beginning to make sense.

Lina was ferociously loyal to Luis and Woolf, but especially to Mr Luis, being a compatriot. They talked Italian to each other, smiling conspiratorially through bared teeth. Lina's canines came to sharp points, and so did her top lip, a W standing on its feet as it were, filled in with bright red lipstick. She dabbed her lips with a red handkerchief to rid them of excess gloss. Then she shook a swansdown puff full of powder round about her face, but no matter how much she tried to avoid touching it, her beard caught some particles of down, and they trembled as she spoke. Rimless spectacles enlarged her soft dark eyes. Her beard was more ample than the hair on her head, and sitting as she did in the reception area most of the day, the lightbulb above her head exposed her gleaming scalp.

Lina and her sister Carmen lived with their mother in Lisle Street, Soho, a well-known red-light district. 'Come, meet Mamma,' Lina said, one day. Walking beside her in Lisle Street, her high heels clicking, hips on a roll, she seemed to be blind and deaf to couples fixing prices on the pavements. Upstairs in their flat, Lina's Mamma sat at a small table in the window facing the street. She was huge and friendly, her English heavily accented. I timed the brisk trade opposite her window. A girl with heavily pencilled eyebrows, accompanied by a man, entered through a door, and ten minutes later, she emerged, her make-up still intact though a layer thicker perhaps; she was ready to stalk the street again for trade. I didn't see the man leave the building. I wondered if Mamma timed her as I did. No, I don't think so, was my thoroughly respectable thought about Mamma. Carmen, Lina's sister, evacuated to Brixton to stay with a friend, claiming it was quieter there, which meant less bombing. Both sisters were trilingual: Italian, French, and English. I stayed in Brixton for a while with friends, the bathroom most likely the attraction – even if we did only bathe in four inches of water. Soldiers, home on leave livened up the nights in the flat. Single people were having sex. How shocked I was!

When Mr Luis' daughter, Asunta, came to the salon, Lina embraced her like her own, and kissing her on both cheeks, she'd whisper, '*amore*'. I found Lina's pronunciation of his name 'Tedesco' very exciting, the way her tongue tapped out the letters 't', 'd' and 's' staccato against her teeth. Sometimes she'd prefix his name with Mister, Signor or Monsieur whichever was her fancy that moment. She wasn't just a receptionist. It was miraculous to hear her soothe irate clients; Lina's greeting was balm for whatever might have ailed them before they stepped over the threshold of the salon – always, her smile banished anger.

My confidence grew as my English improved. On hot summer days, I went with Helen, a new friend I made in the shelter, to Roehampton swimming pool. Helen knew the ropes, knew how to get there, by bus, tube or train. She lived just two doors away from the shelter. Henry, one of Helen's friends, bald-headed and eyelash-free at twenty, had a ten-by-ten-foot deli in Peter Street a few doors away from the back entrance of the Lex garage. Naturally, the war made Henry everybody's friend, probably the hope was that he had pre-war food hidden under the floorboards! Mother lifted her eyes from her knitting, looking my new friends over as they came in and out of the shelter at weekends. Belonging felt good.

Some weekends, Hanne, my old friend from Mannheim who also came to came to England in 1939, joined Helen and I at the Astoria. When the bombing was bad, she stayed the night over in the shelter, sleeping on any bunk that was free. The last waltz at the Astoria was always a calming influence after frenzied quicksteps. It was comforting to have Hanne to walk down Wardour Street with me. Hanne was not reliable that night and looking round to see what kept her, a man was walking beside her. Who was he? I didn't see him dance with her! I expected her to say a prim good night to him at our 'front door'. Bombs were thudding near and far and although ack-ack fire was reassuring, I urged Hanne to take shelter: 'For goodness sake, Hanne, take cover!' Looking back from the ramp, I saw her pressed against the wall smiling up at the man, a befuddled expression on their faces, and both of them heedless, I repeated, 'You'll get yourself killed!' When neither of them moved, I went a few steps up the ramp and shone my torch into their faces. In the morning I asked, 'Whatever happened to you last night?' But all she did was to smile that silly

smile of hers. A mutual friend of ours in Germany used to say
of her, 'Hanne is a little foolish where men are concerned, you
could even say idiotic… no reserve at all!'

The ramp of the shelter led down to the canteen. There was
a radio on the counter where people crowded round for the
news. Dunkirk had happened; when Churchill made his now
famous 'We'll fight them on the beaches…' speech and most
people round the canteen agreed. Churchill had turned the
disaster of Dunkirk into virtue. Rosie, busy serving tea, nodded her head in support: 'Tha's righ'… naah, ol' 'itler won' ge'
us…' The old man standing next to me clenched his jaw. The
shelter people's resolve gave me confidence but, like cast-off
clothes, it didn't fit too well. England was my refuge, not my
country. Soon after Churchill's speech normal chat resumed.
As always, Rosie was teased: 'Come on love, make us another
cuppa, only this time, make i' a 'ot one!' Tea signified camaraderie, I learned.

The large area of the garage was partitioned into several
bays, each sleeping about twenty: two to a bunk. Turning a
deaf ear was essential. I only ever heard snoring, nothing else!
The early morning trek to the lavatories, the sound of shoes
dragging on the concrete floor and official lights leaping at you
while you were still half asleep were consoling, as was the
sound of Big Ben before the news, and newsreaders giving
their names in their well-modulated voices was a solace too.
We were all in the same boat, but unlike in other shelters, I
don't remember us ever having 'knees-ups' or singsongs.

One weekend, Helen took me to a club on a first floor in
Shaftesbury Avenue. She seemed to be at home there, happily
chatting to people; every now and then she flicked her long
mass of gold, curly hair off her shoulders with the back of her
hand, while in the other, she held a drink, sipping daintily, and
tapping her foot to the rhythm of a three-man band in the corner of the room.

At the bar, I sat only on half the stool, with one foot on the floor, ready to run if need be. Girls sitting next to me rested both feet on the cross bars of the stools, elbows on the bar counter. Wearing off-the-shoulder dresses, they smiled up at men standing behind them, the girls untroubled by their roving hands. I am in the wrong place, I worried, and worry sustained, I slipped off my stool and fled through the swing door and down the stairs along the dimly lit corridor. Two men were leaning against the wall in the corridor, smirking and, as one of them grabbed hold of my arm. I yanked myself free and ran to the front door, happily open. In the street, the air was fresh, though Shaftesbury Avenue wasn't a safe haven either; well past midnight, a few male figures hung about, hands deep in their pockets, the brims of their trilbies low, shading their eyes. The shortest way to the shelter was through Windmill Street. I rushed past the eponymous theatre, famous for 'We never close' written over its entrance. I flew across Soho's nocturnal life rather than into it, avoiding eye contact with anyone. When, finally, I ran down the ramp of our shelter, I climbed onto my bunk, unrolled my dank blankets, and slipping under them, I curled into a ball, glad to be there.

Our family independence was near. The war had changed many things in the hairdressing trade. Before the war, few women in the West End were stylists, but I became one quickly, mainly because male stylists were in the forces; mostly, those in civvies were exempt from the army for medical reasons. In the salon, they dressed in double-breasted suits. Women were usually manicurists or shampooists and passed pins to stylists setting hair. Pins were scarce in the war. We had to extract them with a magnet from a pile of dusty hair swept into a heap at the end of a day's work and then we'd pick them out from the hair and wash them to be used again: a filthy job. 'There's a war on…' was a phrase often used when someone tried to get away with shoddy work. After the war,

the phrase 'there isn't a war on anymore' was used as a condemnation when work was thought to be bad.

I practised most evenings after the sirens had sounded. I
lost the fear of air-raids when I was working. The shelter wasn't
far away. On hearing bombs whistling down, it was time to
take shelter. When bombs fell further away, I hurried 'home'
to the shelter, escorted by ack-ack and search-lights sweeping
across the sky. I felt safe in my 'village'. Only a fool would feel
safe sleeping under petrol.

Then one early dawn, we had a hell of a shake-up, the blast
so strong I was thrown off the top of my bunk from a deep
sleep, wearing only my knickers and a sweater. There was lots
of agitated talk round the canteen. Rosie had woken up too.
She yawned and rubbed her eyes, and yawning some more she
put the kettle on. That done, she rearranged her matted hair.
Before the water came to the boil, an air raid warden came
running down ramp shouting, 'Broadwick Street Post Office
had a direct hit!' No wonder I was blown off my bunk! The
Post Office was less than a hundred yards from the shelter.
Smokers began their early morning coughing sessions. Going
back to sleep was stupid; let the day begin now, a lot of us said.
Half an hour or so later, a man, wild-eyed, his arms spread-
eagle, came running down the ramp, yelling, 'The city is on
fire!'

Most of us finished dressing in silence. When Mother and I
went back to our room, we were upset: the house had been hit
by an incendiary bomb. By the time the fire fighters had put
out the flames, all our possessions – such as they were – were
sodden through and covered with soot; nothing was rescued
intact. Talk about down and out! Not for nothing were we classified as bomb victims. Mother and I were offered shelter at
the Salvation Army in Elephant and Castle. We were told to
bring only nightwear and if there was room, we could stay for
a few nights. We slept in a long hall which had mattresses on

the floor along both walls with decent spaces between them. The floor was covered in green marbled linoleum. A coal fire burned on the horizontal wall at the end of the hall and above the mantle hung a plain black wooden cross. Everything was spotless; a whiff of carbolic scented the air.

Back from the Salvation Army, we continued sleeping in our shelter. The next day my mother went to our room to clear up some of the mess made by the bomb, and I went back to work – but first, I walked round to Broadwick Street to see the bomb-damage. 'Lucky there were no workers inside,' the ARP warden said, his arms spread to stop people from getting too close to the rubble. A few of us stayed a while, but others rushed on, heads held high in survival mood. It was a dull, dark morning. The two men who owned the fruit and vegetable stalls at the end of Berwick Street near the bomb damage checked out their chances of business that day. No chance, broken glass everywhere. At work, near-misses were the topic of conversation: '… just two minutes before the bomb fell… I passed by…' We frightened ourselves with lucky escape stories. Talk remained animated as long as no one knew anybody who had been pulled from the rubble.

Nellie, our Irish manicurist, and her Jewish husband Joe, slept in one of the rooms in the warren under the shop. Their claim was that they never heard any bombing down there, 'Slept through the lot – safe as houses where we are!' Nelly said confidently of the solid Regent Street building on top of them. No one except plumbers ever ventured through those warrens. Nellie and Joe became caretakers for Luis and Woolf. Work finished, Joe would slump into one of the clapped-out salon chairs in the staff room in front of wide mirrors, a hip-high shelf running underneath them served as a diner. He would play Patience until Nellie put a meal in front of him, his chin edged into his chest. When he finished eating, he'd push the plate along the shelf and go back to his game. I never heard them talk to each other except for the occasional grunt from Joe to which Nellie raised her eyebrows, a touch of mirth in her eyes.

The staff room area had the rudiments of a kitchen: a sink with a plain wooden cupboard above. A gas ring was placed on a small sturdy table next to the sink. A large table with chairs stood in the middle of the room. A naked lightbulb did its best with the uniquely gloomy, green painted walls. The last time that basement was painted must have been at the time Regent Street was built. During the day, Joe's 'diner' served as a dressing table for us girls making up our faces, coaxing our lashes upward with mascara, toiling at them until the buzzer went. Each stylist had their own buzzer when a client arrived. A look down the list of clients would bring forth either a groan or a smile: a good tipper could be forgiven almost anything, even had she been the owner of a thin head of hair we referred to as 'two hairs and a nit'.

On one of my late evenings, I was in the staff room waiting for my client's hair to dry. Nellie was standing by the gas ring preparing a string of sausages. I was standing next to her, watching. When the lard sizzled in the pan, Nellie placed the pricked sausages into the pan, all except one, which on a whim she slashed from top to bottom with a pointed knife. Sausage and knife still in her hand, she laughed, her mouth wide open and, still holding the violated sausage under my nose, she ogled her butchery and said, 'This is Alex's cunt!' Joe slid his spectacles down his nose, and swivelled his head and eyes in our direction. Nellie laughed defiantly, giving him the 'V' sign, fingers facing inward. What was a cunt? And then I knew; as I have said before, I was a quick learner. But why was Nellie so rude about Alex's private parts?

Alex was South African, tall and fair and heavily pear-shaped. Walter, her husband, often collected her from work, breezing through the front door of the shop as if he owned it.

He was long and lean and he dressed in army style. Having briefly said hello, she told him to wait at reception, and waving back at him added, 'I won't be long'. Waiting, Walter fondled his moustache, twisting its ends heavenward; whether this was a ritual of confidence or embarrassment is anyone's guess. But Nelly was sure that Walter and Alex harboured condescension in their cool blue eyes. 'Snotty,' she said they were and added, 'so what, so I married a Jew, but the worst about them is, they think they purify the air with their breath.' Spot on.

Who could match Nellie's ribald exuberance? Every morning, she emerged from the staff-room, looking spring-cleaned and perky, a beaming smile showing regular, distinctly false, white teeth. Like the charmer she was, she swept through the gangway between the cubicles greeting clients at every opportunity: 'Good morning, Madam!' Nellie was slightly bow-legged, her walk a duck's gait, and she wore tennis shoes for comfort. The pockets of her pink poplin overall bulged with keys, tips, a handkerchief and rubber bands, and often she fiddled and felt for things lost in the muddle. More than once, the desired objects would fall on the floor, rolling or pinging out of sight, and as always the sound of her pet expletive absconded from her lips: 'Fuck'n' hell!' Even Woolf smiled, despite his puffed up persona. From the East End like me, Woolf had got to where he now was without much effort; he had a lah-di-da air – an additional bonus to impress clients. Though fortunate in one way, he was unfortunate with his health. Classified 'grade three' he was exempt from Army service; 'lung problems,' I heard his brother Phillip say to a stylist. I am sure it was true because he wheezed a lot but, anyone in civvies was under suspicion.

The salon buzzed with celebrities, ennobled women, women officers, and FANYs (women in the First Auxiliary Nursing Yeomanry) who drove ambulances and cars for 'Top Brass' – good pre-war cars! One of my clients, a socialite and a FANY, made Nellie the confidante of her love affairs. While Nellie worked on her nails, I did her hair. They talked excitedly about sex, slithering round on their seats, their faces flushed, making sounds of pleasure: 'Hmm…' I think they forgot I was there. Making pin curls in the state they were in wasn't easy, the socialite constantly on the move – had I poured boiling oil on her head, I doubt she'd have noticed. Shockingly, the socialite's husband was a prisoner of war in Japan. When he was released from the Far East, she told Nellie what a nuisance it was. In for an appointment on another day, one of her eyes was black and blue and when I showed concern she said, looking past me to Nellie, 'Don't worry daaarling, I just walked into a lamp post.'

The war raised the status of Luis and Woolf, and Woolf being a good stylist was a good catch for Luis. Tedesco was small and dapper. His bald head was framed with black hair and his broad bristly moustache spread to the edge of his smile lines. His grey hair was never allowed to be more than a glint on his temples and neither was his moustache. I never saw how he kept it that way, but the sometimes obstinate dye stain holding fast to his skin gave the game away. Waiting at the top of the stairs, Luis welcomed his favourite clients in an area no bigger than three-feet square. One arm swept across his waist, the other bent behind him, the flat of his hand against his lower back, he'd bow as near as was possible to his toes while a favourite was ascending, and as she reached the penultimate stair, he would straighten up and with arms spread out he'd boom, 'Madaaam!' Of course he didn't do this all day long, he knew which day specials were coming.

The Lord Mayor of London's wife was one of them, a fashion plate of her time: she was tall and slender and was dressed by Hartnell. Her favourite was his purple-blue suit blanket-stitched with emerald green wool around the edges. War-time make-up was to have a pale Max Factor pan-caked face with not a hint of rouge or grease mark round the nose, observed by her meticulously. Her hair was auburn and hung, still glossy and orderly, in pageboy fashion round her shoulders – even as she was about to have her hair done. She sizzled with style. Luis feasted on her appearance – the very sight of her made him add a few more 'a's to Madaaaam.

Luis Tedesco liked me. I sensed it was because he and I were from mainland Europe and *we* knew how to work, unlike the English, which he suggested by a mere glance at an English girl passing: 'The nine-to-five brigade,' he said, a glint of malice in his eyes.

Although tea was rationed in the war, Luis always managed to have enough to make some for his specials. A furtive giggle made the illegal service legitimate – no one considered a spoonful of tea as sabotaging the war effort. Later, when the Yanks came to England, we did a brisk business in nylon stockings; ennobled clients were as tempted by these treats as anyone, but for women in uniform Nellie cautioned, 'Better not'.

Country clients brought pheasant sandwiches and all sorts of savoury morsels wrapped in greaseproof paper in tin food boxes: egg sandwiches made from eggs laid 'that very morning', and game and salmon pastes bought at Fortnum & Mason's Food Hall. When tips allowed, Fortnum and Mason was my corner shop for an hour but food bought there was utterly unsuited to our lifestyle. What would we know about peaches in brandy when we ate cold fried fish or powdered scrambled eggs? Nevertheless, Father's eyes twinkled when he compared the peaches preserved in brandy to slivovitz, and smiling nostalgically, he said, his cupped hand flying to his open mouth, 'In *Poilen*, we'd knock back a small glassful in one go!'

Quite a bit of swanking went on in the salon. Clothes being on coupons left big gaps in most our clients' wardrobes, but clients who could afford couture clothes had an advantage: they lasted. Silk 'House Scarves', their names printed round the edges, seemed to be plentiful and never left their owners' laps while they were having their hair done. Seemingly, silk charmed women's senses; they stroked them, sliding them through their hands, no matter what was going on above their shoulders. Jacqmar scarves were favourites. I deemed Hermes to be the dullest with its sage green, beige and brown pictures of riding equipment, buckles, leather straps and horses' heads, and I remembered the riding scenes on the mats of my 'kind lady' in Tyler's Green. Was this a fashion fad? No, it was built into the structure of English country life, worn by women familiar with hunting, shooting and fishing, but curiously there wasn't a sign of a fish on those scarves.

A style known as the Victory Roll was especially useful for service women. It kept hair off the shoulders while on duty, and for party times it could swing about freely. Method: comb long hair from the crown clock-wise down the head, tie worn-out laddered stocking round hair hanging forward and down at the back, and then roll hair round stocking; secure with grips, here and there. Anyone could do that for themselves, and it would cost nothing if you kept your laddered stockings and saved the hairgrips. When stockings laddered above the knee they were stopped from running further with a dab of colourless nail varnish. I seem to remember a service for ladder-repair at the cleaners next to the Café Royal in Regent Street'. Also recycled at the time were brown paper bags, neatly folded and put into a drawer, and of course, string.

A real money-spinner was the Bubble Cut. It seemed that women in the western world wanted to look like Ingrid Bergman in the film *For Whom the Bell Tolls*. The style perfectly suited the American system of contract perming: as many perms needed in a year for a lump sum paid in advance. The money rolled in; but didn't some women want their money's worth! It meant more perms than their hair could stand when not enough new hair had grown to perm. Abuse of chemicals was often the norm because something paid would be fought for by women to the detriment of the health of their hair. A good idea sometimes does go wrong.

After the war DIY perming arrived. 'Which Twin has the Tony?' was a slogan for the twins advertising the DIY product named Tony. The good thing about it was that the chemicals for home perms were weaker.

When the worst of the Blitz was over, an occasional bomb still fell here and there, one of the last fell St. James's street near enough to the Quadrant Arcade. The wind of the blast left Luis holding one of his precious cups of tea in mid-air just as he was about to place it before one of his 'specials'. For a moment we all turned into 'still lives'; everything was covered in thick dust, us included. When we realized that no one was hurt, we unfroze and chattered frantically about our lucky escape, with flat hands against our chests and sharp intakes of breath, stating the obvious, '… Cor, that was a close one…' And then the clean-up began.

Rosie swept and wiped surfaces, packing even more dirt into her already black-rimmed fingernails. Shampooing a few heads of hair would have cleaned them up – that is, if she hadn't had such appalling B.O. She was the same Rosie who ran the canteen in the shelter; Lina recruited her when the shelter closed. Rosie exchanged one counter for another, her grey complexion just visible as her hand slid a beaker of shampoo along the high counter.

Luis instructed her to give me as much shampoo as I needed for practising outside the salon. Despite his instruction, word got round that 'the foreign girl' was pinching shampoo. Luis put an end to the tittle-tattle, giving his consent in front of a witness. That didn't stop my heart beating faster; for me, 'foreign' translated into Jewish. But where did these jibes come from? Alex, passing me on the stairs one day said, smiling sweetly, 'There's a dear, do a shampoo for me.' An emergency it was not! It was a quiet spell in the day and she needed to put me down. My antennae fidgeted. How cowardly prejudice is.

Then suddenly Luis, 'my protector', died. I was doing good work by then, and I was far too busy for anyone to stop me from going forward. Woolf was now the sole owner of a thriving business. I was pleased to have a few lessons from him and I learned a lot. On one of his usual rounds through the salon, he passed the cubicle I was working in, twice, turning on his heel to have another look. Short on praise, his about-turn was praise enough for me. More pay and more status followed. My takings went up each week; Mother was quietly pleased. I was now 'Miss Rose!' I had plenty of compliments. *I* knew perfectly well I was still practising, improving my skills. All the same, I took note of my takings, and one day a thought occurred: 'I could do this for myself.'

Earlier, when I was still the perm girl, there had been great excitement at Woolf's. André, who had been working for Raymond in Mayfair, took the clientele he'd made at his salon to Woolf, and importantly he brought along Henri the tinter (nowadays called a colourist) and Jeanette née Gladys, a top manicurist, as well. André's name had been changed from Eric by Raymond – nothing catastrophic in changing names, many in the trade have done that! Raymond was *the* top hairdresser before the war, through it, and after it for a while. He had a natural talent for publicity and allegedly rinsed women's hair with champagne and wore a dyed turquoise carnation in his lapel, strangely ostentatious in the war.

André, content at Woolf's, swanned about flapping his arms all over the place. But what concerned me personally, were his fingers making free with my bum at every opportunity – behind me, going up the stairs to the salon, or just in passing. 'That' seemed never to be out of my life.

A few weeks into working at Woolf's, he was asked to do a perm for a woman in Knightsbridge. Her telephone message *rollers during war?*

reverberated round the salon: she'd heard that André was a miracle worker, and could he perform a miracle on her before she went back to the country, saying what we all knew, how 'awful country hairdressers were'. André had been given a 'royal command'; ten horses couldn't hold him back from that commission. As the perm girl, I was obliged to go with him.

Wireless Permanent Waving Machines meant mobility for clients. Even clamped up, they could walk about, go to the loo or speak on the phone, freed from being wired to those old monster machines we used at Cohens. Though, the principle of making straight hair curly remained the same: chemicals, heat, and protection for skin. The order of procedure most women now know, the freedom of those heated clamps gave women. Timing was according to hair type: it was better to do perms on virgin hair rather than subject an old perm with a new one, the old perm not entirely grown out: dulled hair. I considered the metal rollers too thin in the middle, which often resulted in frizzy perms. My preference was to make the rollers fatter. I wrapped cotton wool over the thin middle which gave a much softer, open curls, very popular with clients but not with stylists.

It would have been good if the machine had belonged to me alone, but those who liked doing tight perms had to unpick the cotton wool first. This didn't make me popular with the staff because unpicking the cotton wool was irritating and time-consuming. In the war, stylists were still doing their own perms, and how they grumbled! Grading rollers for size wasn't exactly part of the war effort, nor were extra rollers easy to get; lose one and it remained lost for the duration of the war. The freedom-based perming equipment was used in most top hair-dressers in London's West End where luckily it had been bought before the war. Interestingly, I was part of specialisation in the trade, which meant doing perms and nothing else. Tinting was the same.

André and I went to the client's Belgravia flat which was on the first floor up a wide, curved staircase beginning with a wooden curlicue, followed by an elegant handrail swerving gracefully to the first floor. The door was open. All the furniture was covered with dust-sheets, except for a dressing table, its deep-slung mirror reflecting a chair and us from top to toe. The chair was covered in apple-green silk. The client sat down, and looking at her watch she tapped the glass and raised her eyes to us, indicating speed. I covered her with a large wrap, making sure she and the chair were protected from the chemicals we were about to use. The internal wooden shutters were open, letting the sun beat mercilessly across the room. Seeing me fan myself with my open hand, the woman looked at the window, then back at me; 'Sorry, they're locked,' she said.

It was time to begin. 'I've already washed my hair,' the woman said. Confident, André asked, 'Cut?' 'No!' the woman replied briskly but more softly, she said, 'I would, but there isn't time, my train leaves at…' 'Shame,' André countered, 'your hair needs a cut…' making the best of her rebuttal. While I was working, he moved about behind me chatting in his usual way, giving me instructions, his arms, as ever, gesticulating all over the place. The perm finished, all there was left to do was to strip off the pads and foil, but before I could complete that task, the woman had developed a fearful headache. 'Would you get me some aspirins, please?' she said, holding her forehead and looking at me in the mirror through open fingers. Halfway down the stairs, two young women and a man stood huddled together whispering. When I was almost on top of them, they fell silent. I walked past them and out of the house, aware of their eyes following me. Belgravia was an urban desert. Not a shop in sight.

I returned to the house without aspirins. André was standing on top of the stairs shouting, 'It was a hoax… a put-up job… Raymond hit me with a knuckle duster… I'll sue him!'

Blood was coming from his mouth and his left eye was black and blue. Much as I tried, I couldn't repress a smile: he had got what he deserved. We passed each other on the stairs, and struggling for breath, he shouted up at me from the entrance hall, 'Get a taxi back!'

In the room, the rest of the foil, cotton wool wads, clamps and metal rollers, had now been stripped from the woman's head and thrown round the room. The woman had gone. I was now alone. Box in hand, I stooped to pick up our equipment, and, as if from nowhere, Raymond came crawling towards me on all fours. Grabbing hold of my arm, he forced me down on my knees. He came close – very close. I gave him a push he could not possibly have misunderstood, but back he came grabbing hold of my shoulders, his hands not altogether certain where they were going, and insecure, his upper body swayed: our faces touched. I felt his wet lips on my cheek. The box of tools fell from my hand. Not feeling safe, I gave him another push, and this time he rolled over, arms and legs in the air. When he managed to sit up again, he slurred drunkenly, 'Should you loosh your job through this little mishap, I will give you a job – any time!' After a couple more attempts to get up, and some more exclamations of 'Whoops', this elegantly clad man fell flat on his back, the turquoise carnation in his lapel unblemished. On his right hand, the knuckle-duster gleamed, and as if to give him strength to get up, he rubbed it into the palm of his other hand. I finished packing and hurried from the flat, leaving Raymond on the floor, puffing and blowing like a toddler attempting new skills.

As I was running down the stairs, one of the women I had seen earlier called up, 'Margarete, are you up there?' In the street, there wasn't a taxi anywhere; I ended up walking. Margarete, I later learned, was Raymond's sister. André did indeed sue Raymond for assault. As I went up the steps of the Old Bailey with him, he said, a touch of bitterness in his voice, 'A fine witness you'll make!' *Schadenfreude* must have been written all over my face. Raymond arrived at the Old Bailey in a bottle green suit, His usual turquoise carnation on his lapel. In the court room, there were two men wearing stiff wigs with grey-white sausage curls and black gowns which swung as they moved and talked. I had never been in a courtroom and seen apparel like theirs. One of them got up and asked the accused, 'Are you Raymond Bassone?' Other questions followed, and then the other man asked more or less the same questions. I don't remember much of what they asked or what the answers were; I only noticed the tone of their voices, one sympathetic and the other less so. Then my name was called out. At the sound of my name echoing round the room, my heart began to pound and my head ached to bursting. Did I speak? I must have done, I was a witness. I don't remember anything more until the judge said, 'Raymond Bassone, I bind you over for assault for one year.' André's case was my first experience of justice in action; I saw the event as unreal because the guard who had pulped the man standing next to my father in Dachau never faced any justice.

When the Blitz on London had become less intense, we moved from Berwick Street to Meard Street into a house with two bedrooms, a kitchen and a living room. The building opposite was twice as tall as our house, blocking out all the light, and gloom was a daily experience. Then, to add to the gloom, Father got ill. Both his legs were bent over and he was unable to walk. Even walking slowly he cried out in pain. Our nights were filled with his nightmares. He'd wake up in a sweat, screaming. I heard Mother comfort him, 'Max, *beruhige dich*, calm yourself, you're not in Germany anymore.' When the doctor came, he said, 'The Dachau frosts have finally caught up with your father.' I was surprised the doctor knew of his experience. Father spent Many weeks in Grays Inn Hospital, a wire cage over his knees to avoid contact with the blankets. Slowly the pain eased. Home from the hospital, he still wasn't out of trouble. It was recommended that he should go to Peto Place for infra-red treatment, at least three times a week. I took him there, being the nearest to hand. Happily, the distances between home, Peto Place and work were not far, but the waiting, together with the treatment, took the best part of a morning. Father still walked at a snail's pace and not having a car meant taking taxis both ways. What a job it was to get him in and out of a taxi.

Booking over my appointments to another assistant week after week was very inconvenient. Woolf was annoyed at having the flow of his business interrupted. When finally I arrived for work, well past lunchtime, I tried to slip down to the staffroom without anyone noticing. When Woolf was at reception, he bit his bottom lip in frustration, and coming a couple of impulsive steps towards me, he stopped dead, turned round and went back to chat to Lina. I knew he couldn't say what he wanted to say: 'Now look here Rose, this can't go on,' and I, looking at him like a scared rabbit, knew it was too late for apologies, however I phrased them. Time off three times a week was too much. No one, even in wartime was that indispensable, I reasoned. Woolf and I were tied to each other by circumstances not of our making. I was afraid to lose my job and he was afraid of losing me. The one reward in this difficult time was my father's complete recovery. It took a whole year, and although Meard Street was as gloomy as ever, our spirits lifted.

When Father was better, the three of us went to Petticoat Lane, not to buy anything but as tourists. What a treat! From open windows above stalls came mouth-watering smells of freshly fried fish and chicken soup, and the sour smell of pickles spiced with garlic and dill, the same as my mother's. I had never been allowed to fish them out from their earthenware crock when I started to menstruate; it was considered unclean in orthodox law. The best-ever smoked salmon came from

Solomons the Deli in Petticoat Lane which kept its shop front open all summer long. Club Row off Petticoat Lane sold live chickens, caged birds, dogs and rabbits. Trade was brisk. Fur coats hung on rails beside stalls – what sort of furs I had no idea. People paddled with their elbows to get to within a hand's reach of a bargain. Smells of cheap soap, crudely tanned leather shoes and handbags mingled with the smells of the milling crowds.

The market packed up at one o'clock. What a racket it was loading the goods onto lorries: stalls collapsing noisily and people using trams and buses to go home; we saw children hanging on to the pockets of their mothers' coats as ice cream dribbled down the children's chins and onto their clothes. Women carried woven straw bags, bulging over the top like soufflés. Hot and flustered, some mothers' coats burst open exposing worn-out button holes and sagging breasts under tight-fitting cardigans, and deplorable were the wrinkled lisle stockings above down-trodden heels. My mother judged harshly, 'No matter how poor you are, it doesn't cost anything to straighten your stockings, and what is more, slovenliness and painted lips don't go together!' My father added to my mother's disapproving words, 'Men walking behind or in front of their wives, leaving them to cope on their own, is contemptible.'

Before long, we moved again to a top-floor flat in a rickety house in Ganton Street, just round the corner from Berwick Street. The Marshall Street public baths across the road were a boon after months of shelter life and our limited washing facilities. It was in Ganton Street that I learned to smoke. Most people I knew did. Determined, I reclined on our battered sofa and practised short puffs in quick succession. Soon, our room was filled with smoke. Father was watching. 'This is not the way to smoke,' he said, taking the cigarette from my fingers. He inhaled deeply several times, and then, pausing briefly, Father exhaled a faint vapour of smoke. More satisfied with that inhalation than I expected him to be, he handed me back the cigarette. 'Now you do it!' he said. After several deep intakes, I felt giddy and everything went round in the room; I scarcely made it to the sink. Father smiled wickedly. I had never seen him smoke before, though way back, as Germany now seemed to be, I had heard him tell a *Landsmann* that he had secretly smoked in Dachau, drawing on a communal fag. Despite my father's aversion therapy, I learned to smoke, though thin vapours were not one of my achievements.

In 1942, the Blitz had ended. Earning more money now, we moved to yet another top-floor flat, but this time as a family, finally together in England. The flat was in a mid-Victorian house in Beresford Road, Newington Green, opposite where Hanne lived with her parents. As said before, Hanne was as good as related to me because two of her brothers married cousins of mine and so we were cousins-in-law. Natan married Rosl, and Eddie married my mother's estranged brother's daughter, Leah. Hanne's and my parents saw each other regularly. It was so good to have them as neighbours.

Our flat was light and airy with an east-west aspect. There were tall trees in the gardens between the houses from the next street; one tree was close to the house, shading our kitchen in summer. Our new home was furnished with empty fruit boxes, which could become anything we needed them to be: bedside tables, kitchen cupboards or a dressing table. Mother put her usual touch to the 'cupboard' under the sink: red checked gingham curtains with a good head for a frill. The kitchen table, the chairs and beds were real furniture, probably bought from junk shops in the neighbourhood. Our sofa, though battered, came with us, looking exotic with its curved legs among the fruit boxes. New for us was a gas cooker with a rack above the burners for plates. Three steps down from our kitchen was the lavatory. Parks and green squares a joy to be near.

Mother's cheeks began to bloom again. She was fifty and pregnant. The doctor said she had a stomach-upset. My mother knew better. Standing by the sink one day, washing up, she called out, 'I have just felt life!' My father had just come into the room and he was momentarily startled by her news. When her condition was confirmed, mother felt ashamed, proof that she was still 'doing it'. She imagined everybody sniggering and making vulgar jokes behind her back, and of course some did. I remember her letting out a dress she had brought with her from Germany, the one Liesel and I used for dressing up and my mother had chastised us, calling us 'naughty girls'.

In the middle of expecting a new life, we were faced with an entirely new problem. Heinie, just home from an orthodox school, became Mother's overseer in the kitchen. He lifted lids from pots and pans when she was cooking, questioning her on ingredients according to Jewish dietary laws. Had she kept pots and pans separate for milk and meat dishes, and wooden spoons? This was a calamitous situation. Mother, always the moderate in these laws made Heinie's pestering descend into a labyrinth of irrationality. My fourteen-year-old brainwashed brother forced his opinions on our mother at a most inappropriate time in our lives, and it seemed that our escape from Nazi Germany had been a trifling affair compared to our present confusion. After many heated altercations, Heinie, barely fifteen years old, left home to join a kibbutz in Wiltshire where he became Harry. It was there that he met his future wife, the same age as himself. When they were eighteen, they married. My parents lost their son, whom they no doubt expected to contribute to the family's finances, at least until such time when Father could get a work permit. The irony was that the orthodoxy our father came from spoilt the pleasure of us all living together. 'Would God want this?' I reflected.

Misunderstandings put aside, we went to see him in that English kibbutz in Wiltshire. Time had not healed the hostility between my mother and her son – no, it had grown. The concept of communal living outside family life was utterly alien to her. In the kibbutz, hens were laying eggs all over the place and it seemed natural for her to ask her son for some. Harry's outrage at that request was so strong, he sought comfort in his girlfriend's eyes without uttering a word in response. He must have been confused by the explosive mix of persecution, religious zeal and newly minted idealism to which he had been exposed; confused by ideas appropriated from the past, dreamed of in the language of the pious for two millennia. Closing the *Haggadah* (Exodus story) they would let forth the deep-rooted hope: *Next year in Jerusalem.* And here we were strangers in yet another land, where gratitude bedded down with humiliation and our dreams of living together shattered.

Father secured an job as a machinist in a handbag factory. However, not yet having a work permit, he was paid half the going rate. We couldn't afford to dwell on the wrongs of it. Friday was payday, and Friday being Sabbath Eve the handling of money is forbidden in orthodox practice, but for us the commitment we had made to our independence overruled religious practice. Father and I put our wage packets on the table next to the flickering Sabbath candles. Forbidden, yes, but if I knew anything about my father, it was that he had a tacit agreement with God and was forever striking bargains with Him; he even joked that He would be delighted to celebrate our independence with us. Earning more than my father most weeks, I couldn't resist teasing him, 'I earned more than you this week.' Father, teasing back, asserted his station in life, 'To a Father, you talk like this?' I loved his attendant smile; that was the way I liked him best, humorously managing his way around life. Then closing his eyes he said the blessing over the *Challa* and long-life *Kiddush* wine. After we had our meal, Mother counted our money and, after calculating her expenses for the week, she gave Father and me our pocket money. Pushing mine across the table, she said, 'Less for you because you get tips.' Acknowledging my new standing in her life, she pronounced me the breadwinner of the family, 'Now I do everyt'ink for you, darlink!' (All 'g' ending words turned into 'k' for Mother). To Father, a little crestfallen with her proclamation, she said, 'Don't be childish Max, you know you have always been our breadwinner but at this moment, times are…' and before she could finish what she was saying, Father's damp eyes managed a smile.

Chapter Sixteen

Valentine's Day

If I wanted to see Helen again, I had to forget that awful club she took me to. Cutting off my nose to spite my face was not the answer. She, most likely, hadn't thought anything was amiss between us anyway, so having thought it through, I went back to my regular Sunday tea dancing. The Astoria had more pull than holding on to a grudge. The Astoria was patronized by well-mannered dancers. Fellas, as we called them – it took me ages to sort out fellas from fellows. Fellas bowed before girls, often theatrically, to have the next dance. Girls would readily abandon their half-full gold-rimmed cups of tea and half-eaten dainty cakes on round tables covered with white cotton tablecloths. Smoothing down their dresses, they'd go down the staircase leading to the dance floor, 'fellas' courteously behind them. At the Hammersmith Palais, a bloke would cock a thumb at a girl across the hall, and if she nodded consent, they'd meet on the dance floor – how coarse!

When the Yanks came to England to help get rid of Hitler, their recreation was to jitterbug their way up and down England. The Astoria would never be the same again – and how English girls loved dancing with the Yanks who threw them over their shoulders and the girls would emerge from under their partners' wide-open legs, their skirts flying and knickers on show. When Joe Loss played 'In the Mood' with its thrilling stops and starts, the 'joint was jumping' as the Yanks expressed it, and the world outside momentarily forgotten. I never tried to jitterbug, my body wasn't nimble enough, but to be more honest, my legs weren't good enough to be on display. I preferred dancing with my feet on the ground. Often two couples were left on the floor surrounded by dancers swaying to what became a demonstration in the art of the jitterbug. Helen was partnered with an American soldier, and before the band stopped playing, he had pulled her up from under his legs, and now facing each other they embraced saying, 'Thanks, partner!' Disengaged, Helen rushed over to me, nudging my arm. 'Crikey, what about their uniforms, soft as silk they are – what a difference from our Tommies!' Helen, as ever, was glowing from under her pan-caked face. 'Water,' she gasped, 'I must have some water!'

One dawn, an air raid warden came running down our ramp in the shelter, shouting, 'The Café de Paris had a direct hit… many dead and injured.' The Café de Paris was in Coventry Street just round the corner from the Astoria. So that was the thump that had made everyone look at each other! Rosie was getting the canteen ready for her morning regulars. 'The next thump will be us,' she mumbled, wiping the linoleum-covered counter. That thump stopped me from going to the Astoria for a while. But empty Sundays were boring, and soon enough, I started going there again in my only Sunday outfit: a brown Gor-Ray skirt and pink-striped blouse. Helen greeted me enthusiastically as I was coming out of the cloakroom. 'Come on then, let's have some fun,' she said, pulling me by the arm.

We went up to the balcony for tea. When the band struck up, a young dark-haired man in a grey Prince of Wales check suit asked me to dance. He stood out from the men in uniform. I must have invited what he said next, 'My suit was made by the Evansky Brothers in their workshop in Brick Lane. My father and his four brothers all came from Poltava in Russia before World War I, and all of them are tailors.' Evansky himself was a hairdresser. Culturally then, we had connections to the East End, so nothing to evade or to pretend about. Both of us were Jews with a history in common. Helen had long left to dance with her American partner.

Dancing with Evansky was awkward and although quick with his feet, he seemed to be dancing by himself, incapable of maintaining rhythm or leading. A few steps into the dance I was on my own, trying to keep time, my shoulders steering his disorderly pace. Several egg-mayonnaises later at Lyons Corner House, Evansky and I, despite his lack of rhythm, became a couple. Even the smell of BO coming from the armpits of waitresses wasn't a deterrent! Romantically speaking, Evansky was struck by me. I seemed to have a face he couldn't forget: 'It's in front of me all the time,' he told me. As the weeks went by, I wondered if the only reason he liked me for was my face. The mirror told me that it *was* indeed pleasurable to look at, but I wanted Evansky to find different aspects of me attractive, more than just standard flattery, to see me as I saw myself when I closed my eyes.

Six months into our relationship, it was Evansky's friend Nati who gave me a sense of myself. Nati was home on leave and the three of us were walking up Cazenove Road in Stamford Hill. Evansky turned to Nati and said, 'I am so proud to be marrying a poor refugee girl.' Nati exploded: 'Proud? You've got a bloody cheek! What do you mean – poor? What do you think you are – rich?' Then turning to me he said, 'He doesn't know what a lucky bastard he is to have you!' That was the first time Evansky had mentioned marriage. I didn't thrill to his veiled proposal, remembering his vacuous heroism when I told him of my scrape with the Gestapo official. I shouldn't have let him take me home, but fate was in a hurry.

Halfway through my mother's pregnancy, our wedding was planned. His parents, Rachel and Marks, came to our flat to sort out who would do what. Up to that moment, we were refugees trying to eke out our living, but to them tradition changed us into settled citizens with a substantial income. Rachel appeared to be unaware of our family situation, demanding way above what we could afford. Haughtily, she fixed my parents with her eyes: 'We have a large family you know, you will have to cater for a hundred and twenty people at least!' A hundred and twenty people! We could never save this amount of money in six months! It was Marks Evansky who noticed our discomfort. 'Stop it, Ray!' he said to his wife. Evidently, he had used this phrase before to check his wife's swaggering talk. Marks Evansky was a gentle man, he saw more than he was ever given credit for. Rachel climbed down from her high horse and promised to pay half. Haughty to the end, lips pressed together, she showed her disappointment at the bad match her son was making. In the event, she didn't keep her promise, conceding only to the usual obligation the bridegroom's parents had which was to pay for 'Carriage and Photographs'.

The idea of having Rachel as my mother-in-law and her 'heroic' son as my husband alarmed me. Whatever date they chose would be wrong. When they chose February the fourteenth I said weakly, 'What about a later date?' Rachel, blunt as ever, said, 'What's the matter with you, don't you want to get married?'

Engaged now, Evansky took me home after an evening out but he never came up to our flat. 'Come and say hello to my parents.' Asking him was pointless. On one occasion he came up but was hardly able to disguise his reluctance, fidgeting in a superior sort of way, legs apart in front of the fire blocking the warmth for everyone else. Still fooling myself, I played at loving him, kissing his hand, snuggling up to him, and all he did was pull away. What was wrong with me? My father wasn't fooled. One thing was certain: the throbbing in my chest was not love, but then how would I know about that? I seemed to be drowning in a hotchpotch of feelings, the most convincing one being that he should at least have respect for my parents. His bad manners became habitual. In pictures with his family Evansky was a jolly fellow and when I was with them, I was obligingly, a jolly girl. I later tore up the picture of him with my family – too much of a reminder how gutless I was. Looking at other young couples, I wondered how they coped.

At work, everyone said, 'How romantic to get married on Valentine's Day!' What was all this about Valentine's Day? I had never heard of it before. More to the point, he hadn't bought an engagement ring. When I told people I was engaged, their eyes flew to my left ring finger, and with no ring present the situation became embarrassing. Despite his mother's puffed up ideas, my husband-to-be didn't have a penny to his name. Finally, Rachel bought me a diminutive diamond ring at the jeweller's in Blackline Yard. I wouldn't have minded any of this had it not been for the Evanskys' uppity ways. When Rachel gave me the ring, Evansky looked on. What a sterile moment that was! After that, to protect myself from disappointment I did what I had always done: fake delight. Whenever I bought a treat for myself and it was admired, I heard myself say, 'My fiancé bought it for me.'

[handwritten note: Doesn't really explain; Husb also a hairdresser By boy consult]

Chapter Seventeen

Mother has Baby at Fifty

Disquiet on the impending-marriage front aside, my clientele was growing. I was fully booked most days. On 25th August 1942, I had a phone call at work: Mother had been admitted to the maternity home in Hampton Court. When I rang the next day, the nurse said, 'She's still in labour, come tomorrow.' I arrived after my brother had been born. Nurses bustled about, stopping to point the way to my mother's room, and when I was almost there a nurse touched my shoulder: 'By the way, we removed some fibroids while we were about it.'

Soon, I was alone with mother. The room she was in was narrow and cheerless with a window high above her bed. She was recovering from the anaesthetic. Her mouth was open and hollow, her teeth in a glass on her bedside table. I waited for her to wake up. Suddenly, she sat up as if from a grave and gave a great yawn which seemed to refresh her. Not yet aware of me, she pulled up her legs under the blankets and cradled her knees with her arms, rocking back and forth, yawning. Moments later her eyes opened, and seeing me she smiled, a shy vulnerable smile as if she wanted to hide the fact that she had a child so late in her life. I longed to know if the nurses were kind to this stranger who spoke so little English, hoping they were untouched by bias. Thrown together in this unusual situation, neither of us could find words, even simple words to say simple things like: 'How are you, Mum – Mamma?' And then some came: 'What name did you give the baby?' Like a tap turned on, Mother's splashed out: 'Hirsch, after my father.' That said, she stretched out her arms and pulled me to her, murmuring, 'Uhele.' At that moment, I felt my mother wanted us to be more like sisters, or better still, for me to be her mother. That was what I believed she needed: a mother.

I have no memory of Hirsch's circumcision, no party, no fuss, nor do I remember seeing my brother on that first visit; he was, the nurse said, 'in the nursery'. Embarrassed, I didn't ask to see him; in any case, I had to rush off to catch the bus. Thinking sensibly, I had to get back to work and make arrangements for Mother's homecoming which the nurse said would be 'next week'. When that day came, Father was waiting in the street for us. He took the baby from my arms and I held Mother's elbow in case she needed help going up the three flights of stairs. In the flat, Father put his sleeping son into his cot, ready under the window in the kitchen. Mother sat down on a chair. The baby now safe in the cot, Father pulled over another chair to sit with her. Embracing her gently, he said, 'Manjele, another son.' Tears flowed steadily down Mother's cheeks and Father, knowing her mind, said, 'Don't worry, Manjele, we'll manage.'

I re-named Hirsch, Jeffrey; it was easier for English people to recognise. Hirsch was strictly Eastern European. I chose the name Jeffrey after a tall, blond army captain who used to pick up his fiancée at Woolf's. How plain I thought she was for him! 'Hello, Jeffrey,' she'd say, dropping her jaw on the last syllable. When I practised speaking like her, it sounded ridiculous; to start with, I didn't have a jaw like hers to drop, I judged spitefully.

Jeffrey's cot was next to the sink, shaded by the tree outside the kitchen window. Our kitchen must have been a bedroom once; telltale signs were left unmolested from an earlier time. The wallpaper was still fresh in the hanging cupboards either side of the chimney breast, as was the shape of a headboard on the wall facing the window. On fine days, the sun coming through the foliage of the tree outside the window dappled Jeffrey in his cot as he gurgled and played with his fingers and toes. When Mother was working at the sink, they talked to each other. I was envious of her intimacy with Jeffrey, just as I had been watching her with Harry. Who recorded Mother's intimacy with me? There are snapshots of her with her sons as babies, but none with me; neither are there any pictures of my parents when they were children. No matter how I've wished for pictorial evidence of them, there is nothing: no images, no intimate details of their childhoods, only a formal photo of my grandparents. Too late for grievances, I calmed myself. Come on, I convinced myself, when you were a baby, your parents were struggling in the middle of the German inflation in the 1920s, you were their firstborn in a new country, and they lived in one room.

Jealousy faded when I had fun with Jeffrey. Every morning before going to work, I threw him up in the air and kissed him in the tender places where babies are kissed until he laughed out loud, and sometimes I'd miss the bus and was late for work. Jeffrey was irresistible, and besides, playing with him made Mother's face light up, made the 'shame' she felt lessen, I guessed.

Soon, like a bomb whistling to its destination, the wedding was three days away and still we had nowhere to live. Evansky was unconcerned. My parents looked on helplessly. Father had a stab at Evansky's silences: 'Intelligent people are often silent,' he mocked. Although I picked up on father's tone, I didn't have the pluck to stop the course of events. However averse to getting married I was, I was pulled into the excitement, rushing about buying things like a headdress I had seen in the window of D. H. Evans in Oxford Street. The last thing I did was go to Rosie Drage to collect my wedding dress. She was no ordinary seamstress. The whole of working and vaguely middle class London Jewry streamed to the flat of the Hartnell of Stamford Hill for her beaded jumper suits, and of course wedding dresses; everything she made was covered with beads. Hating beaded clothes, I had begged her, 'No beading, please!' and she said what she always said to her customers, 'Just a little.' When I said firmly, 'No, not one bead!' she looked disappointed. I had left thinking she'd comply with my wishes. Well, she didn't. Beads were amassed all over the sweetheart-shaped waistband of my wedding dress. Noticing my disappointment, Rosie said, 'It's only a little!' What the heck! The wedding was on Sunday, two days away.

Finding us somewhere to live would have to be done the next day, Saturday. London was still empty after the Blitz, which made finding a flat easy enough. Evansky was a hapless twenty-seven-year old and I was nineteen, and there was me thinking that marrying an older man had advantages. Wisdom was not a word I knew how to use: a person was either young or old, though *Chochma*, the Hebrew for wisdom, was a word very familiar to me. Father used it a lot, often facetiously, about people who thought themselves wise but had only a clever kind of sharpness: 'He thinks he is a *Chochem*!' In my father's eyes, you couldn't be clever and wise, and comparing his own wisdom with Mother's, he declared that she was 'born with it'.

Mrs Rosenberg lived on the ground floor of the house we were living in. Every time Father met her in the corridor, she heckled him, he told us. 'Your Rose must go to the *Mikvah* before the wedding,' she insisted. Nothing was further from my father's mind than ritual baths – he was more progressive than he knew – but Mrs Rosenberg forced herself into my life, and Father, ashamed he hadn't suggested this prenuptial ritual himself, complied. To me, Mrs Rosenberg was a meddling old woman. She arranged the whole thing before anyone could say 'kosher bride', dragging me back to the nether regions of our past. I was dipped underwater, had my long finger nails cut to the quick and a blessing said over my bowed head by a woman who had nothing whatever to do with my life – and, adding to my difficulties, I didn't think the Mikvah too clean. Mother and I were of one mind: 'Isn't clean water running from a tap blessing enough?' To debate this with Mrs Rosenberg was not what we could do. We complied with her because we weren't a match for her.

When, finally, my father took me down the aisle and up the four steps to the *Chuppa* (wedding canopy), it wasn't the me who stood next to Evansky: I already regretted too much. But when the cantor started to sing the blessing, silver goblet in his hand brimming with wine, his chest heaving *appassionato*, and what with the wine dribbling down the sleeves of his ceremonial gown, Evansky and I got the giggles – yes, he often made me laugh. There had to be some advantages. Our levity certainly threatened the solemnity of the occasion. After the ceremony, Marks Evansky asked in his heavily accented English, 'For vhy vere you laughink?' He was a member of Great Garden Street Synagogue. It never occurred to me that we might have shamed him.

The wedding party was at Stern's in Aldgate. Jeffrey, now six months old, was at the party, gurgling and cooing at anyone bending over his carrycot, safely placed on two chairs by the entrance of the dining hall and another two chairs in front of them in case of accidents. The party was very jolly, but in the middle of dinner, ahead of the customary time for speechmaking, Joscovitch, Hanne's uncle, got to his feet: 'I vant to make aa schpeetch!' Before anyone could stop him, he began, 'De dai aa couple gedds merried, de menn is aa Keeinig, and the voman is his Queening…' He didn't get much further. Everyone laughed and applauded so much he sat down defeated without finishing his 'schpeetch', his cheeks red as cherries. Joscovitch's *Stetle* (small town) talk had already been lost – how lost we could not have known in 1943. By then cattle trucks were rolling through Europe packed with Jews: destination: gas chambers.

We hadn't arranged a honeymoon, though we should have had a change of clothes for going to our flat. As it was, we went by tube to West Hampstead station dressed in our wedding attire, laden with presents and envelopes with good wishes, cheques and cash – an average present was between £3 and £5 – crammed into two of Rachel's frayed straw shopping bags. We walked to 84 Goldhurst Terrace where I had rented a room on the fourth floor of a Victorian house with the use of a kitchen on the ground floor. I had paid a month's rent in advance from my tips that Mother had saved in a jam jar for me. The day of our wedding was a crisp, sunny day, but when we emerged from the tube station, the sun had gone down and it was bitterly cold.

In our room, we put our presents on a chair to look at them later. Evansky sat on another chair waiting. To my surprise, I sat myself on his knees, and told him, casually, about my uncle Avrum, and then in the same vein, he told me that he had caught VD but was now completely cured. 'Imagine,' he said, 'I chose a nurse for my first time, thinking I'd be safe!'

Now that we had both confessed, we went to bed. From the experience with Uncle Avrum, I knew what to expect, and I believed all would be well. However, not much joy was had by either of us. Evansky managed to ejaculate between my thighs with me staring at the ceiling. No Sleeping Beauty act as with Uncle, or the time I had pleasured myself, the guilt at the time so great, I had never touched myself again. But now that I was married, surely I no longer needed to feel guilty? I seemed to be frozen sexually and might as well have been circumcised with all the erotic bits cut off. When we woke up in the morning, Evansky rubbed his eyes and said, 'I am enjoying married life.' I marvelled as one does in dreams; rootless and bewildered, I stared into a charade.

A year on, Evansky said something very different about our sex life. He was Brylcreeming his hair one morning and seeing my reflection in the mirror, he said, 'Something is wrong in our marriage. I have slept with women before…' and finishing his sentence he said, 'What we are doing won't get us children.' No time to talk about this now, I thought. I jumped out of bed, washed and dressed, scuttled down the three flights of stairs to make breakfast, and then swallowing and gulping down toast and marmalade and hot tea, I rushed out to catch the bus to my refuge: work.

The owner of the house was a journalist. Most days we converged in the kitchen to make our breakfast. Conversation with him seemed easy; he was skilful at wheedling things out of me, and soon enough he knew that we were Jewish, and I was a refugee. My English was still 'empty'. I struggled to express what I felt with the vocabulary I had. 'Why do dreadful things always happen to Jews? Why Jews?' I asked. He gave me his answer in journalese: 'Jews make news!' 'What news, the kind I brought with me from Germany?' I said, my heart racing. Evansky fidgeted, which always meant in these situations: 'Stop talking about Jewish things to outsiders.' Our landlord left to go to work, but I was still thinking why Jews made news. What made us so interesting and newsworthy? Of course I knew: we killed God; that has been the principle irritant for the West. Hitler picked up these threads and made them stronger with bespoke reasons of his own. Was that why a glacier always stretched ahead of any dialogue I tried to have about the Jewish question, with me eager to melt the ice?

There was a lighter side to my life: when I married Evansky, Solly became my brother-in-law. Solly was married to Evansky's oldest sister Beaty. She was nineteen, twenty-five years younger than Solly. He was a chicken auctioneer who traded in Club Row. He had the gift of the gab; his chatter was sure-fire, he attracted big crowds and lots of money. For ten shillings a morning Evansky and I sat by the stall helping to take in the money; Bernie, Solly's nephew, was his permanent staff and partner. Many times, Solly bragged that the chickens were mostly 'wa'er bellies', a trade term for duds – non-layers, I deduced.

Holding up three chickens, he'd start, 'I won' taike fifty bob,

I won' taike a paand, I won' taike eigh'een bob bu' I'll taike fif'een bob from the laidy wiv the beaudiful eyes… Bernie, pud 'em in the busgid for the laidy!' The 'laidy' would often as not giggle and turn coyly to the crowd: 'Ooah, 'e's a one, ain' he?' But all the same she'd open her purse and give the money to Bernie whose eyes whipped round as if he were guarding the Bank of England. He put the crumpled pound notes into a leather bag tied round his belly – 'safe as houses' he claimed. No sooner was the money in the bag than three more chickens were held up to a newly gathered crowd. 'I won't taike…' said our comic, treating us to some mother-in-law jokes. Someone in the crowd always shrieked.

Sneaky business apart, it was good entertainment, and occasionally good birds were sold. The stint over, all of us went to Ma Evansky, as Solly called his mother-in-law, to the flat in the buildings at the bottom of Brady Street, opposite Bethnal Green Railway Junction. We feasted on bagels and smoked salmon from Solomon's in Petticoat Lane. After lunch, Ma Evansky made room for Bernie to count the money, a few fistfuls heaped in the middle of the table. Ten shillings next to so many notes seemed to me unfair for a morning's work. I stopped helping.

Solly drove a pre-war Rover with real leather seats and a wooden dashboard, beautifully veneered. Being in his midforties, he was too old for military service. Trading with farmers, new-laid eggs 'off' ration came his way, too tempting to refuse. In a spot check at Old Street tube station, he was caught. He was convicted and sentenced to three months in jail. I don't know if the farmer was jailed.

When we stayed over at Ma Evansky's, the trains clanking in the junction opposite were our alarm calls, and if they didn't wake us, the 'bagel boy' did, rattling the letter box. Rachel, collecting a cotton bag full of bagels from the door knob, said, 'That boy could wake the dead!' What a treat the bagels were, crisp on the outside and soft in the middle, nothing like the rubbery things now sold in supermarkets as the 'real thing'. I wouldn't eat them for a sack of gold.

The arch underneath the junction led to Bethnal Green Road where my parents now lived. For me, the arch represented the location Flanagan and Allen sang about so poignantly: 'Underneath the arches... pavement is my pillow, everywhere I roam...' Even now, when I see clips of them on television, Flanagan in his long fur coat with the cheekily up-turned brim of his hat and Allen next to him, dressed like a dummy in Burton's window, trilby suavely tilted to one side, both of them swaying across the stage, a spotlight walking with them, my eyes fill up. Jack, Evansky's older brother, was two years older than him. He read *The People* every day. Ma Evansky wanted him married, but he quashed violently any hint that he should enter into what he thought was an unholy state. 'What do I need women for? When I want sex, I go and ge' id, pai fer id!' he shouted. Whether Jew or Gentile, if someone disagreed with Jack, that someone was an anti-Semite. In his favour is a story he often told. Local youths, influenced by Mosley, taunted his father calling him 'Jew boy' and other names on his way home from his workshop in Brick Lane. 'I'll tell ya,' said Jack, 'they ounly di' i' tha' once, I left 'em bleeding in the gu'er! Naw, I tol' 'em, you'll know 'oo yah dealin' wiv – my favver! And remember, I'm 'is son!' Evansky Senior, according to Jack, had no more trouble from that day forward.

In other ways, Jack stood still, very still. In the twenty years he worked for his father and uncles, one skill sufficed: with basting he began, and to basting he stuck. There was not going to be a handover from father to son here. When the family was together, and talk was about how Jack could improve himself, I suggested he ran a tobacconist. He was now over thirty years old and still living with his mother. In an advertisement, I found a shop to rent with living accommodation. Jack was hysterical, screamed the place down, 'Wha' am I goin' to do wiv all them rooms? Don' taike any notice of 'er, she'll drive you mad!' And as he screamed, my voice rose too, and in no time, I was shaking like an egg in boiling water. Seeing me hysterical like him, he justified himself to the rest of the family: 'You see, I tol' you not to listen to 'er, she don' knoaw wha' she's talkin' abaa', I tell ya, she'll mix ya up!' Exhausted, Jack jammed his six-foot-three frame into the two-seater Rexine-covered sofa, his back to the room. Seconds later, he was snoring his head off.

Jack's hysterical outburst didn't stop Ma Evansky from confiding to me one afternoon. We were sitting by a blazing fire when she inclined her head to me: 'I'd love it if Jack were to find a girl like you!' I rejected her sudden approval of me, and swore that one day I'd make her bow her head for having shamed my parents.

Evansky's Aunt Annie and her husband Sam had a kosher butcher's shop in Commercial Street, off Whitechapel Road, with living space above the shop. From them we got our meat ration plus bones for soup. Annie and Sam were dead straight. Annie would say, 'Wouldn't I give you more if I could?' Sam was English born. On Saturday nights, he sighed at the rowdy goings on in the pub across the road from them, drunks staggering home, and raising his already high-placed brows in distaste, his fine skin stretched over delicately formed bones. Aunt Annie was the only girl among her five brothers. All of them came with their parents from Poltava in Russia. Fourteen grandchildren, the story goes, queued up outside her flat in the building for a halfpenny on Saturday mornings.

Another story was of how Marks Evansky was made a postman in the British army. He had spoken very little English and read even less. 'Any letters for us, Evansky?' soldiers asked him on his barrack rounds. Evansky, a seasoned illiterate, tipped the sack of letters in a heap on the floor. ''ere's you' ledders!' he said, leaving the soldiers to sort them out. I heard him tell this story a couple of times, and each time his chest heaved with mirth.

While the war was still on, Mother became very ill. I was still working at Woolf's. Personal calls were discouraged; Lina took messages and she'd asked whoever was near to pass them onto me. This time, it was Audrey, the second manicurist, who touched my arm: 'Your mother is ill.' I hurried home to my parents. Mother was lying flat on her back in bed, motionless. She had black rings round her eyes and her complexion was grey-white. Standing at the foot of her bed, I went into shock. She was not being a 'drama queen', although she had a reputation for being so in the family. Seeing the state she was in, I felt wretched having half believed what was said about her. How could I look after her when I was earning our living? Father was earning money too by repairing shoes for neighbours and people living further away. Who, then, would look after Jeffrey, now a sturdy toddler?

Fostering was considered. One of my clients told me of a couple who lived in a council house in Croydon with a large garden. The couple were 'good folk', I was told. On the phone, I said, 'If you could take care of my brother, that would be good.' They agreed. Relieved, my hopes soared.

I took Jeffrey to Croydon by train. The couple reassured me: 'Don't worry,' they said in unison, 'we'll look after him.' Jeffrey was standing between them outside their front door. I don't remember the hand-over exactly but the memory of Jeffrey standing in the doorway sobbing into the remains of an apple. I swallowed hard, not knowing what the words were for what I had allowed to happen. It was a freezing cold day. Mother got better, then ill again. This became a pattern: well and unwell.

I held on to Jeffrey's sobbing, the sorrow behind his wet eyes, his running nose, my escape to catch a train back to London. I imagined how he might have felt before he fell asleep that night, how a darkness must have fallen on his young mind away from his mother. I should have done more, given him comfort, soothed him to sleep with tender words, all of them were swept aside when his foster mother phoned me at Woolf's, a call that Lina let me take. 'Your brother isn't settling,' she said. It was a blow, though not unexpected. Then Mother got better and Jeffrey came home.

Evansky became edgy with my little brother. Straight talking about our sex life was not what we did, so Jeffrey would always be between us, the reality of a life I couldn't give him. As long as I was only playing with Jeffrey as if he were a doll, picking him up and putting him down, this was acceptable to Evansky. Going to see Jeffrey was an ordeal. Evansky feigned tiredness, anything at all served as an excuse, football being the most genuine. When he said, 'Look here, your brother isn't my responsibility,' I burst into tears. His refusal to come with me grew like a fungus between us. And our sex life – well, what was there to say about that? With my body I did not worship, and I asked myself why Evansky made it so obvious that he was staying with me for the money I earned by the way he used to roll the cash into a scroll held together with a rubber band, peeling off notes as needed.

My visits to Jeffrey and tending my parents meant more days off. I hated asking Woolf again. 'Yes,' he'd say grudgingly. I had no way of telling him that I was sorry because our troubles were too deep for superficial apologies, but had I been tempted to tell him the truth, I would probably have burst into tears for which he would have to pity me, or to insist that business *was* after all business. I would suffer anything rather than be pitied.

Visits to my in-laws at that time weren't easy. 'How is your mother?' Rachel would ask perfunctorily. When I told her how my mother really was, she said, 'Oh dear,' and quickly resumed chattering with her family. I resented her casual reference to my mother's illness, and my way out was to shut up for the rest of the afternoon. The Evanskys would then ask what they always asked when I was quiet, 'What's the matter with you?

After that, I decided to say, 'Not bad, thank you,' when asked about my mother. Rachel, relieved, said a plain 'Good.' Then, resting her elbow on the table, she'd bury her hand in her mop of grey curly hair, returning to what she'd been talking about moments before. Anyone was up for mockery, anyone better looking, richer or cleverer than they were. The worst of my predicament was that my in-laws knew about our fake marriage, and meaning to tease, Rachel blurted out when all her family were present, 'Fancy not knowing where to put it!' all of them gabbling on like drunks with Evansky taking part in the merriment. Poor sod.

The next time Mother was ill and Jeffrey had to be farmed out, we took him to a children's home in Oldham. I don't know who thought of this but whoever did must have thought that being with other children would be better than Croydon. After we had left Jeffrey in the Home, the last sight of him standing with a nursemaid at the front door, Mother and I traipsed around Manchester in driving rain, looking for a B&B. On the train back to London, the clattering wheels roused a memory: Da-di-da, dadi-daaa-da-da-daaa… again, I had left something behind.

On our next visit to Jeffrey, he was standing in his cot, his hand over his right ear, tears rolling down his cheeks and onto his long nightshirt, with snot trailing snail-pace into his mouth. Mother looked from him to me. 'Oih, Ruchel!' was all she said. No one was about except for a young helper. 'Can I speak to the Sister?' I asked. 'No, she isn't here, she has gone to the pictures!' Then, I heard myself shouting, 'We're taking Jeffrey home!' 'You can't do that,' the helper said, 'he's got a temperature. You have to wait for Sister to give her permission!' I gave her a look enough to make a herd of cows run. 'I want blankets! Now!' I demanded. The helper turned on her heels. A couple of minutes later, she came back with more blankets than were needed. Immersed in our troubles, I don't remember if I thanked her.

Mother and I wrapped Jeffrey up and went to the station. A train for London pulled in as if to order. Jeffrey slept fitfully. In London, we took him to the Children's Hospital in Hackney Road. He was kept in. It took six weeks for him to get better. Antibiotics would have made short shrift of his infection. The hospital was a five-minute walk from where my parents now lived in Blythe Street off Bethnal Green road. Visiting Jeffrey there was easy.

At this time Doodlebugs (V1s) were falling from the sky regularly. The first one I saw was flying under low-hanging clouds over Liverpool Street Station, the sound more of a grumble than the drone of bombers. I had just jumped off a bus. Everyone was looking skyward, transfixed. The bus was trapped in traffic which gave the conductor time to eye the sky. Gripping the vertical rail on the platform, he swung out on one arm, and eyes still upward, as were everyone else's, he declared, 'Gor blimey, it's a toy, ain' it?' Moments later, the plane stopped in mid-air. Rooted to the spot, everyone ducked instinctively, and seconds later, the 'toy' dived and exploded – half a mile away, at a guess.

When Doodlebugs stopped droning, V2 rockets followed – no warning at all with them, they just arrived, lethal like a heart attack. Jeffrey now better and out of the hospital, I remember having a picture taken with him in my arms outside the house in Hendon where Evansky and I had moved when a V2 drilled into a block of flats, not far from us. Jeffrey threw his arms around my neck, his face white as a sheet.

Mother continued to be intermittently ill and her periodic kidney attacks didn't exactly make her a loving Mother. Of all the predictable things to happen, Jeffrey started to wet the bed. Having to cope with wet beds on a daily basis, Mother's frustration peaked. I feared for my young brother, still smarting as I did from the way she had treated me. I warned her, 'If you don't stop your threats and your curses, I will never set foot in this house again!' The room Jeffrey slept in was dark and gloomy, even by day. My parents had moved from Beresford Road because going up and down stairs with a baby was hard for Mother, the age she was. What a pity it was that they couldn't stay in Beresford road with the garden at the back of the house for drying washing.

I visited Hanne and her parents often. One Sunday morning, Hanne opened the door to me in tears. 'What's wrong, what has happened?' I asked. 'Come in Rosel, my mother has just died. Only a few minutes ago, she was dancing to music on the radio – you know, the way she always did, enjoying herself – but this morning she became more breathless than usual,' Hanne said, struggling to get her own breath. With her chest heaving, she continued, 'I told her and told her to lie down and rest – even promising her a glass of lemon tea, the way she liked it, sharp without sugar. And there I stood, a few minutes later with the glass of tea in my hand, my mother sitting up in bed, her dead eyes staring at me. I closed them out of respect, and you know something, Rosel, closing her eyes was good, it helped me to accept; my mother was too young to die. My father predicted she would if she didn't take more care of her heart. Although he loved her lively nature, he'd anxiously watch her dancing around by herself and being afraid for her, he said, "Your spirit is stronger than your heart". Tears were now flowing down Hanne's cheeks. 'If only I had been a moment earlier,' Hanne said, reproaching herself. Then, suddenly, she took hold of my hand and pulled me into her parents' bedroom, 'Come, Rosel, say goodbye to my mother.' Rosa was in a sitting position as Hanne had described, resting against pillows, her black kiss curls perfectly arranged on her rouged cheeks. The perfection of the curls was no surprise to me: Rosa groomed them habitually, always licking her fingers first before she started the twirling, this kind of helped her to concentrate, especially when something she was interested in was being talked about, like dressmaking. Rosa was a keen amateur. Come to think of it, where was Mr Goldberg? Working?

I don't remember Rosa's funeral. Under Orthodox Jewish law, it wasn't usual for women to go to funerals. Although the Goldbergs were not Orthodox, they followed some of its customs 'for the old country's sake', Mr Goldberg said. Like my parents, their origins were in Poland. In the Thirties, Rosa's four sons had left Nazi Germany: three went to Palestine and one to America. Rosa dying in the middle of the war meant none of her sons came to her funeral.

In Germany, the Goldbergs had run a thoroughly middle-class household with Hanne its cleaner-in-chief. She was the youngest of her siblings. They were a comfortable family. Isaak, her father, was a cloth merchant in Mannheim, though sadly, when he came to England, he never recovered this status. He got a job as a packer in a warehouse, and a packer he remained for the rest of his life. How we became friends with them was because Natan, their eldest son, had married my cousin Rosl. Happily, Rosa had known her granddaughter Carmella; the last time she saw her was when she was two years old when we were all still living in Germany. Rosa died before people were carried in jumbo jets *en masse* for holidays to unite with families, old and new. In those days, long distance phone calls were full of omens, and no one I knew could afford them, except for emergencies. An accident or a death was briefly stuttered into the phone; grief was expressed in letters.

Thirty-five years after the war, I visited my cousin Rosl in Israel. Looking through a shoebox, I found photographs of our past, and among them, two letters from Rosa, written in good German. They spoke of her hope to see her family again. In another letter, she enthused about what a beauty I had grown into and, ending her letter, she expressed her hopes again, 'See you soon'. Foraging through the shoebox some more, I found a picture of myself at the age Rosa talked about in her letter. What I saw wasn't beautiful at all, simply a podgy-faced teenager. That was probably why Rosa had said to my mother in our kitchen in Ludwigshafen, 'Look at her cheeks Mrs Lerner, the blood seems to be bursting from them… beautiful!' To which my mother replied, 'Beautiful? Where? I can't see!' – the 'evil eye' was always present in our house, meaning, 'Don't boast about your good fortune or else …'

When peace came it wasn't peaceful at all. True the killing stopped and the soldiers came home, messed up in mind and body, reuniting with their families, expected to be tender lovers after what they had witnessed and done in the fight to rid the world of Hitler. But for us Jews and other 'outcasts' the grieving was of a different kind. Families were murdered without a chance of self-defence. Hanne married Harry Wurzel, a diamond cutter, and a good earner. Ironically, Wurzel means 'root' in German. Of all the names to have when Harry was the only survivor of a large family in Belgium, and as it turned out, Hanne and Harry didn't breed. They had a small modern flat in Beresford Road opposite where Hanne had lived with her parents. She seemed content enough to polish the red tiles to the entrance of her flat. Hanne wanted children, and when none came, she confided in me, 'I think I am like my Aunt Ada, she couldn't have children either.' Having children or not wasn't what I wanted to talk about with Hanne.

A couple of years after the war, Hanne's youngest brother Eddie came to England for a visit. He was one of the three brothers who had gone to Palestine and we had heard that he had met and married my cousin Leah, the daughter of my mother's estranged brother, Adolph. The marriage didn't work, Eddie told me, because she was 'too manipulative'. Eddie came to England to be with his sister for a while, but also to be nearer to Mannheim to see if he could get repara-tions for his parents from the German Government. The out-come of these negotiations I never learned, but what Eddie did find in Mannheim, he told me all too willingly. 'Do you re-member Raphael, Hanne's Italian boyfriend?' Hurrying on, he said, 'He's alive and kicking.' 'Whatever you do, don't tell Hanne!' I advised. But Eddie, fool that he was, told her as soon as he could. 'I am so excited,' Hanne told me on the phone.

That same day, I rushed over to see her before Harry came home from work. 'I'm going to my Raphael,' she said, flames rising from her cheeks. Uneasy about her plan, I said, 'I would-n't like to be you when you tell Harry.' 'I'm not going to,' she said, 'I'll leave after he has gone to work.' And that was exactly what she did.

After Hanne went back to Mannheim, I went to see Harry from time to time in their old flat. He treated me to fresh bread he had just baked with seeds and garlic. 'It's the stuff of life!' he said, a poignant smile playing around his mouth. I sensed I was too young for his woes, and he took to seeing my parents; it was to them he poured out his heart. Harry lived alone until he died.

True, Harry wasn't handsome like Raphael, but then Harry wasn't the villain Raphael was. I remember well Raphael com-ing to the Goldbergs' flat in Mannheim to give Hanne a pair of high-heeled Italian shoes, red with navy blue trim. Being wrapped in navy-blue tissue paper must have added to the ex-citement. I was in their kitchen with the two of them. Hanne was ecstatic. 'They are from my parents' shoe factory,' Raphael said proudly, tears glinting in his eyes. Hanne put on the shoes and paraded up and down on her polished kitchen floor, the shoes, apparently, a perfect fit. Raphael was shorter than Hanne. He could easily have been a George Raft look-a-like, his eyebrows, like Raft's, starting thick beside the bridge of his nose and ending as fine as needles.

When Hanne had gone to Raphael, Eddie spilled some nasty beans about him to me, 'Have I mentioned to you that Raphael was a pimp in the war? Not only did he live on the earnings of women, but he was kept by his sister as well. Remember the restaurant on *den Anlagen*, that classy Avenue in Mannheim?' Raphael had told Hanne the restaurant was his, and she believed him. Confirming his love to her, she wrote, 'Guess what?' the words flying across the page, 'When I arrived in Mannheim, Raphael was waiting for me in the car park leaning against a pink car, waving. I ran to him with arms wide open. When I opened my eyes, I saw 'Hannie' written on the mud-guard in gold letters.'

Eddie's splitting with my cousin Leah took me back to the last time I saw her which must have been when we were two or three years old, at a time my mother was still talking to her brother. I had forgotten her name until Eddie spoke of her, describing her as a bossy woman. 'Like mother, like daughter,' I suddenly remembered my mother saying about her sister-in-law so long ago. 'And now', Eddie said, 'I want to marry you because I can see you're not happy.' What was it about the Goldbergs' sons wanting to marry into our family, and what was Eddie doing, wearing a trilby hat, pressing me back against the front seat of my car trying to kiss me? If only he knew what a turnoff trilby hats were for me, quite apart from his proposal.

One early morning, in the late Forties, our telephone rang. 'Your favver is dead!' Jack screamed down the phone. Marks had died in his sleep while Rachel slept peacefully beside him. In the morning, she got up as usual to make tea. 'Marks,' she said, holding a cup in her hand, 'wha's the madder wiv you? Move yerself!' Rachel re-enacted that scene many times. And then, when it was no longer dramatically effective, she laughed to herself, her voice drifting.

Marks Evansky was laid out on the bedroom floor, a white sheet over his body, his feet to the door. A *Wacher* (sentry for the dead) sat by his side all night, a candle burning beside the body. The next day, the men carrying the coffin had to negotiate their way through a narrow corridor to the front door, crammed with family. Annie was hysterical. 'My dear, dear, brother,' she wailed. Unable to get near the coffin, she stretched her arm over people's heads, and when finally her fingertips reached her brother's coffin, her wailing became a sob. When the coffin was shouldered out of the front door, she buried her face in her hands. At the *Shiva* (mourning period) Jack burst out, 'Fink of i', my favver died with a fimble on his finger.'

It was at Marks Evansky's funeral that I read the prayers in English for the first time. Among them, we thanked God, '… for not making man a woman… for she is like a beast in the field.' Thank heaven for Progressive Judaism.

Chapter Eighteen

The Manicurist

In the winter of 1947, the worst winter in years, Evansky and I had opened our shop in Hendon. The roads were covered with ice and snow well into May 1948. Water pipes froze solid; even water left in pots and in the bath tub. Renting premises in West London was too expensive, and the suburbs had to do, which was disappointing for me. Happily, the shop we found was a spacious area of two shops knocked into one among a parade of utilitarian shops: a greengrocer, a drycleaner's, a hardware shop, and conveniently round the corner was Barclay's Bank. It wasn't convenience that I dreamed of though; it was more of a palatial ambience – but that fantasy went the way of all fantasies.

The reality was we had no money at all, and ironically it was the rough and ready Solly who lent us £3000 for Smith, the builder, to do his best with still rationed materials. On the whole it was a good result, except for some floorboards coming loose from the pitch by the front door: someone might trip. When asked to do something about them Smith said, 'Snags? What snags?' That apart, our shop was light and airy; it had two huge windows rounded at the corners and held in by bevelled white painted beading, though for the moment they were still boarded up.

On one of the freezing days that winter, the wartime precautions were removed. At last our windows were revealed. This took two days. Undeterred by the cold, women arrived to have their hair done armed with hot water bottles to hug or put their feet on. Finally, our massive shop front was revealed – better, I thought, than some shops that lingered on *innovation is crucial discourse*

from the thirties, clad with slabs of Vitrolite stuck around the front, shiny with self-importance. I dressed mine with pale green crossover nylon curtains, remembering my mother's delicate style in the Römer Straße.

What to name our shop? Rose? Albert? Rosalbert? The answer came from our new friends Ted and Grace who we met at a bus stop. They lived in the street next to ours. Ted was a promotions manager at Paramount Pictures in England – how far up the ladder, we never found out, but I reckoned that he must know about these things. His idea was to call our shop *Tudor Rose*, linking my name with the mock-Tudor mansion flats above the shop. Trusting him, I let him take it a step further. 'Why not print your cards in Tudor lettering as well?' he suggested. Our business cards ended up in brown 'ye olde English' script, on a background not quite yellow and not quite beige. Evansky remained silent, shuffling his feet; delighted, he was not.

Clients came in from my West End days, happy that I was now within walking distance for them, and glad not to have to go up West. But new ones from the neighbourhood, though pleased to have a West End hairdresser locally, let me know the privilege they were granting me by letting me do their hair. I knew they were lying when they said, 'Raymond usually does my hair.' This was not very inspiring for me, and not very safe for them, as I put the scissors near their jugular to gauge the length of hair. Of course I was angry being used as a convenience! Apart from that drunken encounter with Raymond, my knowledge of his talents came from a post-war, black-and-white television programme on hair fashion. Gracefully, his fingers placing curls where he imagined they should be, and doing his own voice-over he said, 'A Teezy Weezy here, a Teezy Weezy there…' A brilliant sound bite! Now everyone would know who Teezy Weezy was.

Few people asked for Evansky to do their hair. Instead of learning new ways, leading with me as I had hoped, he larked about. Most upsetting was the time he stood on a chair in the cubicle next to the one I was working in, and unbelievably, he popped his head over the partition and spat down on me – not a real gob, more like a baby dribbling. What was happening here? Better to ignore it, too busy to deal with a 'baby' at the moment.

Although the war was over, staff were still difficult to get. We advertised, offering 'personal training'. By-and-by, we collected thirteen girls, and, as offered, I trained them from scratch. Manicurists were the most difficult to find. Eventually, a dark-haired young woman, under five-feet tall, applied. Lenja and her God entered my life.

Her English was fluent and only slightly accented. She told me she had lived in Warsaw before the war. I was afraid to ask more; the numbers tattooed on her arm said it all. I didn't give her a trial but hoped she'd be all right. If not, I would teach her, I reasoned. She worked awkwardly, but somehow she managed to do a manicure in one and a half hours, longer than it took to do a shampoo and set! When would be the moment I could tell her that she needed help? The number on her arm inhibited me.

Lenja didn't hesitate to tell me more about herself. One day, both of us sitting around killing time, she said with her eyes looking up to heaven, 'I have been in Auschwitz and Belsen,' and with her eyes still heavenward, she continued, 'I was saved on a lorry going from one camp to another.' Did she fall off the lorry? My connections to that time were cattle trucks. But then she said, 'I belong to the remnant who will be saved for the Messianic Kingdom.' 'I don't understand,' I said. Frustrated by my ignorance, Lenja explained, 'Catholics and Jews are the most difficult to convert.' 'Difficult? How?' When I had taken her on, she had told me that she was Jewish. Was she talking about Mrs Hermann's saviour who I'd looked for in the church? It seemed so. Jesus was Lenja's saviour too. Then why was Lenja talking about Catholics being difficult to convert, when they had the same saviour? Catholics, she implied, didn't deserve Jesus, and as for Jews, they were too stupid to live without him. But my father said that Jews didn't believe in Jesus because he was a man. Knowing little about Jews converting, I wondered why Lenja scorned us. Every time she uttered the word 'Jew', her voice was laced with more than a little venom. How come she was so spiteful when she told me that Jesus was love, but more to the point, how did this 'love' fit in with us learning about the massive losses to our numbers as every postwar day passed? I didn't much care about Catholics, they had 'huge numbers all over the world,' Mrs Hermann said. Was Lenja suggesting, I wondered, that the Nazis had been right to vilify Jews – at least, that was what I understood her to mean.

On another day, Lenja rushed over to me before she started work. Dipping deep into her carrier bag she fished out a Watchtower publication of the King James Bible. 'Read it!' she said, 'I'll help you.' I read, asked questions, and Lenja explained. When we came across the sacred texts of St John in the New Testament, it reminded me of the condemnation we experienced in Germany. Firmly, Lenja fixed me with her eyes, 'If Jews had accepted Jesus they would not have suffered.' Some Orthodox rabbis have said much the same, except they replace Jesus with disobedience to God, the invisible one. Not much solace there either.

Lenja tired of people asking her about the numbers on her arm. It was summer, and wearing short sleeves, she covered them up with a plaster, only to be asked what had happened to her arm. Irritated by the plaster hanging off most of the time, she left it off altogether. 'Why should I bother to protect them?' she said to me – 'them' being people who hadn't suffered and been through what she had – 'and on they go while I'm doing their nails, nit-picking about the shortages they endured in the war, boringly going on about how they longed for pre-war luxuries like gold-rimmed glasses for water!' From then on, Lenja's number was exposed all summer long.

But those numbers got to the clients. Lenja was a flesh-and-blood victim sitting in front of them. Although they wanted to know more about her they stopped short of asking her directly. 'Too onerous,' they said to me, 'Would *you* ask her? Where has she been? How did she survive?' In those early post-war years, none of us relished the names of Auschwitz, Belsen, Treblinka. Like shock troops, they forced their way into peacetime.

How dared I question Lenja's faith? As I saw it, she wasn't talking about faith; no, she was talking about blame. Sadly for Lenja, the strength of feelings I had when reading the New Testament didn't make up for the strength of feelings I had brought with me from Germany. Jewish I was born and Jewish I would perish, the Nazis had said. Lenja's forefinger pointed to where the Jews in St. John are blamed for eternity. So that was where it all started! And back my thoughts went to how Germans had been indoctrinated about the Jews two thousand years later, Hitler picking up on the Christian past, subliminally dispensing the religious content. Many had made Hitler their saviour, Mr Hermann a prime example, to the annoyance of his wife.

Lenja's preaching was relentless; I knew so little of what she knew, and curious, I listened. On not a busy afternoon, Lenja and I sat opposite each other, chatting. Lenja's chatting invariably turned into Bible talk, and sure enough, the Bible was already in her hands, and her fingers were turning the pages of St. John where the Jews are condemned, highlighted as villains and deserved to die. Though the potency of the message in the New Testament made me weep, I couldn't connect the blame with the love it advanced. At best, Lenja connected Jewish people in the camps with the Jews written about in the New Testament. 'They were the worst behaved in the camps,' she claimed.

I was back in Germany, feeling ashamed of who I was, and what with the number on Lenja's arm which marked her as a Jew, brought me no comfort. Lenja could have been a writer for Streicher's anti-Semitic newspaper. 'The Jews are our misfortune,' Hitler said. Lenja appeared to be paraphrasing him, but if you reversed the phrase, it was indeed a misfortune to be a Jew in Hitler's Germany. To Lenja, I wasn't Jewish at all – Jehovah's Witnesses were the 'real Jews', she asserted, 'the remnant to be saved'. Sometimes, the muddle I was in brought me pretty close to baptism – anything to rid myself of confusion. What in the end stopped me was Lenja's anti-Semitism, the kind that closed my throat and made me breathless, the kind that travelled across the world and had even influenced H. L. Mencken who was proud to be an atheist and better than Christians.

Allegory was not something I understood. Did Jesus fly to heaven or not, was the question I wanted answered. And did conversion mean you had to hate what you were born into as Lenja did? My father claimed that to be a *geschmad* (convert) was a disgrace, a destroyer of the community, no longer reliable; that accounted for the long silences after he mentioned such a person, his arms apart, eyes to heaven, as if to declare the end of a Jewish life. I see him still, standing in our kitchen in Ludwigshafen, the '*sch*' sound in *geschmad* fringing his lips in repugnance. And here I was, being asked to change into something my father felt was wrong for Jews – the reason we had wandered about in the world for centuries, ending up in hostile lands. Would I not drown in shame if I made such a change? To be rid of conflict, I closed my ears: why not devote myself to what I did best, which was to make women look beautiful and give them confidence?

The letters we had at that time from my cousin Rosl in Israel were distressing. She had information about who in our family had survived and who had perished. Few of my father's family survived because most of them had remained in Poland: his

father, (his mother died before the war), his sisters and brothers, aunts and uncles, cousins, and their children. As he read
out the names of those who had perished and looked at the
pictures he had of them, tears ran down his cheeks: 'If I start
mourning, I will have to sit Shiva for the rest of my life.'

Four of my mother's siblings went to America from Poland
before WWI. The one left in Poland was Chaskel, with his wife
Hella and their two children Heinz and Sally. All of them had
been sent back to Poland, they had come illegally to Germany
some years earlier. Leah, Stupack and their sons went to Lux-
enburg from Worms in the early Twenties. Wherever Jews
came from or went to for safety or a better living, none of
them would ever be safe again in Europe. Having no land of
their own didn't help. When WWII started, all of them were
gathered up by the Nazis as they invaded the countries around
them: East, West and North. Cross a border, doubt awaits you.
It was said that a million people were on the move after WWII.
How lucky we were to be in England, the Channel between us
and mainland Europe.

I didn't tell Lenja anything about my family. I sensed that
her anger was an iron wall around her own suffering which
only her God could penetrate. Other people's suffering, those
who had choices, could not match hers. True.

In the twelve years Lenja worked for me, she slipped
Watchtower pamphlets to clients, quoting scriptures as she
worked on their nails, preaching and working, and as truths
sped from her lips, she licked her fingers, the quicker to turn
the pages of the pamphlets. No gossip, no tales of shopping
expeditions, no holiday talk, nothing relieved the intensity she
brought to her subject. At times, a brilliant smile would open
up her face, but moments later, her eyes darkened, as if in self-
reproach.

Her only other topics were recipes and cooking. When
Belsen was liberated, Lenja's gums were inflamed from mal-

nutrition and, naturally, food became a preoccupation; she conjured up recipes from her head, scribbling down ingredients, weights and methods of cooking. I preferred that chatter to her preaching. But no matter what she talked about to clients, she always finished early. Resolutely, she'd put on her coat, and with a bag full of Watchtower copies, she'd rush out of the shop, still arranging herself in the street, doing up her coat, putting on her gloves, and stern in face and gait she was ready to go from door to door, preaching. Lenja devoted every spare moment to spreading the 'good news'.

Ben, Lenja's husband, had been a private in the British army. It was his unit that liberated Belsen, and that was how he met Lenja. She didn't convert Ben – at least I don't think she did. I rarely saw them together, but when I did, he seemed to treat her reverentially, like a holy object. Lenja made sure I could not delude myself about my marriage. She made me aware more than I already was of my husband's shortcomings, while with her next breath she delivered eulogies to her own, how Ben loved her. I was frugal with my responses as she gorged me with her happiness, and what with the salvation she offered me, I was cornered. To dislike her was not an option and I struggled with forgiveness. From the depths of my being, I dredged up blessings for her happiness. My benevolence didn't last long, and back I was in the rut of conflict. Even exchanging the word 'like' for 'dislike' didn't help, but fear of retribution helped me to come to terms with her. Lenja was a survivor and she had numbers on her arm.

Ben, I imagined, probably hadn't bargained on meeting a Jewish girl who was baptized after he brought her to England, having just snatched her from the jaws of death, linked to the faith she now embraced. I never asked Ben what he thought about his wife's conversion. I'd have given anything to know what Ben the Jew made of it, how he hoped and coped, how he tolerated her becoming a Jehovah's Witness.

I frustrated Lenja. Although I responded to the beauty of biblical writing, my reluctance to convert angered her. She was furious with me, often quoting Isaiah where he promised '… a world in which there'll be no more pain and no more death', words she lived by and believed, eager that I would too. She never tired of urging me to see that there was a second chance to live, and when the last words of that inspirational passage had left her lips, tears stood in her eyes. Realizing that I mistrusted flesh and blood resurrection, Lenja snapped, 'With God, everything is possible!' Seeing me still unmoved, her eyes gazed upwards and then back to earth, and seeing me as obtuse as ever, Lenja ascribed yet another attribute to her God: 'You'll see…God will – God can do anything!' Lenya had a temper and she was her God's great defender.

The one and a half hours Lenja took to do a manicure was no longer acceptable. Clients murmured, 'One hour and a half for a manicure! Really!' It was then that I offered to teach her. Surprisingly, she was compliant. Her hand in mine, her eyes soaked up all I showed her. I don't remember saying a single word of instruction; I didn't have to, she missed nothing. Almost at the end, Lenja withdrew her hand from mine and sighing deeply, she began to tell me her story:

'I was in a line that forked at the top. Left. Right. Life. Death. By the time I was near the top of the queue, I already knew that having a trade helped you to stay alive, and I thought of one, just moments before I was standing in front of the commandant. The woman standing next to him held an Alsatian on a lead, her hands restless as she tried to restrain the dog pulling on the leash. In those moments I saw her perfectly polished nails reflected in the floodlights. Then it was my turn. Smiling sweetly, the commandant asked, 'And what can you do?' 'I am a manicurist,' I said. 'Really?' he said. I started to tremble. I had never manicured anyone's nails before. What if he found me out in a lie? But over the shouting and dogs barking he bent down and whispered into my ear, kind of confidentially, "I promise you, someone will bring you to my quarters this evening, and you will do my nails. Rely on it." Chimneys smoked nearby and the smell coming from them… rumours were rife about that smoke, but we hid in disbelief – no, that can't be true. No one wanted to believe such things. No one! The commandant's smile was constant as he looked over my head at people waiting…' Lenja stopped talking for a moment, and I stopped my intermittent instructions in the art of the manicure. Her hand still in mine, both of us took a deep breath. Then Lenja continued, 'Later that night, someone really did come to the hut I was in. Walking next to that someone, my legs dragged. Finally I was in the commandant's quarters. He had been waiting for me. He towered over me. Straightaway he dragged a stool from under the kitchen table and handed me some tools and a small towel. Then he pulled over a chair for himself and sat down, looking at me, just looking. I spread the towel over my lap and he put his hand into mine. I tried to cut his cuticles, and fumbling around them, I couldn't cut anything at all with the small blunt curved scissors he'd given me, and still I tried, pulling at them as if compelled, when, not surprisingly, a drop of blood fell on his trousers. Not having soaked his hands, his nails were brittle and dry. Come dawn I would be dead, I was sure of it. His hand twitched only slightly in mine, and with me trembling so much, the scissors fell on the floor. Bending down to pick them up, I looked up at him from under my lashes. He was watching me calmly, smiling. We had already learned that these smiles weren't smiles of friendship. Then suddenly he snatched his hand away from mine, and pushing back his chair he took the towel from my lap, got up and dabbed the blood on his hand. His smile now mask-like, he said, "You can go now." His control made me lose mine. The 'someone' who had brought me took me back to the hut.'

My hands lay lame in my lap. Lenja's eyes were swimming in tears. Then, with a great fluttering sigh, she said, 'I am convinced my shaking affected him.' She stammered on, 'The commandant must have had a grandmother who told him to be gentle with trapped animals, but then, when I think of what he saved me for...' Lenja paused again and, holding down her chest with the flat of her hand, she breathed in deeply and resumed her story, repeating, 'What he saved me for was to see a human being in Belsen tear flesh from a corpse, scraping against a bone with his teeth. It was then that I remembered my journey to Belsen from Auschwitz, people whispering to each other and leaning towards them, I heard what I later learned were scriptures. They were Jehovah's Witnesses. They seemed so composed and it was then I believed. And because I believed...'

This wasn't the moment to analyse the commandant's 'compassion', nor Lenja's illusion. In any case, how would I do that, not knowing what belief was? What would I have done in Lenja's situation? Just thinking about her endurance covers me with dread. Survivors have this effect on me. They brand me, scar me.

Another day, Lenja invited me to her flat for tea. It was in a small purpose-built block off the Finchley Road, neatly furnished. The kettle on, she came back to the living room and left a box full of pictures beside me on a table. On her way back to the kitchen, she talked over her shoulder, 'Some of the pictures are of my blockmates taken after Belsen was liberated.' Her 'mates' were lying on bunks, most of them skeletal, too weak to get up, their eyes sunk in hollows. When Lenja came back, she put down the tray, and pointed to a skeletal person in the picture I had in my hand. 'This one died the day after the British arrived...' Lenja paused, seemingly collecting her thoughts '...when food did come a lot of people died because they ate too much, too quickly, and although we were warned not to, they ignored the warnings. They didn't listen, but I was careful…' Her eyes filled with tears again, 'I know I survived because I believed, I listened… The Jews were greedy. And then there was this girl who could be anybody's; she was completely out of control, giving herself to one man after another.' Lenja broke off. Struck by what she told me, the biblical Lot and his daughters came to mind and their ultimate means for the survival of their tribe: after the catastrophe of the destruction of Sodom and Gomorrah, they contrived to lie with their father. Unbelievably, Lenja called the people in the pictures her mates one minute, and in the next they were hateful Jews. How could I relate to this Jew Lenja, who offered me her God when such evil was perpetrated in his name against the people looking out from these pictures? Soundlessly, a curtain opened in my mind: I was at a post-war charity benefit for Israel, and one of the performers (Inger's son who I had known from Ludwigshafen) was singing a song ending with the line '… and what is more, we've even given you your God' to rapturous applause. Why was everybody standing up, clapping long and hard, and why were some people in tears? And why had Lenja broken ranks with us? As I thought about those things, Lenja's voice came from a long way off: '… the cake is home-made', she stressed, 'lemony, fresh lemon and some grated rind.' She was holding a floral plate, a doily peeping out from under her cake.

However Lenja may have confused and distressed me, it was because of her that I read both books of the Bible in English for the first time in my life, the pages of Genesis, the most threadbare. It was she who instigated the religious education I should have had, and her passion which lead me to the writing the Jews were famous for.

It was not until fifteen years later, when I met Mrs Boxer on the steps to our flats, that I felt the compulsion to look at our history again, but this time round, I would leave God out of it. Why, I wanted to know, have Jews survived as a people, and why had they gone their own way after Jesus was crucified, and what was the continuity Lenja had spoken of that the Old Testament led to the New, breaking the bond Jews had with their God and the reliance on His protection for them? Perhaps if I knew more, my trembling might stop when faced with anti-Semitism.

Many years later, when Lenja was no longer in my life, I saw the painting by Stanley Spencer, the one where people rise from their graves fully dressed, pushing aside slabs of stones – in Cookham! So, this was what Lenja believed! Although my feelings about her beliefs were unchanged, I was sorry I doubted her. Who was I to question her faith, wrought from the circumstances she had been in? I have no idea how many clients she may have offended by her passionate preaching during what was meant to be their leisurely time at the hairdresser. None ever complained.

Me, in England, 1942.

I marry Evansky, Valentine's Day, 1943.

Top: *The staff of Tudor Rose, 1949. Lenja, the manicurist, top row, 3rd from left.*
Bottom: *The Lerner family, Bethnal Green, 1947. L to R: Norma (Heinie's wife); Heinie (who changed his name to Harry when he came to England); Mum with Jeffrey; Dad; Evansky and Me.*

Top left: *My father's sister, Blooma, Lodz, 1927. When her older sister died, she married her brother-in-law and became both aunt and step-mother to her sister's children.*
Top right: *Blooma's daughters by her brother-in-law who were gassed at Auschwitz.*
Bottom: *Sarah, Aunt Blooma's eldest surviving step-daughter, in Paris with her sons, Bernard and Morris, and her husband, Henri, 1950.*

Chapter Nineteen

Entertainment with Ted and Grace

Seeing Ted and Grace was a relief from Lenja. Evansky and I had our first ever Christmas with them; the full treatment: the tree, the tinsel, the baubles, the crackers, the Christmas dinner and pudding – all of it so huge. Grace encouraged us to sit by the imitation inglenook, a fire roaring up the chimney, and of course we fell asleep. The moment we woke up Grace stood beside us with tea and fruit cake on a tray. We held our hands against our stomachs: 'We couldn't possibly.' Grace was not dissuaded. 'Christmas comes but once a year', she said, and went off leaving the tray on a table beside us, 'Ted and I will join you as soon as we've finished the washing-up.' On the way to the kitchen, she bumped into a chair, the red tissue crown on her head slipping to the bridge of her nose. 'Steady on, Grace,' said Ted. I don't remember if we wore 'hats'; we must have done, having pulled the crackers.

Ted had been all over the place in the war, but it was India he talked about. On one of our evenings together, he told us how walking over people sleeping on pavements was normal. The more astonished I looked, the more Ted hardened the reality: 'They do everything on the pavement, from birth to death, and everything between.' Was Ted topping the Jewish nightmare, so often seen those days in newsreels and written about in the papers? Was he sending me the message that Jews were not the only people who suffered? I wasn't ready for neutral thinking, not yet.

On another evening together, Ted, in a more relaxed mood, told us how he'd made it in civvy-street after he was demobbed. 'A friend told me of a job going as a front of house manager at the Paramount Cinema in Lower Regent Street. Slapstick, when I think about it: one minute in army uniform and the next in a 'monkey suit'. I grabbed it – a job was a job – and odd though this dress-game was, I had to wear it in broad daylight, to look as if I was 'somebody', but this 'somebody' couldn't afford to eat lunch out. Grace made me sandwiches, but how was I to hide them until lunchtime? Talk about going from grandstanding to absurdity! Imagine me pushing the sandwiches into my trouser pocket where they bulged under the cut-away of the 'monkey' jacket. What a thing to be doing after what I saw in the war!' Ted threw back his head, closed his eyes and fired off several hard 'ha-ha-has'. Not knowing how to respond, I asked, 'When did you and Grace get married?' 'On one of my leaves in the war,' Ted said, giving Grace a generous glance. 'Yes, Ted,' she said, smiling back, 'Remember our lunch party, Spam on lettuce leaves and chunky pieces of sour beetroot?' Ted nodded obligingly. Food rationing continued until 1953.

We celebrated New Year's Eve at Hendon Hall Hotel with Ted and Grace. Streamers draped all over the place like giant cobwebs, and after the New Year was proclaimed everybody was kissing anybody in the crush. But Ted wasn't 'anybody', and having got hold of me he angled his tongue round in my mouth. Looking over his shoulder, I saw Grace standing behind us smiling. Why was she smiling when I was thinking, 'How dare he?'

The next time we saw them, I couldn't meet Ted's eyes. He wasn't put out at all. He merely tried to hold my eyes when I was trying to evade his, not knowing where to look. Had Evansky seen Ted kissing me? He couldn't have, because all he said on the way home was, 'Lovely evening, wasn't it?' I was glum, too preoccupied working out Ted's gratuitous kiss with Grace looking on. Evansky and I couldn't talk about these things, both of us being as green as each other. Doggedly, ignorance remained bliss. Premieres followed at the Paramount Picture House in Lower Regent Street. The film over, we'd go on to The Hungaria, a popular nightspot, conveniently opposite the cinema. Mingling with the famous, stardust fell on me when Stewart Granger looked at me for at least five seconds.

Apart from the Bible, I hadn't read anything. I used to stand in bookshops, bewildered by choice. Which one? I continued reading the Bible, not for Lenja's sake, or God's, but for those indestructible stories, so often still pertinent for our day. *Am I my brother's keeper?* When Evansky caught me reading the New Testament, he was outraged. 'I am not 'aving it,' he warned, 'I'll divorce you if you go on reading that stuff!' After that, I hid 'that stuff' in fashion magazines, flipping the pages when Evansky was in the room. He wouldn't have known the Bible from the telephone directory, but instinctively he knew that what I was reading had to do with Lenja and conversion.

Less risky recommendations were talked about while I was doing women's hair: cultural things, what was on and where. Covent Garden Opera House – a dance hall in the war – had been restored to its glorious status. Margot Fontaine was dancing *Swan Lake*. I went alone. Watching Fontaine was an experience as profound as sitting among the scorched trees in the garden of the synagogue in Ludwigshafen. I was ravished by technique made into art, miraculously performed by Fontaine, especially as the flesh and blood Odile where she held that brilliant smile pirouetting across the stage, her black tutu glittering. The curtain calls, the flowers tossed over the footlights, her bows, and the gold embroidered Royal mono-gram on the corners of the red velvet curtains, shutting away the enchantment… I clapped until my hands ached, and when the audience got to their feet and clapped too with their arms outstretched, it gave me a feeling of belonging – to what, I couldn't yet put into words.

Out in the street, the bubble I was in burst on the pavement. Traffic fumes now dominant, the enchantment faded with every step I took towards Solly's car waiting at the curb. And there he was as he promised he'd be. Now, sitting next to him, he made no reference to where I'd been, and sensibly he nego-tiated his way through the traffic, taking the best way to get to the buildings. 'Everybody is wai'ing for yeah at Ma Rachel's.' His market talk ground in my ears like gears wrongly engaged. I moped all the way to the 'buildins'.

A couple of weeks later, I tried again: 'Come to a concert with me.' 'Okay,' Evansky said, indifferently. I regretted asking, but maybe he'd change his mind on hearing the music. The foyer in the Festival Hall was packed and everyone was flock-ing to their seats. Evansky remarked, 'A lot of people go to these things.' He fidgeted throughout Beethoven's Ninth, and the more he did, the more I wished for his hand to link with mine in celebration of the sounds coming from the platform. That night, I cried myself to sleep. 'You and your fancy ideas,' Evansky said next morning. He concurred with nothing I wanted to do.

From then on I went to 'these things' alone: art galleries, more concerts, the theatre and more ballet. The last time Evan-sky came to the theatre with me was to see Rattigan's *The Deep Blue Sea*. He slept peacefully through the final act, and it seemed that the 'gas' Peggy Ashcroft turned on for her suicide in the last Act had wafted across the footlights towards Evan-sky, so silently and deeply did he sleep. I applauded and filed out of the theatre, leaving him to come round. 'That was a good sleep,' he said when he caught up with me in the street.

More to Evansky's liking were the music halls. 'Now that's what I call entertainment!' he said confidently in front of his family. How could I possibly disagree? They undoubtedly were. We saw them all: Max Miller, early Morecombe and Wise, Max Wall. But it wasn't about one or the other, I should have said but couldn't – too much resentment was flying around for any discussion to take place. Frustration vanished when I worked, laughed, and mulled things over in my head.

Ever on the lookout for that elusive something, I'd sit back on my padded bed-head, looking round the room for an arbiter to sort out our problem. My gaze rested in the dark spot where my dressing table stood across a corner, a construction that served no purpose at all, with its two mock-baroque lamp holders and flame-shaped bulbs, electrically dead. I never did get them wired up. The only thing brightening the darkness was the baby pink tutu surrounding the dressing table, made of cotton organza, washed and ironed damp for maximum stiffness, proud and aloof. I never sat in front of that altar; I did my make-up in front of the bathroom cabinet – a hard silver mirror hardly improved by a north light hitting my face – and lost in the harshness, I tried to find lines of experience. Not a crack anywhere. I hung on to what Evansky had told me he 'couldn't forget'. I should have been grateful for the face I was scrutinizing. I stared into my pupils close to the mirror – of course I couldn't see myself cross-eyed – and thus distracted, I'd hear Evansky calling, 'Breakfast is ready'. This was our routine: he made breakfast and I cooked our dinner and ironed his shirts, folding and smoothing them the way Weiler had shown me, remembering each grunt of his instructions as I flipped a sleeve and coaxed a collar into place.

Despite my misgivings on the Evansky front, I thought his family jollier than my mine. They were a noisy lot, shouting at each other in head-on collisions, more accidentally than out of malice. Their shouting was a subtle language; it kept them together. I weighed their methods against my parents' silence; they felt alone, they often told me, but then, I couldn't tell them that I felt the same. I was married, awaiting happiness. Evansky and I divided our spare time between our parents. My parents resented me staying longer with Evansky's family than with them. Mother must have counted the minutes before we came because when she opened the door to us, she would say, 'Why so late?' Emotional blackmail was not something I knew how to handle, and as for their loneliness...

I was glad to have Rachel to compare my mother with; I couldn't imagine her doing what Rachel did. Numb to my feelings, she told me of the time she'd gone to school to pull up the teacher for chastising her son: "'You!' I said to her, "you can't treat my Albie like that!" ' Not a word of what Albie had done to raise the tempo of the teacher's voice, or hand, as the case may have been when he came home crying. How could I compete with such primal feelings?

But her son seemed still to be dribbling like a baby. After much reflection, I realized that his babyish behaviour had to do with my sexual crippledom, and therefore, no criticisms of mine affected Evansky, no matter how innocent or objective. He refused them as a matter of course. 'This tie doesn't go with that colour shirt' would elicit the retort, 'so and so likes it' and always there was that triumphant sound to his voice. Evansky was part of a clan where little was corrected or challenged – even had I been sexually spectacular. His sister, present when Evansky did his 'baby trick' made light of it. 'Come on Rose, make up your eyelashes and forge' abaa' it!'

And then, in the middle of those shenanigans, Evansky was taken ill with a burst stomach ulcer. He spent six weeks in Wembley Hospital on a drip. Every evening, after locking up the shop, I went there by bus. Shop signs creaked painfully as steely Siberian winds whistled round corners despite the calendar firmly stating it was spring. Eventually his ulcer healed, but a few weeks later he was back to having sour tastes in his mouth. He was only in his early thirties.

Walter Mempris, a surgeon at St Thomas' Hospital, recommended a partial gastrectomy. 'Go on, have it done!' I said. Evansky was on the operating table for four hours. I battled with my conscience: what if he died? I should have let him decide for himself. The nurse I spoke to on the phone said, 'He's doing fine.' That was comforting. On his release from hospital, his surgeon said, 'Your husband is a good patient.' He couldn't have known the turmoil I had been in, guilty to the hilt. Was Mempris trying to tell me something? And then it occurred to me that Evansky might have told him about our sexless marriage. When we left the surgeon's rooms, he shook my hand longer than was professionally necessary, his eyes packed with meaning, as he patted Evansky on the shoulders in a fatherly way. I felt in the wrong again, though glad in another way. Evansky made a complete recovery, and he never had another twinge in his stomach for the rest of his life. His ulcer had excused him from military service.

As Evansky got stronger, and spring finally came, I looked into our situation again. We would never be anything to each other, except for the ties of respectability and the shop we shared. Even that consideration didn't make my loyalty to him into a Royal Performance. Evansky never told me what he felt on a personal level, yet deep down, I longed to hear and see with him. Oh, to be central in someone's life – the raw need of it!

Chapter Twenty

Paris

With Europe now free, Evansky and I went to the South of France for the first time. 'Could you,' my father asked, 'break your journey to see my sister's children who live in Paris?' Sarah, the oldest, had lived through occupied Paris, and the two youngest, Carola and Paula, had survived Auschwitz. Their mother died before World War II and was thankfully saved from the experience of the death camp. Father's younger sister Blooma was then obliged to marry her brother-in-law, which was once a practice in Jewish Orthodox law. Blooma became both aunt and stepmother to her sister's six children, three of whom I was about to meet for the first time, having only known them from photographs.

How Sarah survived in Paris during the war, Father didn't say, but his finger pointed to her standing next to her mother in the back row in a sepia photograph taken before Blooma became her aunt and stepmother. 'Beautiful children, my sister had,' my father reflected, 'she was the most beautiful of my sisters.'

Over some tea, he told me that Sarah had left Poland with her husband and two small boys to settle in Paris, some years before World War II. Then, pointing to the children in the photograph who had perished, he hunted through the box and found a picture of the two little girls Blooma had by her brother-in-law. 'Have I ever told you they were gassed?' he asked. I had never seen that picture before, nor had I known of the girls and their fate. Father broke my silence: 'We lost a lot of family.' And as I remained mute, he said, 'Come to the yard and see the improvements I made to the chicken house,' but both of us lost interest in this. 'I must go home to pack,' I muttered. As long as Jewish persecution was something heard amongst other news on the radio, I could just about cope. More was too much, and what with Lenja's experience still burning in my mind, the excitement of going to Paris cooled.

Peace in Europe set creative talents free, notably at that time, in fashion. Dior's New Look was fluted skirts and jackets with peplums. My excitement returned. My copy of the 'new Dior', run up by a local dressmaker, was made from soft chocolate-brown wool allowing masses of fabric for the skirt. It was thrilling to swirl round and round, my skirt high. Utility-labelled clothes with their minimal use of fabric seemed suddenly a world away. A client of mine offered me one of her hats to go with my 'Dior': a brown-felt beret style with a long, speckled bird feather sticking out sideways. I was in my early twenties and my client was about fifty. She considered herself abreast of fashion. In those days, old and young fashions were distinctly divided. If I refused her offer I might lose her custom. I hovered between embarrassment and obligation. Her hat remained firmly on my head throughout the flight, my head and neck rigid, leaning away from the back of my seat. My client's all-seeing eyes followed me everywhere.

At Paris airport, Sarah's husband Henri met us. Apparently, he had a picture of us, and recognition over, he led us to a small open lorry. The front seat was full of builder's tools and particles of grit collected over time. Henri apologised in French and pointed to our seats at the back of the lorry where there was an array of boxes on top of each other and the two meant for us stood side by side. In no time we were rattling through the streets of Paris, the feather on my hat bending in the wind. So much for my grand thoughts about elegance!

Sarah lived on the fifth floor of an apartment block in the Rue de Couronne. She had been waiting for us outside her front door. We tried to embrace but that silly hat stopped us.

Once inside her flat, I took it off. 'These are my sons, Bernard and Morris,' Sarah said, extending her arm. They were standing next to each other in the middle of the room looking us over like important documents. Bernard and Morris understood Yiddish but couldn't speak it. Evansky's and mine being rusty didn't exactly make our conversation flow either, in fact it was paralysed. My Yiddish had withered in my fervour to learn English. Evansky seemed to be a bystander, his brow puckered in the thought: *what have I let myself in for?* He wasn't coping, but then neither was I. It wasn't about not speaking Yiddish fluently, we understood every word, but with the suddenness of our meeting it seemed as if we had been swept together by a violent storm, and now overcome by stillness, only our smiles could fill the gaps in our conversation.

'Carola and Paula are coming tomorrow,' Sarah announced, pointing to them in the photo on her sideboard, the same family picture my father had. They were youngest of the children in the picture; both of them were dressed prettily with several rows of beads around their necks, and ribbons from brimless head-hugging embroidered bonnets streamed from below their ears. With their heads slightly tilted to one side, their manner seemed to say, 'Aren't we lovely?' 'Their husbands are working and will come after lunch,' Sarah said. Then, urgently, she said more, 'Blooma's two little girls who she had by my father didn't survive… nor did the picture of them. On a collection in Lodz ghetto, they were taken with other children to be gassed. Blooma ran after the lorry, and on hearing her children call, "Mamma, Mamma", she fainted. Blooma was in another "collection" and was transported to Auschwitz. At the front of a queue, she was asked what she could do. "I am a cook," she said, and this being useful, she was selected to live – at least Blooma believed this with all her heart, but by that token many women might have been saved. Then again, if you consider the amount of cooking needed in the camps when most of the "transportees" were gassed on arrival. Perhaps she cooked for the commandant and his family? I believe no one knows. That she survived is all that matters. Wanting to know more is blasphemous. If survivors are able to tell at all, that is miraculous.'

Sarah ended, exhausted, a great fluttering sigh escaping from her chest, having verbalised the unspeakable. There wasn't a space to interrupt her. In any case, I partially knew that story. Sarah then rushed off to make up our bed on the floor in her corridor with an old-fashioned feather bed, the kind my mother used to top up with feathers she'd plucked from the odd goose we had for Passover. As the years passed, that duvet became a dead weight.

Sarah's French was spiced with Yiddish. Out shopping with her was the first time I realized the varieties of Yiddish spoken in the Diaspora: '*a gitten bon jour*!' Sarah greeted her butcher. 'This is my *meshpucha*,' she said, pulling me, her relative, close to her. Eventually the fluency of Sarah's Yiddish moved Evansky's and mine on.

At dinner, Henri looked me over. Glancing over to Sarah at the stove, he said, 'Why don't *you* dress like your cousin, look how smart she is!' 'I am satisfied to have enough to eat!' Sarah said. She was rushing about from stove to table, beads of sweat on her forehead. Bernard and Morris helped her. We had braised lung for dinner, big pieces of garlic floating in the sauce.

The next day, Carola and Paula came as promised. Carola had a mop of Afro-style hair, innocently avant garde for the West just after the war, its colour pale gold like my father's with eyes to match. Paula's hair was curly and black as pitch, matching her eyes. Her teeth were a mixture of silver and gold crowns. When the sisters and I embraced, they sighed, and when we disengaged, tears brimmed in their eyes the way Lenja's did. 'Come, eat,' Sarah said, whether in French or Yiddish I don't remember.

The dining table filled the room entirely; when someone jerked back in their chair, it hit the wall. Evansky said 'thank you' in French when appropriate and then fell silent again. He was very ill at ease; no one was shouting here, no one spoke with bombast. 'Know all, know nothing' was the motto here. I was sorry for him, for myself too. Carola and Paula's eyes glistened throughout lunch.

The meal over, we took our chairs and went into the living room, crowding round a small table in the centre, café-style. Henri and Evansky decided to stand by the window looking out into the street, their ears cocked. Carola and Paula's Yiddish had the warmth of constant usage, speckled with affectionate diminutives for close relations: *Saideschie* (grandfather), *Bubaschie, Tanteshie, Onkele*… redolent of a past I had only heard spoken about by my parents. Then, without any preamble, Carola declared, 'Our *Saidischie* died in the ghetto of hunger, and our many cousins, aunts and uncles…' she said, her arm sweeping through the air towards the family photographs on the sideboard… *wurden vergassed.*'

In one fell swoop, Carola related me to our dead, gave me an intimate vision of our tragedy. Sarah looked at me, then back to Carola, and then over to Paula whose back was bent, her hands covering her face, and then to Henri and Evansky who were still looking out of the window, clearing their throats, clearing the way for words, maybe, but none came. Sarah's boys hung their heads, I assume to avoid the treadmill of sorrow. Again it was Carola who lightened our burden: 'Come, let us hold hands and sing some songs,' at once leading with a blessing for the meal we had, her voice ripe with feeling. All of us joined in the singing, all except Paula: she just cried and cried, and all of us just let her be. The days when my father used to sing those songs came flooding back.

The sisters' husbands, Mariano and Salvatore, came halfway through our singing. Before Carola and Paula arrived, Sarah had told me that they met their husbands, two Catholic friends, on a holiday in Spain. None of us spoke each other's language though we shook hands warmly. Mariano was the friendlier of the two. It was he who tried to join in our singing; a cigarette bobbing up and down between his lips, he mumbled, watching everyone's mouths, trying to imitate the shape our lips made, yielding to our mood. One elbow on the table, his hand cupped holding up his head, he smiled contentedly. Salvatore, Paula's husband – Salvi, she called him – was more reticent: his dark eyes alert, he looked at us in turn, a black oily lock in free-fall over his forehead, his muscular body leaning back on his chair, his large hands flat on his thighs.

Before Carola and Paula went home, they arranged themselves in front of me, nudging against each other as if to say 'We speak as one,' and again, it was Carola who did the talking: 'Please tell *Onkele* we could not do otherwise.' I knew what they meant to say, knowing well enough that intermarriage was not what Jews from a closed society did with an easy conscience. Nevertheless, their petition made clear that my father was now the head of the family. Their declaration gave me a rare insight into the respect given to elders in the past. Father, I thought, will be surprised when I tell him of his new status in the family. A patriarch – at last!

I had my first taste of French bread, both fresh and stale. Going up and down five flights of stairs twice a day for fresh baguettes couldn't be easy, I deduced, custom or not. Sarah never complained having to climb the stairs, weighed down with shopping. When we went shopping together, I wanted to help her carry some things, but she eased me aside saying, '*Non merci*, I'm used to it!' I wouldn't take no for an answer, so she let me help, albeit reluctantly. Her autonomy unsettled me. When we reached the top, she put down the shopping and sighed.

Henri told us nothing about himself. His looks were as mysterious as his past: he was rough-featured with wrinkled eyelids, with reflections of some Mongolian tribe. He had been in the Resistance, and after the war he became stepfather to Sarah's two sons from her first husband, who had been caught by the French police, transported to Auschwitz and gassed. Sarah had managed to send the boys to Free France.

Sarah told me how she survived alone in Paris, and how she met Henri, while we were on a walk from the Rue de Courrone to the Arc de Triomphe. We were just walking when, with a great heave of her chest, she began to tell me how she had lived in Paris under German occupation.

When France surrendered, Paris was occupied without a shot being fired except for a few from snipers here and there, the last protests 'officially' silenced for the duration of the war. Sarah was trapped, alone. Other Jews ended up in Trancy, the collecting camp from which they were transported to Auschwitz. As Sarah said, 'It was good to be alone, less conspicuous, less opportunity for betrayal.' She continued, 'What am I talking about? Betrayal or not, I never saw any of my friends again. Luckily, I managed to dodge the police.'

The only time I interrupted her was to ask about one of the few details I knew at that time, 'Didn't you know the French police collaborated with the Gestapo?' Sarah nodded. 'Who knew anything? The only thing I knew was that I had to survive the next minute, find the next meal, the next doorway to sleep in before night-fall.' Traffic rushed past as before, but now I heard it. Sarah gave me a weak smile. I tried to gauge the meaning of that smile. Was she tired or apologetic? Did she want to continue with her story? I expected her to cry out the way my father did after he came home from Dachau. I waited.

'In those terrible days,' Sarah said, 'you did what was possible. Plans went wrong and things happened so fast, I thought myself blessed not having to worry about my boys. And then it was too late, and I was alone to fend for myself, eating out of dustbins, sleeping in alleyways, doorways, living the life of a vagrant. I looked grubby, and when I caught sight of my reflection in a shop window, I was alarmed: looking too shabby might be dangerous. I decided to disguise myself. It took a while to find my disguise, but then again, what was I looking for? You won't believe the things people throw out, and sure enough, I found something suitable in a dustbin: a big, floppy straw hat, shabby and tattered, and a big silver cross with Jesus on it: their *Meshiach*. I tied it round my neck with string and that was how I walked through the streets of Paris, acting crazy, slouching, dragging my feet, my head lolling and drooping, the hat shading my face. It worked. Passers-by voiced the odd "Tut-tut" and "poor thing". Their pity gave me confidence one minute but frightened me the next. Was I more conspicuous than before?' Sarah stopped in the middle of the crowded pavement, re-enacting how she had walked. Her story made her reply to Henri's criticism of her lack of chic poignant. Even now, as I remember this walk, I wish I had worn sackcloth and ashes.

'Then one night, I accepted a room from a friend, offered to him by a friend who had had his deportation papers. Like all vagrants, he talked furtively: "Had a few nights sleep in a bed… must move on…" and dropping the keys on the pavement, he whispered the address clearly and left. Terrible days they were, who knew who a friend of a friend was? Insider? Outsider? Only a fool would trust anyone, but then a night's sleep in a bed was a chance worth taking: a bed is a bed. The flat was on the top floor of a house. I slept the sleep of the dead, when suddenly I was woken up by violent banging on the door: "Open up! Police! We know you're in there, open up!"

'I fell out of bed. Luckily or out of habit, I don't know, I always slept in my clothes, and despite the luxury of a bed, I'd kept my clothes on. I opened the window, scrambled onto the roof and slipped down a drainpipe into the courtyard of the next house. I knew only one man would follow me because I heard them talking, planning how to catch me: "You break down the door and I'll wait for you downstairs, that way she can't escape. Hurry!" How did they know I was a woman? I was too scared to think. But when the other man caught up with me, I fell to my knees, embracing his.' Tears were bursting from her eyes, as she told me, '"Your friend won't know that you found me, please let me go," I begged him. "I have two children." Then, to my surprise, he detached himself from me leaving me sprawled on the ground. Moments later, I realized I was alone. How long I waited, I don't know. That I was alive was the only thought I had that moment. It was still dark and no one, it seemed, was woken up by the commotion. No hurry for me to leave, but then, a cold wind came at me. Mustn't get ill, must find somewhere for the rest of the night before it gets light. Having decided what to do, I was able to get to my feet.'

Sarah kept going back over things she'd already told me, and I felt that any interruption by me would be like talking through a liturgy. Proving me right she continued. 'The bed I slept in was a comfort I couldn't afford as a vagrant; better doorways and alleyways with rats and cats as your neighbours,' she said ironically. 'Looking the part I had chosen was dangerous in a different way, because I really believed I was going crazy, slipping into a twilight world, half in and half out of madness, and I was hungry, so hungry.' She turned to me and gripped my arm forcefully, 'and then, one day, crazy as I felt, and looking down on the pavement all the time, I kicked a bundle of papers secured with a rubber band. I looked about me, keeping the bundle between my feet. A few moments later, and shivering less now, I casually picked up my find and dashed into an alleyway. Calm at last, I took off the rubber band. Dollars! Was I hallucinating? Had I really gone mad? Perhaps it was a miracle!' Sarah cried joyously, sniffing and wiping her eyes and nose with her sleeve, remembering.

More composed, she said, 'I used that money to have false papers made. And that is how I managed to get to Unoccupied

France and there I was reunited with my sons. Sometime later, I met Henri in the Resistance. Have I told you my husband was gassed?' she said, suddenly restless again. She had – it had been one of the first things she told me after our arrival – but I didn't say, didn't want to embarrass her, though to be honest, I wasn't adept enough in empathetic responses. Silence was best, and nodding.

The next morning after breakfast, she got up from the table and pulled me over to the sideboard and opened one of its a drawers. Rummaging about in it, she found a sepia picture of her husband; holding it between her fingers she murmured, 'Wasn't he beautiful?' Sarah dictated how long we gazed at her husband's image before she put it back in the drawer. Henri had gone down for baguettes.

There was little time to digest all she told me. The word 're-sistance' had mysterious overtones for me. Jews resisting? This was not what I had learned in Germany about us: we were cowards, sly and slippery, and I sort of believed it. Stigma clings. It would take me a long time to work out the image of Jewish heroes, kibbutzniks, and Diaspora Jews, fighting in the war for their adopted countries as citizens, juxtaposed with those who 'didn't want to fight for *them*', as my father said.

I told Sarah nothing of wartime in England. It didn't occur to me that I should, considering my comparative safety then. Up close, the Arc de Triomphe dwarfed the clips I'd seen of it in the newsreels with Germans marching up or down the Champs Elysées, its significance multiplied tenfold as Sarah and I walked fearlessly on that famous stretch of road. Sarah must have seen them marching, the sound of jackboots tolling in her fate, as I saw the columns of the S.A. in Ludwigshafen, feeling their power, hearing them sing of Jewish blood bursting from knives. When next I looked at my cousin, her head was bowed and her eyes wide open as if in search of something.

Without consulting each other, we turned round to go

home. A few steps on, Sarah continued, 'When the war was over, Carola and Paula came to Paris. Amazingly, they survived, but our other siblings perished.' I didn't even feign surprise; Sarah was talking about the sisters my father had told me about a few days before. She continued, 'When they came, we didn't have a lovely time together. It was awful. I was ashamed of them. They behaved like wild beasts sitting with their legs apart in the Metro, laughing at nothing at all, staring rudely at people, shrieking like badly brought up children. I was distraught. We had hardly any money to live on. Henri worked hard for all of us, but I didn't want to be with my sisters. But what could I do? Sisters are sisters. When their behaviour didn't change, I borrowed some money and sent them for a holiday to Spain, cheaper than France.

'Then another miracle happened. They met the two men you've already met, Mariano and Salvatore. They fell in love. Back in Paris, they asked me if they could marry them. I let them. It freed me. As you saw, Paula has a little boy, and Mariano, despite Carola not being able to have children, loves her. It was fated. Perhaps God meant it to be that way. My life in the war was bad enough, but imagining their young lives in Auschwitz... and even then, I couldn't understand why they behaved the way they did, it was too shocking, too distorted. I still can't find the words for what happened to us all. Our family was so respectable. It was the coarseness of their laughter that upset me; I couldn't bear it. I was ashamed that I didn't understand, ashamed not wanting to know them better. How do we heal our wounded souls?' Touché, I thought, my hand touching Sarah's arm. As from nowhere I heard myself say, 'Time.' What a lie that was!

'Tomorrow,' Sarah said, 'we're going to them. They live on the fourth floor in a large apartment block, each in one room with a communal lavatory two floors down on the landing, just a hole in the floor, and neither have running water in their rooms. Carola's window looks out onto a dirty wall. I feel for them; at least I have a water closet and running water in the kitchen. Tell *Onkele*, we couldn't do it any different,' she said, repeating Carola's request. Sarah was talking of our lost culture and its way of life, of its mores she couldn't help but follow. 'To think that the Nazis nearly destroyed us all,' Sarah said, weeping gently. I felt cold, the way I did when my father wept. Something was controlling me.

There never seemed to be the right moment to tell Evansky of Sarah's experiences in the war, in fact I don't think I ever did, remembering only too well his devil-may-care response when I told him about my brush with the Gestapo official. In all innocence, affecting a holiday mood, Evansky proposed taking everybody out for a treat. I don't remember who suggested the Follies, but since it was the popular nightspot on the Paris tourist trail he booked a table.

We all piled into a taxi, including Sarah's sons. Sarah slept throughout the show. Bernard and Morris leapt up from their seats, their eyes popping. Henri showed only partial interest, spreading his lips in that slow lazy smile of his. In the taxi going home, Sarah apologized for falling asleep. It was I who should have apologized to her. I was tongue-tied again.

I didn't know how to make it right, unable as I was to tap into the lives my cousins had left behind in Poland: the diminutives of names, the singing after meals, the traditions Carola had refreshed for me and I should have warmed to. I felt guilty for having rejected what Hitler had destroyed. It seemed as though I was adding to his crime. Truth tossed and turned as I slept, and on waking, I coshed it. Back in England, I hid Sarah's story behind holiday smiles, showing off my tan.

In 1965, I was briefly in Paris. I hadn't planned on seeing Sarah again, as my life had taken a different turn. Like Paula and Carola, I too was now married out. Henri had died. I decided to see Sarah because not seeing her would be worse. I took for granted that she still lived in the Rue des Couronne. The concierge of the apartment block she had lived in wrote down the address of her shop, a haberdasher's.

When I opened the door of the shop, Sarah was sitting behind the counter. After a cheerless greeting, she said, a resigned expression on her face, 'I am sitting in a wasteland made ready for redevelopment.' The building the shop was under was a huge obelisk round which traffic circled non-stop, and with no passing trade Sarah's business had dwindled to nothing. My arrival stirred her into action. 'Come, let's go home,' she said shame-facedly as if she'd been caught out doing something wrong. The shop locked up, we walked to her new apartment.

It was through a courtyard on the first floor, in a better area than the Rue de Coronne. Only one flight of stairs for her to climb, I was pleased to notice. A balcony stretched along the first floor with a row of French windows and rooms leading into one another, gallery-like. It was a dreary day, but the large tree in the courtyard obscured what little light there was. Despite the sullen weather, the building exuded elegance.

Sarah cooked lunch and served me, but didn't eat herself. We said little to each other, so little it didn't even lead to words of comfort, even of the most conventional kind. 'Sorry about Henri,' would have been appropriate enough, but I remembered that Henri hadn't been the love of her life and this stopped me saying something. I had gathered this from one of her apologetic smiles on my first visit to her when she told me, 'Henri does his best for my boys.' Whether I had noticed something gruff between Henri and them, and Sarah noticing I noticed, I don't know.

It was a silent lunch. I ate and Sarah stared at me as if to get inside my head. Even if she could, I didn't want her to; there was too much to explain in my deficient Yiddish, and besides, I didn't have enough emotional power to mull over our past. I was busy with my present, nurturing closeness in another direction, new and exiting. Sarah and I were unable to link arms as girls do in playgrounds, stepping into the future, laughing. I don't know, maybe too many family links had been broken when only our woes filled the cracks, oozing from time to time.

What Sarah and I had in common were the same photographs, hers on the sideboard and mine in a shoebox waiting to be passed on, only to be put hurriedly into a drawer after my death or until the recipients were older and wanted to know more, wanted to show them to their children. 'This,' they might say to them, holding up a picture of an old man with a flowing white beard, 'is my maternal great-great-grandfather… and this couple is on my father's side… the whole family lived in Lodz. Oh, and this is Cousin Fritz from Luxembourg, dated 1936; he was one of six brothers. I understand the whole family perished in the Holocaust – it says so on the back of the picture. And here is an aunt, long dead. And look, this is Carmella, another cousin, in a Purim costume in Haifa, aged fourteen… and here is another cousin; she lived in Tel Aviv. She died young, my aunt is reported to have said; she was sorry she didn't know more about her except that they were first cousins.' So many cousins, lost to each other, lost and not even knowing of each other's existence yet longing for family bonds, the chance to have enjoyed the commonplace things we may have loved and hated – even each other at times – and the agony this brings, and how we learn to live with such things. Yes, these are my regrets. I willl never know these things because distance has trained my soul to behave.

Father stayed in touch with Sarah. Some years after Henri died he received a letter from Sarah's third husband. It was written in good Yiddish. Father cried, 'Look, such beautiful Yiddish, every letter a picture!' It seemed natural that Sarah's new husband should write to my father, the sisters having made him the head of the family. Having married a traditional man, Sarah didn't have to nudge him to write to my father, 'and because of it,' Father said as he was reading the letter, 'she is contented, I'm sure of it!' Obligation pulls manners along: community; continuity. Being childless, I will not continue, I couldn't help thinking. Years later, I received a notice of Sarah's death sent to me by my sister-in-law. It seems Harry and Norma exchanged Jewish New Year cards with her. Sarah lived to be eighty-four.

I look for happy moments for them all among the pictures in my shoebox. In one photo Sarah and her husband Henri, Carola and Mariano, Paula and Salvatore and their little boy, my mother and father, and some people I don't recognize, all of them in short sleeves, are sitting round a long table under a pergola somewhere in Paris having lunch, posing for the camera, elbows on the table or sitting back in their chairs. I look at the picture for a long time. My father is smiling, apparently accepting that his nieces had married out, and I want to believe it was true. What foolish thoughts!

Chapter Twenty-One

Treatment

The trip to Europe changed nothing in our marriage. Coming home meant more therapy, and this time for my body rather than my mind. Over the years, I went from one therapist to another; it was like picking through a bag of pockmarked apples until a good one was found. But how would I know which one was good and who I could respond to? One I remember well sat behind his desk in a room smelling of furniture polish and carpets reeking of vinegar – a method Mrs Weiler used to enliven the colours of old rugs. I was more interested at that moment in how these household tips travelled across continents than in feeding my prospective helper with confessional tirades about my abusers. 'Now, let's see,' he began, his passive eyes wanting to engage with mine – but I certainly didn't want to engage with his. Giving my name and address for his records deadened my world within and there and then I was sure nothing else would be written in my folder – so sure because his face was inscrutable. What mine was I can't say because I was busy scanning his for trust. I knew my time was up when he gripped the arms of his chair to get up. I cancelled the next appointment when I got home.

How emotionally safe I had felt in the war! But when it was over I saw the newsreels of Allied armies going through towns and villages turned into rubble and ruins spiking hazardously up to the sky, and finally newsreels of concentration camps, and one in particular, the now famous clip of an English officer refusing to shake hands with the commandant of Belsen, behind them a backcloth of bodies strewn everywhere, and walking skeletons, their deaths moments away. And the mass graves:

corpses in layers as in a pie, their gaping mouths ready for worms and earth, topped with quicklime the quicker to decompose, 'not to spread more disease' the reporter said. How many more times would I have to realize that my body could have been in that pie? In the war, people often asked me when I was going to start a family, and being married and having tailored my response according to my sexual predicament, a light-hearted phrase was at the ready: 'When the war is over.' I secretly wished it would never end; then I saw on the screen what that meant.

The therapist I cancelled wrote suggesting that I should see a gynaecologist at Wembley Hospital. Feeling obliged, I made an appointment. Full of dread, I waited for him to finish reading the therapist's letter. 'We'll soon put that right,' he said, 'you have what is commonly called Vaginismus, usually linked to frigidity. My suggestion is to stretch you – under anaesthetic of course.' What was he talking about? 'Where?' I asked. Soberly he explained, 'Your vagina – that is, if you want children! I am sure that would solve your problem!'

I seemed to be on a conveyor belt, destination Motherhood, but before I could think through what the consultant suggested, I was at the hospital being stretched. When I came round from the anaesthetic, I had been painted violet between my legs. 'What is this?' I asked the nurse. 'Against infection,' she said. And looking at me with her large blue eyes, they seemed to say, 'What have you let them do to you, girl?' I laughed, kind of happy-go-lucky, in the hope that her eyes would not ask any more questions.

A couple of weeks later, the surgeon checked me over. After the examination, he pulled off his rubber gloves and roared like a Sergeant Major, 'Now you are big enough for a horse and cart to get in.' Getting off the examination couch, my senses turned inward. I vowed. No! No horse! No cart! Not anything! Nobody! Which meant more frustration for Evansky and more therapy for me.

The obligation to have children became oppressive. When pregnancy didn't materialise, the doctor who had married into the Evansky family suggested yet another way. 'Why don't you have artificial insemination?' I plucked up courage to ask him what that meant and he explained the procedure. In shock, I refused his suggestion with an emphatic 'No!' Linking Avrum's sperm with science was surreal. His sperm down the kitchen sink and Evansky's into a sterile container; the whole thing was disgusting! I looked up 'insemination' in the dictionary: 'to fertilize, to impregnate, to pollinate.' What was I, a flower with bees buzzing around me in the shape of men with nurses serving them? The only thing flourishing inside me was outrage. The more I tried putting sexual facts together, the less they made sense.

Evansky, poor wretch, went along with whatever was on offer, gladly accompanying me to my appointments, always waiting outside for me in the car. Seeing me walking towards him with downcast eyes, he sighed, hanging his head. Both of us were silent on the way home. But then, why was I so sure that he wanted to be shot of my problem, my inability to have intercourse? Did he agree with his brother-in-law's suggestion? Evansky and I never discussed my problem. We didn't know how, didn't have words to help us the way people lament with each other over a common cold.

Evansky turned to his mother again about our hopeless marriage, and she, without any qualms, said the next time I saw her, 'You know, you'll make my son ill if you don't let him be a proper man.' I made sure not to be alone with her again.

One thing was good in my life: work. There were even times I forgot about my problem, but I wasn't allowed to for long. More therapy was suggested, and this time with a Freudian analyst. He didn't get far with me either. Apart from waiting for me to talk, he skirted round my problem, probing and waiting for me to tell… tell what? Was I to be a washerwoman, washing away the dirt of Avrum's abuse of me, the dirty feelings ever-present? Again, I was looking at someone across a desk, both of us speechless, except for the occasional leap of breath escaping from my lips, and both of us looking surreptitiously at our watches. All he knew was that I had an Uncle Avrum, and that talking about him troubled me.

More to the point, therapy was expensive and I wasn't rich enough to continue. On my last session with Dr Shaw, I told him I wouldn't be coming anymore, but when he said encouragingly, 'Do come; there is a new treatment I would like to try, it may help. St. Thomas's Hospital then, yes?' I complied.

'Dr Shaw's consulting room, please?' I asked the porter at the hospital reception area. He took me down some steps leading to the basement and pointed to a door down a long corridor. There were thick pipes round the walls, along the ceiling and in the treatment room, a wedge-shaped labyrinthine space with a window dim with dust, no bigger than a car windscreen. A faded Axminster rug, flat and lustreless, lay in front of a black leather examination couch, a crisp sheet and pillow at its head, blindingly white. A one-bar electric heater glowed comfortably enough.

'So you've come,' Dr Shaw said, 'I am so glad.' He looked at me softly, and extending his arm towards the couch, he bade me to lie down. The couch stood against three rows of pipes. The rotund Dr Shaw metamorphosed into Uncle Avrum's tall and lanky frame; his arm extended like a scarecrow's was how I remembered my abuser. The image faded when Dr Shaw sat down on a chair behind the head of the couch. 'I think we have talked enough,' he said, 'let's try this, it may help.' Talked enough? That must be a joke! Secrets were secrets for life, tidily stitched into the mind. If I were to give up this security, I might not be able to live, but that apart, it dimly occurred to me that I no longer wanted to do sex with Evansky, even if I were spectacularly good at it. And what was 'this' that Dr Shaw wanted to try? I went hot, then cold, then hot again, my blood flooding through me. Dr Shaw put a muslin mask over my nose and dribbled ether on it. 'Breath in deeply,' he said. I wasn't keen to do this, because inmates in the death camps supervising the smooth transition of people into gas chambers whispered to the new arrivals as a kindness that if they breathed in deeply, they would die quicker, Lenja had told me. Busy comparing situations, I went drowsy. Footsteps clattered on the stone floor outside the room, some running, others slow and firm and portentous. The water pipes gurgled and hissed. I was drifting away, when with a steady voice Dr Shaw dragged me back to the present. 'Open your legs!' I don't remember obeying his command, but when he dribbled more ether on the mask and repeated, 'Open your legs!' I knew that that was my problem. Over and over, Dr Shaw said, 'Open your legs.' When finally I did, it wasn't without protest. I screamed so loud, I thought I might be acting because nothing was actually hurting me. But then, why was I screaming? What was hurting me?

After three of those 'treatments' I dredged up some more sense. Why should I have to open my legs? I was beginning to understand that this was what I should do for a man's penis to get inside me. But why should I when it was perfectly nice for me on the outside, remembering that first time I'd felt pleasure? More doubt. Had Avrum penetrated me while I was asleep? How had I reached orgasm, which by now I recognised was what that pleasure had been? And if he did penetrate me, why did I not bleed as I learned virgins did and that it hurt, and if it hurt why hadn't it woken me up? But then, how would I know if I had bled when I hadn't put the light on in the lavatory when cleaning myself up? And on I went, going over the same stale but well-remembered sequence of events. Then, as new as could be, a clean, fresh question broke free: for whose benefit was this? The reply came instantly: certainly not mine, not about me having pleasure. That it was just about getting me pregnant was a totally new thought. A heated debate was going on in my head, and on and on it went for years. I named my treatments 'clinical rape'.

All this started with Evansky wanting babies and me having to go through the sordid details. At the height of this sexual exposure, I gave my parents the names of my three abusers: Karl, Ztupack and Avrum, the chief abuser. 'Why didn't you protect me more?' I shouted at my mother and she, wailing, said, 'I clothed you, I fed you, I bled for you, what more do you want from me? But in any case, what you say can't be true. Ztupack left Germany before you were born. You imagined it all!' Father stood by helplessly: 'Have pity for your mother!' I wasn't in the mood for pity. He even tried humour, thumping his fist on the table in mock rage, a smile playing around his lips, declaring his paternal status, the way he had when I cut my hair short without his permission. On that occasion, my mother had stood behind him, waving to me not to take any notice of him. Mother had been my friend then.

I needed time, and work. Cutting hair relaxed me, gave me the focus I needed. After those 'treatments' I went on working as though nothing was troubling me, and I resolved to live the way I was for the rest of my life, an outcast twice over: a Jew, and a defective woman. How could I escape when I was surrounded by such enthusiastic experts protecting the status quo?

Chapter Twenty-Two

Parents' Independence

To be free from the financial worry of my parents, I wanted to set them up to earn their own living. A 'Dyers and Cleaners with Alterations' already existed in Well Street, Hackney, for the price of £200 key money. I jumped at it, and so did my parents. At last to be independent! I treated my plan as an emergency.

My father's 'handbag job' had long gone. It would be sensible for him to change trades. Having trained as a furrier made him a dab hand with a needle. The Evansky Brothers, being men's tailors, allowed him into their workshop to learn the rudiments of tailoring, certainly enough for him to do alterations. Father was a quick learner.

At that time, Harry and I were struggling to establish ourselves, and my being further on than him became problematic. Sibling rivalry over what was right for our parents was put aside. The last attempt to settle our differences on the parental front ended with me shouting and Harry staying silent. We had just finished lunch at our parents' home. Nothing reasonable emerged. My choice was to help our parents to help themselves, and Harry's silence conveyed something more profound: he was jealous of me taking charge. Why else did he say, 'It wouldn't matter what I said – even if you shat in the middle of the room, Mother would think it was wonderful!' Unusual language for my brother. My frustration peaked. I picked up the jug of water from the table and poured it over my brother's head. He had the proof he needed that I was his hysterical sister. Getting to his feet, he pushed back his chair, flicked the water from his face with his hands, and left the room. From then on, my once open-hearted brother froze our relationship. I even stopped buying presents for his children because… actually, there was no 'because' any more.

Some responsibility for this estrangement must go to our parents. They had a way of setting us against each other, praising the qualities of one child that the other didn't have. At that time, I was the one Mother did 'everythink' for. I enjoyed the harmony between us, but as for my brother and I, the biblical Joseph fits the situation: I was in a hole.

One problem solved, another arose: Mother's kidney kept playing up. It had good periods and bad; when it was bad it was alarming. Frequently, she fell to one side losing her balance, though luckily when there was a wall near or a piece of furniture to hold on to. Every attack she had, the shadows under her eyes got deeper, but all that the doctor recommended was bed-rest. Her appearance used to give me a fright on those visits when I hurried home to see her from work. She would be lying there so lifeless and still, I wondered how long she had to live, and then a few days later, she would be better – baffling. I didn't even think I had to speak to the doctor; I don't remember ever being present when he came. In those days, the doctor came, saw the patient, spoke to the spouse and left, leaving a prescription on the table. An emotionally charged message from my father would frighten me into silence; then when Mother got better there was no point in carping on about it.

The shop was still available so we decided to take it on. I borrowed the key money and in no time my parents were installed. Father learned how to write out tickets in English: 'clean trousers', 'shorten skirt', 'press jacket'. Anything plural was more difficult for him as he only wrote Yiddish, written with Hebrew characters, but soon Roman characters flew across the tickets with a flourish; loops and squiggles and a full stop beside the curved stroke underneath his name. 'This is me!' it said.

Mother was his front woman. She priced alterations and gave the day and time for collection. She knew Father's worth, often saying about him, 'He loves what he does so much, he'd be happy to work for nothing!' When required, she did the deliveries, upstairs and down, in blocks of flats without lifts. Back at the shop, she'd cook in the back room, in a ready-made kitchen: a two-ring gas stove, a sink, a small table and a couple of chairs under the window. Jeffrey, at school in Hackney, came for lunch to the shop every day.

Father's first alteration was to shorten the hem of a dress. 'Easy,' he said, but the dress being cut on the bias made it difficult to do without a dummy, yardstick and tailor's chalk. Easier still would have been if the customer could have stood on the work-table, the hem eye-level with Father. He struggled on nobly, the dress lying flat on his work-table. His whole reputation hung in the balance, and having spent hours on the hem, he was close to tears with frustration. 'Time is money,' Mother said. Father had to come to terms with this financial loss. Ever after, he referred to that experience philosophically as *Lerngeld* (learning costs money). He told this tale endlessly in the style of an adventure. After the 'hem calamity', he stuck strictly to altering suits and coats, which he turned into an art form. 'Look,' he'd say proudly, turning a job he had just finished over to the left side, 'if it doesn't look like the right side, the job is no good!' And that was his way for the rest of his life, whether he was cleaning a house, or painting a room, or cooking. Father was the most adaptable of men, happy only when he was learning yet another skill, or any useful thing, discovering the workings of anything, turning an object upside down or inside out, finding the fault, touching surfaces, feeling them, a sense of appreciation on his face.

At last, Father was making a 'livink'. His pronunciation was the same as Mother's; even when he had retired he would ask people he'd never met before, 'Makin' a livink?' Fine for the

Stetle but not for the middle-class woman he met in the fore-court of the flats that I later moved them to in Hove. He and I were on our way out when we met the woman. 'Goot mor-rnink, makink a livink?' The woman pursed her lips in distaste and made a fitting retreat. After reminding him that he wasn't living in the *Stetle* anymore, he said, 'Vhat you know? I see her evvery day – I know her!'

The smells that mingled in the shop were similar to the ones in my youth when Father was working in our kitchen. Then it had been soaking leather and melting wax competing with the cooking smells; now it was cleaning fluid and urine mingling together when garments were steamed as 'press-ups' in readi-ness for the Friday evening, for *bar mitzvahs* on Saturday mornings or weddings on Sundays. 'Press-ups' meant that trousers were not cleaned first. Father dreaded the heavy steam iron bearing down on the flies. 'What a *Stinkerei*!' he'd cry, and although he was sad having to work on the Sabbath, he man-aged secular life quite well; knowing my father, I was sure he had a tacit agreement with God that dreaming about his Sab-bath *menoocha* (peace) was as good as prayer.

By the time mid-week weddings became really fashionable, Father had retired. Tea dances now marked out aspiring mid-dle-class Jews from the rest. The weddings of earlier times, where cooks waited at the door for tips after a rowdy *Cossatzky* (a Russian dance) ended, the celebrations were forgotten. The surprising thing is that there was always some young man who could do this dance – performed crouching, legs strutting from the knees – despite his family having left Russia, or Poland, or other satellite countries two generations ago. Evan-sky, nimble with his legs, did a fair *Cossatzky*. Never mind him being out of rhythm with the music, everyone enjoyed his con-torted clowning.

Mid-week tea-dance weddings in London were celebrated at Gunters off Park Lane or at the Grosvenor House Hotel, a few blocks away. In those classy places, humble origins could easily be lost. Women in cocktail dresses and ever more glorious hats, and men in lounge suits swiftly de-*Stetled* themselves, and it was good business for attending trades. A good few decades later, couples partnered rather than married; the weddings solemnized in our progressive synagogue in recent times can be counted on one hand.

In summer, the window in Father's workroom was a blessing: urine odours were dispersed. But other perils loomed. 'Lifting this iron will give me a heart attack one day!' Father said, after having pressed down its weight on the wet cloth over a lapel, and one day (not a Sabbath) he passed out while pressing a suit. He was rushed off in an ambulance to Hackney Hospital, Mother told me on the phone. I suspect she just opened the shop door and shouted, 'Help!' They were not on the phone; the call for the ambulance was probably made from the shop next door.

Again my appointments had to be booked over to an already busy stylist... not always agreeable. When I got to the ward, I was told that Father had discharged himself, 'Done a bunk' a nurse said, and then, more feelingly, she added, 'Sorry you came such a long way.' 'Well, at least I know he's alive,' I said, venting my fury, 'Where the hell is he then?' The she smiled sympathetically. He was back at the shop of course. 'Why the blazes did I have to leave my work?' I screamed, rushing through the door. 'Be quiet!' he said, coming on with his mock anger, 'Is that how you speak to *e Fadder*?' I could cheerfully have done him an injury. Mother tried to placate us, but as always, after a few more rowdy exchanges she said what she always said when Father and I bickered, '*Cheita troika!*' (They're off!)

Relieved he was alive, I hopped onto the worktable, my hands under my thighs, legs dangling, and asked, 'So *noo*, so what happened?' Father was only too ready to tell, 'From the ambulance I was taken to a bed, and a few minutes later, a doctor and nurse came to see me. Standing at the bottom of the bed, the doctor asked: do you feel giddy? Does your left arm hurt? Do you feel numb anywhere? And between his questions, he was poking me all over and listening to my heart through a tube, and finished with his poking, the nurse wrote down what he said on a board in her hand, and then, looking at each other, and back at me, the doctor said to the nurse, "I tink it must be visalogical," (Father's pronunciation). What? I thought, I'm not stayink here – and, closing my eyes, I pretended to be asleep. The doctor and the nurse gone, and everybody busy in the ward, I took my clothes from the bedside cupboard and went to the lavatory to dress. Opening the door a notch, I waited. When I no longer heard any footsteps, I ran down the corridor and down the stairs and out of the hospital. Clever, eh?' Puzzled, I asked, 'But, why did you have to run away?' 'Ha, you think you're clever! They thought I was *meshugge*. And if you think I was going to stay there and be locked up in a madhouse, *you* must be *meschugge*!' On the bus back to work, I sighed. Whatever next?

On a more serious level, my mother's illness played up ever more frequently, and as a consequence, she became an unreliable mother for Jeffrey. Cousin Rene (Sally and Jack's daughter) and her husband Julian were happy to have him stay until Mother got her strength back. Jeffrey stayed with them for a whole year; it was perfect for Jeffrey to have Rene and Julian's care and attention. Their daughter Ruth, the same age as he, was his surrogate sister. Both went to Moss Hall School in rural East Finchley where pink almond trees lined the streets. Jeffrey thrived in speech and education. Rene, a fervent advocate of speaking good, plain English – she too had a 'Miss Page' in her life, she once told me – was keen that Jeffrey's cockney accent should go the way hers had. Jeffrey, now part of their family, went everywhere with them: museums, day-trips, and holidays to Westgate. Not long ago, he told me that his stay with them had been the best thing in his life, and that at a time when Rene and Julian didn't have money to spare.

Harry and Norma had moved to Liverpool, Norma's hometown, but when they were still in London, their son David, about three years old, had bad stomach pains. The doctor said it was cramp. When Norma insisted that more must be wrong than cramp, the doctor called her an over-anxious mother. In Liverpool, David nearly died from these 'cramps'. Appendicitis was diagnosed, but when he was opened up it turned out to be a twisted gut. A more experienced surgeon and more sophisticated equipment were needed. The doctor doing the operation told Harry and Norma that David's life 'was hanging by a thread'. During the operation his temperature dropped so alarmingly, that hot water bottles filled with boiling water were put against his legs to find a vein to inject, which resulted in him having some nasty burns. 'Help them,' Mother said, wringing her hands, 'You have more than them.' Putting aside our fights, I rushed up to Liverpool.

Harry and Norma lived in a gloomy house in Ashton. A dim, naked light bulb lit their living room. Clearly, Mother was right; they needed and so I offered. Harry was astute and knew where my mission of duty came from. 'And what makes *you* so magnanimous?' he asked. I puzzled over the word 'magnanimous'. I had heard it before but never in that tone.

On the train back to London, David was on my mind: his bandaged legs, his tears, the bleak unfriendly ward with its high ceiling and tall windows, the acres of green linoleum with walls to match. And the icy blast of my brother's feeling coming at me.

It was up to me, it seemed, to make good all that had been lost in migration. My parents had never settled anywhere long enough between the two world wars to save the money to be traditional parents, giving to children on prescribed occasions like births, coming of age, weddings, and when grandchildren were born. Their life up to now had been lived on the hoof. When I had saved up to pay for my wedding, my father talked as though *he* had. Proudly, he declared that he had managed to fulfil his duty as a father. It was more important at the time to preserve his status than make a point about mine. With hindsight, I am glad my head wasn't full of feminist ideas, which would have been a hindrance in our situation. My parents left their parents with nothing more than blessings, but on their way forward, guilt was firmly tucked into our lives.

When family tempers settled, my parents, Jeffrey, Evansky and I, went to Liverpool for Passover in our 'banger'. Harry and Norma now lived in a rented house with a garden. At the end of the *Seder*, Father fainted again. A heart attack, we thought. Harry opened his collar and tie and took off his shoes, while I stared at Father in disbelief. When the doctor came, he gave him a cardiogram. Tearing off the sheet of paper from the machine he said, 'Your father hasn't had a heart attack, he has a hiatus hernia which can mimic a heart attack. But he should avoid sitting low, especially when eating – and having a bit of a 'pot' doesn't help.' Father had indeed been sitting low on a couch; there were chairs enough for three, but not for seven.

When Father realized he wasn't going to die in the next five minutes, he acted very ill indeed. Closing his eyes, he spoke in whispers: could he have a pillow to go under his head? When the doctor asked his age, and we, thinking he was too ill to speak, answered for him, guessing 'seventy', Father slowly rolled back his lids and whispered, 'No… no, Doctor, I em sixte nine!' The effort of authenticating his age seemed to have tired him out, and he closed his eyes even more slowly than he had opened them.

We seemed to be back on track as a family, appreciating and responding to Father's antics as we drove back to London. He was crammed into the back seat with his knees up to his chin with Mother and Jeffrey squashed in beside him. Evansky sat in the front, with me driving – good practice before my test. A full car added to our difficulties; the shock absorbers were clapped out, and so it was a bumpy ride. Outside Luton there was a traffic tail-back a mile long, and Father, threatening to faint again, asked, 'When will you get a more comfortable car?' Mother, dismayed by her husband's tactlessness said, 'Max, why are you never satisfied?' So everything was as it always was in our family: Mother curbing Father's demands. As respectfully as I could, I told him to stop grumbling. Now no longer centre stage, he said, 'To a *fadder* you talk like this?' Laughing, he knocked down the status he had just given himself. Soon after Father's fainting spell, Harry and Norma moved back to London for better job opportunities.

In the late 1940s, Mother's kidneys played up again, but this time she didn't get better. The NHS, now fully operational, took charge of her. At last, her panel doctor (GP) referred her to see Professor Bell at the London Hospital in Whitechapel Road. 'Why hasn't your mother had a urine test?' he asked, looking down at the doctor's letter. 'I don't know!' I said. Further tests were made. When mother and I came back for the results, she was kept in the hospital. 'If I don't operate straight away, your mother will die!' Professor Bell said bluntly.

'Ring in the afternoon,' the sister said. I phoned at regular intervals, ignoring the stipulated time, and got the reply: 'She's not up from the theatre yet. Ring again in an hour's time.' Ignorant of all things medical, I equated length of time taken over an operation with death. The hour was long. 'Yes, your mother is doing fine; her kidney has been successfully removed. You can visit tomorrow,' they said. Her kidney removed? I was in shock.

Mother's bed was at the end of a long ward. She looked peaceful enough. After a few days, I brought her boiled fruit in a jam jar. I fed her and she swallowed each spoonful, mashing the fruit with her gums; her teeth were in a bowl on the bedside table as usual. When she had had enough, she picked up my hand and held it against her cheek, murmuring, 'Uhele...'

The kidney was 'in tatters', the nurse told me. The stone was disentangled from the kidney and given to Mother as a memento. She kept it in a jam jar on the mantel for ages. Jeffrey told me recently that it ended up in a kitchen drawer: 'Every time I opened the drawer, the stone was there, like a root of a plant with the feathery ends cut off.' Seeing my mother on a post-operative visit, Professor Bell said, 'The stone had almost gone through the wall of the kidney. We operated just in time.'

In appreciation for saving my mother's life, I bought Professor Bell a cashmere scarf from Jaeger in Regent Street. 'How kind of you, thank you so much,' he wrote back. I was overcome by his reply. All the unexplored feelings for my mother, feelings I couldn't name, went into the giving of that scarf. What if she had died? With her living on, I could at least go over our life together, perhaps to understand more.

When a place was free, Mother was to go to Walton-on-the-Naze to convalesce. Meanwhile, Aunt Rosie looked after her, giving the scar more of a chance to heal. It was the shape of a hockey stick, from her back to the front, about twelve inches long.

Mother came back from her convalescence a changed woman. 'I have never enjoyed myself so much in my life!' she said, laughing out loud. Her system no longer toxic, her cheeks were rosy again. Like a pearl in an oyster, her stone must have started to grow in 1936 when we were still in Ludwigshafen and she had been taken to hospital, delirious. Medical records from Germany would have helped had there been any, so oral history had to do. Perhaps she couldn't explain with the little English she had, not knowing the word for 'kidney' in English. Mother was of the generation who thought doctors knew best or were even mind readers. She had nothing to contribute –

and for that matter, neither had I. It seemed as though our whole family was tarred with ignorance.

The Fifties flattened the drab Forties and, disappointingly for me, we were still in Hendon. Despite my discontent, Tudor Rose was reasonably successful, and in a bumbling, self-gratifying kind of way, I sent my mother to see her sisters in America, to Reisle in Chicago, and Blooma in New York. There were as many Bloomas then in Jewish families as there are daisies on a lawn. The sisters hadn't seen each other for forty years. When my mother met Reisle, she told me that they were strangers.

I guessed this might have had something to do with Aunt Reisle's son Alan who had come to see us during the war. My parents were then living in Bethnal Green in one of the many streets with identical houses where only the workshops across the top floors were light and airy. Alan must have been disappointed when he saw where his Aunt and Uncle lived. I happened to be with my parents that day. Opening the door to him, I was only too aware of what Alan saw: an unrelieved darkness in the corridor which only lifted slightly at the threshold of the kitchen. The smell of potato peelings boiling away on the stove for the chickens Father kept pervaded the house; a whiff of it surely must have reached Alan's nostrils. To add to all that Mother was ill with one of her kidney attacks; the skin under her eyes was black as soot, a constant symptom of her illness. We were barely sociable, but there Alan stood, leaning against the door frame of my parents' house, looking like my brother Harry's twin, short in stature like him too. So that was the short gene in the family Mother often joked about. Her father was short and so were her brothers who she, small herself, described as being less than five feet tall. Ironically, her sisters were tall.

Sadly, Alan never made contact again. Perhaps he was killed in France. Perhaps he imagined he would show us off to his buddies: 'Come, meet my family', that sort of thing. I had been too dumb even to ask where he was billeted; but then he wasn't at the ready with pen and paper either. It would have been worse if I'd asked him in and he'd excused himself, 'Sorry, I can't, I have to be…'. Alan appeared and then disappeared, without me having felt anywhere near close to him. For me, our relations lived like characters in books, remembered periodically.

Alan's family likeness was striking. Looking at my grandparents' photographs, I used to wonder what my grandmothers, wearing wigs, and my grandfathers with their long white beards, could possibly have to do with me. Years later, looking more intently at a drawing of my paternal grandfather, I could see myself in several of his features: his mouth, his almond-shaped eyes and, particularly, his lips. The drawing we had of him was copied from a picture taken at his wife's grave, covered with snow. In another picture, my mother's sisters Blooma and Chana were wrapped in black shrouds like Arab women; they leaned against their mother's gravestone, expressions appropriately plaintive. The round picture of their mother on the gravestone surprised me: I didn't think images were allowed in Jewish tradition, though I was glad that this one existed because it showed me who my mother looked like.

The only image I have ever seen of my father's mother is in a faded sepia picture of the English side of our family: a podgy woman, no longer young, and worn out from having had many children, I heard later. 'Fourteen she had,' my father told me, and seeing me taken aback, he quickly added, 'but not all survived.' I want images as seen on the walls of grand houses of the aristocracy. I want to stroll through corridors, as I imagine they do, feeling secure in what had been passed on, even to their black sheep.

In America, my mother had her first glaucoma attack. An immediate operation was needed to save her sight; the damage to her eye could be irreversible, she was told. Unfortunately, the doctor wouldn't do the operation until I'd sent the money. It took three days to get there, and by then it was too late for the operation to be successful. 'Worst of all,' Mother said, 'was the doctor asking me if I had the money before he injected me.'

Back in England, I took her to the eye hospital at Elephant and Castle, the only building left standing in the middle of a cleared bombsite. Several visits and many hours of waiting later, Mother's eyes were tested by thin red lines that hopped about darkened rooms. In the end, nothing helped; she went blind in that eye. My treat had gone horribly wrong.

The discovery of my mother's half-brothers and sisters in New York was a complete surprise. I had never heard them mentioned before. She said that meeting them in New York reminded her of sitting on their knees as a child, a welcome image for me of my mother's childhood. My now fifty-five-year-old mother's face lit up and it gave me a glimpse of the little girl she had once been, pampered by her older half-brothers. What did my grandfather's first wife look like? Why had I never heard about my half-uncles? Why the silence? Having been with Reisle, Mother showed no joy, no memories, no jubilation. Reisle was the oldest of her sisters, and one of the first to leave Poland. Her daughter wrote us that Reisle had died soon after my mother's visit. Then contact between us stopped.

PART THREE

Chapter Twenty-Three

Up West Again

Seven years in the Hendon shop had been enough; high time to look for premises in the West End. Happily, a man I thought was insane offered us three thousand pounds for the lease and goodwill of *Tudor Rose*, if and when we were ready to sell. He had heard it was a good business; whoever told him that must have been mad too. Sadly, everybody in the neighbourhood knew that it was me the clients waited for. The staff I trained took some of the strain but no one wanted Evansky to do their hair. I worried that the buyer might not get a good deal as it was me who had set the standard for the shop. I believed that if the buyer didn't keep it up, the shop would be more or less worthless. I was wrong. So what! My standard, his standard, the buyer paid eagerly.

In 1953, we found a shop in North Audley Street. The owner had been a Monsieur Jadot. His lease had come to an end, and so had the style of his shop, a relic of the past. His window-dressing consisted of faded baby blue and pink hairnets, diagonally draped across like fishing nets. On the faded green fascia was written Harmless Permanent Waving, the paintwork so distressed, it could not even be taken seriously as retro.

Servanti, the shop fitters for hairdressers at that time, broke up the cubicles like firewood, and in no time a crystal chandelier hung in the reception area, and flock wallpaper on the walls gave the décor an air of grandeur. Gossip about my new whereabouts travelled fast, and clients who had claimed that Raymond 'usually did their hair' came, looked and booked appointments at once. Looking up at the crystal chandelier they practically swooned: 'Why didn't you tell me you were going up West?' Amazing what a crystal chandelier can do for your reputation. Now I was 'somebody', they implied. I wasn't taken in; I didn't even like the chandelier, or any chandeliers for that matter. To keep them sparkling was labour-intensive. Why have something which needs an army of deft hands to polish and dust?

What mattered most to me was to be in Mayfair, that important square mile which counted in those days. Still better would have been the south end of Grosvenor Square; I fretted that 17 North Audley Street was too near Oxford Street. The good thing was that North Audley Street was less claustrophobic, less suburban. Whichever end of Grosvenor Square I was, I imagined clients coming from different districts and from abroad. In the Fifties the field was wide open for development – lots of scope, lots of fun and lots of worry.

Fashion editors were constantly looking for new names in the fashion trade; hairdressers were included in that search, and, surprisingly to me, the name Evansky now circulated regularly in magazines and newspapers. When I asked a new client who had recommended her, as I had done in Hendon, she said, 'Come on, Rose, you're in all the magazines!' My naiveté embarrassed me, a sophisticated question it was not! I learned to keep my mouth shut and enjoy my new status in the trade. As in Hendon, I trained my own staff, but this time round I hoped Evansky would stick to running the business. The more progressive I was, the more he regressed. His big idea was to bring back Marcel Waving, something he'd learned in the Morris School of Hairdressing before the war. Despite Monsieur Jadot's decor having been laid to rest, his ghost flitted about brandishing hot curling irons.

As in Hendon, clients called Evansky 'Mr Rose' – degrading for both of us. Staff noticed the discord between us, which made getting new staff more difficult. A buzz went round the trade, 'they're always quarrelling'. This wasn't strictly true, though tension did exist, mostly through our efforts to keep what was going on secret. The male stylist who brought this 'good news' was bonding with Evansky; I was a woman, to be needled, and not to be taught by. When I'd had enough of his gossip-mongering, I snapped, 'Stop playing games, I'm not your mother!' He laughed, recognizing a truth, and having cleared the air, made teaching him easier. But then he flirted with me instead. The gossip about us was unsettling.

'You have everything,' clients cooed. Everything? Evansky was stroppy when fashion editors added Rose to Evansky in editorials. Screaming at me, he said. 'I am not 'aving it, the name of the shop is Evansky, get it?' Feebly, I defended myself: 'What do you mean you're not having it? Don't you think editors know who does the photo shoots?' And on and on he insisted that his name should remain as singular as it was on the shop front. Despite his protestations, the name Rose Evansky was now regularly used in editorials.

Driving to work was at times hazardous: Evansky drove and I wailed. It was astonishing that he didn't crash the car. Two minutes away from my first appointment, I speculated whether the lights would stay red long enough for me to put on some make-up. Yes, I judged, and as the car idled beside Selfridges, I dabbed my eyes and applied some mascara, and then foraging for a lipstick in my make-up pouch, I chose the loud orange. A little rouge wouldn't be amiss either; a couple of daubs and I was ready. I was still feathering in the 'daubs' with my fingers when the car stopped outside the shop. With a couple of long strides I reached the shop door, and pushing it open with the flat of my hand, I hurried over the threshold, spreading my orange mouth into a smile.

Half an hour later, Evansky arrived back at the shop, thundering, 'Parking... it'll kill me!' and pausing for breath, he added, 'I don't know what you're going to do but I will be going by tube in future.' It was an empty threat; Evansky loved our new car. After that altercation (one of many) my work was charged with energy; I didn't understand how, or why. Scissors in hand, my aim was strong and decisive. A cut or two later, our wrangles were swept away with the hair.

Evansky and I finally gave up our flat in Finchley Court and moved to the West End, nearer to the shop. Now I really did have everything: a shop and a flat in the West End! And there I would sit in my new flat in New Cavendish Street, on my sofa pouring tea from a silver pot into Spode china, the illusion of riches given to me by Solly in appreciation for his half share in the business. I felt awkward with riches and having spent all the money I had earned on furnishing our flat, I thought myself more of an unfortunate than ever.

The shop opposite our flats sold medical aid equipment. A wheelchair in the window, its chrome wheels glittering under the lights against the backcloth – a deadly black stretched tight behind the chair – reflected me perfectly. At thirty-two, I saw myself eight years on and nearer the end of childbearing age. Would sex still be an issue between Evansky and me?

Meanwhile, we had our Ford Convertible, yellow with black trim, and with our parents now settled in their shop, I could at last have some fun, albeit with Evansky. But wherever we went with our new car, me, the 'dysfunctional woman', travelled with us. Whatever she wore and however she tried to smile her worries away, the more reality bit into her soul. She was the poor one, that sad female who would never grow a life inside her – a shade biblical, I thought much later in my life.

France was our destination. The hood was down and I was driving, a long, yellow scarf round my neck flapping like a flag in the gale. The sun was high. We were on a Route National flanked by trees, their shadows on the road giving the illusion of pools of water, and fast-running wheels imitating streams hurtling down mountains made the illusion complete. Nothing could spoil that illusion, but when a small open lorry eased itself out from a side road, illusion and despair mingled. Was this the way I could end the parody of the life I was living? With that thought in mind, my foot pressed down hard on the throttle and imagining myself dead I screeched to a halt swerving to the left, more like a choreographed dance than an accident – but an accident wasn't what I was looking for. Evansky, the lorry driver and I all got out onto the road. None of us was physically hurt. All that had happened was that the headlights were broken and the door had some scratches, though the door of the lorry had a good biff, dislocating the lock. Evansky negotiated with a garage mechanic nearby. 'The repairs will take four hours,' he said, opening and shutting his hand, flashing four fingers in quick succession. The lorry driver wasn't amused. He began to gesticulate wildly, and making sure I understood his displeasure, he sliced the air with his hand, his wrist flicking at top speed, and with his black eyebrows hopping up and down, he made his point. Looking from me to Evansky, his eyes finally rested on me, suggesting that if he had a say in the matter, he would have me certified. Coming closer still, he exhaled great gusts of breath heavy with garlic and expletives into my face. *Merdè* was the one word of French I understood. Then he turned round and walked away with great lumbering steps. Not a café anywhere; Evansky and I sat on the verge in silence when, finally he asked: 'What were you trying to do, kill us?'

Cannes was wonderful that year. I taught myself to swim in shallow water. I trusted no one to teach me. My reward – backache. Back from holiday, our routine was the same, and I laughed and chatted as always. Nothing was wrong.

Chapter Twenty-Four

The Final Treatment

1956

Three years later, one late Thursday afternoon, I was finishing my last client, advising her on the shape of her eyebrows. Turning her face away from my scrutiny, she said, 'Rose, I don't believe my hair, or the shape of my eyebrows, can possibly be any concern to you at this moment,' and touching my arm she asked, 'what is wrong?' My eyes filled with tears. The last touches done to her hair, I pulled back her chair, and she got up, walked the length of the salon and down the stairs to the cloakroom. When she came back up, dressed and ready by the street door, she looked back at me and waved her hand gently from side to side, level with her chest. Why was she frowning?

The next day, my busiest of the week, I couldn't get out of bed. Crying became the norm for a week. Sleep came in snatches. Crying and blowing my nose was all I could do. I don't know how many boxes of tissues I used. Evansky stood at the bottom of my bed looking at me, just looking. Had he asked why I was crying, I wouldn't have been able to tell him exactly, except that I had a pressing wish for him to share 'my problem'. I might even have fallen into his arms in gratitude. Then, suddenly, the rush to plead and to please was at an end.

'What can I do? She won't get out of bed,' I heard Evansky say. I guessed he was on the phone to his brother-in-law, the doctor whose advice was always sought in a family crisis. Hearing nothing else from Evansky, I knew he was listening hard. Back at the foot of my bed, he said, 'Daniel has suggested a new psychiatrist, a Doctor Benine, who is a consultant at Colney Hatch, the mental hospital your mother was in.'

Stunned, I suddenly realised that I had completely forgotten that episode in our lives. 'But they did terrible things to her – shock treatments,' I mumbled, 'after them she was like a zombie, staring into space. Is that what Daniel wants for me? I won't go, tell him I won't go!' and with all the strength I could gather, I gripped the duvet as if it were an iron bar, screaming, 'No, never!'

When Daniel promised that I wouldn't necessarily have to have shock treatments, I agreed to go. I was to be treated in a large Victorian house run by nuns, across the garden from the main hospital. We were in BUPA at that time. I disliked every aspect of this set-up.

Once I was settled in my room, Dr Benine breezed in, stopped beside my bedside and, opening a folder, he said, 'You are having a nervous break-down, and my treatment for you will be drugs and bed rest.' A week later, I could hardly get out of bed, and going to the lavatory I walked like a frail old woman, holding on to furniture for support. Four weeks on, I could barely stand up. Cleaning my teeth I looked in the mirror above the basin and saw the drugs had done their job. My eyes reflected a less anxious, a less alive, version of me – and, I felt, a less important one.

Visitors came and went. Connie, a journalist who had become a client and a friend, brought me several books, among them *The Second Sex* by Simone de Beauvoir; she clearly thought it would help me. I really tried reading that book, the word 'second' sort of illuminated something for me, but try as I might I couldn't push past the drugs, only snatched meanings here and there. On his next round, Dr Benine looked at the books on my bedside table for a long minute before giving his opinion of me: 'I hope you know that you are not a genius,' and pausing a moment or two, he went in for the kill, 'instead of reading, it would be better if you concentrated on being a proper wife.' Any faint understanding I may have gleaned from

The Second Sex was demolished by the two words 'proper wife'. Many days passed, blank and white. My mouth felt dry but my body was damp and clammy.

Six weeks later, I woke up one morning knowing that I wasn't having a breakdown at all; I was trying to break out! Who could I trust to help me escape? My journalist friend Connie was a possibility. The first time we met, she was in search of a story. Her story about me described how I derided her hairstyle and then illustrated how she could look less like a peasant with her long hair screwed up inelegantly into a bun; that is how we became friends. The other memorable visitor was my brother Harry. The rest were polite; some understood and some didn't. To most, I was having a straightforward breakdown, their parting words to me: 'Give yourself time.' I was upset that they agreed with Dr Benine. I didn't think I was ill, only tired of feeling tired and sure that what was happening to me was my own fault. Evansky added to that feeling by telling me about someone's suggestion that he should 'tie you to the bed and make you submit!' 'Who told you to do this to me?' 'Your brother,' Evansky said, with a smile of pleasure. When Harry visited me, I ignored what I'd been told and held onto the Heinie I had loved so much: the vulnerable, affectionate, ten-year-old Heinie running home from school after Kristallnacht. Again I asked, 'Tell me what happened on that day you came home from school. Had Father already been taken away? Did the Catholic sisters come for you? Did you go up to them? Did you see men demolishing our furniture? Did you hear them? Did they tell you to leave the flat?' Harry's answer was the same as then. 'I don't remember,' he said, tears in his eyes.

If Evansky was right, Harry, the married man, had some accumulated frustrations of his own – was that why Evansky had such a pleasurably smile on his face? Was there more to Harry's tears than our Nazi past? If only we had more time together, we could let go of our hurt and chase the mischief from our souls.

After Harry left, Dr Benine visited. Seeing my red-rimmed eyes, he said to the nun, 'Give her a double dose of medication, she's too agitated,' but then, so was he, hurrying from the room. Alone with the nun, I begged her, 'Please, please, no more pills…' 'Doctor's orders,' she said. At dusk she came back with my pills in a small plastic tumbler. 'Take them now while I am here,' she said. When I had, she left, her habit swaying from the draught made by the door.

Full of drugs, I hung onto the idea of my 'break-out'. 'Doctor Benine, you won't get the better of me,' said a quiet voice among my shambolic thoughts. Whatever mood I was in, it was never to Dr Benine's liking. On another visit, he sidled up to my bed and, looking past me, fixed his eyes on the books stacked on my bedside table, his head slightly raised, his eyes hooded. His look lingered above the reading light, and turning towards me again, he fixed his gaze somewhere between my eyebrows and hairline, and said, 'You have lived without a proper sex-life for many years now, and since you're not able to change, why not try oral sex?' What was oral sex?

I watched Dr Benine leave my room, his arms hanging limp by his body. I seemed to have annoyed him; was pleasing Dr Benine part of my cure? What was I being cured of? Did my resolve not to please anybody loosen its grip? Outside my window trees did what they always did in spring…and back I was to my fragile hopes: could I be new?

Later that evening, the nun bringing my pills said, 'You're going home tomorrow, Doctor Benine is finished with you.' 'Finished' sounded like a judgement, but how glad I was not to have see him again.

In the morning, I was sitting on my bed half-dressed, staring out of the window at nothing in particular when the door of my room swung open. I turned round to see who it was. Dr Benine came in and stood over me. 'I have come to say good-bye,' he said, light-heartedly. I looked up at him, suddenly abject with misery again, my 'fragile' hopes crushed. I lost concentration. Just dressing was an effort. Dr Benine's hand was in his jacket pocket. Something clinked. 'There,' he said, taking out a handful of cone-shaped glass rods from his pocket, 'try inserting these, a different size every day, until you get the hang of it.' In my hand, they felt cold and heavy; nine-tenths was transparent, the rest was crudely finished at what I guessed was the gripping end.

At home, I moped, thinking about what I had to do. The rods were in the drawer of my bedside table, waiting. Two days passed. Nothing. On the third day, I attempted to do as I'd been told. My hands were shaking as I tried to push the rods inside me. Soaked through with sweat, I burst into tears, as one by one these substitutes rolled together into the indent my body made on the mattress. The shame of it all! The following day, I put them into a brown paper bag and into the dustbin.

Though now less burdened, I still jumped every time the doorbell rang. In this state, Evansky persuaded me to let him take me for a night out to the Pigalle in Piccadilly. He invited the staff we still had, to extract any solidarity they might feel for us. What I saw were their pitying smiles and fake sincerity. I knew with clarity that they saw me as a lame duck, and soon these 'leftovers' would leave too. The one thing on my mind was all the money this was costing. Evansky admitted, 'Business isn't good.' That was depressing enough, but when he added, 'No one is busy!' This reminded me of what second rate tradesmen always say.

At the Pigalle, Sammy Davis Junior's performance was noisy and magnificent. His energy was too much for me and when he tap-danced across the stage and sang in the moments he stood still, the band full and rich with brass sounds, I thought my head would burst. 'Please take me home,' I whimpered, wiping the sweat from my upper lip.

On the way out, I saw myself in a mirror: slow faltering steps,

Evansky's arm under mine, his brow drawn and lined. I was sorry for him. What more could he do? Our reflections in the mirror showed the result of eighteen years of wasted efforts: me – the sexual cripple and Evansky – the long-suffering man. I already knew what the staff would do. I would have to start from scratch, teaching new staff. Advertising for stylists in the trade journal was shaming; the best salons attracted staff, considering themselves fortunate to be in a teaching salon.

In the following weeks, I dredged up some more sense. Pills. I must stop taking pills, and then, one day, I did. Even after just a few days without them, I felt stronger. Dr Benine, I thought, I must tackle him. I phoned his rooms and arranged a home visit. My heart was in my mouth as I talked to the receptionist, and when I'd made the appointment I banged down the receiver. That decisive move made me shake uncontrollably. Would he want his rods back? Surely they were not manufactured for me alone? Were there other women like me? Where could I find them, talk to them?

Up to the moment the bell rang, I had no idea what I would say to Dr Benine. Words were jumbled up in my head, bumping into one another. Opening the door to him, my hands trembled. Sheepishly, he walked past me. I felt as if my chest was held together with metal bands. I sat down but I can't remember asking Dr Benine to take a seat. My heart pounded as I looked up at this six-foot-something man and said, 'I have stopped taking your medication and I have thrown away your rods, and I am feeling better because of it.' Then taking in more breath, I continued, 'All I need now is some sleeping pills, and I will do the rest.' No sooner were the words out of my mouth, I questioned what I had said. 'I will do the rest' sounded as if I knew what that meant. Taking my next breath was difficult enough, and holding on to my stomach with both hands, I watched Dr Benine writing out my prescription. When he gave it to me, his hands were trembling. I could barely say 'thank you', but amazingly I was able to say, 'I won't be needing your services any longer,' followed by 'please, will you send your bill straight away.' The words had fled from my lips before I could stop them. Dr Benine fumbled with the lock of his brief-case, and as he was about to leave I said, my hands still clutch-ing my stomach, 'Please, will you see yourself out?' The front door shut. It was done. I had spoken up for myself. I had dared to see my opponent vulnerable and exposed.

Evansky had waited to see results from my treatment. Meanwhile, he told me as often as he could that there was nothing wrong with him, and the more he said so, the more I began to realize that there was nothing wrong with me either. Why was Evansky so determined to prolong our marriage? That was the moment I began to think of leaving him. No more lies, no more evasions. Detonate them, blow them out of my life! Wouldn't it be wonderful not to feel guilty anymore for making Rachel's son 'ill'?

Alone, I could indulge in self-pity, even shout out loud and squawk like a wild bird, arms flapping. If I left Evansky, I'd be lonely. But I was lonely here with him. As if written for me on a clean sheet of paper, I 'read': Stop dragging guilt and fear from one day to the next! To be really alone would be a lesser torment. I compared 'loneliness' with 'solitude' in the diction-ary; not much difference between them, though I judged soli-tude to be less severe, less pathetic, a cleaner ache; it had a more independent feel to it.

As I let go, I knew that Evansky was hanging on to threads. Did he think we were still bound together and what was going on between us was just a bad patch? Incredibly, he planned another outing.

This time, he booked a table at the Colony on Berkeley Square. 'Just the two of us,' he said. Was my hell his heaven, I wondered? I didn't yet have enough stamina to decide which one of us was the most wronged. Let the last eighteen years all be my fault, I sometimes thought. Then an entirely new thought occurred: freedom. I reminded myself that my new thoughts were private and not a matter for debate with Evansky. I'll cope with this, I'll pretend, I'll manage, I'll… and then it was too late to change my mind. Evansky would be disappointed, he meant well, but when I saw his brown eyes smile with pleasure, I knew I had slipped back into a morass of sentimentality. We dressed to go out, Evansky spruced up with black bow tie and I was in the same dress I'd worn on the last outing. Evansky was in buoyant mood. It was not contagious. My dress floated behind me as I followed the headwaiter to our table. Evansky was busy negotiating. 'The best,' he said to the waiter, pressing a pound note into his hand. The waiter bowed and said, 'Yes, Sir.' Where is the money to pay for this? I thought again. Business hadn't improved since we had been to the Pigalle. I was worried sick about money. Where did it come from – and worse, did we live in debt?

The band struck up. Evansky stretched his arms forward, levered me up from my chair, and with his hand under my elbow, he led me to the napkin-sized dance floor. My legs were inflexible. He pushed me back and forth, navigating for a space among the other dancers. I saw us in the mirrored wall: my face was awash with eye-black from crying, and Evansky, lithe and thin, had acquired the hunch-backed look of Groucho Marx – only the cigar was missing. Each time we passed the bandstand, the conductor's eyebrows were raised, his baton flew about in masterly rhythm, and my tears fell on Evansky's suit and, back at the table, onto the food, on the way home onto my dress, and in bed onto my pillow. In between sobs, my nose needed attention – blow, blow, blow. I had now been off work for close on a year. The shop's takings were bad, and as I feared, more staff left, and so did many clients. How would we live? How would we pay the rent?

It took another year before I left Evansky. Who had been

waiting for whom? Had I hoped Evansky would leave me considering the rough time I gave him? Had I not made the move,
he would have let us go on the way we were forever. Sad to
say, I felt that he saw me as his insurance policy, and I saw him
as a porter minding the shop, even when any man would have
done.

Throughout this difficult time my mother had come every
day after lunch to watch over me when I rested and read, or
nodded off. She sat next to the sofa on an upright chair, knitting, the way it sometimes was when I was a child, a feeling so
deep and safe, her presence so still, I knew she knew how to
let me be.

One Saturday afternoon, she was with me when I tried to
force feed Evansky with Erich Fromm, whose books I had
been reading, hoping to share with him things I barely understood myself – modern commerce, its immensity in contrast
to a small shopkeeper, its effect on people. Fromm imagined
for us what we might feel when we walk through large stores,
how small, how overwhelmed we might be by their size. This
was exactly how I felt, overwhelmed. And I remembered reading in the Bible about 'Men of great stature... giants,' that 'the
children of Israel looking up at them and saw themselves as
grasshoppers before them...' (Numbers 13:33). Was this what
Fromm meant? I wanted Evansky to work with me, think with
me. 'Do you ever feel like that?' I asked him. Every page in
Fromm's book had question and exclamation marks in the
margins; strong feelings bumping into words whose meaning
I only sensed. Yet I felt them clustering together in my head,
jostling each other like children wanting attention. The drugs
hadn't quite left my system; I had to take deep breaths to
recharge. 'Do you know what I am trying to say?' I repeated.
Evansky glowered at me. I knew that look, and knew only too
well the sight of his elongated body in the armchair, legs
stretched out stiff, heels digging into to the carpet, the soles of

his shoes on view, one hand in his trouser pocket and the elbow of his other arm resting on the chair, three fingers depressing his cheek to support his head. He almost nodded off while I was talking. Then suddenly he wriggled in the chair, turned back the cuff of his shirt, looked at his watch, and, like a cuckoo from a clock, he leapt up, leaving me in mid-sentence. 'Kick-off!' he cried. The front door shuddered.

My mother put her knitting on her lap. 'What you want, *mein Kind*, you will never have with this man, er paßt dir nicht.' 'He doesn't fit you' – these were momentous words from my mother at a time when divorce still stained family reputations. My mother made me think that she wouldn't mind at all if I left Evansky. Her insight gave me the courage to go forward. My thoughts galloped. This marriage wasn't any longer about sex alone. Why then should I serve myself up on a silver platter for him, when he can't, or outright won't, engage with me on another level? 'Let's learn together' was my constant wish. I had spent years waiting for him to ask me something other than 'Where are my socks?'

Before Dr Benine, I had wondered how I could view myself positively. Face-lift? No. Go on a holiday alone? No. A lover? What would I do with him? Then unexpectedly something harmless happened. I was having a schmooze with a client, when, cutting across what we were talking about, she gave me a long look in the mirror. 'Guess what, Rose? I have just had my portrait painted: a great experience and great fun. Go on, Rose, you try it!' I picked up on her excitement, and, my gaze meeting hers in the mirror, I saw that the glint in her eye was not just the thrill of vanity. I suspected that more went on in that studio than painting! How would I know about this 'more'?

Putting suspicion aside, I booked a sitting. I had no glint in my eye; the painter lay bare what he thought I wanted to see: a vapid, smooth expressionless face more appropriate for the current static cosmetic advertisements: lips in a pout – fuller than mine really were - and my hair sculpted like women who shopped at Dickens and Jones.

Evansky and I once met the painter. For the life of me, I don't remember his name – but he knew his business. Without my knowledge, seemingly dissatisfied with what he had done, he did another painting of me with Evansky. 'Come and see,' he said on the phone. The painter was right twice. The first time, he painted what he thought I wanted to see, but the second time he painted what he really saw: a young man and a young woman, on a blue-black background, next to each other, looking out into the world, fearful and apprehensive, fugitives bundled up in shapeless clothes, their body shapes outlined in thick blue-black strokes. The woman, much smaller than the man, clasped his arm, an anxious frown on her brow. The man was tall and lanky, wearing a trilby hat shading his nose. Electric! It was Avrum and me! As far as I know, I hadn't told him anything. Perhaps the sitting had been like women having their hair done; they talk, hardly knowing they do. The stuff I know about women's lives… I'd give anything to see the 'blue painting' again, perhaps to measure how far I've come.

Where was I to find the girl in the blue painting? Certainly not by making an appointment with a plastic surgeon, yet that is what I did. A little ashamed, I kept the date and hour in my head. Nobody would know but me. I got his telephone number from his wife, a client of mine, pretending it was for someone else. The surgeon welcomed me as though I were still a force to be reckoned with: 'So this is Rose Evansky!' Niceties over, he scrutinized my face. Then, kneading my neck and shoulders like dough, he said, 'There is still a lot of bounce in your skin, nothing to pull up here. Think about why you want it done.'

I left his consulting room thinking about my lack of bounce, emotionally. Walking down Welbeck Street, my supposed frigidity came to mind. I stopped in the middle of the pavement and looked down at my feet, and by extension, back at my life: Avrum presented himself and finally it dawned on me that it was he who had blighted Evansky's sex-life. I had to think about this.

Chapter Twenty-Five

Nothing Familiar

Connie and I now being close friends, a new world opened up to me, one different from my limited certainties of 'right and wrong' which she considered to be guilt trips. Philosophers were Connie's passion; she loved their reasoning that was the death knell of all I was brought up to believe. Don't think, do! Until that moment, my mind-set was plain and simple. I could recognize rights and wrongs by the way I felt; a structure that had been hammered into me so deftly that to mess with it sent my guts into revolt. Yet I ventured to say, 'Wrong-doing feels lousy, and good feels comfortable.' I didn't yet have adequate words for my feelings; no wonder Connie frowned. 'Darling, what can this possibly mean?' she said to most of what I said. I felt self-conscious with my simple way of thinking. But curiosity held me captive.

'I am a twentieth century woman,' Connie announced one day to a room full of people. But what I saw was a high-wire performer working without a safety net, swinging from one emotional disaster to another and, in free-fall, she fretted about some man or other: would he, or would he not ring her, and if not, why not? Endless monologues with me not knowing how to advise her except for some common sense, 'You are a married women and you have three children, and so has the man you're involved with.' 'Oh that… darling, what has that got to do with it?' she said. Connie exposed my certainties as being too basic, while she with her theories, floated above a boiling cauldron about to receive third-degree burns at any moment. Most of what I said Connie rejected as 'Too much of Christian humility.' Knowing only Lenja's version of Christianity, I felt

I had a trinity of my own, vacillating between the Jewish God, Lenja's saviour and Connie's atheism. Feeling thoroughly uncomfortable with all of them, I put them aside as something to think about later, perhaps to understand more.

Connie lived in Blackheath, then a fashionable area of London to which the professional classes had flocked after the war. For such a sophisticated society, a lot of moaning went on about not being happy, and jealousy was not acknowledged as an important ingredient of being unhappy. 'What' said one of Connie's apostles 'is jealousy?' Most seemed to want freedom from restraint. And there was I still banging on about 'right and wrong'. 'You have a right to pursue happiness,' Connie said to me many times, but for me feeling comfortable with oneself was happiness. Those were the moments when you could think at leisure. I wasn't at all sure that I knew what I was saying, because things popped out accidentally without any thought. On the whole, I was an observer.

At the end of a party held by a politician who lived next door to Connie, the eminent man pressed the only too willing Connie against a wall to pluck a goodnight kiss from her lips; an air kiss it was not. Shocked, I reminded myself of being in bed with Avrum and family, something that had happened against my will, but this evening, I was watching the wife of the politician watching her husband kissing Connie in a very public scene. What was I waiting for? The wife to storm out and make a scene? Was she resigned? Did he do this on a regular basis? Sometimes, when staying overnight with Connie, I heard the politician's wife call to her husband from their garden, 'Darling, come and look how beautiful the roses are this year.' I was captivated by the ease with which they could play the domestic game, with him nibbling at titbits outside their marriage.

I was now moving in a world where not only old-style morality was out of fashion; manners and modes of address were changing too. My staff stopped calling me Mrs Evansky and I became plain Rose. Breaking that convention was meant to grant me the privilege of being one of them.

When I told Connie my secrets, her advice was, 'Don't tell me any, you know I can't keep them,' and sure enough, she'd blurt out confidences not meant for other ears. I was about to be dragged away kicking and screaming from ghetto-thinking. Do anything, eat anything, say anything, be with anybody, change partners – indeed, have one for each day of the week! Would I, could I, do that?

In that newly minted morality, Connie tutored me: 'When an affair is over, a signal should be given, like tapping the side of your nose with your finger.' I listened attentively. As the Sixties left the Fifties behind, my association with Connie opened a future for me unprotected by marriage. Though it had been close to disastrous, it was my safety valve. When dangers loomed, I could preserve my dignity with 'I am a married woman!' Without this protection, I felt lost. The structure of misery had its uses – that is until my future arrived.

On a not very busy day, Connie came to the shop bringing glad tidings. 'Darling,' she said, 'I have arranged a dinner in Soho for you and me, my neighbour and his friend Cannan.' The neighbour was one of Connie's 'flirts'. Both men were married and had children, as of course did Connie – nine children in all. Were we playing at being an extended family living in an African village?

I was to appreciate Soho in ways I had not during the war; now there was haute cuisine among the sleaze. Cannan had suggested L'Escargot. We were early and the restaurant was not yet filled. We could have any table we wanted and chose a round table in a corner. Connie's 'flirt' looked across the table at me with his large, brown, hangdog eyes. He repeated these looks, now and then, as the evening developed. Looking at Cannan's hair, I remarked, 'What a bloody awful haircut you've got!' He snapped back, 'I've cut it myself with nail scissors.' 'It shows,' I replied. Worse, Cannan was eating snails! Faintly, a protest tapped my conscience: they're not kosher! Though no longer eating kosher myself, I always went back to the holy directive when judgements were needed. Snails were definitely out, even in someone else's mouth. Just their breath might contaminate me!

Cannan then turned back to Connie, picking up where they'd left off, tearing each other apart in argument. So stirred was Connie by the heat of the debate, she pulled out the white kid triangle from her jacket which had been covering her cleavage, and keeping it in her hand, she waved it about like a flag, quoting and fighting the battles for her cherished philosophers, a confection of pronouncements none of which, I sensed, had anything to do with what was really going on, but had everything to do with who would take whom to bed that night, and where: I knew my Connie. There was still time for me to make the excuse that I was tired and had to work next day, but like a dog following its master, I was held rapt by what was going on. I was spellbound.

The 'where' was Cannan's flat, bang in the middle of Curzon Street, rented for him by the film company he was working for at the time as a writer. No sooner was the front door shut behind us, Connie disappeared to another room with her 'flirt'. When had they arranged this? Moments later, through the partly open door I saw them on the floor, the very moment her 'flirt' was disentangling himself from her grasp and she was whispering, 'Do you love me?' Without replying, the 'flirt' stood up, threw on his jacket and rushed out of the flat. The door clicked to. Not knowing what to do, I went into the kitchen and consulted the plughole in the sink. Later, Connie told me what I already knew.

Cannan appeared not to have noticed what had been going on but composure had to be regained by us all. Connie and her 'flirt' weren't, after all, dogs doing things in the middle of a street. More to the point, I couldn't link her high-minded talk with the action on the ground.

Recovering her poise, Connie started to talk frenetically to Cannan as if what had just happened was no more momentous than clearing her throat. The agenda was to discuss the 'flirt's' marital situation, the coldness of his wife, her lousy cooking, her posh accent, the worry she had attached to an ordinary meal she had just cooked, anxiously asking the guests, 'Is it all right?' A genuine critique of the 'flirt's' marriage may well have been their aim but, as they chattered on my interest waned. I had heard it all before. Seasoned listeners though hairdressers are, by two-thirty in the morning I was beginning to feel the strain, and feeling uncomfortable, I undid my bra and slipped under the cover of the bed I had been lounging on. Cannan sat on my bed, and Connie sat on the bed opposite, a gangway between them, their arms taut and hands fig-leaved behind them, feet gesticulating on the carpet. I was floating off to sleep, their chatter growing more distant by the second, and thinking, 'Why don't you call a taxi and go home, Rose?' when suddenly Cannan bedded down next to me, saying, 'Move over.'

Connie was in a rage. She pushed the bed she was sitting on next to ours and said, 'Why can't we all sleep together?' at which Cannan pulled the blankets over us, whispering playfully, 'Let's keep her out.' Connie, of course, had told Cannan about my virginal state and, although I was shocked, it didn't surprise me that she had broken my confidence. Not knowing what else to say, I mumbled, 'Only cuddles.' Cannan complied.

In the morning, I was somewhat bewildered. Connie was prancing about nude in front of Cannan. I couldn't stop staring at her pert breasts, her proud upright posture as if directed by a sculptor. All I could see were the faint, pink scars running down from her nipples, the only justifiable cosmetic surgery she ever had. Connie was less than five feet tall and, until the surgery, she had huge breasts, which she practically had to carry about in her arms. That had been just the beginning: soon, addiction to plastic surgery followed.

Late for work, I left Cannan's flat in a rush. In the street, a cool wind blew about my head: something familiar at last. What would my father say? But more importantly, my shop was falling through the floorboards and we didn't have the money for repairs. In fact, it was beyond repair and needed more than patching.

A couple of weeks after my rite of passage, Cannan phoned me at the shop. 'There is a Mr Cannan on the phone for you,' our receptionist said. Her face flushed and with eyebrows raised, she handed me the phone. 'Hello, Cannan here, do you remember me?' 'Yes,' I said. I hadn't expected a follow-up. 'Could you meet me in Shepherd's Market for a drink?' 'Yes,' I said again without hesitation. Clients were coming and going, and the receptionist, nosy as hell, was listening hard, her ears on fire. At the pub I had my first Bloody Mary and probably my last – but not my last meeting with Cannan.

When we met, we talked marriages: how I had worked with Evansky for eighteen years of my life, my determination to free myself from Dr Benine, his ways of treating me, trying to cure me… I can't remember if I gave Cannan the details of my treatment; not quite sure whether I was ashamed for Dr Benine, or of myself. We talked endlessly about regrets, and how that I wanted to make a dent in the world and failed, and how we would heal ourselves, get over disappointments – and, of course, about Uncle Avrum, the reason I only wanted 'only cuddles'. Cannan listened with care. Talking about his marriage was more difficult. There were three children. Not quite the same situation as my shop, which could be closed down if needed.

During this time, Connie frequently came to the shop. On one occasion, she was wearing sunglasses. 'Why the dark glasses?' I asked, 'the sky's black.' But then so was Connie's eye. When she took off the glasses, she said, 'Look, darling,' lifting up her face the better for me to see, 'look what Jim has done!' 'Why did he do it?' I asked. Connie talked herself out of blame with a few rushed sentences while I thought, 'Oh God, he hasn't caught her in bed with his best friend, has he? Well, so far, so terrible.'

Connie had an affair with one of her husband's colleagues, virtually under Jim's nose. Jim guarded his honour, and his ownership, Sicilian-style, and if he hadn't, half of Fleet Street's journalists would be nursing black eyes. Matey with his colleagues, he wouldn't hit any of them, so blacking Connie's eye killed two birds with one stone: staying a regular chap, he rid himself of chauvinistic anger.

In our enlightened times, honour and possession still counted for Jim and, old-fashioned though he was, he coveted his neighbour's wife in broad daylight. Jim was wont to slipping out of his house and going next door to satisfy his natural impulses, and satisfied, he slipped back to his own house, so nonchalantly it seemed he had just gone out for a bottle of plonk. My father had a phrase for such goings on: 'You can't sit at two weddings with one behind.' And what about Connie? Free thinker though she thought she was, she still trembled at the thought of being found with a lover; 'Will you cover for me, darling, if Jimmy phones?' she would ask. I became her accomplice simply because I didn't know how to say no, or if indeed I should. Perhaps the life Connie lived was better. This, that, or whatever, beyond doubt and beyond conscience, I fell in love with Cannan.

As we settled into our cuddling and talking mode, he told me what he loved about me was the decisive 'yes' I had given him over the phone, and he continued to extol that virtue to our friends. How was I to live up to this view he had of me? It wasn't how I knew myself. What did I know about pedestals and seduction games? 'I love you' was not a phrase I ever used as a statement. What I liked about Cannan, in contrast to Evansky, was his newness – so new, and so different it was like a blow, and stunned as I was, the thought of losing him began to hurt. I had never felt such pain, and in the pain, love flourished. 'Opposites attract' was something I often heard my clients say. My world had spun out orbit. I knew that just cuddling and talking wouldn't make me into a flesh-and-blood woman. Still hesitant with my body, my priority wasn't sexual rewards, but what about Cannan? A good listener, yes, but what did I have to do next?

Weeks went by and spring was close, and I was thirty-nine. Meanwhile, Cannan called me Rosie, yet another exotic appellation. I loved myself as 'Rosie'. So firmly did Cannan establish that name, hardly anybody dared to call me Rose again. I liked its endearing sound, though it was nothing like 'Uhele' my mother called me: that was holy. When I came to England, the sound of the long German 'o' in Rosel in the mouths of the English was an offense to my ears, Rossel, Rousel, so ugly in its cockney pronunciation, I cut off the 'l' and became Rose. How could I have known Rose was common? 'After all,' I said to Cannan, 'Princess Margaret's second name is Rose.' 'Yes, but it was always thought to be common,' he explained. My education about the English class system had started.

My bolt-hole in my publicist's house – a blessing after I had left Evansky – was not a place to conduct an affair. My room was in her basement, facing north. No sunlight ever reached down to my window. It was cold by day and sweaty in the evening when the electric heater was on. Connie knew a couple who lived on the eighteenth floor of Camden Hill Towers in Notting Hill Gate. She took me to one of their monthly open-house parties. The townscape from their window was magnificent. All the flats were maisonettes with balconies, one side faced west and the other east. Shortly afterwards, a west-facing flat on the fifteenth floor became vacant to rent. 'What about it, darling?' Connie said, 'Why should Evansky live in luxury in New Cavendish Street in your flat, while you go mouldy in that basement?' Connie's words rang true enough. She persuaded me to move. Heaven, that place mortals long to live in, could not have been better. Without Connie, I might have caught dry rot in that north-facing room. But before living in 'heaven', there was the question of how to get there physically.

\

Chapter Twenty-Six

Hannah's Help

My cousin Rene changed her name to Hannah. 'I hate the name Rene', she said, 'awful when people assume it is pronounced like the French Renée. Too affected for me. No, Hannah suits me just fine.' With her new persona she berated me for having an affair with a married man who had three children and was a Goy to boot. Her morality, and that of others in my family, bothered me; a cacophony of objections came at me. Years later, when Cannan did meet Hannah, he said, 'Pushy woman, your cousin.' Never mind what he said about her, I needed her help. I liked the way she sensed my emotional needs. Hannah seemed to know what I'd come for even before I did.

Her friend Bella was part of her plans for me. Bella was the head of the Amsterdam Family Planning Association and was very fierce about women's suffering. Hannah enthused, 'You must meet Bella, Rose; she's a fantastic woman! We talk deep into the night, and for the first time in my life I don't care what Julian thinks. Of course, he feels threatened by her and rushes up to bed breathing fire, but I don't care!' 'What do they talk about?' he asked me when I was cutting his hair. How could I possibly tell him that they were deliberately tearing apart his manly pride? There was some right on Hannah's side; Julian did try to make her his possession, but Hannah, with Bella's help, coped better. Bella had done sterling work. Another time and another haircut, he revealed what he thought about his partner's wife, 'I hate intelligent women!' Being more confident these days, I said, 'Really, Julian, I thought you liked me!'

The scheme that Hannah and Bella were hatching for me was that I should get myself pregnant by Cannan, and then leave him. An alarming suggestion - more like a fire engine racing to a blaze! 'I'll think about it,' I said, but what I was actually thinking was I'd better fix myself up with a Dutch cap. Those were new thoughts for me: who should I go to? No hurry; just cuddles and talk were still de rigeur between Cannan and me.

Hannah and Bella's relationship thrived. Either Hannah went to Amsterdam or Bella came to London, which is where I met her. Her English, though accented, was perfect. Talking about her work loosened her anger. 'For years I have listened to women who have never had an orgasm in their lives, and moreover, when their men fall on them, they have no idea what is going on. Calvinism!' Bella declared lifting her eyes to heaven, assuming I understood the enormity of what she was saying.

Bella invited me to come to Amsterdam to stay with her. I chose to stay in a hotel. At dinner we talked, but when the dining room filled up, it was too noisy for intimate talk, and we decided to go up to my room. It was well past midnight. Bella would not go, and as dawn spread over the horizon, I grew anxious. We lounged on the bed, pillows piled up behind us. Bella did most of the talking. Then, breaking off, she smiled at me, lifting her brow questioningly. What was she asking me? I had no idea. When her arm stretched out to embrace me, I jumped out of bed and fled to a chair, crouching, embracing my knees. Would she think me narrow-minded? I was at the stage of wanting to be broad-minded, so back to bed I went, my body stiff with dread. Bella was alive to my feelings. 'Relax, she said, 'I won't harm you. But, let me say this: it doesn't matter where love comes from, as long as you have it sometime in your life.'

Bella was married and had three daughters. 'My husband,' she said later that morning 'is well instructed in the art of making love to a woman. When first we slept together, I placed his hand on my clitoris.' So that is what it's called, I noted. Bella's directness gave me a jolt; feeling confused was a treat compared to her proposal. Hannah had briefed her on my 'condition'. It seemed that I was now a property under new management.

After lunch, Bella took me to a Calvinist neighbourhood in Rotterdam. 'Behind these clean, crisply ironed curtains is a lot of suffering,' she said, nodding her head very slowly. Back in her flat, we must have talked more about universal suffering. I may have mentioned the Holocaust, though I didn't much in those days, preoccupied as I was with trying to be a sexually functioning woman, but it seemed that Bella could help me spiritually too. She was resting on her chaise longue under the window, half bathed in sunlight, and saying nothing in reply to my remarks on suffering she stretched her arms straight above her head, wrists crossed, her eyes looking upward saint-like as in religious paintings; Bella was simulating the suffering Christ. She held that pose long enough for me to get the point. Compared to Lenja, Bella was a silent evangelist. I felt anguish as I did with Lenja. What, I asked myself, were gas chambers compared to the Cross?

Bella must have told her husband – I don't even remember his name – about me being a virgin. He hastened over to London as if he were a paid-up member of a virginity cult. His intention was to seduce me, Hannah told me later. What was I, a land to be conquered? He nearly succeeded: as Bella had taught him, he almost brought me manually to orgasm in my car but in that split second before losing reason, I considered that I'd be obliged to him as I had been to Avrum. I pulled away from him, switched on the engine and drove him to the station. 'Get out, get out!' I shouted, pushing him out of the car. Poor sod, he nearly fell on the pavement.

From Hannah's good intentions to Bella's instruction, the whole thing was too intimate, too incestuous, too like an exhibit in a peep show. I reflected and, now clear what I didn't want, I drove back to my bedsit. I swallowed the two sleeping pills my publicist had left for me on the pillow with a note:

'Sleep well, love, Pam'. After I had left Evansky, she had got into the habit of doing this; it was helpful that she understood.

When the nameless man went back home without having staked my 'land', he told Bella he was in love with me. At that point she threw him out, and the idiot upped and went to Australia. From there, he wrote passionate letters to me. My pulse didn't quicken. I stuffed his letters leaning against each other for support into the upright shelves in my little desk to read perhaps another time. I never did. 'One thing is for sure,' Hannah said, 'Bella is far too strong a woman for him.' Hannah's adulation of Bella was in no doubt, but meanwhile, with Cannan hovering in the wings, anything they now said fell on deaf ears.

One evening, when I got home from the shop, Bella was in my room. She had her husband's letters in her hand, fanned out. I'd hardly shut the door when she said, 'No, it wasn't your fault, he is a sixty-year-old fool, dreaming foolish things.' Had Bella really considered me a willing participant in this thicket of intrigue? I looked at her, astonished. What was going on around me felt more like a hunt, with me being run to ground with the cry, 'Open your legs!'

No, my helpers' plans for me cleared my head. What I now needed was Hannah on her own, and when she was, mugs of tea in front of us, I went straight to the point. 'Where can I get fixed up with a Dutch Cap?' 'Doctor Goldstein!' Hannah cried. 'She is the best gynaecologist I know. She'll sort you out!'

Doctor Goldstein was a woman of about sixty-five, crippled with arthritis. I gave her a thumb-nail sketch of Avrum and me. A couple of sentences on, she asked, 'Did you feel pleasure?' At last, some sense! Her question went to the heart of my troubles: pleasure mixed with guilt. I was lying on the couch. Looking up at Doctor Goldstein, I saw nothing complicated in what she said; it was as plain as her face. 'Let's have a look,' she said, one finger up my vagina while her other hand rested on a stick. Satisfied that physically all was well, she fitted me with a Dutch cap. Then, pulling it out again, she said, 'Now you do it.' So naturally did she say this, the guilt amassed over the years ebbed away. Free at last, I would do what millions of women did everywhere. Doctor Goldstein limped to the front door with me, smiling. I walked out of her house, the roaring traffic in Finchley Road now a soft hum.

Settled in Camden Hill Towers, Dutch Cap in place, I hoped that Doctor Goldstein having named my problem meant that I'd be free of it. It seemed I wasn't. Cuddles were still the norm no matter how much I was in love. What was I scared of? Cannan knew about my uncle but not about the orgasm I'd had. And being, at last, at the brink of one, all I managed to say was 'No!' What did I imagine would happen in those moments – an in-depth analysis? Facing the end of my sex life before it even began, I remembered reading a book called Virgin Wives by Leonard J. Freedman. The category I came under was 'Sleeping Beauty': the 'prince' who'd awakened me was my uncle: grotesque. Myth and Taboo, one a legend and the other the guardian of moral codes: both had edged themselves into my life. Would I get rid of them? Often I did.

Three years on, Cannan filled his Fiat Estate with his personal belongings, drove to Notting Hill Gate from Somerset, and unpacked in my flat. My life changed in a way I could not have imagined. Cannan's children came to look me over and I became a common-law stepmother. That wasn't easy either for any of us. Love was demanding, from being childless to being a stepmother; Myth says they are awful and there I was with yet another Myth to handle. Instrumental in Cannan moving to London was that his wife wouldn't let him have her and a mistress. In a more trusting moment, he told me what she said when he left home: 'Now she can wash your socks!' So far, so exciting. Except for my parents, I didn't see any of my family, and for the moment, I kept them and Cannan strictly apart.

I was free to do as I pleased. Then my father sprang a surprise visit on us. Without any fuss, he sounded off in our paradise about Moses and the burning bush. I don't know about the burning bush, but it was me who was on fire! Father could see he wasn't getting anywhere, let alone beyond the foothills of Sinai, never mind the Ten Commandments! When he sensed he couldn't part us, practical as ever he suggested that Cannan could at least make a settlement on me, and going further, he said, 'I know of a furniture manufacturer, and his daughter was entangled with a Goy.' I didn't want to hear anymore. What was he saying? That it was fine for me to be the mistress of a man as long as there was an exchange of money? I escaped into the kitchen, separated by a glass partition. A grave would have been more appropriate. I was thirty-nine years old, and about as independent as I had been in my mother's womb.

'Well,' I said, going down in the lift with my father, 'Are you satisfied now?' Father fell against the lift wall, flushed and exhausted. He knew he had made a mistake and overreached himself. I felt sorry for him because he had blundered into Cannan's world without having any idea of what that world was. Cannan was merely amused, listening attentively to my father's oration, but I knew that Father had lost the advantage. He had been talking to a sceptic and an atheist, a man crackling with English education and manner but, despite being a sceptic, he knew the Bible stories backwards, and here was this Jew telling him one of its stories. Like a lot of Jews, my father most likely thought the Hebrew Bible belonged to Jews alone, and in my panic I said, 'Where did you think you were, in a Stible wagging your finger, invoking awe?'

Back upstairs in my newly established Habitat-styled flat, I was mindful of every word I said. In fact, did we say anything? Would my father now be thought of as a crafty, grasping, extortionate usurer? When I first came across the catalogue of definitions for Jews - now marked 'obsolete' in English dictionaries – my mouth dropped open. Was my father now seen like those portrayed in the Nazi film? Had these definitions of Jews come from Christendom? And wasn't Europe open-mouthed after the Holocaust? I was aggrieved to think the man I was involved with might have read these definitions and agreed with them; why not? I braved the thought. The phrase 'the kiss of Judas' is still in circulation, affixed to anyone who betrays a cause, or a person. I wince every time I hear it on the radio, or see it in print. Perhaps I should think of it as politically neutral, its origin too obscure in a now largely secular Britain to be religiously potent. But however small the flicker of the 'crafty Jew' may have been in the mind of my lover, why did my father have to fan that flicker? I wasn't confident enough to suggest to Cannan that my father had other attributes and it certainly was not the moment to defend him. Cannan had been a spectator of two anxious people embarrassed socially. It was torture for me not to trust Cannan entirely, and far too risky for me to speak openly about anti-Semitism, beaten as it was into Western sensibilities no matter what other affiliations individuals had. Besides, I was so lit up with love and Jewish neurosis, I couldn't tell them apart. But then, whom could I trust with my doubts? Even if I dared to open my heart to Cannan, would a torrent of puss gush out, and more to the point, would he have the right antibiotic? And if I were to go back to my family and tell them of my torment, wouldn't they have sneered and scoffed, 'What did you expect, understanding?'

The year I met Cannan, I didn't send out cards for Rosh Ha'shana. I was triumphant, hoping I had finished with all that and was now free to do as I pleased. The following year, no one sent me any cards. I felt as if one of my limbs had been torn off. Letting Cannan into my life was an epic move. I had opened the gate of a closed society and walked out into a new world, ignoring the warning my father had given me so long ago. Despite his feverish suggestion of a 'settlement', the reality was that I might as well have been turning a pig on a spit for Passover.

Then, early one afternoon, there was another ring of the door bell. Cannan opened the door. 'Yes,' I heard him say, followed by my mother's voice, 'I em Ruchel's modder.' God, I thought, it can't be, but I was instantly relieved that she had come alone. Mother was at ease. She took off her Russian style astrakhan hat and her coat and passed them to me, a smile beaming from her face. I led her to a comfortable chair, and she pulled out her knitting from a bag, and with her face composed, she started to knit, that peaceful activity she was never without. Her visit seemed so easy compared to Father's, and looking several times from Cannan to me she said to me in Yiddish, 'I like him because he likes you. At last, someone is a Mavin – (connoisseur) - of you.' We had tea, and soon after she left, content and smiling. Mother left a good feeling behind.

More than anything, Mother wanted my Father to forgive me. On one of my visits to them, Father grumbled about what was wrong in his life, and soon enough it became clear that I was part of that 'wrong'. He went on about me being with a Goy, and a few sentences later Cannan no longer had a name and was just 'he'. That was when I began to hear. Annoyed, I said, 'He' has a name!' Father went into the kitchen, busying himself, clanking about in the cutlery drawer. Mother called after him, 'But she's heppy, Max, more heppy than she was mit dem Yid!' I was looking out of the window when Mother whispered to me, 'Be patient.'

Trusting Goyim again wasn't going to happen in my father's lifetime; that much I knew, but it didn't stop me from dreaming. In one dream my father was dying and Cannan was with the rest of the family at his bedside; my father held out his hand to Cannan and he took it. I had often imagined this in daydreams, while drying myself after a shower, making up my face; anytime, anywhere at all. When do nocturnal dreams and daydreams melt into one, as do our moments of joy? I don't think I was sane in my paradise in the sky. Sure, I had seen the sun reflected against buildings thousands of times, but walking down Bayswater Road was as if I had seen a slab of sunlit stucco for the first time. That magnetic glance, a commemoration of that moment, that blinding flash of light when you know that nothing in your life will ever be the same again. My world was bezaubert, enchanted

As the years passed, Hannah and I fell out often and never did become reconciled to each other, despite her knowing all my woes. I remembered the faith I had in that trustworthy, practical side of her; the way she used to lead me up to her small bedroom, clean and cosy with a sidelight for reading. Settled in bed, I'd hear her running up the stairs and into my room, a hot water bottle held to her chest. She would place it under my duvet and then go over to the window to draw the chintz curtains, and lastly coming back to me she would kiss me good-night whispering, 'Good talk, wasn't it? Sleep well.' Those were the moments I felt safe with her, and I'd sleep peacefully all night until the sun filtered through the cretonne curtains in the morning.

After Julian had gone to work, we'd have breakfast and chat, looking out on their well-kept garden, the sun on the bare terrace. We talked about Connie, a cousin on her mother's side whom she rarely saw. 'You've met her, haven't you?' she said. 'Yes', I said, 'a couple of times.' 'Well, that makes two of us.' After a pause Hannah resumed, 'Imagine, not having seen Connie for years, this woman phones to tell me that Connie is dead and would I come to the funeral. I felt ashamed of myself, not knowing what had been up with her. Only four people were at her graveside: her brother and me, and two strange women, one of them the woman who had phoned me. Connie had no children. Ceremonials over, the women who phoned said, 'Your cousin was a good person, we loved her, and she made us laugh a lot.' Tears were now running down Hannah's face. 'And I thought she was as common as muck,' she said regretfully.

When I got stronger emotionally, I presented more of a challenge for Hannah. Often my doubts loomed long before she arrived on my doorstep. Would we be able to stay friends this time? When I opened the door to her, she said with perfect directness, 'I am a survivor!' After wiping her feet on my doormat, and now inside the house, she gave me one of her bear hugs. Stiff in her arms, I wondered what she had just overcome. I discovered that she delighted in her mastery of me when she said, 'Come on, don't be afraid to hug me back, let go!' And back we were, with me deficient in spontaneity, all that old stuff I hoped we'd buried and she now reminded me of why we had stopped speaking the last time round. And, as then, precious moments were lost. In truth, whatever Hannah's hurt was, I could not have helped her; she needed to be the perfect helper. Ultimately, I was not the woman she would have liked me to be, the one she knew she was losing as I became more successful in my work. I would never be standing by a stove, a couple of children hanging onto my skirt, the suburban housewife she so proudly claimed to be; and then, being in disagreement with that aproned woman she was, she reached out to another self, 'But, I am perceptive and I know my limitations!' All Hannah's declarations were made on our respective doorsteps. Another time, arriving on mine, and barely through the door, she said, 'Compromise, you have to compromise in life!' I wish I could have picked up her thread, but the truth is I needed to look up 'compromise' in the dictionary, and the doorstep was not the moment to do so. When I did, it told me that I had already been compromised in my aunt and uncle's bed. What was Hannah's woe? How good our conversation could have been.

On my way home, I remembered the Hannah when we were both much younger and she had struggled to understand the relationship with her mother. Casually, one day I said how alike her mannerisms were to her mother's. She stopped dusting the leg of a chair, looked up at me and burst into tears. 'I would give anything not to be like her and one day, I will succeed.' 'But Hannah, you won't, you wanted your mother's love so much, you gathered in all she was, bad bits and all,' I insisted. Then Hannah said, 'I've made my peace with my mother, I had the best of her, that vivid side of her.' That afternoon, we actually exchanged a couple of phrases without contradicting each other. 'Life's a bruiser,' I said, and she agreed, 'You're dead right, it is!' I added, 'But laughing helps.' 'I'll say it does!' Hannah said. After we had tea, she said, 'Let's watch Fiddler on the Roof, I've got the video.' We had a good cry at the end, Jews going to different parts of the world after a pogrom. Paradoxically, we felt nostalgia for the closed society portrayed, that love of tradition destroyed in the war, its mores now repudiated. Later, we talked of something less poignant.

All we agreed on, and all we didn't, came to an end when in her early seventies, Hannah fell gravely ill. We hadn't seen or spoken to each other for ages. I wrote to her to say I regretted that we hadn't come to a better understanding and wanted to acknowledge the contribution she had made to Jeffrey's life, and mine. I said how grateful I was and apologized that I had never really thanked her properly, and most likely neither had my parents. She rang me and said, typically unsentimental, 'Yes, it is true about Jeffrey, but he fitted the bill at the time. I had aborted twice. Besides, I loved Aunty Marie [my mother], the way she did things; she was so clean compared to the way things had been at home. I wish she had loved me back. She didn't know what she was missing!' Then, suddenly, Hannah's vigour waned and she began to cry. I wished that we could embrace in one of her bear hugs, and this time it would be right and we could talk as we should have talked when life was still abundant before her. But on the phone, she hurriedly said conciliatory things, that she had been arrogant about her health. And as she spoke, I wondered if she remembered the time she danced around in my garden when I was lame with arthritis, showing me how mobile she was. How I had wished then that she might just feel a little pain! And as she spoke, I knew she knew all that I'd been thinking and had wished on her in the past. And now I wished she had more time, and more strength.

Now that Hannah is dead, she's still part of that defenceless side of myself, and I am unutterably sad that she needed me that way. I would love to have been more to her before she died, to go back to the time when Hannah was young and vulnerable, the optimism she had when we sang our songs together on the top floor of her parents' house in Hackney Road, with Mascha looking on dolefully, thumb in her mouth, listening to her sister singing 'Stormy Weather', and to my rendering of 'Ich liebe dich', each of us repeating our songs until the other was word perfect in the other's language. And how over the years, she remembered that Sunday morning, how precious those moments were to her... the need to remind me of it, and how we advanced into chitchat when the morning's entertainment came to an abrupt end, and she shrieked, 'To buy, to buy, to buy' until her mother came through the door and said 'këufen' in Yiddish. How vivid all this is to me again.

Chapter Twenty-Seven

Time for Reflection

Before we moved in together, Cannan used to go home at weekends. I then had time to go over events, advantages and disadvantages, gains and losses, stormy telephone conversations with Evansky over who owned what. Me: 'You go. I've worked for everything in this flat.' Evansky: 'You are a destroyer. It's you who wants to break up the marriage, and, no matter what you say, I'm staying here.' He did.

Then another phone call about whose shop it was morally. Me: 'It's my shop; I built it up from nothing.' A long silence. Me: 'Are you there?' He revived, and thundered down the phone, 'It's mine, it's mine, it has my name, and I will never let you use it!' Me: 'But that isn't fair.' Evansky, now short of breath, gasped, 'I think... I think... I think... I'm going to have a heart attack.' And down went the phone with a bang. We had equal shares in the shop, and I no longer had the grit to start up with a new name nor did we have money enough for lawyers to haggle the rights and wrongs. And so it was that I was obliged to work with Evansky for another seven years.

No sooner had I left him, he had a woman in tow. I was surprised that I minded. Despite his frustrated life with me, he had always sworn loyalty to me, saying, 'I'll never leave you, I'll follow you to the ends of the earth.' I believed him, was even grateful to him for enabling us to live our sterile life. The moment I was out of his life, he walked about with The Connoisseur under his arm to show me, I presumed, that he knew a thing or two after all about the Arts, ballet especially, where he befriended prima ballerinas and although this was true, his boasting began to grate. 'I am making a film with Elizabeth

Taylor,' he announced, and yes, he was indeed an extra in one of her films in a non-speaking part.

But strangest of all was that later wherever I lived he would move there. He even bought Cannan's house in Brighton after we'd moved to the country. A couple of years later, he moved back to London. 'Julie wants to choose her own house, doesn't want to live with your ghost looking into her life,' he told me on the phone. 'Good for her! I said, not knowing what else to say. Suddenly, Evansky was in a hurry: 'I'll ring you again, soon.' I wished he'd never ring again. His calls merely served to rub salt into old wounds: how potent he was sexually; that he was 'a sexual athlete'. These calls upset me for days, leaving me alternately sad and glad: sad for myself because they reminded me what a sexual cripple I had been, and how guilty I felt for having deprived him for so long. When he had children, he laughed in my face, full and rich with happiness. When in the shop, I seemed always to be near when staff or clients congratulated him on the birth of his children, my misfortune open and raw for me to see in detail the barren woman I was. When his wife left his newborn son in the shop for an hour or so to do some shopping, I was mistaken for the real mother. 'Congratulations, Mrs Evansky!' said a client who had not been in the shop for ages, not knowing we were separated.

What were his phone calls really about? Certainly not about our bad old days! As an introduction, he always asked after my family, and in turn I hooked into this mawkish stuff and asked him about his. On another one of his calls, I changed the subject, wanting to reminisce about my achievement, the innovation of the blow-dry. A long silence ensued. Had he fainted? 'Are you there?' I repeated. If we were still friends, as he declared we were, why couldn't he acknowledge the contribution I made in our business? The longer I lived with Cannan, the more poignant Evansky's phone calls became. Provocatively, he'd ask, 'How is D.? Working?' No innocent question, this:

Cannan hadn't worked for some time. Chasing the famous, Evansky knew Cannan hadn't been making headlines in the arts columns. I vacillated from yes, to maybe, to soon, to I don't know, knowing that my awkward replies would be read with precision.

A good many years later, Evansky died and made it to the obituary page of *The Times*: a third of a page, a large picture of him framed with text. Who could have written this? Thinking back, I knew: it was the man who used to come to see Evansky in the shop after we had divorced. He would bolt down the stairs to the office, a folder under his arm, and when I was in view he would look daggers at me. 'Who is this man?' I asked Evansky. Grandly, he replied, 'He is my art adviser, an associate of the Fine Art Society.' 'But he looks daggers at me. Why?' Evansky wasn't forthcoming, but I knew with certainty that this art adviser must have doubled up as his 'Agony Uncle'. Reading down the obituary, I was sure of it. Apart from saying that Evansky had 'bought me out', I was obliterated from the page. In one way I was grateful because this art adviser went on in the obituary about the basement we had converted into a 'Cupid room', obviously described to him glowingly by Evansky as a great design achievement. It was the most embarrassing mistake I had ever let happen: plaster-cast cherubs smothered with gilt embracing each other, set in an opening of a dividing wall. Why would a fine art adviser fall for such a naff idea? By the time Evansky had met his art adviser, the shop had been redone, and he could well have spun him a tale that the cherubs were originals picked up on one of his trips to Italy.

I looked at Evansky's picture a long time. It took me back to the time he'd gone on holiday alone to our old haunts in Italy. He wrote me a letter saying that he missed me, and that going to 'our' old haunts was a torment for him. I felt appropriately sorry, I even had a lump in my throat until I read,

'Lots of people on the beach told me how good-looking I am. "What a face! Why aren't you an actor, or a model?"' And that was what Evansky eventually did most successfully: Einstein and Toscanini look-alikes and non-speaking parts in a couple of films – notably, Indiana Jones. I wish we had known where his talents lay when we were struggling to be together.

Being busy with my hands left me free to think, and sometimes I would say what I thought to a client while cutting her hair. What we talked about can only be guessed at now, but two different women handed me books: one was Connie and the other was Bronwyn Pugh who married the aristocrat, Viscount Astor. Both women said, 'I think you'll understand this, try.' One was Huxley's The Perennial Philosophy, and the other, Eric Fromm's The Fear of Freedom. Laughing, I said, 'Me? Never! My English isn't good enough for things like that.' Those two books were the first books I had read properly since the Bible. I needed a dictionary close to hand; two big words together and an eternity would pass before I could work out what they meant in context. Embarrassingly, I still have both books: almost every page has exclamation and question marks in the margins, wildly drawn next to instinctive recognitions. Evansky warned me that I was easily influenced. By then, I was worlds away from his jibes.

I learned to be comfortable with being 'influenced'. Some years later, in the library at the Spiro Institute, a Jewish secular college, I was scrolling down a dictionary when my finger stopped on the entry 'Philistine'. An archaeology scholar whose liturgy classes I went to was browsing through books next to me. Thinking out loud, I said, 'Who were the Philistines really, apart from having the pejorative label of a non-cultured people?' 'Oh yes', he said, 'all I can tell you is that they turned a fair pot.' His answer changed the way I thought about the labelling of peoples. But why did I still want to know our story, why couldn't I let it go? Truth was, if I didn't know our own story, how would I understand other's stories?

In the middle of my dense life between Evansky and Cannan, Jeffrey reached school-leaving age. I went to see his head mistress to ask if he could stay on at school for further education. Stirred up by the books I read, I wanted Jeffrey to benefit from what I had learned just by reading. Jeffrey didn't want to stay at school and I didn't know how to go about these things, perhaps talking it over with him first. The headmistress wasn't helpful either, leaving me to think that Jeffrey wasn't good enough material. I wished I had told her a little about his childhood, but that needed a know-how I didn't have at that time. All was solved when our parents said, 'Let him learn a trade.' That was what they knew about: trades, portable trades. My shop was a ready-made opening. Jeffrey met his future wife, Yvonne, in my shop, both of them just fifteen.

When my life with Evansky ended, Jeffrey's life began. I needed him to be like a rock, to be old before his time, to be my right hand, even to replace me. My thoughts weren't his thoughts. One day I found him sitting in the staff room like the other employees, talking with them as if he had no connection with me. I lost it and threw him out at a moment's notice. A fateful day. Yvonne and Jeffrey left together, minutes after I had shouted, 'Get out of my shop!' I didn't know who to weep for first: my desperate impulsive self, or my startled young brother. I have repented ever since, but that kind of damage doesn't mend easily.

My mother had a warning for everything life throws at you. When Harry and I were still children, and bickered, she always cried, 'What will happen to you, when each of you is in a different corner of the world and neither will want to know about the other?' This was hard to imagine when the fire still glowed in our range and the smell of cooking was so reassuring. Whatever the strength of my action the facts remain: I went too far.

What I did parted me fatally from my brother, making another of my mother's warnings appropriate: 'A family is all right until the strangers come!' Was I the stranger in our family?

Chapter Twenty-Eight

Makeover

The Sixties arrived precious and adorned: women in flowing dresses with flowers in their hair, the Laura Ashley country-girl look displayed in her shop in Sloane Street, the street known for its elegance rather than the romantic look she revived, using her own fabrics. By contrast, Mary Quant launched her miniskirts; apart from Dior's New Look in 1947, this was the most significant fashion since the end of the war. Girls were free to stride rather than walk daintily, but regrettably whether legs were long, fat or short, fashion dictated and the mini was worn by all: and forward they went into the world leaving behind the stultifying mores of our yesterdays, when 'don't' was a girl's chaperone. Freedom, that multifaceted phenomenon, pushed restraint out of the way. Reassured, girls took to the Pill which made pleasure less sinful, and whatever else was considered sinful in those days was abandoned. King's Road came to define the era; just having a friend living off King's Road had value. More and more new cars mobbed the roads, Minis among them, niftily nipping in and out of traffic.

As this new generation detached itself from the past, Art schools all over England disgorged exceptional talents: fabric and dress designers, (self-taught fashion photographers outside that norm) artists, graphic designers and architects – and of course the Beatles – transformed how we saw and heard. A lot of the talented converged in London's Royal College of Art: possibilities abounded. When Hockney became famous the world over, my friend Audrey Levy, a fabric designer in the 1950s, said to me, 'All of us knew that he was the best among us.' England was on the world map, happy to be envied after the dark days of war and post-war austerity. Carnaby Street was no longer the dingy street I used to hurry through in the war years. From where we lived then in Ganton Street it was a short-cut to Regent Street. Sadly, clothes coupons had limited value for shopping sprees which were fantasies at best because nothing of note was in the shops. And now, the whole world seemed to go to that pedestrian precinct with its colourful clothes hanging outside shops just moments away from Liberty's, and no one was rushing to get to somewhere else. Just being in Carnaby Street, you had already arrived. Thrilling!

Alan Fletcher, the graphic designer, and his wife, Paola, were my neighbours. Driven by talent, he often pointed out what was graphically superfluous. Once when Cannan and I were having supper with them, he drew our attention to letterboxes with the word 'Letters' printed on them. Irately, he said, 'What do they think they're for – to piss through?' Although his example was crude, it made scales fall from my eyes. With attitude like that, he changed the logo of the Victoria & Albert museum leaving out the left leg of the 'A', the omission so subtle its demise is hardly noticed. Yes, I learned a lot from my neighbour. The Art of Seeing Sideways was what he called one of his books; looking sideways is what many people do and Alan confirmed this with images in his book.

On a personal level, my status in being addressed formally as 'Mrs Evansky' changed, and I became 'Rose' as mentioned before. As Rose, I acquired a pair of spectacles with emerald green frames. Like it or not, I was 'in', and with my visual ideas enlarged, I asked Peter Moro, an architect and a friend of Connie's, if he could makeover our shop. 'No,' he said, 'but I know an architect who can, he mostly does renovations.' That same day, he took me to Gordon Bowyer's studio. From the open studio door, Moro pointed to a bald man bent over his draftsman's board: 'That one,' he said.

Our now shabby shop – I called it 'falling through the floor-boards' – was not complementary to being 'in'. Still with my mend-and-patch approach, I pestered Gordon: had he thought of 'this' or 'that'? He was miles ahead of me. Good-naturedly, he told me not to worry and suggested that I should go out and enjoy myself. At that point, I made the connection with how I dealt with women who didn't 'see', who didn't trust me when I wanted my way with their hair to give them confi-dence. An often-used phrase was 'my husband won't like it'. I would get rid of that, and soon these women understood and 'saw' with me, looking into the mirror at themselves with their own eyes. What fun it was!

Now more clued up, I knew that our shop with its crystal chandeliers and flock wallpaper was utterly outdated. Cool, clean functional looks opened up a new era of shop fitting. A lot of money was needed for that look; in fact our shop 'needed gutting', Gordon said. Who would lend us money? My guardian angel turned out to be the wife of the director of the Scottish Commercial Bank, and it was she who persuaded her husband to see me. Facing him across his desk, I wondered, 'Why would he lend eleven thousand pounds to a woman who had just left her husband and was still working with him?' Apart from a short lease, we had no other credentials. Could it be because I had used his daughter, who was trying to get into modelling, for a photographic session? Did this soften the banker's heart? My hope was that I looked confident in my Bonnie Cashin coat (bought in better days) as I promised to pay back the loan in three years. How I would do this I had not the faintest idea, and I truly hoped my doubts didn't show. Apart from the shop having to be gutted, it would have to be closed for a whole year. These days, shops are practically done overnight with gangs of builders working at top speed.

While the shop was being gutted we rented a basement in Lansdowne Row, off Berkeley Square, from an old colleague

I'd worked with at Woolf's. It was windowless and smelled damp. We lost eighty per cent of our clientele and half of the best staff I had trained in the fifties, among them Leonard, the most talented. One practice night he had taken hold of my arm and took me over to a 'model' whose hair he had just cut. With both of us standing by her, Leonard demanded, 'I want you to tell me what is wrong with this cut.' 'Wrong?' I said, 'There's nothing wrong with it – it's perfect!' No sooner, it seemed, had I said 'perfect' when Leonard joined Vidal Sassoon and with him went Nigel Cohen, an apprentice like Leonard. They were friends, I discovered. On a different practice night, Nigel too had wanted to know what I thought of the 'model's' hair he had just done. Well, he wasn't a Leonard, but remarkably Nigel became a publicist, acquiring the name of Justin de Villeneuve.

When Leonard left Vidal, he opened a small shop in Duke Street, parallel to North Audley Street. That didn't last long. A couple of years later he established himself in Upper Berkeley Street in a five-storey 18th century house. Justin became his publicist, and he found a sixteen-year-old model called Lesley Hornby. Leonard and Justin turned Lesley into Twiggy. She was fresh, unaffected and talented – worlds away from the models who dominated the glossies with their unapproachable snooty (though madly attractive) looks. Leonard cut Twiggy's hair into a softer version of the Twenties' Eaton Crop. Justin made her a household name, as she still is to this day.

In Leonard's big house, Daniel Galvin had a floor to himself. He was a brilliant colourist and innovator, his most influential invention was a new method of doing highlights which became known the world over. Gone were the days when see-through plastic bags were fitted tightly over a head of hair, and armed with the finest of crochet hooks, colourists would poke through the flattened hair and pull out small strands of hair – pure guesswork! Daniel's method was not: selected strands of hair were placed in tinfoil squares and covered with cream

bleach. Then they were parcelled up in the foil, accurately dis-
tanced from each other, and left until the desired tone of blond
was achieved. Daniel's silver-foil parcels and my blow-dry
have become classics.

After Leonard left Vidal he surprised me with a visit to our
shop. Not much small-talk took place, he seemed to urgently
want to tell what me he thought of cutting hair, 'I've always
wanted to tell you that, I preferred your free-style method of
cutting hair which, in my view, achieves a softer look; section-
cutting is mostly done with the stylist's head down, concentrating on the next section of hair to be cut. Your way, you can
always run your hands through the woman's hair between
snips, allowing you to see how things are shaping up.' 'How
nice of you to tell me,' I replied, 'but to be honest, section-cut-
ting is easier to teach because not all stylists have the gift to
hold on to what they have in mind to do.' When Leonard left
I remembered a couple of words he'd used in connection to
Vidal: 'fed-up' and 'stiff'. Perhaps Leonard just needed to off-
load to someone before he started out on his own, seeking reassurance, maybe.

Clare Rendlesham was my client and editorial benefactress
who, surprisingly, had stayed with me in that damp basement
for a whole year. When the shop was ready and Clare came in
for her usual lunchtime appointment, the electrical circuit was
being tested for the last time; lights flashed on and off, and Clare,
standing suitably still, allowed that theatrical moment. With her
blue-fox hat covering her ears, she looked like a Russian aristocrat about to go on a sleigh ride, and I, anxiously standing next
to her, awaited her pronouncement. Finally she said, 'Brilliant!
Marvellous, Rose,' her chin dropping in amazement, as her
glance fanned across the décor. The fact that her glance lingered
at all lifted my spirits. She was a critic to be reckoned with.

The makeover of our shop was minimalist, the way most
shops are done now, forty-odd years later. The Sixties wiped

out the garish contemporary colours of the 50s, and, excitingly, our shop was cool and serene in black and brown with a white terrazzo floor softened with straight teak trim round the mirrors, separated from each other by white Formica surrounds. Some lighting was concealed in each workstation and a few spotlights beamed into the mirrors dramatically bouncing back on clients and operators. Stainless steel surrounds for back washes and hydraulic chairs made hair-washing feel like having it washed in bed: neck-cricking was definitely out! At the back wall of the shop was a window overlooking a dirty wall; a constant frustration. Now the window was treated to dried autumn flora, lit up and pressed between two sheets of textured glass, warm and welcoming to anyone who entered the shop. The cloakroom was stripped of its powder-room image and all the rest of those frippery things women are supposed to like, such as sweet-smelling sprays advertised as Fresh Air. Thank heaven, Muzak was not yet the norm. The hum of dryers and conversation was music enough. Nevertheless, a few clients wondered when our shop was going to be decorated.

With Clare's approval, Mr Jadot's ghost was finally expelled from the shop. On a more personal level too, I was liberated from old symbols of success I thought I had to strive for: mink coats, diamonds, those kinds of things I now can't believe I ever aspired to. The moment of liberation came at a fashion show at Grosvenor House where I mingled with the big names in the fashion world, my mink stole round my shoulders. I bumped into May Routh, a fashion illustrator who could sum up the latest trends on the catwalk with a few pencil strokes, who said to me in as few words, 'Rose, nobody wears these things anymore!' Deliverance, at last!

In the shop, I was radical which meant that I educated women about their hair, showing them how to keep it in order between haircuts: 'Wash, shake and rough dry your hair, and then finger it into the shape it's been cut to, helped along with the hand dryer.' Big rollers made a difference too; I was getting somewhere with the softer looking hair.

One Friday lunchtime, Mrs Hay had an appointment for 'straightening'. As a junior rolled a trolley laden with chemicals, brushes and dishes towards us, I said to Mrs Hay, feeling her healthy curly hair in my hands, 'Why don't we try something less harmful?' 'Less harmful is fine with me,' she agreed, and as if I had been doing this for years, I picked up a spiky plastic-hairbrush and a hand dryer and started rolling a wet section of her wet hair around the brush, followed by warm air from a hand dryer held in my left hand. I knew how to do this because I had seen barbers use a hand dryer and brush to dry-style men's hair. This could be for women, had been my next thought. The more sections of wet hair I rolled over the brush, the easier it became, and soon part of Mrs Hay's curly hair looked smooth, as if it had been brushed through from a set. Exciting!

I was still rolling away when Clare came in for her usual appointment. Standing behind me, she said, 'What aare you doooing, Rose?' Half thinking her tone critical, I said, 'I'm just trying to...' and, before I could finish my sentence, she was gone.

Clare gone! Unthinkable! What had I done to make her rush out of the shop? Where had she gone? Paranoid, a never-ending cycle of reasons gripped hold of me: had she regretted her loyalty to me in that airless basement? Had our shabby gowns offended her? Had she remembered the time when I told her what our perm girl had said in the staff room about what a pity it was that Hitler hadn't gassed all the Jews? What was I thinking of, telling Clare what Jews talked about only among themselves? A long minute later Clare advised, 'If she's a good permer, keep her; if not, sack her!' So like Clare – straightforward. But where had she gone, I wondered? Vidal Sassoon, I was sure of it!

Then I heard brisk footsteps click on my new terrazzo floor; Clare and Barbara Griggs, the feature writer of the Evening Standard, were standing behind me. Clare said to Barbara, 'Look what Rooose iis doooing!' and seconds later, they were gone. I watched them hurry down the shop and out, and as Clare climbed into a taxi, she flicked her hand at the driver, indicating haste.

That afternoon, Barbara did a piece in the Evening Standard on the 'Blow Wave' as she named it, with graphics of clock dials showing time saved at the hairdresser. Important to this story is that we had recently installed twenty new hood dryers. Evansky protested, ''ave you gorn mad? We've just spent two thaasand paown on new hood dryers! What do you fink we're goin' to do wiv' 'em? Frow 'em aaht?' The dryers had certainly become redundant at the strokes of the clocks with the stationary hands in Barbara's piece. Evansky did have a point; the dryers were rarely used after we'd perfected the technique of the blow-dry. Women were happy to pay the same price for a BW as for a shampoo and set. From a business point of view, the BW was more labour-intensive than a set; stylists were committed to a client for up to a half an hour – that was money! Half an hour or so under a dryer left a stylist free to do other things – though, the weekly shampoo and set became more or less redundant. Forty years later the blow–dry is still on the price list at every hairdresser's, an innovation that has endured: curly, straight or permed hair, all can be blow-dried.

In my dotage, I am still in the habit of looking through the windows of open-plan salons where more often than not a young stylist is doing a blow-dry, wielding hairbrush and hand dryer in exactly the same manner as when the technique was first devised. Sometimes, I find it very tempting to go into the salon and tell them that it was me who innovated the blow-dry…

In the past, I had often wished that Vidal had been my brother, because he often behaved as though he were. Cheekily, appointments were made for his models for me to do 'something new' for them. Of course my hands went limp. Having heard our 'Makeover' was wonderful, he asked to see it. I agreed, warily, and he came, not just looking from afar but closely, at every nook and cranny. Vidal, my honorary brother was thorough. The next day he phoned again: could he have our architect's name and number? Several month later he phoned again but this time, it was to ask me out for dinner. Although I had told Reception not to give my home number to anybody, they gave it to Vidal – but then Vidal wasn't just anybody. Where we went I don't remember but what he offered I do: would I be interested in running a salon he was opening in New York – me in New York? And back I went to my old self: the 'pushing a pram woman'. That deeply disappointed self, that pathetic woman who disabled herself in a man's world, emotionally ready to abandon the race to stay at the top in her trade. To be out there needed a touch more of testosterone. No, New York was not what I wanted at that time; 'I'll make you a star' was a popular phrase used by top hair salons in the sixties: it pulled in new staff. Maybe Vidal thought he could strike a deal with me on the star front, that I would jump at the idea of joining his outfit - no - what I wanted now was to see stars on high, romantically.

In any case, I realized that top women hairdressers would never be 'stars' nor be numerous. Somewhere there is a press photo where I am the only woman among thirteen men hairdressers – a rarity then and largely this situation has not changed in the hairdressing world. It no longer made me cross that women preferred men to do their hair rather than women. Having once seen a woman reaching deep into a male stylist's trouser pocket, pushing down a pound note as a 'tip' made me connect why in the long run I didn't have a chance – and besides, I was already too old. When I was doing Molly Parkin's hair one day, she offered me an editorial in the magazine she wrote for, to hail me as a woman hairdresser who liked doing the hair of women in their prime – women like me, or Mrs Exetor, a model who represented slim elegant woman, her steel-grey hair gloriously and suitably quaffed by me – yes that is what Molly meant. Mrs Exeter was hardly ever photographed: a sketch sufficed. Wish I remembered the name of the man who drew her for Vogue. Molly's suggestion was too sudden. I refused. I shouldn't have; she spotted a gap at the top end of the trade where young male hairdressers seemed only to 'see' model girls, much like Mary Quant whose miniskirts were worn tastelessly by women of my age. Sharing a taxi with Quant after a photo-shoot we were in with Hockney et al, I asked her about sizing. 'I love your clothes,' I told her, 'but nothing you make fits me.' 'Yes, I know,' she said, 'American sizing is better, I'm working on that.' She was not fazed by what I said, the opposite, she was utterly professional.

One Friday lunchtime, I was giving Clare my new cut: long sides and short at the back. Her head was bent down for me to work on; then, slowly lifting up her head she looked through the mirror at me and said, 'I am having lunch with Vidal today, hurry.' That was the last time I saw her. What Clare needed were good pictures for Vogue. Vidal was her man.

The photograph of Vidal which best illustrates the difference between male and female hairdressers is one of him with his model showing off his new cut. They are standing opposite each other in profile, him as a latter day Pygmalion. The model Vidal used was Grace Coddington. As far as I knew she was a natural redhead. His models were invariably dark-haired. Whether he cut a wig for Grace, or she let him colour her red hair black to show off his cut is anyone's guess. All that mattered was the end result: stunning.

I wasn't marketable in that way; my place was behind the chair. That was where I thrived, took risks, made women see with me, opened up their ability to see what I saw for them.

At best, my strengths lay in the Before and After features I did for Vanity Fair, lots of them – good ones! Why did I never cut them out to keep? There were pages and pages of them every couple of months. Maybe I hoped Evansky would – now that was a silly thought!

A good few months after I had given Gordon Bowyer's name to Vidal, he phoned to invite me to the opening of his Grosvenor House salon. Coming through the door, he embraced me, 'My favourite woman!' As more guests came through the door to be embraced, he promptly let go of me. My special moment was over. Then Gordon took me to one side and said in a low voice, 'I have tried not to repeat too many details from your salon.' His revelation was an eye-opener. Why was he apologizing to me? He didn't have a contract with me and could work for anyone he pleased. That method suited Vidal: he was a good tactician, knew what he wanted and how to get it.

Some reassurances came for me from women who didn't want to be defined by the 'Vidal cut'. 'Look at me,' some said, having come straight from Vidal's salon to ours, 'I've been obliterated! I don't want my hair to be a label for Sassoon.' In some cases this was true; his cut didn't suit women universally. In a way this defined what I was good at: revealing the woman so that she could be told after I had done her hair how good she looked. As Vidal once said of me, 'Rose makes women look beautiful.'

Although Evansky and I were finally divorced, we still had to work together and this became increasingly frustrating. I couldn't manoeuvre between the two men in my life, each pulling me in different directions: one redundant, the other compelling. 'Give less', said a therapist I went to a couple of times for direction. The 'less', in the end, was my career.

One Friday evening, I left the shop to catch my train, saying good night in the usual way. I felt cowardly and sorry for

Evansky who would have to explain my absence to the staff on Monday morning. Well, he wanted to be the boss and the best thing was to leave, I reasoned. Had we arranged a ceremonial farewell for the staff they might have run off leaving Evansky to cope with an impossible situation. Thinking this way made me feel a little more comfortable and less of a traitor. But how would I ever feel comfortable having left my emotional till wide open.

On the bus fidgeting through Park Lane and round Hyde Park Corner in the rush hour, I went over my attempts at being a tycoon. The first time I had tried was in 1952. Someone had talked to a well-known shirt manufacturer about us and a meeting was arranged. The director sat behind a huge desk in a large, drab office, partitioned with walls that reverberated when doors opened and shut. A listener sat a 'bishop's move' away from the director. Evansky came along to the meeting, but it was me who laid out the plans. The director appeared to expect Evansky to do the talking. Disconcerted that he didn't, he looked from me to Evansky, who struck as neutral a pose as he could. The interview was a washout. Nothing substantial could be accomplished with us, said the director's resolute rise from behind his desk. Although we were young and good-looking, as a business team we were as frail as tissue paper.

Females in the Fifties were not yet striding to the top in the business world, except cosmetic queens and dress designers, and even then their set-up was like ours: a woman working 'behind' her husband, giving a picture of respectability, though some I knew of were shrews at home. What was I saying? I wasn't a shrew at all; I wasn't deft or subtle enough with language for that. Yammering was more my style, endless monologues, words rambling to nowhere.

Several years later, I tried again and went to see Richard who had started the first hairdressing chain outside the hallowed square mile of Mayfair, simply named Richard. We knew each other from our East End days, the way tradespeople often do after venturing out from tight-knit ethnic groups. We met at his flat which was a clone of his salon style: black-and-red Vitrolite and white walls. It wasn't a home at all, more like being wrapped in a Nazi flag. Before Richard came into the room, his wife appeared in the doorway. The fact that I had never met her didn't stop her from saying, 'Do you know…' and without pausing for me to answer, she volunteered, 'every time Richard opens another salon it's as if he were having an orgasm!' I had enough trouble concentrating on what I wanted to say without having to think about Richard's orgasmic trajectories, metaphorically meant or not. Maybe this was the way fashionable people now talked, exposing themselves to each other, loose with words and flesh, as I had learned from Connie.

Richard seemed to know me better than I knew myself. He was a short, stumpy man with black hair and eyes the blue of a Mediterranean dawn. He came straight to the point: 'Rose, I hope you know you are not the type to expand. Besides, I'd kill you, wanting more takings each year. I know your work, you don't compromise, and when you expand, you have to water down your ideals a bit!' When he saw how disappointed I was, he added the corollary, 'Even if I did back you, there is Evansky. I wouldn't back him!' Ouch.

A few years later I saw my last tycoon. He doubled up as an MP and I met him at the House of Commons. By then I was in two minds about my plans and dithered in response to his questions. I didn't mind him seeing through me; sensing that I wasn't totally committed, he got up from his chair to let me know the interview was at an end, and holding out his hand he looked over my shoulder. Oh, another Vidal! This time, I didn't follow his eyes – I didn't really care who was coming through the door, even had it been a king with a posse of princesses! Disappointment didn't last too long this time, and I consoled myself with the quip that tycoonery was not for me.

Later, when I was no longer working, I went to London to see Caroline Charles' dress show where I met Jerry, a former colleague of Vidal. We chattered on in a lacklustre way about our trade, its highs and lows. Then, unexpectedly, Jerry said something comforting to me, 'You know, Rose, you never had the right man behind you.' He crystallised more than twenty-five years of my life.

PART FOUR

Chapter Twenty-Nine

Close to Nature

Knowing what I didn't want, I gave up my career and threw myself into living next to nature with Cannan at Godleys, our cottage in Sussex, surrounded by seven acres that could in the late Sixties still be bought for a song. We had nine years of flattening bumps, creating a vegetable patch, and feasting on what we grew. In hot summers I languished in a hammock held aloft between two greengage trees. Never since have I eaten greengages like that, sweet with soft skins, not like fruits now bred with tough skins for better shelf life. Some of the trees cracked in a colossal storm. Omens? I didn't believe in them.

My life was now a blend of baking bread and making jam from fruit trees growing all over our garden, including a crooked quince-tree outside the kitchen window still abundant with fruit from which I made jelly, a very old-fashioned taste. The rest were plum trees no longer in their prime, and we selected the best fruit from them. I cooked and sewed, and the smell of baking bread enriched my life. I rode a bicycle for local journeys, flying down hills as in Ludwigshafen, but now this experience gave me other enjoyments. Riding a bicycle in preference to using our car, I heard dogs bark and birds sing, flies and bees droning beside me, and my travel companions were spirals of midges. When I got home, I told Cannan about these things. I felt a peace I had never known before, acutely conscious of being free from anxiety. I had shut out the world and that patch of land we lived on became my refuge, all of it initiated by Cannan. 'Come and share my life with me,' he said.

I was so happy, I forgot everything: being Jewish, having a family. Only my parents were reminders of the past, and I saw them regularly. There were other things I saw; after waiting the best part of a day, a butterfly slip from its chrysalis, and on another day, sitting on a bench in autumn, the view of Blackdown in the distance, a purple horizon meeting clouds tinted by the sun on its way down, different from summer sunsets. Then it set behind a majestic oak tree, still youthful and golden and high, and the moon came up glowing in the darkness, moving the way our family always has, abandoning homesteads and finding new ones in other lands. Sometimes the mingling of these thoughts lacerated my peace. Had I the right to be homesick when I was so happy?

There was so much to enjoy: eating the eggs from our ducks and chickens; the walks in the woods a few paces from our house; the copse beside our lane exquisitely carpeted in spring with bluebells, their colour so intense and unique to me, no other blue since has ever pleased me so much; the cows grazing in our fields, and calves slipping onto the grass. Cannan stood at the fence watching. I went over to be with him; his eyes were filled with tears. We waited for the moment to pass before we went back to the house.

There was life in decline too. Once, stuck in our lane in the car behind cows being led home for milking by Farmer Bailey, Daisy's rear was up for scrutiny, wrinkles I never imagined in such places, and to add to her troubles, she tottered behind all the others cows like an old woman wearing high heels. Not yet, I petitioned, not yet, holding onto the fact of just being middle-aged, and momentarily I let go of the steering wheel, my hands in a gesture of holding back time.

The country suited me, and I embraced it whole-heartedly. I learned the differences between the plants and the trees and the weeds, and being tranquil I started to read. Finished with one book, I asked Cannan, 'What next?' But reading was irritatingly slow for me. I had to look up the same words many times and still they wouldn't stay in my head. The possible cause of this could have been that I had not spoken or read German for thirty years, and learning a new language I needed both languages to crosscheck. But then how could I have spoken the language of the country England was at war with, the shame I felt about anything German, connected as it was with my Jewish experience in Nazi Germany. With my English now on its way, I was ready to rescue my first language, the kind I had only a glimmer of when I heard it in the garden of the synagogue sitting under scorched trees, listening to poetry.

Sure of what I now needed, I went to the German-English bookshop in Wigmore Street to buy books: first an all-German dictionary and an English-German dictionary. Then, feeling inspired, I chose Schiller, Goethe, several little pocket books of Heine's poems and, ambitiously, *Katz und Maus* by Günter Grass. Freud in German was a must too – why Freud? I was ready to reflect on all the therapy I had had in the past.

To be practical, I devised my own dictionary with exercise books, copying out meanings of words from the English dictionary into mine. I soon had more than one exercise book; page numbers and the words in question I underlined in my dictionary and in the book I was reading – though in the book the pencil line was very faint and easily rubbed out after my final check. Gradually my vocabulary grew and I began to have a feel for words, and most important of all was why and how the same words were used in different contexts. It was thrilling to recognize my 'new' words in conversations around me, and when brave enough, I used them myself. Jubilant, I celebrated each new word like a birth.

It took a while to make sense of my language, so deeply had I buried it. Being in touch with German again was poignant. I was upset that I needed the two dictionaries to refresh my own language and although my German had come back to life, I would never be a simultaneous translator the way a German Jewish friend of mine was. 'Please can we speak German?' I asked her excitedly, and soon enough I was struggling for words, but no sooner was the word needing translation out of my mouth, out it came from hers.

Many of Heine's poems were written to be songs; the most loved by me was Die Lorelei. Remembering it from my school-days, and having found the words again among his poems, I began to sing the tune: Ich weiss nicht was soll es bedeuten dass ich so traurig bin... (I don't know why I am so sad...) All at once the German language was beautiful again and my eyes filled with tears, and lost were the ways in which the Nazis used the same and similar words for ugly purposes. So words were what you did with them, how you placed them, loved them, treasured them, gave them away to heal the human spirit. 'Forgetting' my language, I seemed to have numbed an entire way of understanding and what I hadn't realized was that I had been practising a kind of racism with me at the helm of two languages, determined to keep them apart.

Difficult though it was, Freud's Beyond the Pleasure Principle in German was a gift; reading about 'hiding' pleasure, keeping it secret from the status quo, my heart quickened. With the book open on my lap, I exclaimed, 'How come he knows me so well?' How sad that I hadn't read Freud before, but what a solace Doctor Goldstein been to me – she must certainly have read him! Coming across the Id was another find and again I said out loud, 'Ach, das Es ist doch the Id!' Another mystery solved. How useful that might have been to me in the past instead of having my body bullied into submission, albeit unsuccessfully. Body and soul together, I discovered, educated my emotions – that cumbersome dough kneaded into shape by poets. Still deficient in English, I had spent my worst emotional moments in a language vacuum, knowing neither German nor English well enough to help me identify my feelings.

Full of such cheer, I fancied love was a soft option compared with the shop. I can handle it, I thought, a touch too confidently. In no time, so it seemed, heaven's door was blocked, locked up. Little things began to upset the harmony Cannan and I shared. We bickered over how to do domestic tasks: his way, it always needed doing again. His way, my way, what was the difference? It wasn't about doing something well. That hoodlum, power, squatting between us made our life no longer like a line in Drei Groschen Oper (The Threepenny Opera) so heart-rendingly phrased: 'Ich schützte sie und sie vermehrte mich (I protected her and she made more of me).' Every time I played the tape, I held fast to its tender allusion, albeit ironically meant in the opera. I couldn't make more of Cannan because he wouldn't let me, and when nothing changed, I felt less myself.

Being a one-car couple highlighted the scraps we got into. I kept house and Cannan worked from home, and often he would ask in the morning, 'Are you going to Cranleigh today?' and I'd say, 'I don't know, I haven't planned my day yet.' 'What do you mean, you don't know?' and in no time I was shouting, losing the simple words needed to solve a simple situation, and every time it happened, I got caught. One day, after another one of these stupid scraps, it crossed my mind that these were Jack Evansky's tactics. But this couldn't be, Cannan was an intelligent man, surely we could sort this out? When the 'tactics' continued, I roared, 'You have the mind of a philosopher and the emotions of a navvy!' I felt pleased with myself, thinking I'd made a breakthrough. I spent days thinking what I could do to stop the bickering. Then I found that simple word 'if', as in 'if you are going to Cranleigh, could you get me so and so?' and I hoped this two-letter word would bring back our harmony and stop us from tearing at each other. Living with Cannan became an obstacle race: one thing put right, another popped up. Nothing was learned. He vandalized what self-esteem I had – though bickering did sharpen my wits. I speculated on a million 'ifs', but finally I had to admit that the battle for reason wasn't going to be won because of love; that might well be a casualty and die in the battle.

Foolishly, I believed that if I didn't feel pain I wasn't in love, and no matter how I tried to deploy words to change the way we spoke to each other, our senses deadened. Walking in the woods across the field from our house scuffing up autumn leaves, the romance of spring was near, but romance was not what I craved; something more important was missing: mental intimacy. Listening to the crackling of dry leaves under my feet, I found what was wrong between us: I was no longer cardinal in his life, and we were no longer extraordinary to each other.

We dealt with our despair, each in our own way. He found someone new. I could not believe that life was like the inside of a conjurer's cloak where all the birds had flown. How beguiled I had been by tricks, but now when he held me captive and told me about her, his voice rich and full, mine lost its music. What dribbling nonsense fell from my lips!

A sea of tears later, I was cleaning out a cupboard in Cannan's office when a row of empty whisky bottles rolled together. Had our house tilted on its clay foundations? If it had, then so had Cannan. He was failing in the world, and he'd made me believe that his drinking was purely social, but what I saw was a man drinking enough alcohol to fill a moat, full enough to drown in. In my dreams giants nipped my arm; a truth emerged when I woke up knowing that the monsters lay trapped in whisky bottles. As Cannan poured the liquid into glass after glass and the Plimsoll line on the bottles dropped lower each week, and new bottles were opened ever more frequently, he grew out of control. One evening, he finalised a day's drinking by smashing the empty glass into the fireplace. I escaped into the spare room to sleep.

Even the solace of his affair slipped from his grasp. I didn't understand that any of this was connected with drink, or to the promises we made to each other. One night, a fox went berserk in our chicken house: Cannan hadn't locked them up. In the morning, the cockerel rushed about distraught; and so did my alcoholic. This was what AA told me he was. My calling AA was something of a miracle, considering how ignorant I was about drink. They recommended I should join Al-Anon, the family support group. I did; laughter and tears were shared and understood.

Anticipating my 'recovery' (his was his business, AA advised), I dreamed I was swimming across the world underwater with my eyes wide open, making large confident breaststrokes to the shore above pebbles in many shades of grey. I remember thinking, even while I was still dreaming, 'This dream is Truth.' At that moment I woke up. Licking my lips, I tasted salt. Crying in a dream? Could this be? It must be: my cheeks were wet. Had I been awake only moments ago? Was this dream the 'ordinary unhappiness' Freud offered to patients as a general introduction to analysis?

Whatever kind of love was now on offer, I was immune to it. In the end, all that was left was a sob, like that physical lurch men do when they can't give way to grief. The glow that had warmed us in the beginning had fused, gone for both of us. It was hard to admit that our physical life together was at an end, having mutually entrusted each other as its caretakers.

What to hide and what to tell the children? In the beginning, having stepchildren had seemed easy: they came and I cooked, and I served them gladly. My shop was now a distant memory, but as Cannan drank ever more seriously, the 'detachment' which Al-Anon suggested I should practise failed me. I continued in my old ways, carrying on the familiarity I'd enjoyed with his children because what I offered was accepted readily. I grew confident believing I had a place in that family. Not having children of my own, I had no yardstick with which to measure motherhood, that kind of love, that kind of pain, that kind of involvement. Even Cannan was deluded. Stepmothers? How old-fashioned! Did we not live in propitious times when the edges of family life were beginning to blur? As more and more families were overwhelmed by new mores in an ever increasing cycle of marriage break-ups, fresh attitudes had to be found to deal with ever more extended families, so why not us? I felt that as long as I kept assuaging Cannan's guilt for breaking up his family, life would be good.

What had followed some years later was of a different intensity. What we still had to face was that I was the woman who made Cannan's children choose which parent to live with. I responded to what I thought Cannan wanted me to be to them. This left their mother sighing in the shadows. With no shop now, I was free to perform at being better than their mother. Had we imagined that we were sitting under heavenly clouds, convinced they would never turn into rain? What a pile-up of emotional stuff we had to deal with in the years ahead! But for the moment, life was novel and I liked the novelty though I knew deep-down that we were living on borrowed time. All the same, I continued to mother them because it pleased their father. How stupid was that!

When Connie visited us at Godleys, she sensed that not all was well in the Cannan household, and with eyes harbouring glee, she said, 'And I thought you led a charmed life inspiring Cannan to write!' Most women who came to the house suggested this with their overbearing manner towards him – they could love Cannan better than me. An old friend of mine showed me how: she attempted to engage with him in a heart-to-heart conversation in front of me, her eyes moored to his, her finger pressing between her breasts. Cannan fled, besom in his hands, to sweep up autumn leaves. My 'friend' and I watched him through the kitchen window, his back bent in harmony with the melancholy day. After a few moments of silence, my 'friend' gave me her opinion of the man sweeping. 'Ah', she said, 'all he needs is a little bit of loving.'

We had made promises to each other that we would live in a little white house with brown furniture, a whim once uttered after we had made love. Although our house was redbrick and not white – red or white, our dream was over. Connie's observation was right. Nothing was 'charmed' about our life anymore.

Chapter Thirty

Compensation

Throughout this turmoil, I continued to see my parents. I had been able to move them out of London to Hove because the post-war German government, led by Adenauer, legislated that Jewish victims of Nazi Germany were to be compensated for loss of property, education and health. In the late Fifties, my parents' claims came through, mainly for my father's health, the physical and mental anguish he'd suffered in Dachau, and for belongings, such as they had. A good thing this legislation was too, because Sketchley dry-cleaning vans were running round the neighbourhood collecting and delivering work, while my mother still went up and down stairs, laden with suits and coats over her arms. Just thinking about it made me wince, but she never complained; like Cousin Sarah she just sighed. My parents by this time were well past sixty, and chain cleaners were too much competition for them; it was a battle they weren't going to win. Despite Father's good work, his customers defected for quicker service. Their shop no longer paid its way.

The amount of the compensation was £3000 exempt from English income tax. Certainly enough for my parents to lead a more comfortable life! I received £800 for loss of education. Harry was not included in this scheme, because he was still of school age when he arrived in England and able to continue his education in a Yeshiva, a Jewish religion boarding school. At the time the money came through, Cannan and I and his children were living in a three-storey Regency house in Brighton. I commuted to London and kept house at the same time, with Mrs Dockings helping to keep the house in order.

In 1964, Cannan became restless without a project, and it was then that we moved to the country.

I had caused offence in my family by wanting to move my parents out of Bethnal Green. The family's worry was that if they left the neighbourhood they'd be lonely. 'Rubbish!' I said, 'What neighbourhood? Aunt Rosie is dead. She was their neighbourhood!' Besides, I knew my parents' dislike for the slummy surroundings, particularly the corner shop they declared schmutzig. What they couldn't fathom out was how the shop owner could dip her black-rimmed fingernails into a barrel of pickled cucumbers one minute, and the next grab hold of a globe of cheese and press it against her bosom to cut off a wedge from it, all without the intervention of soap and water. Singling out this unpleasant practice, my mother highlighted Germany's good qualities. 'In Deutschland, everything was so clean,' she said, a smile of nostalgia on her face, momentarily forgetting why she was in England.

With the money from Germany, I had bought a flat in Hove for £3250, in a complex of flats three-storeys high, beautifully planted gardens arranged around them, designed by Eric Lyons. He had designed the Span Estate in Blackheath after the war; Connie had lived there. We paid £2,500 down and I took out a small mortgage for the rest which left £500 plus a weekly pension of eight pounds. Then I worked out a gift-free allowance to top up their English pension – happy with the thought that they would never have any financial worries again. To waste the money on a holiday treat, as was suggested, would have been profligate. My parents' life in Hove would now be a never-ending treat, I liked to think.

I hired a small van for the move. The most useful furniture my parents had was a three-piece suite bought at the Times Furnishing Company, the poor man's Heals at that time. They already had beds and I added to the basics with some new pots and pans. The rest was dumped. To save our fares, I had the suite loaded last onto the van and arranged it like a living room. With the top-half of the door at the back of the van open, we said goodbye to Blythe Street. 'Go on Mum, wave,' I said, as we drew away from the street. Instead of waving, my mother leaned her head against my shoulder and patted my arm. My father looked on, pleased.

Over a weekend, I had painted the flat white; being newly built made painting easy, no preparation was needed. The £500 left from the lump sum was enough to re-cover the suite with durable checked fabric from Heals, in different hues of heather. Splendid! I made fitted sheets and duvet covers from old flat white sheets. Curtains, I made from black and white striped ticking with bright yellow zigzag binding above a broad hem. New furniture came from Stag, early MFI. My plan was for easy maintenance. Father loved it all, except for the dark brown carpet. 'I have to sweep it twice a day!' he moaned. Trendy though I thought my decor was, he had a point. When Cannan and I moved house, our yellow carpet didn't fit the new house we moved to, and so my parents' brown carpet was changed to yellow. 'That's better. More friendly,' Father said cheerily. My mother loved her new life because I'd chosen it – another reason for my brother Harry being angry with me, though this time I knew I was right; setting up our parents was both practical and good.

And so was their life, very good. Visitors were in and out of their flat, and often my visits coincided with theirs; mostly congenial meetings, except for Mr Josephs, the Shohket/Moil (kosher slaughterer/circumciser) who Father knew from his Shul. The two of us meeting agitated my father, notably when Mr Josephs asked where I lived. This was no ordinary social dialogue. The panic in my father's eyes was apparent. Had I told him Horsham Mr Josephs would have known there wasn't a Shul there, and in Orthodox language that meant I was under suspicion: either I was not observant enough, or worse, I was married to a Goy. Mr Josephs' keen blue eyes were challenging for my father as they darted from him to me. To save the day, I lied: 'I live near Brighton, it's a good walk!' Nearness in these circumstances is relative. Orthodox Jews have walked to Shuls all over Europe in all kinds of weather not to break the rules of riding on the Sabbath, be it in a horse and cart, or a car. 'Near Brighton' made the distance from a Stetle situation a short walk. My father exhaled audibly. I was glad to have saved his feelings, but to be frank I felt as if we were in the presence of the secret police. Mr Josephs' influence on my father was skin-deep, not at all my father's real spirit. I liked father best when his relationship with God was more of a struggle; it seemed to make him more human, more Jewish.

I had one more brush with Mr Josephs. When my father had phlebitis and was unable to go to Shul, Mr Josephs suggested, 'This is what we'll do: we will hire a wheelchair and pay a Goy to wheel him to Shul.' 'What?' I said, 'My father can pray at home!' Father didn't know where to look. Mr Josephs must have known he'd gone too far because he sensed that I no longer agreed with these outmoded traditions. For once I didn't feel guilty; Mr Josephs' plan was offensive. I believed Mr Josephs dominated my father, and in turn my father tried to dominate me. I liked to think my grandfather Chuna Aaron wasn't like this, having learned to have regard for him through the gentle letters he sent to his nieces and nephews in England before the war. They talked of their uncle left behind in Poland with respect and affection. I needed this to be true.

Driving home that evening, I went over all the things Hitler told the Germans to hate us for. Mr Josephs didn't have to add much to an already existing bias. I disliked him for making me dislike him. And why did my father make it his business to make me familiar with Biblical texts and stories in the Talmud of how children should take care of their parents, even if they were found in the gutter? Did he point this out to my brothers?

I never asked them, but to give my father the benefit of the doubt, he probably passed on to me things that Mr Josephs had reminded him of. It was certainly not what my father had done for his parents; he couldn't have in the circumstances they lived in. But why tell me and not my brothers? I already obeyed that commandment.

All this made me think of other things I did that my father objected to. When I first read the New Testament, he warned me that people go mad when they think too much about such things. Did he mean people, or just women? I never heard my father mention Maimonides, the twelfth-century rabbi and philosopher who advised that women and children should not be acquainted with holy texts because they would be wasted on them. These guidelines were picked up by men through the ages, my father included. When reading Maimonides's Guide for the Perplexed, I came to the passage where he said that 'women are weak-minded'. Furious, I slapped the book shut. Why should I get steamed up about the misogyny men practised? Why should I be a mute partner, barred from the riches men considered theirs alone? How could I make more of myself? Perhaps by understanding that men who tried to make more of other men were men of their time? To throw aside the good things Maimonides said would be as unfair as he was to women.

I celebrated some of what he wrote: 'The religious life does not find its essence in obscurantism or simplistic solutions that affirm piety at the expense of reason, and it is better to live with irreconcilable problems than to find tranquillity in solutions that are intellectually spurious.'

My eyes pricked in recognition, and I felt what I was supposed not to feel, or have the sense to understand. I once had the temerity to tell an Orthodox rabbi I had gone to for advice on which books to read, how much I loved the writing of the prophet Isaiah. Cutting me short, he said, 'He wouldn't have considered you!' His wife was pregnant with their fourth child, all within the space of five years. That morning, he told me that there was only one issue over which he would divorce his wife, and that was, he said in a clear voice, if she didn't stick to a kosher kitchen. We hadn't been discussing domestic arrangements.

That spring, the rabbi invited me for Passover. His parents-in-law were there too. His wife and mother-in-law wore Shei-tels (wigs worn by Orthodox married women) and their Hebrew was fluent. Mine was a stuttering mess. I felt awkward among them. His father-in-law noticed my unease and ha-rassed me: 'Sitting on the fence won't get you anywhere, either you join us or you leave us.' We looked daggers at each other. I shouldn't have come; we had nothing in common except for the qualification to be gassed forty years earlier. Yet why did the rabbi's father-in-law poke his finger at me so malevolently? What did I say to anger him? Was I disrespectful, like the way Mother and I used to laugh at Father? But Father, more often than not, had laughed with us, relishing the religious tug of war we were in at that time.

On my last visit to the rabbi, we were in his office when his wife appeared looking ragged and worn. 'Three things', she said, 'One, I haven't slept because the baby kept me up all night, and you will have to take over.' I don't remember the other two things, because she threw me a look of such con-tempt I knew it would be foolish to continue using her hus-band's library. On this last visit, I learned that the rabbi knew nothing about Christianity in relation to our persecution. 'No,' he confirmed, 'I know nothing about it, you probably know much more than me.' How smug, how insular, how arrogant!

When I saw the rabbi and his family for the last time they were outside their house on their way to Shul. In the middle of saying our goodbyes, the wife lifted up the long string of colourful wooden beads I wore round my neck with a limp hand. 'Where did you get those?' she asked in a tone suggesting their irrelevance to her life. Undoubtedly, I lived in the realm of the trivial: a husband-snatcher and a gossip, and, most important of all, dangerous to know. It made me think of Charlotte Bronte who pleads in *Shirley*, 'Men of England, what have you done to your women?'

Chapter Thirty-One

Tea and Cake and Stories

Whatever my thoughts were on the misogynist front, they did-
n't yet fit into what was going on around me. Old ways of
thinking stubbornly remained; even when my life in the country was no longer charmed, I still enjoyed going to my parents.
At leisure in Hove, my father began to tell me how he and
Mother had left Poland, the country they called Daheim,
where Jews had lived from the ninth century. Father's stories
used to come like sudden rain, and at other times he'd look
up as if he were searching in an attic to find treasures stashed
away long, long ago, and a story would unfold.

And now it's my turn. Father is in our multipurpose room
where he often debated with himself while working. He'd hold
up a shoe under repair, and moving his head from side to side,
he'd turn it over in his hand to inspect; then, pausing, he'd
sigh, and sometimes just plaintive sounds escaped while
Mother went in and out of the room, folding washing, sweeping, making their beds, smelling my cot, and Father, hardly
knowing she had gone, talked on.

These memories were good, but years later I read about the
plight of Jews in Poland down the centuries and the circumstances of their flight to Germany and other lands. I knew very
little about the huge numbers that went to America, except
from seeing the iconic Ellis Island film clips, and from popular
Hollywood films, and particularly from America's involvement in both world wars. A trusted Polish-born Jew – a lawyer
I consulted for getting compensation from Germany – gave
me a different view of Jews, explaining that they weren't all
peddlers or horse traders. 'You know,' he told me, 'the Poles

didn't always have the advantage over us; my father climbed high on the economic ladder in Lodz. Poles seeking employment in Jewish factories had to have some Yiddish.' I laughed out loud at this news.

But however well some Jews did in Poland, business was brisk for false papers because Russia was an ever-present threat for Poles, and for Jews. I was about five years old when I heard my father talk about forgers, saying 'easy money' with a mean smile on his face. Most people must have known one – how could they not with such a large Jewish exodus from Eastern Europe – and, as is famously known, boats didn't always dock in the right port but disembarked in London or Liverpool, even when the journey to New York had been paid for. 'So what?' my father joked, '...as long as the forger wasn't out of pocket!' At the age I was then, irony escaped me.

Recalling the humdrum life in our attic room was reassuring until I heard my father's disembodied statement: 'Why should I fight for them? It wasn't my country!' That phrase has lived in my head all my life. I used to think Jews were cowards: always on the run. Only recently, after reading a book called *Tsar Nicholas I and the Jews: The Transformation of Jewish Society in Russia, 1825–1855* by Michael Stanislawski, did I begin to understand why Jewish men dodging the army played such an important part in Jewish migration to the West.

When Poland was part of Russia, her edicts regarding Polish Jews were the same as for Russian Jews; even when Poland was briefly independent; fear of being press-ganged into the army continued. The Tsar's intention was to make subjects of all the peoples of Russia; Jews living according to Torah, their law, interfered with his plan. The way to remove these 'interlopers' was to lure them into the Russian army. Apparently this was done by stealth and torture, and finally with forcible conversions to Christianity. To force grown men to relinquish their religion proved too labour-intensive; less clumsy was to focus

on children. Significantly, Jewish men known in the community as Chappers were appointed to catch them. In the period
between 1827 and 1854, some 70,000 Jews were conscripted,
of whom 50,000 were minors, some as young as six. These men
and children were lost to the community forever. Being press-
ganged into the army turned out to be a life sentence for them,
and the loss of their identity.

There was some cause for celebration; not all measures for
Jews were cruel. In 1844 general education was introduced to
add to the singular study of the Talmud and Torah. Living
without rights in the Pale of Settlements in Russia continued
and the system of the settlements instituted in 1791 was not
abolished until 1917. The Jews had lived isolated there, as Isaac
Bashevis Singer wrote '… hardly knowing what was going on
in the world outside'.

Eastern European Jewish men found ways of avoiding the
army: lying about your age was easiest, Father told me on one
of my visits. Army service could be avoided by giving false
ages, as was made crystal clear to me reading my mother's
birth certificate. Even so, my father served in the Polish army
as a tailor to officers. As other men did, he found a phrase to
support his actions: 'It wasn't my country,' he said in connection to army service. I doubted that my father knew the grim
details of earlier times, but if he did, he never told me the pre-
cise circumstances from which this phrase may have sprung.
For my father, real learning came from the Torah, and news
of political troubles came to Jews from outside, filtering
through communities by word of mouth in Yiddish. Both my
parents were illiterate in their host country's language, not unusual for many others.

Jaroslav Hašek's novel The Good Soldier Šchweik illustrates
a particular attitude of Eastern European conscripts (not necessarily Jewish) in the 19th and early 20th centuries. My father
wouldn't have known Hasek's novel, but he mimed Šchweik

perfectly, a mischievous smile round his lips saluting his superiors. Yes, my father was Šchweik! Now in England, his play-acting was merely entertaining as he was in no danger of being marched back to barracks for insolent behaviour.

An account of a Nazi atrocity perpetrated on Polish soil in World War II highlights the plight of Jewish statelessness through the ages. A resurgent group, mostly Jews, was being shot into a pit. A rabbi posted on the edge was ordered to recite the Kaddish (prayer for the dead) continuously until all the bodies had fallen. A man and a woman in the group were lovers; she was a Pole and her lover was a Jew. Before the woman fell, she cried out, 'Long live Poland!' She had a country to die for. I was reminded of Weiler and his dislike of his Eastern European brethren, the possibility that they might spoil advances made by German Jews, and worst of all for him was how they had tortured German into Yiddish. No less displeasing was how they displayed their Hasidic ways of dress; how scruffy they must have appeared to him: crossing borders illegally as most of them did, could not have been an elegant affair. However, whether scruffy or not, these 'poor relations' were welcomed in soup kitchens by German Jewish women.

Cousin Sarah from Paris had already told me about my parents' life in Lodz. 'When your father decided to leave the old country, it was assumed he'd take a wife,' Sarah revealed, 'the girl he was engaged to didn't want to leave home and the matchmaker arranged a meeting with another woman.' A detail Father never told me.

Visits to my parents also meant freshly baked cakes ready on a wire tray, the divine smell greeting me full on. Mother would sit on an upright chair, knitting. I felt like a small child waiting for a treat: cake for tea, and a story. Still with his apron on, Father would sit in his chair, legs apart. 'Where shall I start?' he'd say, chuckling. Then, clearing his throat, he'd begin. 'Oh yes, I know. I was invited for afternoon coffee to friends and friends of friends and God knows who else. Looking over the gathering I wondered which of the women there was for me. Then the matchmaker, seeing how awkward I was, escorted me over to a young woman who wore a hat with a high crown and a deep brim –only her chin was visible. I had a problem: how was I going to see her face when I was a head taller than her? Worse still was that her head was bowed which made me think of all the matchmaker jokes of last resort brides on offer – cross-eyed, limping and humpbacked women. None of this was true of the woman standing in front of me, and all at once the outlandish jokes faded. All the same, I had to tell them something when I got home! Encouraged by the matchmaker, your mother and I shook hands. Both of us were now covered with embarrassment – and still, I hadn't seen her face! Not knowing what else to do, I bent down and looked under the brim of her hat.'

Father, now in a jocular mood, mimed the scene and looking over to Mother he said, 'What did I see you may ask? Well, look at your mother now and you'll see exactly what I saw!' Mother's eyes were fixed on her knitting, her face in flames. 'Blushing or not, I decided that she was the one for me, the one to take with me to Germany. 'Noo,' Father said cheekily, 'did I make the right choice or not?' He picked up his story again: 'When we left Poland, I promised your grandmother I would look after her daughter.'

So, they didn't just up and go easily as is said in some history books. Listening to my father took me back to my childhood, how I noticed their tears, the difficulty they had leaving family behind, and I began to listen more carefully. 'Yes, three hundred of us made for the border. The ground was boggy underfoot, and sometimes our feet sank ankle-deep. We were lucky,' Father digressed, as he often did when telling a story, 'a few months earlier, your Aunt Pessa, at the very same spot, wasn't so lucky. There was a lot of shooting on the border, and she had the misfortune to get a bullet in her leg. What an Och und Weh that was, I can tell you! When your mother heard of the shooting, she fell to the ground, doing her sackcloth and ashes act: up and down she went like a ship on a rough sea. Pessa was taken back to Lodz to have the bullet removed. One thing is for sure, there were doctors who kept stumm about such things. Pessa was a hero. As soon as her wound healed, she dared again, and this time she succeeded, and with a small child! Did I ever tell you that Pessa belonged to the Bund?' Without waiting for a response, Father started marching back and forth, a fist by his chest holding an imaginary axe over his shoulder the way devotees of the Bund (General Jewish Workers' Club) did, according to him. 'She was the strong one in that family, she could have gone far, and look how she ended up, marrying that lump, Avrum, a good for nothing, a decorator, who spent the money he earned on cigarettes and going to the pictures. His family always came last. If anyone asked where Avrum was, we always said, 'probably at the Lampeles!' Father was using the Yiddish euphemism for the pictures. 'Oh', I said, remembering, 'little lights'. Acting cross, Father said, 'Now you made me forget where I was!' 'Come on, Daddy', I jollied him on, 'you know exactly where you are. Come, finish your story.' Being eager to listen, digressions and all, I put up with his ways, but what made my heart give a thump or two was that my parents knew what a rotter Uncle Avrum was.

No surprise, my father knew exactly where he was. He clasped his chin as though there was a beard to stroke, a gesture Hasidic Jews make when thoughtful or content. 'There we were, finally across the border, endlich in Deutschland! The guide took us to a large wooden hut with benches round the walls and extra chairs stacked on top of each other. We were glad for the rest. All our boots were muddy but your mother's were worse than anybody's. I knelt down before her and cleaned them with my handkerchief. People knew we weren't married, and what they didn't say in words, they said with their eyes – engaged couples didn't behave like that, touching a woman's ankles before marriage! I felt more awkward than ashamed. Gott alone knows what your mother must have felt!' Then, turning to the flower box outside their window, he said, 'I must change the plants.' Moments later, he faced the room again, 'They whispered among themselves, looking sideway at us,' and as Mother's face seemed to be on fire again, a wave of affection took hold of him. He had to embrace her, that instant! This way, I imagined, he could link the past to the present.

My father's affectionate nature is a strong memory for me, it made much in my life good, helped me to forgive. Although his straight talking embarrassed Mother, she never once contradicted him. She seemed to be satisfied with his version of events. Finishing his story, Father said, 'Next stop Berlin, and from there, to Worms.'

I often wondered what kind of witness of their past my mother would have made. Only once did I see her rebuff him. He was telling a story, she was knitting as usual, and finally the moment came when he had to touch her. She was counting stitches, and Father being a nuisance, she took one hand off her knitting and smiling up at him gave him a gentle slap on his cheek. 'Go avay!' she said. Eyes back on her knitting, she cried, 'Look what you made me do – I've dropped a stitch!'

Nothing she did or said offended him; the opposite, her modesty attracted him, and her irritation with him merely aroused him. I used to think that Father wanted more of a sparring partner, but generally he enjoyed what she was. His only criticism of her was 'she expects too much from people, thinking that if she gives, people will give in return. When this doesn't happen, she suffers.' 'Yes,' I said, 'I've noticed. I feel the same.' Father appeared to be surprised.

Contrary to this benign description of my mother, she wasn't always passive. Many times she endorsed the claim made by Jewish women down the ages, 'To live with a man is to learn a page from the Talmud.' What a help this 'learning' must have been when her husband was wilful! Women's analysis of men was a task taken as seriously as men took the Torah, and, further aggravating these tensions, men patronizingly stuck to their view of women: 'The test of a good wife is if she is able to disentangle a disorderly skein of wool patiently.'

Another visit, another story, and more cake. 'Eat, eat,' Father said, imitating the fabled Jewish mother, putting yet another piece of cake on my plate. 'Look at that,' he said, 'am I not as good a baker as any woman?' By that he meant he was more like a pastry cook than a baker. I think my father could have been anything he set his mind to. Mother had taught him all she knew, and when he could do what she taught him, he retired her. She seemed to enjoy her well-earned rest.

Father was who he was, lovable, kind and humorous – and, as I was to find out, a bit of a rogue. The amount of the German pension was not fixed. In the excitement of getting everything together, I didn't read the small print (did I ever?) that the pension would increase with inflation. Not knowing this, I asked him every now and then if he needed more money. He assured me he didn't. Though puzzled, I went on saving, just in case, and as it turned out so had Father. When I retired, I had saved enough money to buy an annuity for my parents. Over the phone one morning, I told Father about my savings. 'I don' need id!' he said with pride. 'What do you mean you don't need it? Do you live on air?' I asked. Apparently not, 'I have saved seven t'ousand poun'!' he said. 'On the allowance I gave you?' 'Yes,' he said. When I told him that the allowance I gave him was a gift and tax had to be paid on it by me, he dismissed the whole thing as nonsense: 'I saved the money for you!' and having acquitted himself, he added, 'all you would have done was to spend it on Schmattes!' Dead right, but what a rascal you were, Papa!

Now Father wrote out cheques for charities and considered himself on the way to becoming a Rothschild. Unsolicited, he'd say, 'Mein bank is de Barclay bank!'. Quick, I thought, I must get him to make a will, at least to get my money back. What a battle it was to get him to sign! I don't think any member of the Lerner family back in Poland had ever left such a document. After his death, the will was nowhere to be found, nor was the solicitor's name who had dealt with it, and I didn't have a copy of it. Father's disregard for legality cost me three hundred pounds. What did my father and I know about intestacy? The lucky thing was he didn't put the money under the mattress. The fact is that both of us were still peasants at heart.

Another visit, another story and cake. 'Have I ever told you how we lived in Lodz?' 'Yes, you have!' I said. I needn't have bothered to say anything, because he hadn't heard me. It didn't matter, I loved his stories even told twice, and on he went: 'Fourteen people in two rooms, girls and boys together. My mother and father…' and before he went into details, he chuckled the way he always did, his whole face lit up as he imagined what he was going to say, one hand palm up or down to illustrate the situation. 'We slept, one on the table, another under the table, and yet another above the stove. Furniture was used as room dividers; cupboards and wardrobes were special places wide enough for two where my mother and father slept,' he said, a respectful expression on his face. 'One night I heard my parents talking. "Chuna, what are we going to do about our girls, what will become of them without a dowry?" they cried.' I knew this situation well: no dowry, no husband. 'But what could a poor scribe provide,' Father said, excusing his father, 'writing a few mezzuses?' (miniature Torah scrolls fixed on the right doorpost of Jewish houses) When Jews came from Eastern Europe to the west, they looked for these symbols on houses to connect with Jews. 'You can't make a living from that, let alone save up for a dowry! Anyway, my sisters took their lives into their own hands and left home to live in furnished rooms near their work; machinists they were,' (Lodz) was the Manchester of Poland), 'What a disgrace! Young women living alone when they belonged to a family whose father wore Peyis and whose mother wore a Sheitel!' (The curly side-locks and wig were signs of what an extremely Orthodox family my father came from).

Father wasn't as outraged as all that; he was feeling retrospectively, replicating attitudes that were held in his youth, the shame they all felt. I thought of Father in his early years in Germany, well on the way to discarding the old ways, his hand running over his chin as he said, 'You see, I don't have a beard but I am still a Jew!' Who was he talking to when Mother and I were the only ones in the kitchen? At a guess, away from the confines of a closed society, I suspected that my father wasn't as bound to the views he now expressed. He never wore the eccentric apparel of Hasidim, nor did he observe the Biblical injunction regarding the style of hair. Clean-shaven, he looked like everyone else in the street. Although he never admitted his lapses consciously, they were more visible than he knew, or wanted to know. Minor festivals like Chanukah were remembered halfheartedly. We didn't even own a Menorah. The first few lines of mau ozur were sung and Chanukah faded back to antiquity without me ever making a connection with the club I belonged to, known as Maccabee after the eponymous hero's struggle of the Hasmoneans under Judas Maccabee. The Purim festival was only a word to me, not something to be enjoyed by dressing up and painting your face, and mostly the phrase Purim Spiel was used to describe a farcical situation, or a tragic one, the emphasis being: this is no Purim Spiel!

The next time I went to see my parents, Father opened the door to me and said, 'I am going to Israel to see my sister Blooma.' His fervour surprised me, as did his opinion on the *Guardian* newspaper I had recommended him to read instead

of the *Daily Telegraph*. 'O.K, so I'll read the *Guardian*,' he said.
A couple of weeks later I asked him, 'Well, so what do you
think of the *Guardian*?' expecting agreement. Giving me a
quick look, he said, '*Anti-Semiten – alle!*' 'What do you mean
by 'all of them'?' I asked. 'The tone they write in about us
makes me think that nothing has changed since the Holocaust:
as I used to say in the Hitler years, anti-Semitism is a Gentile
illness, and as we are now able to defend ourselves, they don't
like it – what Chutzpah they have!' he replied. It seemed to me
that my father was angry having to point this out to me, and
now that he drew me back into his mindset, I thought of Shy-
lock, Dreifuß and Fagin and how I used to read the names
without noticing how they were portrayed. Critically numb, I
had stayed that way for years. I must have appeared absorbed
in these thoughts because Father prodded me and gave me a
rundown in his imperfect English of news he had listened to
on the World Service during the night and what he had read
in the paper before I came that morning. Thinking of the effort
he made, I regret my impatience with him, how I stopped him
from telling me what he had learned. 'Don't bother with English, tell me in Yiddish,' I said. I suppose I didn't want to lose
the homely sound of the Yiddish I understood so well, and the
way Father used to read me stories from Sholomalikim, the
scornful Yiddish writer, and how he swore me to secrecy not
to tell Mr Josephs, his ultra orthodox friend. 'And another
thing,' Father said, interrupting my thoughts again, 'don't
worry about the fare money, I saved up for it sewing hundreds
of buttons on suits and coats for a local tailor. For next to
nothing, I tell you! But who cares – as long as I can go to Israel.' Why Mother wasn't going with him I didn't find out; I
was too involved with Cannan's drinking at the time. In any
case, Mother was still able to look after herself. All the same, I
kept an eye on her. I can't remember helping Father to get his
ticket or taking him to the airport, but then he was only in his

early seventies. For once, I had nothing to worry about. The two weeks he was away raced by. The card he sent arrived after he came back, and a good thing too, because neither Mother nor I could read Yiddish.

Back from Israel, Father told me how irritating his sister had been. More to his liking was his favourite niece Rosl. They shared the same sense of the ridiculous. 'Yes', he said, 'laughing with Rosl was better than crying with my sister. Whenever I wanted to go out, she'd hang onto my jacket holding me back. "Don't go out, don't leave me," she'd say. She stifled me; but to tell you the real truth, my fear was that she'd ask me for the picture of her two little girls – you know, the ones that were gassed. I was afraid she'd go mad if I gave it to her. She knew someone in the family had it, but not who.'

I inherited the picture of the two girls whose names I didn't know. When Cousin Sarah in Paris told me about them, she didn't refer to their names either; they were just Blooma's little girls, her half-sisters and cousins rolled into one. From time to time, I come across the black and white picture of them in my shoebox. I look at them, imagining Blooma checking her girls' appearance, like mothers everywhere, the final tweak to the bows in their hair before the shutter release buzzed. They are standing next to each other wearing identical dark dresses with white Peter Pan collars, their hair parted on one side, dark bows holding back thick clumps of hair. Both girls are wearing knee socks and their shoes are tied with what look like satin bows. The arm of the older girl is round the shoulder of her younger sister; both of them are looking shyly at the camera. They would be roughly my age now had they lived. As ever when I look through pictures of family I have never met, I speculate about bonds we might have made, kept or broken. Blooma was the only one of my father's sisters I knew by name, the one he talked about most. They wrote to each other regularly, that is about four times a year.

'I surprised Rosl,' Father said, pulling me back to his story, 'she came to the door rubbing her eyes, hardly believing what she saw. She excused herself for having just woken up from her afternoon sleep. The whole flat was in darkness.' I had the impression Father didn't understand about darkened rooms in hot climates, just as we, after the war, didn't understand when we sent parcels of heavy clothes to Israel when what they needed were refrigerators. At the time, their request was thought to be an extravagant demand. 'What a Chutzpah!' my mother said, never having had a fridge herself. Rosl called my father the affectionate Onkele. She was Pessa's daughter, so no blood relation to him. I remember him making her a fur jacket of black astrakhan way back in our kitchen in Ludwigshafen, nailing the damp skin to Mother's baking board to stretch and dry the pelt and Mother crying, 'Oih, how will I make my Challas for Shabbes?'

'Tell me about your apprenticeship with the furrier,' I asked my father when next I saw him. At once, he plucked an incident from his mind, but before he started to tell his story he reminded me, 'You know, I started work when I was eleven,' and when I nodded yes, he looked upward and smiled as always, amused by the images in his head. 'Yes... I sat cross-legged on the work table practising, sewing off-cuts of fur together, blowing hairs out of the way, blowing and sewing, and often while I was eating my lunch not daring to stop eating for fear the manager might shout at me. He did once, I tell you; the walls shook! But that wasn't because I was eating – no, it was because I cut the fur on the hair side! I never did it again and so I ate and blew, and when the hairs got into my food I just ate them.' Father then showed me the stitch he had learned as a boy by laying two bits of material edge to edge, then sewing a row of small running stitches on each piece of material, holding them together top and bottom with a bar stitch; then, delicately, he pulled the stitches together so as not to pucker the material. 'Now,' he said, putting the sample of his handiwork on the table next to him, 'machines do it.' Looking upward and smiling again he cleared his throat and began to tell me the story of the manager.

'Every day, at dinner-time, he flicked bits and pieces of stuff off the work table, and when it was free of dust he took a cloth from a drawer in a cupboard. Shaking it free from its folds, he laid it ceremoniously on the empty space, smoothing and stroking it flat. Then he laid a knife and fork opposite each other and a glass at arm's length for water. But most important of all, he put his gold pocket-watch, flap open, next to the knife. Ready, he sat back in his chair, fists on the edge of the table, waiting. The same time every day, a woman – his mother she was not – came with a basket over her arm, a white embroidered cloth over the dishes. Gently, she lifted two bowls and a plate from the basket and put them on the table, and lastly a big spoon for serving the food. The smell of it made my mouth water. I had just eaten a salt-herring and bread for my dinner.

'The manager ate at a leisurely pace but every now and then, the woman sitting next to him took tiny morsels of food from his plate and popped them into her mouth. When they'd finished eating, they schmoozed and laughed inches away from my feet. A little while later, the manager looked at his watch. "Hmm," he said, "half an hour exactly," and satisfied with the timing, he and the woman got up from the table and went into the small room next to the workshop, shutting the door firmly behind them. God knows what they did in that room!' Father said, giggling like the schoolboy he should have been then. I imagined him sitting there with his golden curls, watching. Throwing conjecture to the wind, he said, 'Never mind what they did in that room, the boss nearly had an apoplectic fit! You should have seen the way he paced up and down shouting, "A whole hour for dinner!" His shouting was of no use: times were changing. The manager belonged to the Bund, which for the boss was like sticking needles into him, and both of them being Jews they couldn't exactly kill each other, could they? The boss, furious or not, had to put up with the changing times and he suffered in silence – but if looks could have killed!' Father said, chuckling.

On another afternoon, dusk had turned to darkness, and times had changed for my parents too. The glow of light from the flats beyond the shrubs of Park Gate was just right for storytelling. We had finished tea and Mother was at the day centre she now went to, so Father was able to tell me another story. We were sitting opposite each other in armchairs, and Father was looking down at his knees: it was a different mood entirely. When finally he began to speak, he told me something I never knew. To put me in the picture, he said, 'You know when I lived with the Mamme at Eva's, and Harry was a boarder in the religion school and came home for visits?' 'Yes, yes,' I said impatient for the new story. 'Imagine, when after a couple of visits Harry's Peyis were growing. I was in shock. Picture it, my beautiful boy with Peyis! Just looking at him gave me a fright.' Father rubbed his knees with flat hands. 'What could I do, complain to the rabbi who, I was sure, would punish my child if I complained? With every visit, Harry's Peyis grew longer. My heart ached from indecision and I made up my mind to stop the ache. The next time Harry came home, I cut off his Peyis with my tailor's shears. The hair fell on the floor with my tears; I was thinking of my father's Peyis and I wondered what he would have said. What I did cut me in two.' Father's tears ran down his cheeks and down his shirt. Giving his nose a good blow, he continued, 'The rabbi was too rigid, too old-fashioned. When Harry went back to school without Peyis, the rabbi sent me an ultimatum: either your boy lives according to my rules or you take him home! Home? I knew living with Cousin Eva was only temporary – she'd already done more than enough for us – and what with you not wanting to stay with the Cohens in Dudley… I thanked God for Jack and Sally… agreeing to give you a home. Thinking back, the pain still grips my heart, how unbearable the whole thing was, and how I blotted out the way my child looked.' Then, saying no more, my father bent forward, kneading his thighs with his fists, tears flowing. What made me feel dreadful was that I never appreciated how difficult my wanting to come to London had been for him.

Seeing how painful this episode had been for my father made dealing with the Orthodoxy he returned to difficult to understand. I decided not to probe any further; he had told me enough. As I saw it, Peyis and beards seem always to have been a crisis for my father's identity as a Jew. Challenging him on his insecurities wouldn't be helpful, and with me having married out nothing rational was going to ensue. I knew that trusting Goyim was always going to be a problem for him: how dare I trust them after what happened to us in the Holocaust?

'My dearest, precious brother,' Blooma's letters used to begin. Every new paragraph began with yet another endearment as if to fix affection to the page. My mother mocked these endearments, thought them overdone. In one letter, Blooma said she was coming for a visit to England. Father prepared me, told me how old-fashioned his sister was, and how she still upheld old traditions. Whatever was going on between my father and me was shelved; that way, I could be around to see, hear, and help. Blooma came with her fourteen-year-old son, Aaron. All was well until she spilled my parents' past over their present – in particular –by claiming that the girl he was originally engaged to had been a better match than my mother. Casually, when Father was out shopping, Blooma said to my mother, 'You weren't the one he loved.' So there was more to the story Cousin Sarah had told me in Paris.

Blooma's status as a survivor from Auschwitz made normal criticism of her inappropriate, but Father stayed loyal to

Mother: 'Blooma, you can't talk to Marie like that! We have been married far too long for you to face my wife with your foolishness.' For Blooma this was no foolishness; what had happened sixty years ago was to her as if it had happened yesterday. When I called in on my parents one afternoon, she was out with my father and Aaron. Alone with me, my mother spoke in whispers, 'Blooma wants to sleep with Aaron in the same room as her, honestly! I saw her cuddling him and he was patting her neck. She blushed bright red when she saw me watching.'

Would I ever know what really happened? Mother was getting forgetful, exaggerating events, and she angered easily. Further involvement on my part was unpalatable. In despair, Father told me, 'Your mother said one thing and Blooma said another, and they ended up screaming at each other. Of course the neighbours could hear, the walls are thin, and when I told them to stop screaming, Blooma got in a huff and threatened to pack her bags and go.' When I heard what had happened I was confused and so was Aaron, watching and hearing everything, but some of what Mother said must have been true, because next time I visited my parents Aaron's camp bed was in the spare room where his mother slept.

'The final outcome of this Geschichte,' Father said, 'was that Blooma, after another shouting match with your mother, packed her bags, and standing next to her luggage, hands on her hips, she waited for me to take her to Victoria Station. After a very unpleasant journey, Aaron threatened to die of hunger if I didn't buy him a hot dog from a stall in the station forecourt. So, what else could happen? I was upset enough without him wanting to eat non-kosher! I was glad when the train started to move, I wanted my peace.' After Blooma's visit, my mother's memory loss got worse. Our laughter ended abruptly. Father rang me at least three times a week, and as Mother's senility got worse, twice a day.

A couple of years later, Blooma died of cancer. I have no idea how Father coped with his loss. I didn't dare ask; climbing the Himalayas might have been easier. But in the end it is dreams that count: longing woven into letters, understanding from afar, choosing words to console, to mark concern. When Mother was still well, long before Blooma visited my parents, my father read out the letters he received from her, the same endearments mocked spitefully by my mother. Finally, her jealousy had an outlet. Apart from us children, my mother had no blood relations in England. Often she would say to me, 'Your father's cousins are very clannish.' Defeated, she got round her envy and found the phrase to describe her feelings. Out came her new name for my father's cousins: Deine holzene Meshpukha (your wooden family). Most of my father's cousins being in the furniture trade made Mother's phrase pertinent and Father and I laughed heartily with her.

Father, no longer a tourist passing through his faith, shaped his life to his liking, reclaiming the ways of his father, but he did go a little peculiar. He did a dreadful thing, a tribal thing no longer appropriate for our times. He wrote a letter to Harry about his wife Norma, declaring that she came from 'bad blood'. I was dumbfounded. Harry, too upset to be rational, was sure I had helped Father write this letter. 'You must have done,' he said. 'What?' was all I could muster. The rift between my father and Harry and Norma was total, and of course with me too. Years of enmity followed.

The one good thing in this family mess was that I had moved my parents to Hove. My reward was that my father was happy with his life and often told me how 'fulfilled' he felt. Conveniently, the synagogue was two minutes' walk from the flat. He did the morning service every day, enjoyment written all over his face. Father really believed that he sang like one of the famous cantors, the brothers Kosovitzky. It made him happy to believe this – harmless really.

Yet despite his joy, Father served God in isolation from his family. Having written that dreadful letter didn't help. Both his sons lived in London, and I was 'buried in a hole in the country' as he put it. One of the saddest things I remember my father doing was lighting the Sabbath candles himself. Mother could no longer be trusted with matches. One Friday, cutting hair in Hove, I decided to pop round to see my parents; not to see them, even just to say 'hello', was unthinkable. I parked my car in the drive under their kitchen window and ran up the stairs two at a time. Opening the front door I saw my father already enveloped in his Talith, the tapes bound round his left arm and the phylacteries resting on his forehead. He swayed, his lips shivering in prayer. The candles had been lit, probably moments before I arrived. I felt like a ruffian barging in on the ambience he had created. Mother stared through me – not one of her lucid moments.

Chastened, I fled. 'So how come you are tearing yourself away from something so warm and familiar?' I chided myself on the way home, 'you are not exactly going home to any warmth.' Driving through the countryside created the space I needed for the two sides of myself, leaving my otherness and the religious baggage safe with my father. But hadn't I wished to tear that baggage into shreds and chuck it on our compost heap in the hope it would change into something fine and new? At first, when I moved to the country with Cannan, my life was religious in a different way: digging, pruning, grubbing out old shrubs, planting new ones, shifting soil, levelling ground. Yet despite this, my emotional ground was uneven, no longer level between the life I'd chosen and the soil I pottered about in. I was not as transformed as I thought I was, hardly even knowing that transformation was what I wanted. An alien I was and an alien I had stayed, a weed on the perfectly kept lawns of the local riding fraternity. Conflict between my new life and the old sired a new voice: 'Duty, stop nagging me!'

In the fifteen years my parents lived in Hove, we had only one family Seder. I helped Father prepare for the festivities, as I always did even when I didn't actually join him; thinking about this, I don't know how I managed not to. For the preparations, Father produced a much thumbed manual with instructions for the yearly 'spring clean' as I called it, much to his annoyance. 'What do you mean a spring-clean, Pesach is Pesach, no?' Part of these preparations was the instruction on how to clean surfaces: 'Take a scrubbing brush and hot soda water and remove every particle of dirt etc. Rinse with clear water...' and so on; clearly this was meant for earlier times. When Father started to scrub the Formica top with all his might, I thought for God's sake, has he lost his reason? 'Why scrub Formica?' I asked, and he, truly furious, stretched out his arm, finger pointing to the door, he shouted, 'Go! Leave my house!' This time, he was really angry; this was serious stuff not said with his usual mocking tone. I left him bent over, scrubbing brush held down with both hands, his elbows articulated over his Formica top.

When I returned, he was himself again and we collaborated as always. I made the traditional Kneidel (Matzo balls) from a recipe in Robert Carrier's Great Dishes of the World – less solid than Mother's – and Father made the chicken soup and stuffed fish, all the while keeping an eye on me to make sure I kept milk and meat dishes separate.

That night, Jeffrey came with his wife Yvonne and their two small sons. Harry and Norma came without their sons. Jeffrey's youngest son fidgeted throughout the proceedings, taking his Kippa off his head, and I dedicated myself to the task of putting it back on. On, off, on, off – in the end, I won this battle of wills. That 'win' caused an emotional typhoon inside me, uprooting a network of contradictions. We all seemed ill at ease with each other. Father stuck strictly to tradition, overseeing, pointing, selecting the little heaps of symbolic food on the ceremonial plate to be touched and mentioned in turn, reciting blessings, and maro (bitter herbs) were eaten to remind us how bitter life was under slavery. No amount of sentiment given to this festival of freedom could help the epic move needed to resolve our family muddle; sticking to what happened three thousand years ago was simpler than dealing with our problems that night. Whether Father felt remorse for having sent the offending letter, I don't know. The formality of the Seder saved the evening, but I wanted more, much more: phone calls the next day, the excitement of having been together, going over jests between courses, laughter. None of that happened. Worst of all was when Mother showed affection towards Harry, and he, unable to respond, his face red with embarrassment, looked across the table at me and said, 'You can see I have a problem here.' Harry's lips brushing against Mother's cheek could have been the sign for change, but for that to happen courage was needed.

After the years living contentedly in Hove, what a terrible moment it must have been when my father noticed my mother's disorientation, the start of her senility. The more the illness advanced, the more Father didn't understand it. 'I will make her better, I will!' he'd say obstinately. Lucid moments did occur; he told me about them on the phone. I witnessed one of them when Father had phlebitis. He was resting in bed, the affected leg on a pillow. Coming into their bedroom, I saw Mother rewinding bandages for the sores on his legs, sitting on a chair facing him. Looking at him thoughtfully, she said, 'Max, don't go, I need you.' This left even me thinking I had imagined her confusion.

Chapter Thirty-Two

Women

I had hoped that moving from the country would change our situation. I found the nearest thing to a perfect flat in London: a top floor flat in a mansion block behind Baker Street. It had an east-west aspect and a small balcony facing west, the tree tops of Dorset Square visible above the houses. We were lucky: the previous owner had left the best bits, and cupboards galore. Nothing much needed doing except for a lick of paint here and there. Cannan came and viewed it; I packed up our chattels at Godleys, and sold the last car we ever owned.

Now living in London and no longer having a plot to keep in order and water, I began to cut hair in our bathroom, four half-days a week starting at 2 p.m. I enjoyed intelligent conversation with women who appreciated the sparse service I offered, happy to be liberated from 'hairdos'. Before I started, I walked briskly through Regents Park, past the bandstand, on to the zoo and out again through the rose garden, its gusts of gorgeous smells coming at me when the wind blew my way. Twice that pleasure was marred, once when a bomb exploded under the bandstand, which I missed by exactly three minutes. The other time was when I saw Cannan sitting alone in a deckchair, furtively looking round before he gulped some whisky from a flat half-bottle. I didn't want to catch him red-handed; ashamed, we were unable to undo the turmoil we were in, I walked on.

But when the affair he was conducting was slow to end, I choreographed my own Kristallnacht giving way to something I had never done before: drink. I downed a third of a bottle of whisky, glass after glass after glass in quick succession. Then, from a Habitat kitchen unit in the corridor which was used as a drinks cupboard, I took out glass after empty glass and smashed them against the cupboard door at the top-end of the corridor, three metres away from where I took aim. Once every glass was smashed, I stepped into the bathroom, lay down on the floor and curled up, waiting for oblivion. A fragment of stray glass blinked near my eye. Clutching it between my fingers, I scratched away at my wrist, and before I drew blood my senses went limp.

Almost asleep, I heard the front door shut. Moments later, Cannan stood on the threshold of the bathroom. Though fuzzy-minded, I knew I wanted him to be upset, show me he cared, embrace me perhaps? Was I dreaming? Cannan behaved like a paramedic, advising me to get off the floor and to be careful not to step on any glass in case I cut my bare feet. I stayed where I was, and as if from miles away, I heard Cannan's shaky voice, 'Samaritans?' This soothed me. I stayed on the floor. He was in charge, I thought vaguely. More activity on my behalf: Cannan swept the glass against the wall and then urged me again to get up. This I did on my own, levering myself up on the bath. Then he led me to the living room and made me sit on the sofa. 'Rest while I make you some coffee. It will be instant,' he said, 'you know I'm not good at making the real thing.' Back we were with obstacles and evasions. I sipped the coffee in silence, its bitter taste appropriate for the mood that moment. Cannan, not sober himself, suggested we go for a walk round the park 'for some fresh air,' he said, 'it will clear your head.' What about his head? So his problem was mine, and again I found myself in a sacrificial situation and glimpsed a pattern; I was unable to walk away from our situation and as always I felt responsible. Like my father, I must and would make things better.

I agreed to the walk. We made our way past the zoo. Some couples were holding hands – a sharp contrast to what we were doing; we just hung onto each other, bodies close, shivering. What price a human touch!

Tracing what led to my despair, I have to go back to when we still lived in the country and Cannan's affair was at its height, when I looked for, and found, drafts of his letters to her and her replies to him. When she was in London, they stayed at Blake's Hotel; this he had revealed to me in a moment of drunken pride – in fact he had invited me to meet her: 'You'd like her', he said. What was I, his mother, to give my approval – applaud them? By now, my common sense was way below my squalid emotions, and no sooner did he speak, I obeyed. I went to London to stay with my cousin Hannah with the sole purpose of chasing them. 'Don't go,' she said, but I replied, 'I must.' 'To achieve what?' she asked. In a hurry, I left her question unanswered.

'What is the room number of –?' I asked at reception. Upstairs, I opened the door without first knocking, and stepping inside, I imitated the casual way people then spoke: 'I've come to see who would do what with whom.' Then I remembered that this meeting was similar to what he'd asked his wife to do when I first met him. She too complied. Poor us.

At dinner, the 'lovers' had eyes only for each other and she cremated him with her gaze. Is this what he wanted me to see, their passion for each other? Despite the evidence before me, I asked Cannan pathetically, 'Where do I fit in this set-up? It was you who wanted me to meet her,' to which he said, 'No, not this evening, you go back to your cousin in Finchley.' I stayed.

What was wrong with me? I was a forty-five-year-old woman who had fallen in love for the first time, with the emotions of a teenager, who couldn't handle rejection, who was convinced their love would last forever.

After dinner, the lovers went up to their room. I remained seated at the table wondering what to do next. When the waiter asked me if I wanted some more coffee, I knew that he knew the situation I was in. Embarrassed, I looked away. Like hairdressers, hotel staff get a sense of what is going on around them. I decided to go back to their room but this time, I knocked. Cannan opened the door and ran straight back to the bed where they'd already been. As they were now cradled in a three-foot wide bed, the only one in the room, I bedded down on the floor in front of the wooden sofa, first grabbing the two scatter cushions displayed in each corner of the sofa: one for my head and the other to hug – and, as it turned out, the cushion I hugged absorbed the banging of my heart. No other sound until Cannan's lover said, looking up at him, 'Do you think she has brought a pistole with her?' He was enchanted by the way she pronounced 'pistole'. Her instinct was right: had I brought I gun, who knows what might have happened? She knew what was going on, her nervous giggle told me, but Cannan, oblivious of any danger, tightened his arms around her and said, chuckling, 'I think not.' I lost control.

I got off the floor and went over to their bed and waited until they got up. She pulled a chair to the middle of the room, and Cannan, clothed in his underpants and socks, depressed the edge of the bed. I sat opposite her on another chair. My thoughts went from one fact to another - but then, so did her gaze, straight to my large knees, and there her gaze remained like poisoned darts. The short skirt I was wearing gave her an opening: 'You are still attractive and you could easily find someone else.' My hands began to tremble and, rushing over to her, I put them round her neck, and she, getting hold of my hands, removed them. Then, getting up from her chair, she went over to the phone and asked for another room. They left, leaving their clothes in the wardrobe. Cannan walked behind her, a trace of appreciation for the drama etched on his face.

Alone, I drank the whisky they'd left behind straight from the bottle. My regret was that I didn't have a pair of scissors with me because, my urge was to cut their clothes into shreds, in particular, her midnight blue satin caftan, embroidered with crystals and mirrors: I imagined her prancing around in it to tempt his ageing body like Abigail did to please the aged biblical King David. She was twenty-seven years old and 'she wanted a child', Cannan told me at a later stage, and trying to appease me, he added, 'Anyone would have done, even a syringe.' Did he really hope his quip would amuse me?

The night passed somehow. In the morning we had breakfast together in their room. She ate with relish. 'I love English breakfast,' she said, and after a few more mouthfuls, she continued, "This was supposed to be my holiday – and she spoiled it!' Her face now taut and angry, she told me the reason why they were together: 'I only want the bits of him you can't mend'. Guilty, I took the blame readily. What she had said was true; our physical life had ended before he met her - of course she could please him better than I could! – and back I was with my sexual crippledom and gone too, was the hope it could be mended.

On the bus back to Hannah, I went over the night's events. Why was I in such a hurry to obey Cannan's wishes? Why did he need me to like her? Ah! Suddenly I knew – that is what victims do, they play their part – and that is why I was up to my neck in their affair. I decided not to tell Hannah; this shabby mess I would have to deal with on my own. Resolute, I got off the bus that went to Finchley and waited for one going to Victoria station, and home to Godleys.

A walk in the woods might help, it always has in the past; kicking over autumn leaves made me think of all the treatments I had. None of them enlightened me: Doctor Goldstein was the only helping hand I had, she knew what ailed me, said her smile, her hand encouragingly on my shoulder. None of my treatments had anything to do with affection or being lovingly coaxed to please and receive, and when finally, at the age of thirty-nine I had the good fortune to fall in love, I needed to hold onto what I thought I had achieved with an iron will, which for me, apparently meant, putting my hands around his lover's neck.

Leaves rustling underfoot dared me to go nearer taboo: taboo, boohoo, you victim seeker, you pleasure thieving you! With overwhelming sorrow I heard the sound of ripping where my heart had written a perfect score. Time to move. To escape the mess I was in, I put the house on the market. London would be better. Our house was sold within a week. A lot of people wanted our idyll.

Work would stop my endless search for answers. In the past, the way out of problems often solved themselves while I was busy with my hands. It was then that I started cutting hair in the flat. Perfect. Earning money again was good too. Twinned in thought; the days were not entirely taken up with Cannan's drinking and my weeping: he now wrote for television. Though still drinking, he was immersed and occupied. Who will ever know why people drink? Watching Cannan's decline into alcoholism made me jump to conclusions: not enough cuddles in childhood, disappointment with himself, the break-up of his marriage. Broken homes in our day were merely a forecast of the deluge to come. Whatever the reasons, our guilt corroded our strengths. Even while we lived in our idyllic surroundings, Cannan was tanked up with drink and the more he drank the sadder I became.

Baker Street had been less isolating at first, but then, tired of walking round the side streets constantly thinking about what I would find when I got home… Cannan's drinking became my addiction too. 'Detachment' as AA recommended for partners of drinkers failed me. Though cutting hair in our bathroom was a good distraction, I could help but be involved. Working time over, Cannan and I went to AA regularly. With his sense returning, he became a 'dry' alcoholic, but with all the habits of an alcoholic still intact: the air was thick with longing for a drink because 'life was nothing without it', he told me, and I held on to that ever-present threat. At one of the AA meetings, a woman sitting next to me said, 'If you prayed a little more, it would help you.' The certainty with which she addressed me took me aback rather than forward. In Cannan's 'dry' period, I reflected coldly on our life: how an inebriated mind, piquant with sentimentality, shows what shallow waters love can be fished from.

My senses returned when I met Mrs Boxer on the steps to our flats, a while after my smash-up. We greeted each other warmly, but when the warmth in her face turned to a frown, and she asked, 'Are you all right now?' I smiled weakly and fled, leaving her standing there, her frown growing deeper. It never occurred to me that she had heard the racket going on over her head. Drink and having a mistress in tow are not emotionally affordable, and with trust and illusion absent, I initiated the sale of our flat in London and went looking for a house in Hove. Crescy, my step-daughter, got a post at Sussex University, and she already lived in Brighton with her son Fergus, then four, and in nearby Lewes lived my step-son Nick with his wife Philippa and their son Robert, also four – additional reasons for us to move back to Hove. Having made a profit on the sale of the flat, we could do the work needed on the house we bought, and so we were back on track with a project in hand; that was what we were good at. Living by the sea again was healing too, her varied moods and behaviour, her violence, her stillness, her rushing and gushing, blatant and honest.

My thoughts were forever trying to catch up with how life was before Cannan drank. Forgetting wasn't easy; thoughts and dreams of Godleys dominated, of how the new owners had ruined it. Every dream was the same: walls barring the way, the staircase abandoned in high grass, doors blocked or locked, explanations expressed in slow, yawning motions. I still dwelt on those blissful days with Cannan: by-ways and unexpected views of steep cliffs and far vistas – that is where I loitered with him by my side, and at every turn, my need to tell him what I had found, and heard, and seen.

When I had lost him to drink, I cried to yet another therapist, and as I overflowed with grief she stroked my head, pivoting hers in almost a full circle suggesting a journey round the world; with raised brows, her eyes full of regard, she whispered, 'Where in the world do you find this happiness?' My therapist was Arthur Koestler's first wife. She seemed to know why I was crying.

In one way, it was the wrong moment for me to leave London because I wanted to go to classes on Jewish history at the Spiro Institute, a secular, cultural outfit in London, rather than a religious one. Losing love was easier than losing Jewishness. I wanted to know the stories behind Biblical tales and the opinions held by scholars. Before our course began, the lecturer said, 'We must acknowledge that we Jews came on the scene a long time after other civilizations.' That was a surprising revelation for me. Spellbinding!

Jewish history and baubles didn't go well together. In Hove we celebrated Christmas every year, and despite Cannan's professed atheism, Christmas decorations were the norm. 'Don't take any notice of what I do,' he said apologetically as he put up greenery and baubles in different colours on twigs. But I did take note, cultivating resentment because I didn't have the courage to claim my own tradition in their midst. I was seemingly addicted to living in the margins. What did a few baubles matter around the house? I rationalized. But baubles apart, Cannan and I were fighting with invisible fists to defend what we didn't really believe. We were swept along by celebrations in case we were thought of as emotional skinflints, mean and tortured, doubtful and lonely with each other. 'It was good of you to bother so much,' he would say; 'I don't mind, really I don't,' I tried to say generously. Had Cannan held a glass aloft declaring 'Happy Chanukah to Rosie' in front of his family I would most likely have been embarrassed, but then how do I know when it never happened? Thinking on these things, tears come to my eyes, telling me of my lack of courage.

In our early days together, Cannan's children used to go to their mother every Christmas, and that was of course right. But with Cannan, despite his dislike for the false aspect of what was supposed to be 'the season of good will', I saw a man regretting that he had lost his children around him on the day that mattered: Christmas Day. And so the disappointments of his life were held under with drink and jollity. Guilty myself, I ached for Jewish celebrations, but less painful was to avoid them altogether. Forget who you are, I counselled myself.

Nevertheless, in 1995 I celebrated Passover in our house for the first time with cousins and friends from the synagogue I now belonged to, and most important of all Cannan joined us, wearing a skullcap. I was nervous – when was I not when Jews and Christians seemingly respect each other? My neurosis aside, it turned out to be a good evening. Hans, one of the synagogue members – a refugee like me – led the service. When he invited Cannan to join us in reading from the Haggada (Exodus story), Cannan told me the next day how touched he was to be included. 'I was determined that you should have this at least once in our house,' he said. And I knew that he knew what I'd thrown to the winds. And that was good.

I married out not to defy my father but because I believed that Cannan and I met on an accultural plateau. Neither of us had bargained on the emergence of my hunger for Jewish history, and he, despite his protestations, belonged to European culture, its literature infused at every turn with Christian sensibilities, distilled and high-minded, supported by sublime music and poetry that still plucked at his heart. Wriggle as we may, Jews are the same, weighed down by their history, a people hitherto without a land, The Wandering Jew, half myth, half reality, often having to leave material things behind; who they were and how they learned was rolled up in the Torah scrolls, rolled and unrolled and read with a silver hand pointing to the text, no matter where they lived in the world.

But why do some Jews get 'lost' so obligingly, mulishly putting aside the contribution their ancestors have made to Western civilization? And why have they allowed the world to feed on their heritage for centuries without any protestation, a piracy the Western world so badly wanted to forget after the Holocaust, not necessarily out of malice, but more out of a kind of exasperation that we have survived as a people, known to them so well from the Bible, established in their minds as an obstinate people who weaved in and out of their lives? For God's sake, what are you still doing here pestering our conscience? Obliging though a lot of us are, it is a hope that anti-Semitism, that light sleeper, will go into a coma and never wake up, and what happened to us will slip into mythology as a tantalizing truth.

Harbouring these thoughts, I have often agonised: would it not have been simpler for the world if our remnants had been found on an archaeological dig, cleaned up and displayed under a glass case in a museum, and when appropriate a scholar might reverentially hold up a shin bone, elucidating to students: '… this specimen…'

Chapter Thirty-Three

Time Smiles

For Cannan and I, and for my parents, the good days were over even before we had left Godleys. Father had cancer of the prostate, Mother's senility was getting worse, and Cannan was drinking again with me running between them trying to mend the ills of our lives. My father tried too. Many times, in the middle of my visit, he would heave himself up from his chair, his face clenched in pain and declare, 'I am going to make a cake!' He could still lose himself in activity. I think he knew what he had, but I lacked the bravery to share the truth with him, barely able to think about it. I had heard only of successful prostate operations, and Father, talking to other men, compared methods used on them. He was sure he'd had the wrong operation, and I believed what he wanted to believe.

Once, walking together on Western Road, Brighton, my father, his face set with resignation, said, 'What I've got will never get better.' We had just come out from Steadman's, the chemist. I didn't agree or disagree. Maybe he was wrong and he would get better. For the moment, denial was useful. I pushed aside the thought of him coping alone with his thoughts, never mind his pain. Actually, I was like him: frightened. Both of us were addicted to doubt.

Father was on medication and I didn't even know what it was. Alienated from the rest of my family, I talked to no one and bumbled on alone. Then, one night, he cried out in pain on one of my overnight stays. I called the doctor for a home visit. He arrived cross and irritable. Would have to pretend he came for nothing! Hell no, I thought and, with a tremor in my voice, I said, 'My father is in a lot of pain!' Cutting me short, he said, 'Technically this can't be, because his stomach is not distended,' and saying nothing more, he went to the door, leaving me to cope with a man moaning in pain, and a senile woman walking round the flat wringing her hands. 'Give your mother another sleeping pill,' that doctor said, shutting the front door forcefully. Somehow, dawn came.

'It burns like a fire!' Father said, coming into the kitchen where I was. Resolved to get to the bottom of his problem, he said, 'I'll go to a specialist. I'll pay. Make an appointment!' At the specialist's we sat opposite him, Father at his most positive while the consultant looked down at his notes. How much longer could we deny the look in the Consultant's eyes while Father was still trying to extend the lease on his life? Father got dressed, pulled out his chequebook and said to me in Yiddish, 'I don't want he should send me a bill, I like to pay straight away.' He knew. At home, we waited for Mother to be brought back from the day centre. I stayed another night.

None of us slept. Mother was charging round the flat again, and this time she ricocheted in the passage from one wall to another, screaming, holding her head. Father and I looked at each other, helpless. I stayed another day, and as the situation got worse, I stayed half the week.

The bad in our life got worse. What with Mother's confusion and his cancer, Father's behaviour changed. On my next visit, something entirely new happened. We were having tea, sitting opposite each other in our usual chairs. Looking at me long and hard, Father cleared his throat and summed up my life as his child. 'I have to admit that you are in every respect a most reasonable person, excepting for one thing: you chose to marry a Goy.' He appeared to be deeply moved. My heart gave a few thumps, and when the tears in his eyes didn't fall I knew something was up because he just kept on staring at me. 'Have I got a spot on my face or something?' I asked, not knowing what else to say. Without batting an eye he solemnly declared, 'When I go to my grave, I shall tell my father what you have done.

When Father went too far in anything at all, Mother always tempered him. Now, with her no longer able to be his helper, what my father held against me turned into a malignant wound, vicious and deep.

Driving home that afternoon, my vision blurred. Did Jews believe such things? The dead talking in graves? I cried picking peas, weeding the garden, dead-heading roses, and while doing these things, I learned the pangs about Jews and inter-marriage down the centuries. Father would never see across that divide. Before Mother's mind went, she'd dismissed Fa-ther's attitude and tried to pacify him: 'Max, the old world is dead, now is a new world.' It wasn't any different from what my father said to his sister Blooma when he brought her to visit us in our house in Hove. Blooma, in queenly fashion, had walked through the corridor with Father behind her, and me behind him. She had looked around our spacious house, up the stairs and around the rooms, her scrutiny catlike. Father seemed to know what she was thinking, and poking her in the back, he said, 'Blooma, this isn't the Stetle, you can't tell chil-dren what to do any more.' Blooma was apparently baffled that I didn't offer her a room in our house, but had I, the mix of cultures would have hospitalised me. I thought of my cousin Sarah, the simple way she had made us a bed in her corridor; for us to have stayed in a hotel would have been as strange to Sarah as water running up mountains.

However distressed I felt, decisions had to be made about Mother. After that dreadful night rampaging round the flat, Father and I had to cooperate in our usual way and talk about getting Mother into a home. I looked through the Yellow Pages: lots of homes in Hove. I viewed several, most of which we couldn't afford even with the council paying half. Then I found Mrs Abbot's which could be afforded. How could

Mother's transfer be arranged? Whichever way we did it would be a wrench for Father, but more importantly, Mother was, at times, still aware of her surroundings. Usually, when she was collected to go to the day centre, she'd hang on to the key of the flat with such ferocity no one could prise it from her hands, fear and suspicion the only things left in her head. Father and I looked at each other: she'll know. Being in a twilight world, her removal from home would have to be an act of violence, however we chose to do it. Pacified by such thoughts, we agreed on our plan. One last component of this dilemma consoled us: Mother hung on to the key every day. A veil fell over our conscience.

We agreed that the next evening, instead of coming home from the day centre she would be taken to Mrs Abbot. This is what we did. I stayed that night with Father. In the morning I heard him weeping, and following the sound, I found him, his head leaning against the fridge door. 'I've done it, I've done it, I let her go, I wanted her to go… and all that after I had promised her mother I would look after her.' Again and again he said, 'I did it.' Then like a bolt from the blue, he joined two traumas in his life together: Dachau, and giving Mother away. Like some forgotten refrain, he repeated the account of the journey from Munich to Dachau, the changeover from passenger coaches to cattle trucks; this time, his arms were not on Mother's and my shoulders for comfort, he just patted the fridge door with his hands. I let him grieve. I grieved. I stayed another night.

In the morning, I went to see how Mother had settled. Mrs Abbot said that I could see her only through the crack of the door. In shock, I obeyed. Mother was sitting with three other women in a light room, the sun filtering through voile curtains. All of them seemed quiet and well-behaved, their complexions grey and lifeless. Mrs Abbot was hovering behind me. It never occurred to me that my mother might have been more

drugged than usual. Mrs Abbot's tactics became clear: she did-
n't want my mother to be more confused than she already was,
still living as she was in her mind at home. 'If she doesn't see
you,' Mrs Abbot said, confirming my suspicions, 'your mother
will settle down more easily,' which meant that she would be
easier to handle. I resolved: I must get my mother out of Mrs
Abbot's clutches!

Father's and my reasoning had been rather simple, I decided. We thought that he would be able to see her every day
without constant surveillance of her – dressing, washing, feeding her, taking her to the loo – no need to watch her every
move, especially when she turned on the gas stove without
lighting it and then leaving the kitchen when he was out shopping. An accident would surely happen was our sensible approach. I could see her when I came to see him, and in between
we would speak on the phone as usual. The consequences of
our plans were not as ideal as we had worked out, or hoped.

Passover was early that year and Mother was still with Mrs
Abbot. Mr Josephs invited Father to join him and his wife for
Seder. I was glad for Father. For once, I felt kindly towards Mr
Josephs; he lived his way and I lived mine, I concluded unsuccessfully. While it was still light, I gave Father a lift to the
Josephs' house. I drove to the corner of their street, near
enough to see him go inside. When the front door opened I
saw Mrs Josephs welcoming my father. He walked into the
house, easing himself against the wall for support. I knew he
felt awkward and I remembered the difficult moment when I
took him down in the lift after he had declared himself to Cannan. But this time the smile was different; in the lift, he had
merely been embarrassed, but here in Josephs' corridor his
smile was pained. I ached for him. Perfect and imperfect, he
was my father.

When next I saw him, he told me how everything at
Josephs' had been just as it was in der Heim and how sad he

felt going home to an empty flat. I was afraid to embrace him; going near was to admit something I wasn't yet ready for which meant I was hanging on to the memory of us laughing and bickering and Mother calling out 'Haita Troika!' Our patterns of behaviour with each other had changed so little in England, but all of it changed with Mother's decline, leaving me to evaluate my father's phone calls, both playful and annoying. His calls to come at once meant that he was at death's door – that I didn't drive into a tree when he made this call was a miracle. Inside the flat, he would be sitting up in bed crying, the tears streaming down his cheeks. When I asked him why, he said, 'I am crying for my life.' After many such calls, I began to wonder if my father was a character from a Chekov play – more a matter of Chekov imitating life rather then my father knowing about the playwright.

Another time, the same request and the same frantic drive, but this time, rushing into my father's bedroom, I found him sitting up in bed smiling. 'What the hell do you think you are doing, making me think you are dying?' I yelled. Ignoring my anger, he said, 'I feel better now that you are here.' It was then I knew that this was his way of telling me he had not been able to cope with what Mother had become. I hated the idea of dismantling their flat, something I had hoped would last and last, at least until he was taken out 'feet first' as he used to say, and so I contacted the Jewish Welfare board. The social worker who came to assess our situation appreciated the state my parents were in and found a place for them in a Jewish home in Hemel Hempstead. It was a complex of buildings for different stages of aging and states of health. Mother was to go into the senile block, and Father into the normal section with a room of his own, light and sunny. Before the move, Father tackled the social worker. Pulling up his chair to the arms of the one she was sitting in he said, 'Look how nice my home is, maybe we can arrange something else, maybe I can stay here,' a lift in his voice. Looking round the flat, the social worker said, 'Yes, Mr Lerner, I can see how difficult it must be for you to leave your home.' Father had tears in his eyes and the social worker, looking at me sympathetically, said, 'You know that having your wife back at home is not an option anymore. It will be much better for you to be among Jewish people.' Good comforting talk.

The social worker said all I couldn't say, and with a deep sigh, Father finally acknowledged the unavoidable. 'Gut, so I go to London,' he said in a tone that suggested he was making a good career move. I was sure that going into a home wasn't what he had ever thought about or imagined. As always my father was resolute and optimistic. I didn't have the heart to disillusion him. In those last days in Hove, I hoped he'd be surprised by death while shopping in Western Road or, best of all, at the end of morning prayers at the synagogue.

Sooner than we thought, we were picked up for the journey. Once he had settled in his own room and Mother in her house, Father and I walked in the grounds. Eventually we said goodbye to each other and I promised to see him soon. When I looked back he was talking to a man, his arms gesticulating all over the place, and smiling, he turned sideways to face the man: Father's friendly body language. Good, I thought, he's absorbed. I walked on, waving, with my back to them. Relieved, I rushed to get the bus to the train station, feeling that I had left him in a good mood. He was going to do the prayers, he told me on the phone that evening. The man he'd been talking to was a visiting rabbi.

On one of my visits Father asked to be taken to see Mother. By then he was heavily sedated and not too steady on his legs. I took him in a wheelchair to Mother's house. It was a sunny day. A lot of patients were on the terrace sitting in their wheelchairs, the sun reflecting off the chrome wheels. The terrace was too crowded for Father to join the patients with his chair, so a nurse wheeled Mother into the dayroom where Father was waiting expectantly. On seeing her he reached out to get close to her, but the wheels of their chairs clashed. All he was able to do was to stroke her head, his arm outstretched. Mother no longer knew him; she just sat in her chair uttering obscenities. Father sobbed.

Back in his room, I told him what the doctor said to me, 'Alzheimer's disease destroys the inhibitory factor in the brain and there is too much aluminium on the brain. The hope is that twenty years from now, we may know more. In the meantime, they just sit.' Father was deaf to explanations. In a way, so was I. To hear my mother screaming obscenities, her mouth distorted in anger, was more than we could bear. I don't think Father went to see her again. 'All I have cherished in your mother is dead,' he said to me on the phone.

When Father was first in the Home, he resisted taking medication. On my next visit, we lunched together: four to a table, each resident had a separate little dish for pills next to the salt and pepper. Father saw me look at them. 'I don't care anymore,' he said, 'now I take everything they give me.' It upset me to remember how he had fought to manage without medication; 'I'll try without them,' he'd often say when still at home.

On another visit, the matron told me that he had fainted one morning before he started prayers. 'Why was that?' I asked. 'Pills and whisky don't go together, don't buy him anymore.' I hadn't; I was as surprised as she was that he took a nip.

Father's life was now well organized but he was no longer the free spirit he had been. The matron's stiff bleached hair above gaunt pale-powdered features made her unapproachable. I once dared to ask her if Father needed to be asleep every time I visited. Crisply, she replied, 'Doctor's orders!' Information was sparse; he was, in fact, on morphine.

Looking down at him sitting asleep in a wheel chair, his chin digging into his chest, I thought of my regular visits to Alcoholics Anonymous with Cannan and the family support group Al-Anon I went to regularly. Beyond Father's slumped body, I saw his former upright figure rise up behind him, standing in our kitchen in the Wrede Straße, warning me about Goyim and drink. Awful though it was to see my father in the state he was in now, I had at least less to pretend to him about. Had I been foolish and told him of my life with Cannan when he was still well, he would surely have said, 'I told you so!' I preferred to think of my father, upright and well, full of exuberance and with a towering will for life.

Mother too was no longer my mother. In the time of her early confusion, I attempted to revive her memory by testing the flair she once had for mental arithmetic. If anyone in our kitchen in Wrede Straße asked her to multiply or subtract a sum, the answer was out of her mouth seconds later. Alone with her now, I put up my hand: 'How many fingers?' The blank look in her eyes humbled me. Would there had been something to embrace, something to talk about, something to regard, her eyes less numb and empty! I was an orphan but could not yet mourn. Even worse was that Father blamed me for breaking up his flat. His pain had turned him into a spiteful man.

On my next visit, Mother, sitting in a high-backed chair, looked like a disabled five-year-old, shrunken and blind, her eyes no more than slits. I stared at her, hoping she would die that moment. When she slipped down in the seat flat onto her back, the seat contained all of her. The young Asian male nurse moved to prop her up, and seeing the futility of it, I said, 'No, leave her as she is.' A rush of logic surged through my mind: perhaps God agreed with me that she wasn't his creation any longer either, and I needn't feel ashamed. But the nurse's look brought me back to reality. If only he could understand why I had said what I did. As my mother wasn't wearing her own clothes anymore – the patients wore each others' as it was easier for staff to grab hold of anyone's, incontinence needing haste – her identity slipped away altogether. No matter how many Yiddish songs the matron sang to her, she couldn't sing life into her, the way she and Father used to listen to a record, both of them humming along. I wasted those moments, never asked them what they remembered as they smiled and sang along with the record. Seeing my mother as she now was with the matron kneeling in front of her chair, smiling up at her holding her hand, sharpened my deficiency in pity. The matron was black and spoke a sing-song English. Working for the Jewish Welfare Board, she had learned Yiddish songs, a natural addition to her skills. There was some comfort in knowing my parents were cared for in a way I could never have managed. Seeing me distressed the matron used another skill: 'You go home, my dear, we work in shifts, we'll do our best with your mother.'

On another visit, one of the nurses was cradling a patient on her lap. 'Who was she?' I asked. 'An opera singer,' she said and added, 'she has such a lovely nature.' 'So are there differences in the behaviour of Alzheimer patients?' I asked. 'No, this patient had a stroke.'

I have often had dreams of my mother but the one most vivid is one in which I was on my way to the towel rail next to the garden door to wipe my hands. She was sitting between two shrubs on my blue round-backed office chair, smiling, waiting to catch my eye. Wiping my hands, I noticed her hair was still dark, and her cheeks were rosy and full and still smiling at me good-naturedly with all the time in the world. When she spoke, her voice was gentle and soft as goose down. 'Come here,' she said, 'it's fine where I am,' and other words I've lost from that dream. For a split second I expected her to call me 'Uhele', the way she did when she woke up from her cat-naps in our kitchen in Ludwigshafen, asking me if I had done the things she asked me to do while she was napping. There was a pink hue about the dream: the escalonia was in bloom, and, as ever, Mother was wearing her overall.

It was taken for granted that Harry, living nearer to the home than me, could visit more often, and be more to hand for emergencies. He fed our mother every Sunday lunchtime, he told me. Mush was all she could now manage without her teeth. 'Your mother,' the sister told me, 'has thrown her dentures down the lavatory.' Believable. Harry told me he would have liked to put a pillow over her face. I understood. Then one morning he phoned. 'Father is dead.'

The day of the funeral, Harry revealed, 'It took three weeks for Dad to die, and I was with him most days. We sorted out a lot.' Nothing prepared me for this abrupt disclosure. 'Ah well,' I thought, using a survivor's trick, weighing gains and losses, 'we had good times together, Father and I'. But as the days passed, I realized that I had been excluded from my father's deathbed, this most primitive of rituals that all peoples observe. How could this be? Did our father not ask to see me, even in a whisper? And where was Jeffrey, our English-born brother I had wronged and for whom no apology on my part could ever make it right, it seemed? Had Jeffrey held onto the grudge against me after all?

Harry gave the rabbi of his Shul the outlines of Father's life. The rabbi didn't know my father, yet he spoke of him as if he did: a eulogy for an unknown survivor. He lifted my father to heights I didn't remember him by. No, you are not talking about my father; you are ennobling him because he was in Dachau. At his grave, I thought of my father coming home from Dachau a frail, broken man. Of course this was part of him, but it wasn't the whole man. And now it had been decreed that I had not been part of his life, no longer acknowledged as his child because I had married out. Listening to the rabbi, I was battling with forgiveness. Harry had chosen a martyr's role for our father. What I loved most about my father was his spirit trailing after his fallible self. The rabbi glorified him as Christians have glorified Jesus: the sinless man.

Three years later, Harry phoned again. 'Mother is dead.' The way he said 'dead' was like a bang on the head for something I ought to be sorry for. I had wished for her death, as he had. Nothing will ever be as intimate for me as my mother licking my eyes open to get ready for school, the way a cat licks the eyes of her kittens after they are born. Having wanted more from my mother widened the gap for neurosis. I am sorry I didn't know how to comfort her more in her decline; I was attentive, of course, but intimate? When she could no longer wash herself, I helped her into the bath, washing everything except her genitalia. It seemed as if the door of taboo shut in my face. 'You do it!' I demanded of my blind mother, her eyes grey with cataracts, her whole body almost afloat in the bathwater, but somehow I managed to get her out and I dried her without having attended her private region. Maybe it was because I had to face from where I came, not having given birth myself.

On the day of her funeral I tried to embrace my brother for comfort, hoping that our mother's death would finally rid us of our differences. Harry wrenched himself away from me, his face twisted with anger. Who was I to presume such intimacy? I raced back to our childhood to find that generous child everyone loved.

The day after the funeral, we were sitting Shiva. It was then that I learned from his wife about the fifty-year-old grievance Harry had against our mother. What should have been a celebration of her life, how she triumphed over difficulties, became in fact a condemnation. Not mentioning our father's infamous letter to Harry about her, she laid bare her judgment on our mother. 'Your mother,' she said, turning to me, 'took the ten marks Harry was allowed to take out from Germany.' When I'd recovered, I said, 'What in heaven's name do you think we lived on when our father was in Dachau? Do you think some serious saving took place in the years of boycott?' In an equally retaliatory fashion, she said, 'Whatever the circumstances, no parent should take money from a small child. I wouldn't!' I flinched. It wasn't the moment to ask for understanding or to describe the scene I'd witnessed on our way to the train station, when Heinie gave the ten marks to Mother, that poignant moment when he forbade us to cry.

When did Harry begin to doubt our mother? When did he tell his girlfriend? Was it when they first met, both of them just sixteen? When did she give him her version of that event? Did he change his mind, wanting our mother to be more heroic and refuse his offer? Did his girlfriend want to mother him and erase the love he had for her? Was this why our feelings had run like sores for so long? But isn't that what happens in most families often throughout their lives? Some families are more robust than we were: nothing was talked over after we came to England. The war forced its way into our lives and another kind of survival took over, and then it was too late for reconciliation. Harry and Norma had married in 1947 in Liverpool, her home-town. Evansky and I opened our shop in Hendon that year. The builders were still working to finish for the busy season before Christmas. Money was tight, very tight, and going to Liverpool was out of the question. Maybe that is when my estrangement with Harry started; I didn't move mountains to be with them for their wedding – strange that I don't remember even being aware of their plan. Was I already out of their life?

Harry now being senile, my loss is total. I look at pictures of him before he came to England. I connect him to me as we were then, affectionate with each other. Before my brother got ill, I almost believed that we could again be to each other as we had once been. That speech he made as an eleven-year-old boy, playing at being my big brother, the big photograph he took with him to England. Why do I go on wishing for how we were after the passing of so much time? When do such wishes stop hurting?

On a more optimistic level there was a chance for Harry and I to connect again at a time when our parents had been dead for some years. Away from the diligence required by faith my mind was crawling with questions, and I thought his would be too because he often said he didn't believe in God. I looked forward to us talking, surprising each other with our views. I deferred to his knowledge of Hebrew, and not going to Shul myself at that time, I presumed he was religious. Apparently I was wrong. 'I go to Shul for identity and nothing else,' he declared. Many Jews have a need to explain themselves because Jews and God are generally thought of as being twinned together. When I asked my brother to recite Psalm 23, 'The Lord is my Shepherd', into a tape in Hebrew, its original language, he said, 'I hope you don't expect too much because I am not cultural!' I adjusted accordingly, hoping that the fluency of his Hebrew would pull things along.

What a treasure Harry's tape turned out to be! He was practising lines and metre, murmuring to himself again and again – and finally out came the cry, 'Adonih Roih Lo akhsar...' so heartfelt, so honest and passionate, he connected me to the past in language and spirit.

Harry, you didn't know yourself at all.

But then neither did I. Healing moments have always surprised me. When I had put my parents into a home and cleared their flat, I gave my father's ironing board and the last calico apron he made for himself to my stepdaughter Crescy who was setting up home herself. Many years later, she gave me back the apron, frail from constant washing. 'I thought you'd like to have this back,' she said. I was touched.

I long to remember the moments German words changed

into English for me. When did Liebe become love, and when did Haß become hate? Hunger didn't have to become anything else; like Hand it only needs a different pronunciation and a capital H. When did I start using the word compassion? I don't use it much, because nowadays it is too easily associated with facile talk in claims by people who have lost the religious impact of the word and are embarrassed to feel strongly. For me, it has always been Rachamim (mercy), the Hebrew word containing the word Rechem (womb), mercy at a time when death looted and pillaged new life in great abundance. How close I still was to the word startled me when Harry, Jeffrey and I were standing at my parents' graves for the yearly ritual of repentance between Rosh Hashana and Yom Kippur. Harry was reciting Kaddish. On the intonation of Rachamim, the three of us broke down, surrendering to that rasping, guttural sound coming from the vicinity of the heart. How glad I was not to be alone!

PART FIVE

Top: *Me, 1961.*
Bottom: *My friend, Nancy, in Blackheath, 1964.*

Top left: *Rosl, Aunt Pessa's daughter, marrying Natan Goldberg in Germany, 1936.*
Top right: *Carmella, Rosl's daughter, in Masquerade costume for Purim, 1950, Israel.*
Bottom left: *My cousin, Bertel, Rosl's brother, in the uniform of the Palestine police, 1938.*
Bottom right: *My mother's brother, Chaskel. He was was found twitching on a pyramid of corpses by a nurse in Auschwitz. His first wife and two children were gassed in Auschwitz.*

Top: *With Cannan, at Godley's, 1969.*
Bottom: *Advertisement, 1957.*

Top: *Reunion of Father's family in Paris.* Left to right: *Mother; Father's niece, Sarah; Father; Sarah's sister, Carola; Carola's husband, Mariano; Paula's husband, Salvi; Sarah's second husband, Henri; Paula and her son; unidentified.*
Bottom: *A picnic on my visit to Rosl's family in Israel, 1978. Natan (far left) is reading in Hebrew and all are paying attention except for me.*

Top: *We return to Hove. Cannan's family (left to right): his sister, Diana, with her son-in-law and baby; son, Nick; daughter, Crescy; Cannan; Me.*
Bottom: *A rare meeting of me and my brothers.*

Top: *Cannan in his later years.*
Bottom: *Me at home in Hove.*

Chapter Thirty-Four

Orange Blossoms and Petrol: Israel

The years had piled up, and still I hadn't visited Israel. Why? Because Uncle Avrum had still been alive. When he died, I understood why I hadn't gone before. I feared our eyes meeting, bringing back the memory of marbles clattering on the wooden floor, his hand on my back pushing me towards the front door, and bringing back the effect he had on my life. I was saddened that Aunt Pessa was dead, although remembering her playful smile, I still wondered about her inert body lying next to her husband while he used me, and Rosl to my right – had they woken up and quickly shut their eyes in disbelief? Now, with him out of the way, could Rosl and I talk about this, free ourselves of the shame we shared, that is if indeed she had seen my body rising from the pillows? I decided to go.

In the spring of 1978, President Sadat of Egypt and Prime Minister Begin of Israel shook hands for peace: a good year to go to Israel and renew family connections. On the plane, I compared other peoples' suffering with mine and decided that nothing had really happened to me. After all, I was going to the land where survivors of the Holocaust lived to lighten my troubles, and where oranges and lemons grew and sandy beaches waited.

Rosl, Carmella and Natan met me at Tel Aviv airport. Natan drove. Breathing in the soft air, the smells of orange blossom and petrol hit my nostrils, one intoxicating, the other repugnant and getting stronger as we passed the oil refinery on the way to Haifa. How unexpected, how mismatched, I thought, breathing them in through the open car windows. In the joy of seeing Rosl again after so long, I held her hands and remembered them instantly: her long nails and elegant fingers, the softness of them, compared to my short fingers with my nails bitten to the quick as they were in my youth, Rosl forever urging me to stop biting them. I said, 'Your hands are not a Rotman feature, are they?' Natan momentarily took his eyes off the road and looked at me. 'So you come from an intellectual milieu,' he said. What was he talking about? I was just remembering and saying things as they occurred to me.

The rest of the evening was practical. I was to sleep on the narrow sofa in their spare room. The moment my head hit the pillow, I knew no more until the sun woke me up in the morning. I heard Rosl and Natan speaking German, but I was still too woolly-headed to concentrate on what they were saying. When I joined them in the kitchen, nothing important was being said, just talk about breakfast and the night's sleep and Natan telling Rosl to warm up the coffee for me. All at once, I was back in our kitchen in Ludwigshafen where our coffee was kept warm on the range and where it sometimes boiled over, the smell of chicory less glorious than real coffee. I felt truly at home, and glad at the same time that Natan spoke English as Rosl didn't speak any. In German, she asked, 'Do you want a boiled egg?' 'No, thank you,' I said, 'just toast, please.' 'We haven't got a toaster,' Natan said. 'Will bread and butter and honey be O.K.?' That too was like home a long, long time ago; we only had toast when my mother put some bread on a long fork in front of the grid. England had changed a rarity into a daily experience.

Natan was retired. When the sun rose high, he pulled up the blind on their balcony and lay back on a straw armchair, his face lifted to the sun. Rosl and I got on with family talk, conventional to start with: 'How is your Mamma and Papa?' More came slowly when I got used to speaking German again. Happily when I got stuck in the middle of sentences Rosl finished them for me; a few days later I could finish them myself.

Meanwhile, wherever Rosl went, I went: to her daughters Ronit and Carmella, their husbands and their children, grand-children and a great-grandchild. Natan had Buerger's disease and had to have his 'bad' leg amputated, my Father had told me a while back. I was prepared, but seeing the reality was rather different. At home, Natan's false leg leaned against the wall next to his bed, and when he needed to go to the loo a crutch was to hand for him to hobble to anywhere in the flat. Picking up his 'leg' one day, it felt as if it was a sack of coal, and Rosl, seeing me astonished, showed me how it would be for Natan to walk were it not weighted. Bending her body as horizontally as she could, one arm up in the air, she said, 'You see? This is how he would walk if the leg were weightless,' and holding the pose she laughed heartily. I was not surprised she laughed, because my father would have too, the pair of them quick to see absurdity.

Their car was adapted to Natan's disability. At weekends he drove us to pine woods for picnics, and all the family came, three cars following each other. They talked a mix of German and Hebrew. Although understanding every word in German made me happy, Hebrew was a strain, endlessly having to ask what this or that meant. After we got home, Rosl said, 'Eget Tours will take you to historical places.'

Another day, Natan took Rosl and me up Mount Carmel. On the way to the top was Haifa University, stark naked with no foliage to soften its appearance. Natan remained in the car while Rosl and I looked around shops selling tourist stuff. In a gap between two shops, I looked down at the view below where the traffic moved silently on the coastal road, the silence set off by the sea drenched with sunlight, glittering ostenta-tiously. The shop we had just been to belonged to a Druze Arab. He had given us the Christian message. Rosl, indifferent to all of that - and to the view – shrugged her shoulders and said, pulling at my sleeve, 'Come on, I see this view every day from my kitchen window!' I was still looking at the view, lost in thoughts, and blurted out, 'Are there prisons in Israel?' Incredulous, Rosl said, 'I think you need a psychiatrist!'

In my imagination Israel had been perfect: a land only to be worked over by willing Chalutzim (pioneers). This was how I, and many others, had perceived Palestine in the Hitler years and there it had remained in my mind unmolested ever since, though Rosl too had her own share of illusions. While I was staying with her a scandal broke out where geriatric patients in a home were treated roughly by nurses. 'Unheard of in our land!'Rosl cried out. We were two of a kind, both our heads still filled with ideals. Another day we were walking through a busy thoroughfare in Haifa; a beggar in rags sat on the pavement cross-legged, a few coins in a cap between his knees. Rosl looked at me looking at the beggar and said, 'You see? The poor are here too.' Perhaps seeing a beggar in Israel was a kind of justice telling me that we belonged to the same human race after all with the same mistakes, the same failures, the same disappointments all peoples have. Victims are so busy being victims they haven't time to do anything else except ward off danger, Israelis and Palestinians both.

Zvika, Carmella's husband, took us to meet his Palestinian friend who owned a restaurant on a hill around Jerusalem. I was pleased to see them shake hands with neighbourly warmth. That was in 1978 when Sadat was still alive. By 1984, the year of my second visit to Israel, the Israeli/Palestinian situation had deteriorated. Having shed some of my illusions about Israel, I asked Zvika about his Palestinian friend. Leaping forward in his chair, he said, 'Friendship between us and the Arabs is no longer possible, I see them coming from a long way off, and I am sure it's the same when they see us.' Tapping the side of his nose with his index finger, he showed me that he knew how the situation between them now stood. I listened, understanding two things: one, that it was a political/religious hangover from yesteryear in Europe, and two, that Israelis were thrown into the consequences of this hangover, while the Palestinians were paying the price of Europe's endemic anti-Semitism which they had adopted readily. Zvika saw the cautious behaviour on both sides, while I saw Helmut turning away from me after he had been indoctrinated in the Hitler Youth and given something to hate. Political situations can be defined in the way we order steaks: medium, well-done, or bloody. Helmut ended up as a guard in Dachau. Was it shame that made him drop his eyes before my father? Was Helmut decent after all? Were his dreams as powerful as ours were, hoping for safety elsewhere, as he was with Hitler's dream of a Thousand Year Reich? How will we, can we ever, claim justice for our dead so ignobly slain?

When the day had cooled and the shutters were up, Rosl and I talked. Most urgent for me was to check my mother's story about the woman who suffocated her baby. Rosl, eight years older than me, knew more family history. 'Who was this woman?' I asked her. Although this event had happened some sixty-odd years before, it was as fresh in her mind as if it had happened yesterday. 'It was our grandmother!' she cried. When I wanted to know if she had been arrested, Rosl laughed one of her many spirited laughs at my earnest attitudes. 'What do you mean? Our grandmother went to the rabbi for solace and he promised her that God would give her another child next year! Hah,' she exhaled, 'and He did!' 'What about the secular law?' I blundered on. Rosl eyed me again: 'You know you are really quite stupid. The rabbi was our law!' When she fully realized how naïve I was, she said, 'You know, I really think you have just fallen from the heavens!' and that said, she left the room and banged the door behind her.

A few minutes later she came back, 'Well, are you still thinking about Jewish history?' 'Yes,' I said, 'there is something else I want to know.' 'Ja, tell me,' Rosl said, leaning forward, a trifle patronizingly. 'What do you know about Uncle Chaskel? What happened to him in the war and what do you know about a torn-off piece of packing paper with Yiddish writing on it in verse form?' 'Oh that. He sent it to my mother when he moved to New York. When my mother died, I found it half sticking out from an envelope in a drawer. I couldn't make sense of it because Yiddish is not easy for me to read, nor was it for my mother. So I sent it to your father, hoping that he could.' 'No,' I said, 'he couldn't read it either, and he put it back into his box with all the other papers related to his life: marriage documents, bills, and a newspaper cutting about David, Heinie's son, a prize he won for writing a essay. Remember David? He stayed with you.' 'I should say I do! I couldn't get it into his head that our water was rationed. Just thinking about it annoys me. When he finished showering, he paddled in water up to his ankles. Thank goodness our flats have terrazzo floors. Now let's talk about something else,' she said.

'Yes, let's... tell me more about Uncle Chaskel.' Rosl was more than a little perturbed. 'If you really want to know I'll tell you,' – she didn't wait for my reply – 'When Auschwitz was liberated, a nurse noticed a skeletal body move at the top of a pile of corpses about to be bulldozed into a pit. That 'moving' body was our Uncle Chaskel. She took him down from the pile and nursed him back to health as best she could. The good thing was that they got married and went to live in New York. Uncle Chaskel wanted to be near his sister Blooma and his half brothers. But for all his wife's devotion, he didn't live long.' Rosl broke off. When I asked what had happened to Uncle Chaskel's wife Hella and their children, Sally and Heinz, Rosl cut across my question and like an expletive she shouted into the room, 'GAS!'

When Rosl was calmer, I went back to Uncle Chaskel's poem, perhaps to joggle her memory some more. 'When I cleared my parents' flat after they went into a home, I didn't find the poem anywhere,' I said, and trying to convey my disappointment I lamented, 'Why didn't I snatch his writing from my father's hand? Why didn't I preserve Uncle Chaskel's words, perhaps the most deeply felt in his life?' Bursting into tears, I concluded, "Survivors' stories trail around in my head begging, "Help me, hear me, remember me."' Rosl nodded in agreement, her head bowed, tears falling into her lap.

Another day, more talk with Rosl. I hoped we'd manage to talk about her father. At the time of my 'treatments', an abusive exchange of letters had sped between my parents and her. Her father then still alive, I didn't care what they said to each other. With hindsight, it must have been depressing for her to look at him, knowing what he'd done. I waited. Rosl stayed silent. Then almost at the end of my visit when we were talking generally, she startled me. 'Are you all right now?' she asked, and saying no more, she looked up to the ceiling as if in thanksgiving. 'I've done my duty', I took her look to mean. I said a simple 'yes'. Soon enough, we continued to talk about make-up, our likes and dislikes. I had given her a jar of Estée Lauder foundation cream, too dense for my skin. 'Thank you, I love Estée Lauder!' she said, the same as 'louder' is pronounced in English.

Ronit, Rosl's younger daughter, confirmed my suspicion that her grandfather may well have 'touched' her. We had stopped on the steep hill outside Rosl's flat, Ronit standing lower down than me. We were on our way to the post office while the rest of the family had gone to the flat. Looking up at me, Ronit said, 'He was bad.' I don't remember how he came into our conversation; as far as I know, I hadn't provoked her judgement on her grandfather. I longed to know why she thought he was 'bad', but I didn't have the courage to ask her outright; the question 'Did he molest you?' remained unsaid. Every time family pictures had been included in a letter to us and Avrum was holding one of his grandchildren in his arms

I had suspected him. No, I couldn't really tell her that. Although he was dead, his presence was between us. I was sure Ronit knew more than she let on. Perhaps Rosl had told her about my experience with him. No, that couldn't be! Ronit was only a baby when Rosl and my parents exchanged those abusive letters. The worst of the whole Avrum business was not what actually happened, but how we all slept together as a family that night. No one knew that, not even my therapists. Though child abuse is now commonly acknowledged, I believed that I was the only one in the world this had happened to. Avrum had broken a taboo and now I know why pearls of sweat stood on his forehead when I ransacked his pockets.

On another day, Rosl took me shopping for chocolates, boxes and boxes of them as presents for their doctor she was frequently on the phone to, her Arab cleaner from down-town Haifa, nurses, and other people who supported her with Natan's illness. On the way to the bus, Rosl complained about the rubbish lying in the bushes, empty plastic bags tossed aside full of air, blown there by the wind. 'No one cares,' she said, apologetically. I didn't think it worse than anywhere else. On the bus, she pointed to a second floor window in a modern block of flats: 'Carmella lived there after she was married and Ilana, my first grandchild, was born there.' There was nothing to distinguish that block from any other in the town: flat-fronted, anonymous, purpose-built flats for new immigrants coming from Nazi Germany in the Thirties, and others more hurriedly built after the Holocaust. This made me think of people's need to mark places and spaces where eventful things have happened – and going back to ancient times, how our patriarch Jacob marked the stone he laid his head on the night he dreamed of angels going up and down a ladder.

The chocolate shop's interior was old and worn and chipped, the gloss on the dark brown fittings dimmed. The counter had several indents where hands had been placed in them thousands of times. The woman now touching those well-worn dips said to Rosl, 'Can I help you?' – or I supposed it was, not knowing any Hebrew. Three attractive middle-aged women were serving, hurrying past each other in the narrow gangway behind the counter, fetching and putting things back in the cupboards behind them. All three had thick black hair and white flashing teeth. They knew Rosl well. On seeing me with her, they came close together, asking questions which Rosl translated: Who was I? From where? Engeland? Was I in Israel for good? They pronounced the 'g' in England hard, like Yiddish-speaking Jews. Then, smiling brilliantly, they focused on me, forefingers placed between their breasts as each declared in turn, 'Turkey,' 'Persia,' 'Iraq' – countries that had done a tit-for-tat when Arabs fled Israel after it was created. The only way we could have said more to each other could have been in Yiddish or German, of which the women knew not one word. When we left the shop, I asked Rosl 'Is their Hebrew good?' 'Bah,' she said, her face drawn as if she had swallowed something very unpleasant, 'dreadful accent!'

Haifa was an Ashkenazi enclave and all Rosl's family spoke German; even the men who married her daughters spoke some. The city was full of survivors from Eastern Europe whose families had perished in the death camps. I recognized elderly German Jews walking up and down the mountain by their gait, stiff and dignified; they wore narrow snakeskin belts holding up their trousers and wide short-sleeved shirts gaping around old arms. It was hard to imagine them as Chalutzim (pioneers). Most were probably contemporaries of mine. Some must have been running around in Ludwigshafen wearing shorts, hoping what we all hoped – to get away from Nazi Germany. Natan was not a Kibbuztnick, but two of his brothers had been. Rosl mocked her husband's flat Hebrew accent. 'Attaaaa,' (you) she imitated him and went on to tell me, 'Although Natan's Hebrew is grammatically correct, he might as

well still be speaking German.' His English was the same, heavily accented but grammatically perfect. Rosl spoke Hebrew like
a Sabra (native born Israeli), her children said proudly, but she
couldn't write it, not even a cheque. She and I had this in common. It had taken me years to learn how to write one out in
England; pretending I didn't have my spectacles with me, I
asked the assistant to write out the amount, and continuing
the pretence, I signed my name with my eyes screwed up.

As I had already suspected, Rosl didn't read Hebrew either.
Whether out of nostalgia I don't know, she read German magazines about Royalty and celebrities, believing every last word
said about them. Looking at her, I said, 'Really?' and she
replied, 'They have souls too.' Yes, my socialist cousin was sentimental. I wasn't talking about their souls; I was talking about
the magazines inventing 'truths' about them. For God's sake, I
thought spitefully, what a long time to stay adolescent! Then I
remembered how long it took me to dump my picture album
full of film stars.

I was shocked by the xenophobic feeling I had in Israel. I
was sort of cut in two: when in Israel I felt English, and when
in England, I didn't feel English at all. Truth was, I didn't feel
indigenous anywhere, so playing at 'being someone' was getting round a dilemma. When I came across people in Israel
who had a grudge against the English, this strangely divided
my loyalties. It was Natan who pricked my pretension. 'You
know, Rosel,' he said one supper time, 'I know the British very
well, I was here when camp survivors scrambled onto the
beaches and were refused entry to Palestine, so don't tell me
about the British, I worked for them!' He had skewered me like
a kebab, but his keen blue eyes showed tolerance, one Diaspora
Jew knowing another. Rosl told me he had spied for Israel. As
Natan spoke, I was back in Ma Evansky's front room in the
days when Palestine was still under the British mandate. Jack
Evansky, in one of his more coherent moments, was reading

The People. With a sudden jerk he rested the paper on his lap and shouted into the room, 'Bleedin' anti-Semites!' Ernest Bevin was then the Foreign Minister in the Labour government, and he was thought to be resistant to the establishment of a Jewish State.

'The whole of Israel is an archaeological dig,' Rosl said one day, assuming I knew what she had just been talking about on the phone to a friend in Hebrew. Walking brusquely into the kitchen where I was, she continued, 'Who we were has to be proved! Do we – have we ever existed? The search is relentless,' Rosl said, practically screaming at me. What self-laceration! What doubt! But then, I would know about that.

Natan had read Mathematics in Heidelberg. When he first came to Israel, he got a job as a clerk in the port of Haifa, most likely because of his English. I never asked if he rose to be a manager. I had the impression his grandchildren, born in Israel, didn't know the full extent – the depth of his loss. When, after the war, Germany paid reparations to Jews, Natan refused to enter into that fray. We had touched on the subject of taking money for livelihoods and lives lost; we didn't get far. 'I didn't want anything from the Germans,' Natan said, hobbling on one leg, crutch under his armpit. 'Pride,' Rosl said, after he left the room, 'Er ist so… had he taken money from the Germans he would have to face what he had lost.' Natan's eyes were like his mother's, astute, inquisitive, and to his children he was Abba (father). I watched him listening to them; he hardly ever took part in their conversations. When they'd gone, he'd take off his false leg and sit in his armchair watching television, kneading his stump. Rosl, looking embarrassed, said, 'Natan, it isn't nice to let Rosel see you like this.'

We never talked about the war in Europe, but in Israel its aftermath was everywhere: everyone I met had a story to tell. The pain was discernible and so was their exuberance: we are alive, and we have survived! The whole of Israel was a wound, everyone debating, everyone a Member of Parliament, in a café, a bus queue, just about anywhere, angry and blasé in turn.

When Palestinian bombs exploded in Jerusalem and other places in the country, I looked at people in the street to see if they were alarmed. 'How many dead? Where? Is it safe to go out?' I asked. Shaul, Ronit's husband, noticed my distress. What counted for him was the explosion that morning. 'You can't behave the way you do!' he said to me, 'If everybody were like you, everything would come to a standstill.' Having lived through the Blitz didn't help me when here in Israel Jews were being targeted again.

Nerve-endings were exposed. Whoever you were with and wherever you were, everything stopped for the news: on the hour, every hour, and in between for emergencies, every incident repeated even while people were enjoying themselves. 'Be quiet, the news!' was the neurotic refrain. Nothing phlegmatic in that command for people who lived continually in crisis in a country much like a village where most knew someone who had been killed or maimed. Only the weather report showed a constant sunny outlook, accompanied by a ripple of high ding-dong sounds, smug and complacent: sunny everywhere, tomorrow and tomorrow and for the rest of the summer. I longed for rain.

After the war was over in Europe I used to speculate, 'What if Rommel had marched into Palestine?' It was a thought I used to frighten myself with. I never asked Rosl if they'd feared this too. As I've said, I was two people in Israel, one moment attached, and the next a bystander.

'I fought on the Golan Heights,' Shaul told me proudly. When next we met, he caught up with me on our way to his flat, pulling at my sleeve. 'What I don't understand is why more Diaspora Jews don't come to live in Israel!' Mystified, I said, 'Into this sliver of land? It defies logic!' Shaul didn't have enough English or German for us to communicate, and a good thing it was, too. Rosl cut our arguments short. 'Mach Schluss!' she'd say, knowing her son-in-law. Being an ardent socialist she disagreed with Shaul on land-for-peace policy. She was a moderate but he remained adamant about making Israel safe with Jerusalem as its capital. No surprise that tears stood in Rosl's eyes when Shaul spoke of Jerusalem, that ancient longing we all had for it in the Diaspora. For Shaul, capturing the Golan Heights was just part of keeping Israel safe. Next time we met, he started without any preamble, and barked at me with as much German as he could find, 'If you had lost your family in the death camps like I have, taking part in the battle for the Golan Heights was constructive because the Syrians used the Golan to shoot down on the kibbutz inside our border,' and he continued, 'What would you in the Diaspora know about these things? And Perez, he's a softy; he'd give away our back yards if we let him. That was what my family had to do – they lost everything, and their lives!' Shaul's eyes burned with anger most of the time: I think it was his way of grieving, burning the past. I was sad we couldn't console each other, but then, he lost more than I did. Ronit and he held the same views, but she knew how to show regret for the plight of the Palestinians and often said so when I was with them: 'Yes, we have to take that on; not all of them fled after independence, some were pushed.' Shaul fell back in his chair after his outburst, exhausted. Ronit bit her bottom lip, concluding, 'I hate the way the Palestinians got the rough end after the Holocaust.'

Going to see them another evening, I could see what drove Shaul. He cared for his home in a way unusual for a man, touching furniture in passing, checking plants for moisture. When he sat down, he got up again, like a lover in pursuit of the real thing, his hands tenderly touching things, his eyes roving, patrolling his domain. His children, a boy and a girl were his crown. Shaul was short, plump and passionate; despite our disagreements, he touched me. When Rosl's family argued, she looked from one to the other and when it got too heated, she always said, 'Mach Schluss, you'll wake up your Abba. In any case, I am tired of translating everything for Rosel.' Natan had long gone to bed with a book. He read biographies of the founders of Israel, one after another, and then read them a second time, Rosl told me.

When Rosl and I were in a car or a bus, she always pointed out kibbutzim: when they were built, what they grew. 'They were our stepping stones,' she explained. Her grandson Ofer added more to Israel's development. 'Modern Hebrew,' he said, 'is a miracle: a dead language brought back for modern life.' I hadn't really thought about it before, but when Rosl asked the taxi driver at the end of a fare, 'How much do I owe you, Adoni?' I felt faint: a taxi driver addressed as a lord? Blasphemous! Although I didn't practise our religion, Hebrew seemed to me to be too holy for daily usage: fancy saying, 'Do the washing-up' in Hebrew!

After another siesta, Rosl and I talked of the time when we still lived together in Germany, of old friends we had in common and those who had perished. Then suddenly she said, 'Genug, genug – I've had it up to here,' her hand sliding across her chin, 'Tag und Nacht, on the radio and the television, what the Nazis haven't finished, the Arabs will! Come, let's talk of other things.' Rushing from the room, she came back with a family photograph of her mother, father, brother and herself arranged in a crescent, my brother Heinie, about two years old, sitting on a round straw table on a cushion in front of them, his hair arranged in a coxcomb, the curl ending in the middle of his forehead. 'I loved Heinie so much I changed the photographer's grouping to have him in the picture. Yes, he was sweet,' Rosl murmured, passing the picture over to me, 'look!' 'I have this picture too,' I said. She hadn't heard me. Not only do I have the picture, but I was present when she chose Heinie to be photographed with them.

She was then sixteen, and Heinie, I believe, was the sibling she would have liked to have had. She didn't love her brother Bertel. Avrum, his father, made him into something unlovable. Apart from his mother, no one in the family liked him. Pessa pleaded for her son and fought his battles for him, though mostly the battles were with her husband. The harmony she sought was never won. Defeated, she used to claw at her neck, muscles taut.

Bertel became a sergeant in the police. He had two children from his first marriage to a Jewish Moroccan woman. He abandoned her and the children when they were still small, and 'never saw any of them again,' Rosl wrote to my parents. This tallied with the only snap Aunt Pessa sent us of them: him and his wife, a baby in his arms. They looked happy, I thought, conventionally, looking at that photograph over the years. From the rest of the family, we had pictures at regular intervals: Carmella's school days, birthday parties, weddings, anniversaries – but never from Bertel.

On my visit to Israel, I met him after a gap of forty-three years. Rosl made a special lunch for our meeting. Talk was jagged yet strangely familiar: sexual innuendoes at every turn, just like his father, and as he talked on, he vigorously rubbed his dog's back. Ida, his second wife, saw my distaste. 'He always talks like that, I'm used to it,' she said. I ached with disappointment. The only continuity here was that the boy had grown into his father. It was only for my sake that Rosl invited him for lunch. 'I rarely see him,' she said. 'He is jealous of me; of what, I don't know.'

Bertel spoke in German to me. I was curious to know about domestic violence in Israel, to get a response other than his eyebrows arching at every opportunity for sexual overtones. Nothing except a postcard joke emerged: 'It is women who abuse their husbands – with rolling pins!' he said, laughing triumphantly. Then, impatient, he whispered to me, 'Come home with us to see where we live,' and Rosl, having heard, said coldly, 'Good, then I can have a sleep.' Bertel and Rosl barely said Wiedersehen to each other; he left her flat and walked down the steps to the street, his dog pulling on the leash. It was Ida, his wife, who waved a placatory goodbye to Rosl from the pavement.

Bertel's police van was parked a few cars downhill from Rosl's flat. Seated in his van, he said, 'Before we go to my flat, I must pickup some recruits and drop them off at the training centre.' He was their instructor, but not that evening. As the youths filed in, the van swayed alarmingly, and it didn't stop after they sat down. Jumping up and down, they shoved each other, sparring, falling back on each other's laps, and as the van turned round corners they laughed out loud. I was relieved when they were dropped off. Bertel seemed pleased with their frolicking. 'They are a good group,' he said as they walked in groups through the glass door of the training centre, still cavorting.

Bertel lived in a tiny flat on the top floor of a narrow block of flats. On his sideboard was a lone picture in a frame of him and his parents on their arrival in Haifa, behind them people disembarking down the gangway of the ship. The photograph was badly developed, their facial bones were skeletal and deeply shadowed, the busy photographer leaving negatives in the developing solution too long or not long enough, I guessed. 'There was no one to meet us,' Bertel said, seeing my glance lingering on the photograph. I had never seen it before. The year was 1935; Aunt Pessa, Avrum and Bertel were the first of our family to leave Germany in the Nazi years. I was preoccupied with the thought that the man sitting on a chair rubbing his dog's back was the boy in the photo who had just got off the boat, his straight fair hair fringed on his forehead, a familiar image I remembered.

I was very bemused by Bertel and his dog. Jews and dogs? What a quaint idea! But quickly I re-arranged my thoughts: he is a policeman, stupid! Ida made us lemon tea. Between noisy sips, Bertel unloaded his resentments against his sister: birthrights and money. Ida nodded in agreement, each nod an endorsement of what her husband said. She must have heard these tales of jealousy a thousand times. 'Daddy liked her better than me' was the implication. What else was he jealous of? Perhaps being younger than his sister didn't entitle him to any reparations from Germany. Minors who went to school in the country they emigrated to lost out on the money. If they had employment during the Nazi times before the war, this entitled them to a pension. The people I'd worked for as a domestic were scrupulous in paying national insurance. When my documents arrived from Ludwigshafen, the precision with which the entries had been made were all the more remarkable because Ludwigshafen was heavily bombed, the IG factory a ready-made target. Pensions for domestic service, the category I came under, was the lowest. Rosl's was higher; before she left for Palestine, she worked for several years as a sales girl for Tietz, a Jewish department store in Ludwigshafen. As was famously known in the Jewish community, Tietz, the owner, had a 'nose job' done to disguise his – so called – Jewishness, unusual in the thirties. I went to see her there once, ensconced in her stand selling embroidered handkerchiefs, arranged and pinned round an arch like flowers. Her lovely hands rested on the counter waiting for trade. Rosl's time with Tietz qualified her for a substantial pension.

Being in Israel was not easy. Ja'acov, another policeman I met on my visit, hurried away one day from a gathering to a meeting. The agenda was to find out how Arabs thought, how they ticked. It sounded unfair to me, though I thought it better than torture. God forbid Jews should do such a thing! To Ja'acov I said, 'What do you want to find out that we Jews don't know already? If you can't reverse the Jewish experience, you had better go to Auschwitz and pick up a handful of soil.' Ja'acov puckered his brow and left. Rosl told me later that evening that Ja'akov had lost practically all his family in Auschwitz, and because of it he was trying to find a Hebrew surname to give him back his identity, make him more secure, less vulnerable.

On another day, Ja'acov took us on a trip to an arty village, the narrow high street full of nothing in particular. On the way we passed a road-block where Arabs were being frisked, a look of pure hatred in their eyes. It made me think again of Helmut, one of my touchstones on humiliation, but that was different because we, the Jews, were then marked out for de-struction. Arabs and Jews were thrown together out of a kind of despair after the Holocaust, European conscience in a tight knot, barely knowing what else to do for the best, and so Palestine was divided. There seems to be no neat way to achieve justice. Oppressions begets oppression; as I watched the eyes of the Arabs, their arms stretching over the roof of the car, I longed to tell them that no matter how they thought of themselves now, two lots of victims were living in Israel, jostling each other on the way to justice, each believing their cause and their idea of God the best. What a miserable holi-day I was having.

I only went on one Eget tour, to an ancient burial chamber filled with sarcophagi, hand-sized holes gouged out at the back just big enough to seize the treasures left for the after-life. I laughed – so what was new about stealing? I seemed to be the only irreverent person in the group. Then I remembered that I was on a guided tour. On the bus to somewhere else, we passed cultivated land; when we got to the border the land be-yond was barren. A Jewish-American woman sitting next to me billed and cooed at what she saw from her window, 'How wonderful Israel is… from nothing, they made the desert bloom!' The guide looked askance; he must have heard these eulogies many times over. 'Yes,' I said, 'but with a lot of West-ern know-how, ingenuity and money – American money –

and from masses of charity functions in lands where Jews lived.' I would not have said anything like that to an outsider. The guide rewarded me with an ironic smile; sentimental he was not! I imagined we could have had a good gossip about the heated arguments between Jews on his coach. No matter from which country Jews come, they argue among themselves, forever tapping into their anxiety.

My family let me go alone to Jerusalem. The idea that I wanted to go alone to see a friend was nothing short of a betrayal to them; 'Are you sure you'll be all right?' they said. Shaul took me to the taxi station, Rosl's words of caution in my ears. Taxis didn't leave until they were full. On the way passengers were let off at prescribed stops – a kind of private bus system which ought to be taken up elsewhere, I thought.

I stayed with an old friend whose mother came from Mannheim, which seemed to be a good enough bond for us to be friends. Eva had been in England on a university exchange and I met her through cutting her hair. When she went back to Israel, her husband stayed on in England for a while doing some research at Sussex University. He stayed with us for a weekend at Godleys. At dinner, Avi had tried to be a drinking man attempting to keep up with Cannan, but he was ill at ease with alcohol and got drunk on very little. Avi's background was in Poland. After the Germans had blitzed the country, he and his parents went backwards into Russia in a lorry. 'Wonderfully adventurous for a boy of eight, every day a different place,' Avi the sophisticate said. I didn't believe in this story as an 'adventure'. He looked alternately from me to Cannan: how was this story to be told? Sanitised, or the real thing? When finally his look fixed on me, I had decided on censorship. Avi understood. I knew the problem with these measurements: you watch for the ice to form over the listener's eyes, by which time you are paddling in your overflow, and you vow never to be tempted to speak out again. Better to simmer emotionally than slobber all over the place, incoherent and out of control.

My father dealt with such situations with his guts. My friend Connie was staying with me when he came for tea one day, their meeting purely accidental. Despite Connie's empathetic view of recent Jewish history, I can't say I was overjoyed with their meeting. Ages before, I had told her that he had briefly been in Dachau. Faced with him now, she floundered, 'Oh Mr Lerner, when the camps were liberated and I saw the newsreels I couldn't stop crying.' My father, sitting next to me, poked me in the ribs, mumbling in Yiddish, 'What does she want?' and having said how he felt about my friend, he left the room. I didn't know what to say to her, except that my father had been rude. I wasn't grateful for her empathy, because my father mistrusted her tears; he wasn't the kind of Jew who allowed Goyim to pity him.

In Jerusalem, Ilana and Avi lived in a lovely house, 'an Arab house,' Ilana said, meaningfully. The significance of this dawned on me much later. Jerusalem I also knew as Jerushalaim, the way Hasids pronounced it in my youth. Whirring washing machines and coffee percolators did not articulate Jerushalaim for me. Hasids in the street weren't ancient enough either; their black caftans had evolved in a cold climate over the centuries, having had to switch from flowing garments suited for the heat to more substantial cover for Eastern Europe's icy cold. When, after Russian pogroms and the Holocaust, they had to go back to where they had come from originally, mysteriously they seemed to have lost their common sense: fur-trimmed hats with the sun beating down on them? Even the shukhs (souks) weren't old enough for me, nor were the open drains running through Bethlehem. Jericho came nearer the mark; that really was ancient, steeped as it was in the Samson myth. When Eva and I looked down on it from a high plateau, every house seemed to have black holes for windows rather than panes of glass. The heat, the heat... I couldn't endure it; I felt ill and faint, thinking I had suffered sunstroke. I imagined the ancients praying for rain, beating drums imitating raindrops. I begged Eva to take me home, back to European Jerusalem and its comforts, and to a doctor. 'You have vertigo,' he said, 'nothing life-threatening.'

Some of my family's political opinions were expressed in the way they dressed. I wore Indian tat bought in London. I couldn't work out why they looked at me suspiciously; I loved my Indian tat. Finally, the penny dropped: what I wore was too much like Arab clothing. Maybe that was why Hasidim were reluctant to change back to their original clothes. The women in my family wore belted dresses in the heat as if they were still living in cool Europe. Wearing my flip-flops disconcerted Carmella. 'Have you no shoes?' she asked. Bemused, I remembered a friend of mine sending me a postcard from Turkey where she was searching for Goddess history. She knew the postcard would interest me: two Jews sitting on benches in an exquisitely decorated synagogue with delicately coloured walls and Hebrew scriptures written all around the room on borders below the ceiling. The men lounged on wooden seats, dressed in pantaloons with long scarves wrapped round their heads, the way men are still dressed all over the Middle East. What a tangle this dressing business had become!

Another day after breakfast Eva stood by the kitchen window putting the last touches to her make-up before going to work. She was holding a hand mirror close to her face, pinching colour into her cheeks with a look so intimate I guessed she had a lover; she was admiring what he saw. Then she hurried off, taking her four-year-old son to school on her way to work. Alone with Avi, we finished breakfast; he could tell I guessed their situation. Eva and Avi's hospitality confused me and made me feel I shouldn't have come, but Avi had planned a trip for me. After breakfast, he took me to a well on the fringes of Jerusalem. Arab boys and girls were socializing. The girls drew water and the boys loitered, flirting with them, in a scene which could have been the biblical Jacob and Rachel meeting at the well. This setting rooted me to Israel more than the modern hotchpotch of little poshed-up villages selling trashy artefacts that my family took me to.

It took me a long time to get used to everybody being Jewish; Israel seemed to me to be like a ghetto without walls surrounded by enemies. Rosl still cooked Eastern European style. Carmella seemed to have a need to apologize to me for her own Middle Eastern cooking. 'I don't cook like die Ima anymore,' she said, 'but will you come to my Seder?' 'Of course,' I said. Curious, I wondered how her Seder would end. In the event there wasn't even a beginning that I recognised: no candles flickering on the table, no Seder service, and no Haggadas. Crucially, I missed the poignant phrase uttered for centuries by Diaspora Jews around the world after they closed the Haggada, 'Next year in Jerushalaim', that most potent symbol of hope nurtured since the destruction of the temple in Jerusalem two thousand years ago, the beginning of Jewish exile.

On another day, I was alone with Rosl in the kitchen preparing supper. Natan was watching television in the living room. The kitchen window above the sink faced west and the sun was drowning in the sea. I clasped the edge of the sink, watching as night came quickly. The moon turned to white gold, its soft beam across the sea and stars pricked the darkness. Long ago, dreamers must have sat on the mountain Rosl's flat was built on and seen the same spectacle I looked at. 'When I consider thy heavens, the work of thy finger, the moon and the stars, which thou hast ordained...' the psalmist wrote. Rosl was tapping a tin of smoked fish onto a plate. 'Come, Rosel, let's eat, I want to watch the news,' she said and called Natan who came hobbling into the kitchen, leaving the television on. We ate at the Formica-topped table, its legs splayed out like a spider's. An assortment of biros stood in a mug next to a letter rack still holding the letter I'd written before I came. The fridge hummed, then stopped, then hummed again. Streams of Hebrew, for me like babble emerging from ancient times, came from the television, when suddenly the singing of Hallelujah broke through the babble, like bells ringing. 'Hallelujah…' Rosl sang along jubilantly as she put the plates on the table. 'What is the matter?' I asked. 'We have won!' she cried out excitedly. Israel had won the Eurovision song contest.

There was other news: 'Oih,' Rosl sighed, 'a bomb has exploded in downtown Haifa. Again and again we have to be careful and search. Check, check, check,' she concluded with one of the few words she knew in English. Natan looked anxiously from her to me. After the news Rosl suggested we go to visit some friends they knew from Mannheim. 'No,' Natan said, 'you go and take a taxi. In any case, I want to go to bed with my book.'

At the friends' house their television was on too. 'Halelujah' was being played over and over, along with commentaries about how the song got to the top and snippets from the singers' lives. A glow of pride was on everyone's faces, so child-like; the Semtex exploding about us seemed in comparison to be a dead star. Rosl spoke mostly in Hebrew with her friends, and then suddenly she said in German, 'We must learn to live with the Arabs. I pray for this every day, and hopefully they will want to live with us in peace.' I seemed to be a child again hearing disembodied phrases. In the taxi home, Rosl and the driver were talking about the explosion while it was being discussed on the car radio and one of the driver's hands flew off the steering wheel, gesticulating wildly, and the rasping sound of his Hebrew overpowered the modulated sounds of the newsreader.

My holiday was over. The night before my flight home, Shaul took me and my luggage to the local depot in downtown Haifa, which meant that I didn't have to go through Israel's formidable security checkout at the airport. Shaul appeared to be friends with the staff; lots of laughs, and camaraderie was expressed in Hebrew. By now I recognised Hebrew words like 'thank you', 'good bye' and 'sit' – which I learned comes from 'Sabbath', to rest – and of course Shalom and many other words that are the same in Yiddish. It wouldn't take long for me to learn Modern Hebrew, I thought longingly, but realistically my thoughts were already at home in England.

Shaul brought me back to the noisy surroundings of the depot and coming close to me he said in German, 'Sorry for shouting at you.' 'No apology needed, I understand,' I replied. The next day, the family came to say goodbye and those who couldn't come phoned from work. On the plane, my tension eased: nothing but sun, a blue sky, and a droning machine.

Home from Israel, it took me a long time to distance myself from the country's politics and the doublespeak of my emotional responses to its modernity. Rosl's letters were less confrontational and less unsettling, until one arrived to announce that Natan had died. Her grief was decidedly Eastern European in its lamentations as she berated her fate. 'What have I done to have been given this fate?' was her cry. Several years on, her letters maintained the 'why', 'what' and 'unfair' offensive against her fate. She was inconsolable. In the end I ran out of comforting phrases; then, abruptly, her grievances ended. Fate had blessed her with two more great-grandchildren, and at last my letters could be celebratory.

Not long after that, Rosl wrote that her brother Bertel had died, merely a statement of fact without any softness or feelings for her sibling. I was disappointed; a flash of memory came of my cousin Bertel as a boy in knee-length trousers, stubborn and clumsy, and hated by his father. As my letter of condolence flopped down into the post-box, tears welled up in my eyes, my feelings in chaos. On the way back to the house I agonized that real feelings for my family always emerged when I looked at their photographs with space and time to remember, and as soon as I was back inside I opened my album and looked at the black-and-white snapshot of Bertel that Aunt Pessa had sent us from Palestine when we still lived in Germany. He was in shorts and was wearing a fez, the uniform of the Palestinian Police. He was standing at the corner of a street with shrubs fronted by railings. He stood with legs astride, a strained expression on his face, his body casting a short dark shadow to his right: it was midday in Palestine. And I thought of my cousin in a legendary way, as an exile anywhere in the world.

Rosl's German was perfect and on a whim I thought I'd write to her in German, hoping she would forgive the bad construction of my sentences. It was good practice for me. After two years I got lazy and took to phoning her every now and then. On my last phone-call to her, she said, 'I had a letter from Joscovitch last week.' 'Who?' I asked, shouting down the phone, and when she repeated 'Joscovitch' I said, 'This can't be, he has been dead for forty years.' And down went her receiver with a bang. I rang Carmella at once. 'Yes' she said, 'die Ima hat Alzheimer's. She still lives in her flat and is being cared for day and night by a devoted Filipino who is paid with Ima's German pension. Yes, everything is in order.' Blessed be the memory of Conrad Adenauer. Now, with Rosl gone, I have hardly any contact with the family; the pull is not the same. Rosl evoked my childhood and is part of my story, living and breathing and laughing around me. I admired her.

Chapter Thirty-Five

Back to Germany

When I lived in England and I remembered Ludwigshafen, I always seemed to be standing outside the baker's shop on the corner of Wrede Straße, a Linzen Torte displayed in the window on a glass stand, the smell of newly baked bread and cakes wafting out at me as customers went in and out of the shop.

On the third floor window of a block of flats, opposite the baker shop, lived a girl from my class. She had two thick blonde plaits, hanging on her back, the ends held together with huge ribbon bows, freshly ironed, a different colour every day. Hitler had been in power for two years and I wondered what I was doing walking home from school with this girl, and what she was trying to tell me when she stretched out her arm directing my eyes to the Nazi bunting drawn across a window, saying, 'That is my room!' Was it then I grasped that she was the perfect example of an Aryan girl as characterized on posters, smiling, perfect teeth on show, plaits flying every which way? How I ached to have her confidence and other things I did not yet understand, both of us being just thirteen years old.

And still at that corner, I looked across to the Bierstube from which raucous laughter had come and where I had stopped dead on my way home from the Weilers' the morning of Kristallnacht, when my legs had functioned again in the hope that my father might still be at home and, going back to the beginning of the Nazi era when hope was still alive and overtook bad yesterdays, and on to the day, I deliberated outside the Bierstube over which way to go to the Gestapo, straight up Wrede Straße, or right, towards the Schiller

Straße? The foreboding I had! Anything rather than go to the Gestapo to have my fingerprints taken to identify me as a Jew. And still on that corner, I remembered the day I was caught in a snowstorm on my way to school, the snow so dense I got lost. Yes, I must go back to Germany, the place where I lost my reason to trauma.

The first time I went back was as a tourist, in the mid-Fifties when Evansky and I were still married. He wouldn't have known how I felt, but then neither did I. It was a brave enough decision to return, considering that some Jews wouldn't even fly over Germany after the Holocaust. France was our destination, but before that I wanted to visit Hanne Goldberg in Mannheim where she now lived with Raphael. With no aim other than that, we drove to the border of Germany; at least, that was how it seemed to me, though we must have planned it because visas were needed.

It hadn't occurred to me that I would need reassurance on this visit, but if proof were needed, the sight of a policeman on the border confirmed that I did. My heart changed tempo; I could barely breathe.

When we arrived at Hanne and Raphael's restaurant, Hanne had little time to greet us; she was bustling about serving at tables, though she did manage to take a couple of snapshots of us between orders, while Raphael just sat around smoking a cigarette in a holder. So this was the life she had left Henry for! One way or another, Raphael was still being kept by women. We left, waving goodbye to Hanne, and she waved back with her free hand, while with the other she placed a menu in front of a customer. Raphael was still sitting in his chair, curls of smoke rising lazily from his cigarette.

Hanne and I had lost touch with each other; the fact was I didn't want to condone the callous way she had left Henry. Comfortable talk with her would now be difficult. But when her brother Natan died, conventions articulated what she had become. Her letter was written on black-bordered paper in an envelope showing the same reverence for death. I imagined she'd be wearing a black armband for a month. I don't remember Jews ever wearing them; their sign of mourning was to have the lapel of a garment rent (nowadays that is only if mourners agree), but Kaddish was paramount. After that letter, I only heard about Hanne from my cousin Rosl, her sister-in-law. It was to her she told of her happiness. When I was with my cousin, she told me how she saw through Hanne's 'bliss' with Raphael and how she disapproved of her marrying him. There was nothing to covet here except Hanne's fluency in German.

Hanne had about ten years with Raphael before he died. Not long after his death, my cousin Rosl told me over the phone, 'Hanne is in love again with a man thirty years younger than her.' Years later Hanne surprised us again. 'You know something, Rosel,' my cousin cried down the phone, 'even now, after twenty years together, their relationship still works. He's good to her, even after her stroke. What a bit of luck,' Rosl said enviously, 'he looks after her like a son, a misfortune set in gold. Every old woman should have such a jewel!'

The second time I went to Germany, Cannan came with me. We had planned a holiday in the Rhineland. I didn't want to be a nuisance; my healing was taking longer than I had anticipated, but having committed myself to going I decided to fold away the past. Why waste the present? I thought sensibly. I joined Cannan in praise of the Rhineland as we stood in a meadow knee-deep in wild flowers. I willed myself not to tell him of the time in 1935 – my last year at school – when I had been in such a meadow with my class, sitting alone on coarse grass leaning against a rock, watching and listening to the rest of the class running about playing hide-and-seek, eating, chatting, and shrieking. Cannan and I were seemingly having a pleasant time. He was being nostalgic about the field we were standing in, full of wild flowers not sprayed to death as they were in the fields surrounding Godleys. Was I supposed to think that good things were happening again in Germany? Why then was I resentful of praise, begrudging wild flowers smiling at the sky? Did I want the earth to be sick because Nazis might have relaxed in the long grass with their lovers, delighting in nature's glory? Would I want acid to fall on this glory? Why did I want Cannan to be inside my head weeding and pulling out my ugly thoughts?

In the Schwarzwald (Black Forest), we stayed in a great wooden house, its resinous smell made more pungent by hot stoves. German visitors came in and out, as harmless as soft curtains moving in a gentle breeze. Walks in the forest were signposted efficiently; Cannan impartially observed how typically Teutonic this was. I tested my safety again: could the gentle breeze turn into a gale? Yes, gales of greetings for Adolph Hitler in Ludwigshafen, and in Germany all over. In Worms, I led the way to 7 Kyffhäußer Straße, the house of my birth. The moment we got there, Cannan walked around, curious, while I sat on the hillock opposite the house, the way I did as a child watching people come and go and staying where I was because Totzel told me not go too far away. Lost in thought, I looked at the house for what seemed like ages. Then, dreamlike, I crossed the lane for a closer look in the footsteps of my childhood. And I remembered the garden overgrown and dried by the sun, shrubs and flowers as tall as me, the smell of them near my nose. The front door was on the side of the house, and truly nothing had changed. Then, as if a fire were behind me, I rushed into the house and up the stairs, past two young women on the landing, their hands pressed against the wall, their eyes wide open. As I bolted past them up the narrow stairs, one of them called after me, 'Who do you want?' and my mouth said, 'Is Totzel in?' The women, their eyebrows now in flight, blinked in disbelief. A moment's hesitation: where was I? Shaking all over, I did an about turn and ran down the stairs and out of the house. Cannan was waiting: 'Where have you been? Suddenly, you'd gone.'

The third time I went to Germany, I went alone. By then, I had read eye-witness accounts of the Holocaust, and the more I read of them, the more I wasn't sure who was in most danger of being the target of my anger – any Gentile would do, or any thoughtless Jew. Out would come my impromptu lectures on Jewish history; it was me who would keep our dead alive in their heads. I was force-feeding my opponents. I pushed, attacking, fighting, raging, accosting anyone who crossed my path, accusing them bluntly of connivance, giving reasons why they should wake up, having only just woken up myself from a sleep so deep it shut out awareness.

Standing in Wrede Straße, I looked at the hole where our block of flats used to be. My first thought wasn't for the people killed by the bomb; no, I was thinking of cockroaches and bed bugs. Had the bombs finished them off? I kept staring into the hole when Mrs Hermann and Liesel came to mind. The block next door to number 40 was as I remembered it: modern for the 1930s. The demolition men had made a clean hole of where we had all lived, like a tooth pulled out from a crowded mouth. I rang the ground floor bell next door. 'Ja?' said a woman's voice through the entry phone. 'Do you know Mrs Hermann who lived at number 40?' 'Ja,' she said, 'she lives on the fifth floor.'

No lift. Breathless, I arrived at Mrs Hermann's front door. She scrutinized my face with her mouth open, a habit she had when she was in doubt about something. I helped her, 'Yes, it's me, Rosel Lerner.' Finally sure, she said, 'Oh yes, it is indeed Rosel Lerner, come in.' Leading the way to the kitchen, she pulled out two chairs from under the kitchen table, her arms stretched out in welcome. Sitting opposite each other we waited for words, perhaps to say something about the state

Ludwigshafen had been in after the pasting it had from Allied bombing. I couldn't go near any of this, and certainly not the consequences of the Hitler years, despite Mrs Hermann's attachment to us..

Then, politely, Mrs Hermann asked, 'How are your parents?' I mumbled something; I was busy thinking about the morning I came home from the Weilers after Kristallnacht. Not until this moment had I given any thought as to why Mrs Hermann hadn't come out from her shuttered flat when I was howling just under her kitchen window. In fact, I never saw her again, even to say goodbye before I left Germany. When Kristallnacht was in progress, her indifference to anything Nazi must have cracked; finally, they must have terrified her. Looking at her now, her eyes down, I remembered the reasons why we never saw her again: by 1938 association with Jews became more dangerous, and having joined the Habonim my interests had changed.

When Mr Hermann joined us, I thought the chance of any conversation we might have had was lost, but Mrs Hermann lifted up her face to me and leaned forward, saying, 'The bombing was so terrible Rosel... and Liesel was under the rubble... and dead... they pulled out from the rubble!' Having only just been able to tell me the way Liesel was killed, she fell silent again leaning back on her chair, gnarled hands on her knees, head down, and Mr Hermann, who had said nothing, spread the silence into every crevice around us. I became aware of the worn-out corners of the oil cloth on the table which reminded me of ours, perpetually worn out until my mother decided that the bare table was better because it could be scrubbed with soda water – cheaper and better for removing grease – when Mr Hermann interrupted my thoughts. He was levering himself up from his chair holding on to the edge of the table, and standing, he threw me an empty look, and out he walked of the kitchen, leaving behind the smell of a thunderous fart. Mrs Hermann's eyes followed him until their front door shut. How did they cope in the war, I wondered, divided as they were politically and spiritually? There were only two people who could tell me: Liesel, and she was dead, and the other one was sitting in front of me, overtaken by the grief I had reminded her of.

Halfway over the bridge to Mannheim to see Lotte, I remembered that I should have asked Mrs Hermann what had happened to the two Catholic sisters who took in my mother and brother after my father was arrested, but there had been too many things to reclaim from her trembling lips. Walking on, I thought how Lotte would be when she and her family had been trapped in Mannheim after the war started. Hanne Goldberg had hastily told me at the restaurant that eventually all the Jews from Mannheim and Ludwigshafen were transported to the collecting Lager (camp) in Gurs, inside the border of Southern France.

With thoughts of Mrs Hermann and Liesel still on my mind, I went through the Schloss gardens and on to the information kiosk under a huge tree near the train station to ask how to get to the synagogue where I had arranged to meet Lotte. I asked the woman in the kiosk, 'Where is the synagogue, please?' At the word 'synagogue' my voice shook. The woman in the kiosk seemed not to notice my tension and went on merrily, 'You speak real Mannermerisch!' I was convinced I was speaking Hochdeutsch (standard German) not the local Mannheim dialect! With the warmest of smiles, the woman directed me to the synagogue as if to a monument of Frederick the Great, and mollified by her calm, I relaxed. With a friendly 'Auf Wiedersehen' she handed me a street map.

I set out through familiar streets and beyond to an area I had never been to before. Mannheim had been severely bombed and the district I was going to had been rebuilt after the war: long streets, dead and lifeless, reproductions of pre-war architecture and earlier styles. Turning the map this way and that, it seemed I had to do a sharp right turn into a shorter street. To my alarm, a Star of David came into view on the roof of a large suburban villa. I looked at passers-by, but none seemed to care where I was going; nor did they seem to be bothered by the Star of David. But I was walking on broken glass.

The front door of the synagogue was shut. I rang the bell and moved uneasily back and forth from the front door – was anyone watching me? – when a head popped out from a side door of the villa. Cautiously, the man asked, 'What do you want?' 'Lotte!' I shouted, more firmly than I thought I could, 'I am an old friend, a very old friend.' Moments later, the man opened the front door and led me to a brightly lit hall. 'Welcome,' he said. The pews and the Torah ark were made of pale wood and the walls were white. The man left me and walked down the aisle and stopped at the second pew from the front; bending over a dark-haired woman, he whispered into her ear. With a sudden jerk, the woman turned round: Lotte! Was this really her, that black-eyed beauty with a mass of black curly hair and a waist so small, a large pair of hands could embrace it? Now, her hair was thin on top, dyed black and flattened against a shiny scalp, making her ageing skin look pasty. Face to face, two dumpy middle-aged women examined each other closely, sighing and crying, looking for their youth. Lotte was more tearful than me.

The service over, Lotte took me home to her flat in Brookner Straße. We didn't have lunch straight away. She was tense. Without preliminaries she started to talk about Gurs and on to when the war was over: 'When we returned our German neighbours were amazed, "So you've come back?" The bigotry of complete strangers was understandable but the people we had known well and who had lived next to us? God, that was unbearable! My father tutored me in how to cope, "We have to bear it because we have nowhere else to go; shouting at them won't get us anywhere." ' Lotte's first husband died in the camp. When she came back to Mannheim, she married another survivor, a friend of the family, much older than herself, who had been in Theresianstadt. He was a German Jew, much like Weiler, clipped in conversation, stiff-upper-lipped and courteous. He spoke Hochdeutsch, the like of which I had not heard for a very long time and seemed to me more like a foreign tongue; thrilling too, because it reminded me - and always will - of sitting among the scorched trees in the garden of the synagogue listing to poetry. Lotte, I noticed, was not too impressed with her husband's Hochdeutsch; mischievously, she sprinkled her German liberally with our regional accent.

Lunch was Kalte Platte (cold cuts). Lotte's husband was composed. After lunch, she and I sought comfort in armchairs in the sitting room. Her husband remained at the dining table, turning the pages of a newspaper spread flat on the table. Every now and then he lifted his eyes in our direction.

Lotte and I talked as though we were alone. What I had always wanted to know was what women did in the camps when they menstruated before their cycle stopped altogether from malnutrition. No sooner were the words out of my mouth, Lotte leapt up from her chair, pointing to her upper arm, 'Injections! Injections! Hormone injections!' she shouted, her face flushed with anguish, and out came the horror of life in the camp. 'Rats as big as cats, running past our heads and feet, and the food we got dogs wouldn't eat, and worst of all was the constant threat of being moved to somewhere we didn't know, nor to what. Our Lager,' Lotte continued, 'was a collecting camp from which people were transported to where we didn't yet know,' she repeated, staring through the window at a monolith of a block of flats about thirty yards away, her body rigid, arms taut against her chest.

The story she told me next was unexpected, considering the circumstances she had been in. She had made her way to the barbed wire which separated men from women and, somehow or other, she found her husband and both of them had managed to get through the wire. 'We were together… a miracle happened: I conceived, despite the injections!' Lotte said, jubilantly. Another mixed blessing, I deduced.

Then Lotte left the room in a hurry. When she came back, she was holding a photograph in her hand. Without hesitation, she pushed it under my nose. 'This is where you'd have ended up had you not left Germany.' Her finger stayed on the black-and-white photograph showing a desolate place under a sky full of black clouds and wooden huts either side of a muddy trek. A woman was pushing a barrow, its wheel grooving the mud. The photograph was diagonally streaked with white.

I tried to think of days less menacing. One of the last girly things Lotte did for me before I left Germany was to show me how to apply mascara. 'Look,' she had said, handing me a mirror when she'd finished, 'you look just like Käthe von Nagy.' Nagy was a Hungarian film actress working for UFA, and I was, according to Lotte, her lookalike; that was certainly enough to please the sixteen-year-old I then was. But thoughts of our youth fled when Lotte continued, 'My rescue from the camp was another miracle. To this day, I have no idea why I was singled out from a long queue, and even less idea who the man was who discreetly crooked his finger in my direction to come to him. Was his finger a mirage? Had my eyes tricked me? I decided I had nothing to lose.' Lotte's hands gesticulated restlessly.

Her husband looked on anxiously. 'No more questions,' he said, slapping his flat hands on the newspaper. I had only asked one, but his look told me I had been too curious. 'My daughter was born in Free France,' Lotte continued, ignoring her husband's anxiety. Leaving the room again, she came back with a black-and-white snapshot, a back view of her with her daughter, aged about nine, walking on a pavement somewhere in

France. The child was a dark-haired, long-legged girl, as tall as her mother. I looked at the picture a long time, imagining, and while I was still looking, the doorbell rang.

A tall, good-looking young woman walked through the door. Lotte, her face full of joy, announced, 'This is my miracle child.' Her hair had a wave to it and was black which suited her translucent alabaster skin. She made herself comfortable on the sofa. I don't remember her name but I remember her giggly laughter and the way she teased me about my German – 'sweet' she said it was.

An hour later, the miracle child's daughter arrived. Miriam was beautiful the way Lotte had been, petite, though less vivid than her grandmother. Nothing difficult was talked about except for me wanting to know what her school days had been like. 'Normal,' Miriam said. She was part of the generation after the Holocaust. When the war was over, Germans, I gathered, from Miriam, 'bowed their heads in redemptive mode – in fact, classes were taken to the sights where the Nazis did their foul deeds.' And more haltingly, Miriam said, 'I was… kind of revered.' Lotte, continuing in that mood, added, 'I have a German woman friend who listened to me patiently after we came back, and like my father, she taught me control, which was to enlighten the perpetrators with only one thimbleful of horror at a time, and with lots of spaces in between. Any more will defeat your purpose,' she said, though at the moment of telling me of her experience, Lotte's delivery had been like a flamethrower. Me, not being a perpetrator gave her the freedom to speak out. I was an Unsere, an insider.

Seeing Lotte, I found out that my emotions were as deranged as hers, though mine, I hasten to add, had less reason to be. Whatever their size, traumas are similar. On my way back to Worms, I looked out of the train and saw the names of the villages my father and mother went to as peddlers – then, Worms.

In my youth, I passed the cathedral often, dreading the solemnity of booming bells, solemn and joyous. Marked out as 'other', I used to sit outside the classroom (a worldwide Jewish experience in the Diaspora) with one other Jewish girl until the Christian Religion class was over. How I was 'other' was then a bland thought. Now, knowing more, I felt I was taking a risk going through the once forbidden portals of the cathedral, especially on Good Friday.

The cathedral was packed to the rafters. Before the Passion began, the priest gave a short address. 'We must remember Dresden, Hiroshima, Auschwitz.' Tears pricked my eyes: was I feeling the real thing? Forgiveness was what the priest said we should practise. Was this a formula or a command from his heart? Did he really want to understand why we'd been hounded? How would he change our predicament, when in the Christian New Testament, carte blanche is given to hound us till the end of time, if not with swords then with words, the intention being to correct our erroneous ways? Angry, I waited for the priest to prove me wrong.

A large black wooden cross was carried by two men dressed in plain clothes to the front of the altar. The cross was twice the size of the men: an overpowering symbol. The Stations of the Cross were recited and soon we were at Calvary. I was gripped until I heard, '… and the Jews denied him, calling out, "Crucify him".'

Here it was, the same old stuff: the priest's preamble was a formula! Was the Pope's exoneration from our 'crime' of deicide also a formula, or a genuine change of heart? I imagined myself shouting into the congregation, 'I am a Jew and I am listening to you!' And with all their eyes on me, I would ask them, 'Am I still the thorn in your flesh or is this drama you are enacting like old boots too comfortable to throw away?' A joke came to mind: A Gentile meets a Jew in the street. 'Is it true you are a Jew?' 'Yes,' says the Jew. The Gentile slaps the

Jew's face. 'What did you do that for?' the Jew asked. 'You killed Jesus Christ!' 'But that was two thousand years ago!' 'Yes,' says the Gentile, 'but I have only just heard it.'

I had long stopped following the drama of the service. I was looking about me as I had when watching the cinema screen in 1938, when the audience had complied, their smiling faces lifted up towards the screen. Hitler had stretched out his arm as if in a blessing, and, as then, the people here in the Cathedral were swallowing their Saviour's body mouthful after mouthful, 'the light and the truth'. I was sure they felt themselves 'saved'; they looked softer, empty of woe, milder and less beleaguered as they walked back to their pews. Who in their right mind would give up this peace, this flood of feelings carrying away sin? And here I was in their midst refusing this Jew who became their saviour and their God in all its visibility.

The service over, I placed myself across the road facing the great door of the cathedral. The congregation spilled out onto the pavement in complete silence. I have no doubt they felt saved, but was I safe? I wanted to rip out my soul, but which one? The rational one, or the one I'd suckled from my mother's breast? Where could I find what we had lost?

The nearest thing to a memorial I have been to is Yad Vashem on the hills around Jerusalem, surrounded by Israeli soldiers guarding the Jewish tragedy. I have not yet had the courage to make a trip to Auschwitz, crammed with fresh ashes from bones. In Worms, I tried to find evidence of our loss in the Jewish cemetery, the oldest in Europe. I struggled to read the Hebrew without vowels on the tombstones but with no success, except for some dates of burials. The Crusaders had come this way and the age of the cemetery and those dates on the graves fitted with that history.

Lost in thought, I forgot the way to the Judengasse (Jews' Lane). I asked a man passing, 'Die Judengasse, bitte?' He repeated it after me, his features squeezed together, sour. Who, the crumpled mess suggested, could still be interested in that? Though irritated, he pointed the way. 'The synagogue and the Judengasse are not far from each other,' he said, less perturbed. Had I provoked him deliberately to test my feelings and in turn his? I had, after all, a street map in my hand. I would never really know how he felt when it was now against the law to be anti-Semitic in Germany, but his face was evidence enough for me that old resentments lingered on.

The Judengasse was bombed in the last days of the war, but it was restored more pristine than it probably was in its time; no memories there, and on I walked to the synagogue. No memories there either; I most likely never went there as a child. Come to think of it, neither did my father; he most likely went to a Stible where Eastern European Jews prayed and studied.

The synagogue was refurbished to its former glory. The Rashi chair stood at the end of a long table from where he had taught. Rashi was a Jewish scholar who lived from 1040 to 1105. People milled about inside and out, and down steep steps to the Mikvah, their flat hands against the curved wall to steady them as they must have done centuries before, women holding up their long skirts with their free hands. The Mikvah was like a dungeon: hard to imagine bathing in that cold, dank and airless place. I shivered at the thought, and quickly blessed modern plumbing.

Back in the men's section, a man and a woman stood in front of a bookshelf holding open a Hebrew prayer book. The man turned the pages, reading. We nodded to each other: Yes, we are Jews. With our eyes full of tears, we looked at the people milling around the room, when the man said, 'Look, all of them tourists.' The couple left abruptly. I would like to have known their reasons for visiting Worms. Maybe they were conducting the now fashionable 'search for roots'; they were a lot younger than me.

It seemed that Hitler had succeeded in making the Wormser synagogue into a museum. The notorious one was in Prague where Torah scrolls were collected throughout Europe as the possessions of an 'extinguished people'. The visitors in the synagogue around me were blue-eyed with straw blond hair and the babble of Nordic tongues echoed round the walls. Refurbished though the synagogue was, it looked unused: no tell-tale patina on chairs or walls, or a chair suddenly pushed aside from Rashi's table in a disputation, or the accumulation of candle grease on the holder, dried as it ran down. But most curious of all was a guide wearing a Kippa. Totally at a loss what to think, I asked. 'Are you Jewish?' 'No,' he said, 'I am employed by the council.' Yes, the Wormser synagogue was indeed a museum. Looking for more evidence of its past, I found Rabbi Holzer's name on a list of rabbis who had taught at the synagogue. After my parents died, I found their marriage certificate signed by Rabbi Holzer – that was a surprise, having thought they were married in a Stible.

From the synagogue I walked until I got to a roundabout. Wedge-shaped houses at the end of each street made a star pattern. On one house, a pulpit curled round a first floor window, ornate like a ring. The plaque underneath read 'Luther preached here.' Now I could imagine living in the Judengasse at Easter time, when the congregation emerged from the cathedral and crowds listened to Luther's sermons, spiked with his formidable anger against the Jews. Luther's conviction was that the second coming of Jesus could not happen until all the Jews were converted, a belief extant to this day in the church. Conversion of Jews to Christianity proved to be elusive in Luther's time, but when they chose to convert to Christianity – to gain entry into German society – Luther had long been dead. Two hundred years later even Luther, to give him the benefit of the doubt, might have recoiled at what the Nazis did to the Jews.

Back at my guesthouse I collected the keys from the bar. Two dark-haired men were sitting on stools facing each other. One was talking very loudly to the other, 'Look at yourself, can't you see that you can never be a German? Surely, even you can see the difference between us.' The dark-haired man slid about on his stool and said nothing in reply; he just stared at the loud-mouthed man as if obliged. The strange thing was I couldn't imagine a Jew sitting with a German at a bar – a café maybe, but a bar? I was there long enough to hear the 'silent' man order another drink for both of them in heavily accented German. Was he a Gastarbeiter? Perhaps he didn't understand all the loud-mouthed man had said. I lay awake a long time that night. Eventually, sense prevailed; I had, after all, a British passport.

The following Sunday, I walked to 27 Römer Straße where we had lived for five years. I turned round and round several times, trying to recognise something, anything. Where was the place where I had thrown parcels of food into the cellar, and where my mother taught me to smile and count and where my brother Heinie was born? I needed to see the reflection of myself in our shop window of how vain a five-year-old I had been, how I noticed my firm arms, the poses I struck, and how startled I was when my mother called me for Mittagessen. All of it gone, replaced with a complex of police housing.

That Worms had been bombed surprised me; there was nothing industrial there that I knew of. The Roman wall had survived and was still upright..Less ancient was the cathedral and the Denkmal, a memorial to Luther and his co-scholars involved in the Reformation. Luther stands isolated from them on a plinth in the centre, the bronze green with age.

Hungry, I made my way to a restaurant I had noticed opposite the cathedral. Outwardly the Bürgers (middle class) looked like Bürgers anywhere out for Sunday lunch. I was in a time warp. Although hungry, I didn't enjoy my food; instead,

I bored holes through the Bürgers' heads with my eyes. I wanted to scream at them, ask them what they did in the war. Were you glad to be rid of your Jewish neighbours? Where did you think they'd gone? Did you see? Did you hear? Are you sorry? Do you understand? Be telepathic, damn you, acknowledge me! I relived what they wanted to forget. Dissatisfied, my emotions ran on. Was I unhappy because they seemed not to be, laughing and chattering, their children's sudden cries of temper like children anywhere? Could this be 'anywhere' after the Holocaust? My thoughts distressed me. I walked through the streets begrudging their life and their laughter, and looking at men, I changed their civilian clothes into Nazi uniforms.

Despondent, I went back to Mannheim to be with Lotte. The state I was in, I couldn't understand how she could live among Germans. After lunch we went for a stroll through the Planken (the main shopping street) as in olden days, passing the space where I thought the shop was where Trudel and I had photos taken, where we had laughed into the camera. I regretted not having pursued her whereabouts after the war. The truth was I never knew her family name; like a famous person, she had just one name: Trudel.

Lotte and I walked up and down the prescribed stretch of road, a tradition upheld all over Europe from Baden Baden to Moscow and beyond, and I remembered the strip of concrete in the grounds of a Baden Baden hotel I had been to with Cannan which was for the sole purpose of strolling back and forth. Cannan and I had been mesmerised: the strip of concrete divided the back of the hotel from the orchestra, housed in a shell-shaped sphere. A string of shops selling luxury goods flanked the tables set back from the windows at the back of the hotel, shaded with blinds like eyelids. We had chicken vol-au-vents and coffee and watched couples parade, dressed in fashionable ensembles. One couple stood out from all the others. The woman was dressed in rich blue from top to toe with an umbrella to match, tapping it lightly on the concrete as she walked. The man beside her was dressed in a white suit, white spats over black and white shoes, top-stitched alternately white on black and black on white, and above the brim of his Panama hat, a plain black band ended in a masculine slip-bow level with his ear. The brim of the hat swerved slightly upwards on one side. From a black cord round his neck, a monocle dangled animatedly in rhythm with his steps, and for balance, his fingers gripped a silver-topped cane. I had asked myself: What did they do in the war? How did they serve the Nazis? No, I decided, they were a couple of film extras for UFA, disciplined by a director's commands booming forth from a megaphone. They were well past middle age: it was possible they had belonged to the Hitler Youth, or were they offspring of a grand Prussian family, connected to the army? That they may have been tourists never occurred to me.

Back with Lotte, strolling down the Planken was more fun; we could dart to shop windows for distraction. When we came to the end of the shopping area, Lotte turned on her heels and said, 'Now we walk back again!' I had forgotten this ritual, and turning round, the green dome of the water tower came into view. Mittel-Europa was on its best behaviour again.

Staying in a hotel gave me freedom. I could go out on my own, browsing through familiar streets, and leisurely walking to the Planken, when I remembered shopping with my mother before I went to England, and how excited she was, able to fulfil a wish I had: 'I have enough money to buy you the blue-and-red sandals in Salamanders (an upmarket shoe shop) and the raincoat at...' But if I went on thinking about my mother and me in the Planken, it would lead me to the day I had to leave her in Germany, and worst of all that I had never asked how she coped after I left. I wasn't prepared to feel shame, and walking on I came to the Kaufhaus, a department store on the corner where the Planken ended and Breite Straße began, and wanting to escape from my thoughts, I walked in to have my hair done.

Waiting for the assistant, I time-warped again, so it was no escape really. Women, young and old, appeared like slides. I mentally stripped them naked and dressed them in the style of the Thirties. Young shampoo boys I turned into members of the Hitler Youth. I spent my time questioning the 'slides' while the assistant questioned me, 'How much hair do you want off?' 'Whatever you think,' I said carelessly, my eyes fixed on people around me, asking myself the same questions I had in the restaurant. Was I obsessed? I saw them only as forms to be filled in, ticks in the appropriate boxes: Yes. No. Did you or did you not participate in Hitler's orgy? I drilled holes into heads while assistants washed or cut their hair, and the pins being poked through rollers became instruments of torture. Still in a trance, I heard my assistant say a charmless 'Danke' as she placed my bill on the work base. I paid and left.

To the assistant, I must have been a boring tourist and nothing more, but she couldn't have suspected the damage I did in my mind to the clientele. In the street, I knew that the only harm I had inflicted was on myself.

Another day, I turned sharp right at the Kaufhaus into Breite Straße, less elegant than the Planken. It had been a very busy thoroughfare, long and straight, leading to where the River Neckar meets the Rhine, and just over the bridge and beyond was the suburb where my friends Ruth, Lina, Eva and the Bergs had lived – an embarrassing reminder of my last unhappy days with them before I went to England. With my back to the River Neckar, the Schloss was at the far end of the street. This was a popular backcloth for photographing friends and families, and it was where Kurt told me dangerous things; a lick of emotion, hot and familiar, crisscrossed my guts. At sixteen I had walked through the crowds and darted into the fleapit of a cinema, past the notices forbidding my entry. Gigli sang '… forget me not…' to Magda Schneider. I was lacerated emotionally, but despite the risks, I sat through the film a second time. What had the Nazi flags hanging from buildings outside, dripping like blood, to do with a sixteen-year-old's raw emotions as she looked up at the screen from the third row in a flea pit, tears rolling down her cheeks? Exhausted, after the second viewing I walked home having to think of a lie. I lied a lot for my pleasures.

The following Sunday I went back to the spot where I thought the fleapit might have been. I rushed up Breite Straße like a dog chasing after a fictitious hare. I had to find the fleapit. Was I ill? Standing where I thought it had been, reality pushed out the past like a tide: a shoddy street came into focus, forsaken and closed off to traffic, buildings with shops beneath, colourless and drab – not yet, it seemed, treated to postwar renovations. Men were strolling in the middle of the road in disorderly rows, a defeated army wearing crumpled suits, their lips pressed together in fortitude, their arms folded behind their backs, hands crossed at the wrists like convicts, no conversation between them. They didn't look like people walking in the Planken. Again I guessed they were Gastarbeiters. There was not a woman in sight. I stared into the sun. When I looked back, my view of the street was fuzzy and blurred. I stayed were I was, remembering the time I'd walked home after I had seen the 'rat' film thinking I had caught the Nazi illness. With hindsight, I looked for the essence of that era to find a stain in myself, how far I had been sullied by Nazi ideas. There appeared to be no barrier in my mind. Who would I hunt down? Who would give me that frisson of hate to anger me beyond control, beyond the choice we all have?

Another day, I walked confidently down the Planken to the water tower and turned left into the Augusten Anlage, a wide avenue where trees towered like cathedrals and smaller ones fronted substantial residential villas set back from wide pavements. When I was young the people who lived there were out of my reach; I had only ever looked down that avenue, never daring to walk through it. I imagined people pointing their fingers at me, shouting to go back where I belonged. I knew of a girl who lived in one of those villas. Habonim gossip had it that she bathed and changed her knickers every day. Although she was Jewish, she never came to our club; she was too different from us. But for me she was a mirage, her clothes so wondrously arranged in perfectly contrasting colours, so easy on the eye, and so thrilling – diagonal stripes met in the middle of a jumper like arrows. I saw her once or twice, shopping on the Planken. Considering the fate we shared, it was strange I didn't even have the courage to speak to her about her clothes, how that magical fit and that tactful soft mould for the body might be achieved. Nothing I had ever worn looked like that. For her, every day seemed to be Sunday, I thought jealously. When I am rich, every day will be Sunday for me too. Kristallnacht happened a few months later.

After the war, my thoughts turned to people I had known, and known of, and I thought of her especially. How was she brought low? Had she run on the double through dem Himmelweg (way to heaven), the name the Nazis euphemistically gave to the tube through which their nude victims were whipped into the gas chambers? Schnell! Schnell!

When Lotte and I kissed good-bye, I whispered into her ear, 'Now, you must come to me – soon!' Her daughter took me to the station. There was time to spare for a coffee. We chatted for a while, and soon from the lips of the Wunderkind came the whine of how difficult it was to live with her mother. This tale I didn't want to hear. I was glad to get on the train, glad to get away.

Chapter Thirty-Six

Lotte's Visit to Hove

In August that same year, Lotte came to visit me. No longer running a car, I took the train to Gatwick. I waited at the barrier at the end of Lotte's flight gangway and saw her before she saw me. Her eyes moved along the line of people waiting. The moment she saw me, she rushed forward, her shoulders hunched, high heels clicking on the terrazzo floor, tears gushing from her eyes as from a watering can. But the moment we'd embraced, the ground between us was parched: Lotte, having no English at all, made my switch to German too sudden. There were practical things to sort out: collecting her luggage, getting her ticket. On the train to Brighton, Lotte, as usual, mingled Hochdeutsch with our regional dialect, and since I apparently still looked dull-witted, not having maintained the practice I had in speaking German six months before, she said impatiently, 'You know, this is how we spoke!' 'It can't be!' I said obstinately. 'Come on, Rosel, you know we did!' she insisted. There is nothing like the German language to stir me up when I need it suddenly; always it manages to disrupt my senses, and I know that as long as I live, I'll be an immigrant, neither language helping the other when translation is needed.

At home, Cannan joined us for dinner. Lotte and he had French in common and were able to make small talk. I was anxious, suspecting that Lotte wanted more freedom away from home and her husband's reserve. Although Cannan had read a lot of Holocaust stuff, face-to-face with a survivor he seemed to be tongue-tied – we shared this. Criticizing his own culture was one thing, but admitting to past attitudes held towards Jews by the Establishment must have been uncomfortable, so reserve was necessary, else it might bring down Western civilisation as we knew it. I understood this. I had long wanted Cannan to understand more of the situation Jews were in. Over the years, I had learned that talking about Jewish issues in front of our family and friends was to be avoided. To seize hold of the real Jewish question, all of us needed to have greater intellectual and spiritual craftsmanship to keep us socially buoyant. Even for those who have lost religious beliefs or never had any, attitudes towards Jews are a constant. To relinquish the religious thrust of the last two thousand years which has soaked into Western culture, we would have to look more bravely at ourselves. The simplest example is how many times we still hear people ask, 'What is your Christian name? Fine, if you are Christian, but it is irksome for us Jews, Muslims and Hindus. The strange thing is that 'Christian name' has never become absorbed into the German language: Vorname, bitte (first name please). Another example is how carelessly 'the kiss of Judas' is used to describe betrayal.

To be fair, living with me those last two decades must have been like living on the edge of a precipice. No longer an appeaser, I had for some time now argued the Jewish case in our house, but with Lotte present, the conversation round our dinner table was all over the place. Lotte picked up my anxiety and made enormous efforts to keep talk neutral; 'No suffering', my look demanded. She spoke of her time in France as if she had gone there for a holiday, her eyes moving from me to Cannan.

The next day, where I went, Lotte went. Whatever I did, she was watching, perhaps to see what we had in common so that we could be more at home with each other, how we did things, little things we might remember from our past. At the local butcher, she looked round the shop like a stray cat scans a house before she decides to make it her home. She looked over the meat on display. 'The cuts are different at home,' she said, 'and there isn't the variety of sausages for sliced cold meat.' 'That you'll get at the supermarket,' I said, knowing perfectly well that she knew this. When washing up, I mopped a saucepan with a sponge first before I used a tea cloth. 'That is what I do,' Lotte said. So we did have things in common.

Walking through Brighton's Regency area, I gave Lotte historical dates: she was bored. She refused to go into the Brighton Pavilion altogether. 'I've had enough of museums,' she said. 'I understand,' I replied and added, 'these days, the whole world seems to be a museum.' We began to relax with each other, but I wished that I had a family to share her with, to break up the duo and mix things up a bit.

One morning, Lotte and I chatted in her bedroom while she creamed her face and neck. I was amused at the extra care she took as her hands slid down to her bosom. Lotte thought it was no laughing matter. 'I'm nurturing myself,' she said in a serious tone. But what I meant to share with her was the irony of both of us trying to retrieve the irretrievable. For Lotte, all life was devotional, so no tittering; I felt bad about my lack of reverence for her feelings.

August 1983 was humid: not a breath of air for days. Maybe it would be cooler by the sea? Not much difference. We walked along the promenade. No frivolous conversation passed between us. I don't know which was worse, the humidity or Lotte's sombre mood. We were together: Lotte, the sea, and me. There was no danger of strangers being affronted or embarrassed, and without her anxious husband watching over her she repeated what she had told me in Mannheim. The rhythm of her delivery was the same, word for word: the injections, the appalling food, the rats, the loss of hope. Talking on, her bosom heaved helping to free her of her troubles, but her mouth articulated every syllable equally, every word with the solemn intonation of a funeral march, relentless and uncompromising. I was with her every step of the way. It could have been me – why her and not me? We could have been to-gether and now that we were, I listened. Survivors need serial empathy. On the bus home, she laughed, she was even merry! When the bus passed Brighton's East Street in slow traffic and she saw the milling crowds, she said, 'I want to go there, it looks lively.'

The following days Lotte was more restful to be with. Then, abruptly, she said, 'I want to go to London,' adding peremptorily, 'I'll pay.' At the butcher's it was the same: 'My treat!' There was no arguing with her; I felt she would break if I insisted that she was my guest. So to London we went. The humidity was even worse there. The air hovered and quivered above the traffic in Knightsbridge. I had booked a bus tour from Harrods. The bus was waiting outside the store, earphones attached to every seat. When the bus started to move, Lotte looked out of the window, listening attentively to the German commentary. Then, suddenly panic-stricken, she jumped up and down, her voice shrill, 'The earphones don't work!' They were put right at once. Tiny things seemed to upset Lotte's equilibrium. The earphones now working, her eyes hardly moved; they had more of a stare than a look. Tower of London, Buckingham Palace… I didn't see much either; I was watching Lotte.

The tour over, she highlighted not a single thing she'd seen; nothing seemed to have been of interest. She might as well have turned the pages of a picture book. For Lotte it had been just something mandatory she had to do as a tourist, I fancied. The compensation she'd got from Germany for loss of property and suffering endured during the Nazi era made a difference to her life, as mine has for me. But having money doesn't necessarily change panic attacks. When Jews are threatened, I feel threatened. Lotte and I were the same in that private part of ourselves that knows the stark reality that you can never not be a Jew. Hide? What for? They'll find you anyway. Only recently I had learned that the American German family, owners of IBM, invented a punch card with all the particulars needed to find every Jew in every crevice in Europe to support their still beloved Fatherland. Yet despite this kind of thoroughness, some people hid Jews at great risk to themselves.

I had arranged an overnight stay with a friend in Notting Hill Gate. When we got there Lotte was unable to say hello, panting, her chest heaving. 'I am feeling bad, really bad,' she said, enunciating each word like an elocution teacher. I was not surprised having seen her through the crack of her bedroom door squashing herself into a corselet, pulling her middle together like a Christmas cracker – ridiculous in this heat, when loose clothes for women were readily available. Lotte still wore the collars of her shirts outside sporty jackets, as we did in the Thirties. As calmly as I could, I told her to go upstairs and undo her corset and lie down for a while. After a few murderous looks at me, she did as I suggested; I was amazed she hadn't linked the corselet to her feeling faint, and wondered why she wore a corset at all. I could have been more thoughtful and helped her to undress, but she was so proper, and being in a friend's house, I was busy being anxious; I was convinced we were a nuisance.

Recovered after her rest, she agreed to go back to Knightsbridge to look at the shops at a more leisurely pace. A glance from the Knightsbridge exit of Hyde Park was enough: with one look at the shops across the road, she said, 'Boring. We've got all these shops in the Planken. Come, Rosel, let's go home.' Sea air already in my nostrils, I agreed. I apologized to my friend; she was good about our change of plan.

Coming out of Brighton station, the sky was blue and the air fresh. The rest of Lotte's stay was more enjoyable. Once I felt Cannan had no obligation to participate in her visit, I relaxed and so did he. Lotte's favourite view was Lewes Crescent as seen from a good way back on the seafront below; 'it is fab-

ulous,' she said. The weather held. We spent the remaining days
of her visit sitting on benches facing the sea, re-living pre-war
days in Germany when we belonged to different Jewish youth
clubs: she to Hashomer (the guards), more to the left, and I to
Habonim (the builders), more to the centre. Both furthered
the pioneering spirit.

'How important all this seemed to us then: left, right…
stumbling footsteps to anywhere, and whatever club we belonged to was not a guarantee we'd end up in Eretz Israel but
any country which would let us in,' Lotte said. Then suddenly
she was tired of talking about our bygone hopes, and to finish
what was still on her mind she said, 'For all too many, neo-
Zionism that resurrected ideology taken from ancient Biblical
texts died with them in the camps. Those who survived needed
solid ground, not evocation, and then, something real did happen: Israel. The nations voted, spoke at last.' And that said, she
wept. We were, after all, of one mind. We looked across the
sea, still as a pond.

Lost, gazing out to sea, I thought of Israel, populated as it
was with two lots of victims, and since little has healed for either of them, hatred proliferates, the fine line which turns victims into perpetrators stretching until the thread to truth
breaks, and we, the Diaspora Jews, have to listen to criticism
of our new country as she steps in and out of her conflicts and
joys, her mistakes, and sometimes her achievements.

Lotte and I seemed to be thinking telepathically about ex-
tremists and their viewpoints on the 'Promised Land' dogma
so often expressed distastefully in the Western press. 'Imagine,'
Lotte said, 'how I feel living in Germany, wishing that Israel's
self-defence could be judged more sympathetically and not as
if she'd been established for centuries. My nerves always get
the better of me and I pray that our country will behave perfectly, and that the Palestinian people will want to share our
ancient land with us and merge their knowledge with ours,

and to understand what happened to us Jews in Europe, and for us Jews to appreciate what has befallen the Palestinians since 1948 as a consequence. You must remember that I live in a land where a lot of people are still starched rigid with silence on that subject.'

Then, laughing throatily, she said, 'Remember the woman I told you about who warned me not to confront perpetrators with too much? Only last year,' she continued, 'I failed miserably. A Christian woman tried to get me to believe in the virgin birth, and the Three Kings bringing gifts for baby Jesus. Well, I thought, now or never! Her certainty annoyed me, and I told her that the 'three kings' were guests attending Jesus' circumcision.' 'That was daring,' I laughed. Lotte was unstoppable. 'I've been looking behind the Christian story for years, and ours, seeing the way these stories have been tidied up to suit the politics of the time. Sure, I told the woman, but I wanted to say more.' 'That would have been more than a thimbleful,' I teased. 'That's true, but sometimes I get so mad listening to them, the way they hid their faith when Hitler was in power, and now that he's gone, they're hailing the Pope. One thing I'm sure of, people need something to love and something to hate, but most of all something to cheer about – anything!' Suddenly she hissed, 'I hate religion!' How far she had come in the last six months! 'Let's go home and have some crumpets," I suggested. Lotte agreed: 'Kein Problem,' she said, getting up briskly from the bench.

The next day, the sky was blue and a breeze cooled the heat of the sun. 'Let's have lunch out,' I suggested, 'very good fish and chips on the Palace Pier,' and so they were. After lunch, we walked on the promenade past the Angel of Peace, the monument dividing Hove from Brighton. We sat on a bench facing the sea again, the wide promenade behind us. We talked about easier things than we had done the day before, though just as pressing: nostalgia. Was it Lotte or was it me who started to sing a pop song from the Thirties? Singing together, la-la-ing our way through when the lyrics deserted us, we laughed and cried, and embarrassed by the strength of our feelings we covered our faces with our hands and rocked back and forth on the bench, and the more songs we remembered the more came to mind. The sea splashed over the pebbles and the sky was high and clear.

Crumpets for tea was getting to be a tradition with Lotte, and I considered that a daily helping of them with butter for one week wouldn't add much to our already rotund figures. Lotte decided that the perforations on one side of the crumpet were an utterly magical repository for the butter. Tea over, she licked her fingers before we went through my family album, the first half frequently having captions under pictures saying 'perished in the Shoah' (destruction). Lotte's face lit up when she saw Trudel's picture. 'I knew her!' she said excitedly. Not knowing her family name, our hold on her slipped, but not my memories of her, the times we had together in her bed-sit where she lived alone and, unbelievably in 1937, had a record player, and how we listened endlessly to Richard Tauber singing Ich küsse ihre Hand Madam und träum von ihren Mund in the impure sounds of those 78 recordings. How I wished that Trudel had written a dedication at the back of the photograph she gave me of herself, and how disappointed I was when she didn't; the shame I felt when I wrote it myself, the falsification ever a reminder of my need for Trudel's affection that I might have got from an older sister. But no matter, Lotte read it as true. Before I stuck the photo down, I photocopied the back 'To Rosel from her beloved Trudel for an everlasting memory' dated 18.12.1938, just four weeks after Kristallnacht. Lotte broke my thoughts: 'Maybe she was from a different town.' 'Hm.' I grunted.

We were hanging onto threads and with a shrug of our shoulders we gave up. I was doing the washing-up and Lotte was drying when I told her of the Weilers' encounter with Rabbi Wexler, and how Weiler disliked Eastern European Jews. 'You know, prejudice goes both ways,' Lotte said, a little agitated, 'In the camp, I slept next to a Polish Jiddene and it was she who elbowed me: "Come Maidele, I'll teach you Yiddish. How can you be a Yiddishe girl if you don't speak your mother tongue?"' What Lotte said didn't require a quick yes or no, and on a whim I asked her, 'Tell me, did your family pray in a Stible?' She laughed out loud: 'Don't be ridiculous, Rosel!' Ignoring her tone, I said, 'Does this mean that if Hitler had not come to power we would never have met?' 'Probably not,' Lotte answered playfully, and then added, 'But if you'd had the bad luck to have remained in Germany after the war started, all those divisions would have been sorted out on the cattle trucks.' Lotte and I had similar views on Jews being angry with each other.

Then she changed the subject: 'By the way, did you know that Edgar Wexler was the son of the rabbi in Ludwigshafen's German Jewish synagogue?' 'The Wexler who lived above the Weilers?' I asked. 'Yes', she said, 'he was a boyfriend of mine... went to America just in time, I think.' 'Oh, did he?' I said vaguely, still thinking what Lotte had said about the cattle trucks. Her anger hurt me a little. I was back with the hierarchy in suffering, and continued thinking about the differences between Eastern and German Jews, and about Edgar: could he have been my boyfriend? I knew him only from us passing on the stairs; either he was going out, or I was coming in on my way to the Weilers. He knew what my job was because he often saw me scrubbing the stairs on my knees, moving aside to let him pass – no straightforward move, that. He was a good-looking blond youth with intense blue eyes. He too was out of my reach, much like the girl who changed her knickers every day. We never spoke, only nodded the time of day. With hindsight, I am surprised how well I knew my place. I didn't know of any German Jews marrying Eastern European Jews; any marrying out they did was to Germans and in huge numbers, frequently ending up converting to Christianity. The more Lotte and I talked about these things, the more I suspected that Mrs Weiler may not have been Jewish, remembering how her husband ground his teeth, unable to meet her eyes when he came home from Dachau. What was he grinding down? Was it what his wife had to go through because of him? That a Jew was after all just a Jew and nothing else, and that there was no way he could obliterate what he was, and must throw to the winds any hope of total integration in his beloved Germany?

Lotte's third husband 'died of old age' she told me in a letter, '… in the end Terianstadt and its aftermath was too much for him.' Lotte was not alone for long; now she lives with an echt (real) German man who was fourteen years old when the war ended. 'Does it work?' I once asked her when we spoke on the phone. 'Yes!' she said. 'Tell me how,' I asked. Lotte seemed to know what I meant: 'We respect each other's heritage, I do my rituals and he does his.' 'But do you ever celebrate together?' 'Why complicate life?' was her final comment on the subject.

Lotte clarified how accommodating we all were in the Diaspora, as her new partner must have been, silenced as he most probably was by his country's ill-chosen direction. We are not yet what we read on the label of some honey pots: 'A blend of honeys from around the world specially selected to give a balanced flavour and a golden colour.' Isn't this the essence of what fashion does these days, defining a multi-coloured society? Nothing idealistic here, just a mix of outward appearances imaginatively and intoxicatingly presented, ignoring differences. We see Negroes with yellow hair, white people with dreadlocks, models clad like harem girls swishing up and down the catwalk – every possible ethnic influence inspirationally displayed. Could this really change our hearts and minds, or is it just about an elaborate seduction for making money? I wished there could be a real change of heart, not just air kisses fluttering around cheeks after fashion shows. Who knows?

Although talk of catwalks makes light of our differences, no two people have the same reaction to an experience. Lotte lived in the very thick of Nazi times, whereas I only skimmed over that cauldron of evil, and fortunate as that may have been, I still can't acknowledge who I am publicly. When will I say to the taxi driver 'To the synagogue,' or ask for a stamp to Israel at the post office without my heart banging, anticipating a look of disapproval from the person sitting behind toughened glass? Hitler's politics did a good job on me. So thoroughly has his ideology affected me, I long to topple the confidence of Jews who have defected to what I think is cloud-cuckoo land. I want to scratch that fragile jewel they think is their freedom and set it in the context of Jewish history. What do couples in mixed marriages talk about after they've made love? More often than not, each other's origins. Good or bad, these are their credentials, no matter what they think or pretend they've become. Getting 'lost' in mixed marriages, should we not know each other's backgrounds more thoroughly than we do, before we leap into what we imagine we choose out of liberal thinking, that bland no-man's land of cosy mobility? Mixed marriages are a lifetime's study to find out what we mind about, how deep or shallow our roots really are. I have never said 'I am proud to be Jewish', because it suggests latent shame and ignorance. I can't imagine my grandfather feeling pride: he was his beard - was his Peyot – was the kosher food he ate, was the commandments he honoured throughout his life that God was One.

Chapter Thirty-Seven

Acceptance

Old now, my reading is mostly connected to recent Jewish history and its related outcomes. Cannan has often said, 'Why don't you read for pleasure sometimes?' He knew what that meant after having read Martin Gilbert's Holocaust himself. I agreed with him; it isn't always a pleasure to read Jewish history, but reading about it gives me perspective. How did men and women in the street allow Nazi beliefs into their lives? How was Helmut persuaded that his Jewish neighbours were Untermenschen? And when he came face-to-face with my father in Dachau was it a flicker of shame that stopped him from beating him up?

Perhaps, meeting other refugees might help to console my wayward Jewishness. It was more painful than I allowed myself to know. Belonging to the Progressive synagogue made me understand the Hebrew words residing in Yiddish, and generally – be it for good or ill – to understand a little better that invisible God we have, cutting and pasting him into our history. How hard it is to understand His absence when He is needed.

It was my task to get hold of refugees who came, like me, to England before the war – most of them were not known in the Synagogue – but get them I did. Ten in all. One woman chose to sit next to me. While everyone else was talking about getting a coach trip to somewhere yet to be decided, the woman next to me gave me a nudge with her elbow and then her hand shelled so no one else could hear, she whispered in my ear, 'I have been through the camps.' After a self-served tea from my dining table. My home-made cakes were a success: lots of 'ums' and 'ahs'. Tea and cakes over, we went back to our own chairs again. And settled, the coach trip was considered more seriously. The woman next to me nudged me again and loudly she said into the room, 'Do you really think I want to sit here listening to this drivel about arranging a coach trip?' And having had her say, she got up and left without a word of apology. I didn't even get the chance to take her to the front door, so quickly did she get away. There was a lot of throat clearing after she'd gone. When I read Theo Richmond's book Kronin, I realized that the woman who rushed out of my house was an interviewee in his book. I had the impression that meeting us devalued her status as a witness.

Part of that gathering should have included another refugee, but when I invited her over the phone, she said, 'No, you come to me!' 'What, all of us?' 'Good God, no,' she said, 'just you, that would be nice!' I had never met her before and I supposed she wasn't up to going out. The next day was hot and sunny. Later that day, I strolled over to her flat in one of the many purpose-built blocks in Hove. She lived on the sixth floor. Long before I got to her front door, I smelled mothballs. When she opened the door, the smell of camphor was so strong I was sure she had bought up Woolworth's entire stock.

The moment we sat down, her face was set tight. 'What is there for us to unite about?' she said, disagreeably. 'That we have survived,' I suggested. She said nothing in reply and I imagined that she was too convinced, too emphatic and too old to face the past. The windows in her living room faced west, and the sun that day was very strong – so strong, even the Venetian blinds didn't block out the glare. Without any prompting from me, she gave me a blow-by-blow account of her journey to Auschwitz from Westerbork in Holland. I had, after all, come in the role of a refugee, and she could therefore dispense with small talk. Coming straight to the point, she said, 'Once we were squashed together in the cattle trucks, it didn't take long before we were de-civilized. *Die Stinkerei war schrecklich – entsetzlich,*' again, and again, '*entsetzlich…* women in smart hats crouched, relieving themselves where they stood, and urine trickled out from under men's trouser legs.' Still looking up at the light, she slowly moved her eyes in my direction, pulling me into the stench. Seeing that she had succeeded, she turned her head back to the blinds.

I looked round her room. On her shelves were a few books on the Holocaust and some sepia family pictures on a pretend mantle, a two-bar electric fire below. Who looked after the pictures when she was in Auschwitz, I wondered? Then turning back to me, her eyebrows raised, she said, 'Tea? I am going to make tea!' I followed her into the kitchen to help. 'No!' she said, firmly, letting the water run over the used cups, leaving the tea and her lipstick stains intact. I insisted on taking the tray to the living room and we sat down. Our cups tinkled on the saucers, but hers was now leaning to one side in the saucer, her forefinger and thumb tight round the handle of the cup, and almost empty, the remains of the tea came up to the rim about to dribble into her lap. I tried to take the cup from her hand, but she held on to it with an iron will, in much the way my mother held on to the front door key of their flat before she went to the Day Centre. That 'iron will'. I also read about of a camp survivor who reported, 'Lose your mug, and you lose your life.' Gently, I managed to disentangle the cup from her hands, and she went back to looking at the blinds, a soul lost in grief.

The next time I saw her, she was sitting alone in a café, thoroughly at home, her elbows resting on the table, her eyes looking about her, expectantly. Her appearance told of an elegant past. She was wearing a chic sleeveless dress, the fabric in a bold black and white design, and she seemingly didn't care that the flesh of her upper arms was hanging away from her bones. A headband made from the same fabric as her dress held together her fine hair. 'Hello!' I said. She looked up and through me. Perhaps she had gone the way of my mother, but then, how come she managed to get herself dressed as perfectly as, I assumed, in her past?

There is a certain helplessness we feel when listening to people's horror stories. 'Come, let us hold hands and sing some songs,' my cousin Carola had said. I believe singing helped to spirit away the things she had seen. I feared her pain because it is a terrorist, even second-hand. However sympathetic we are, we avoid involvement.

Now well and truly filled with horror stories I've been told and have read about in books, confirmed by images in the media showing atrocities meted out before and after the Jewish Holocaust at regular intervals around the world, I know that those who have lived through such horrors will, in the long-term, be alone with their pain. How many have the facility of the Pope who uttered instant forgiveness for the assassin who made an attempt on his life? Is his 'pardon' a tuning fork sounding out other souls?

Some of the most haunting pictures on the television screens in more recent times were when Yugoslavia was being torn apart: women and children in a field, abandoned in the pouring rain with no shelter, the camera scanning that scene, repeated on the 24-hour news for a day in the middle of our lives, unimaginable deeds, descriptions of mutilations, human beings in colourful robes wasting away before our eyes, the colours of the earth and the skeletons returning to it. The newsreader warns us that we may be upset by these images. How do we understand this concern for us? Is it so that we can go on pretending these events have nothing to do with us, that we can confidently buy the new car offered in the next commercial to ensure that the global economy flourishes? And when we are told that we suffer from horror fatigue, are we glad to know our responses are blunted? How else could we go on living? Are we not still full of illusions, imagining we have evolved and are just a hand's stretch away from perfection? When those pictures have lost their impact, do we feel baffled by our impotence, and are we not glad to throw the horrors back to where we are certain they belong – to the razzle dazzle of prehistory?

How readily people pointed their fingers at the Nazis after the war – it was they who did evil and it was they who said the Jews weren't people at all. Capitalism, Bolshevism – those were evil! And what of Pontius Pilate? – he just washed his hands. But what of modern Israel, that Goliath with a two-thousand-year-old grievance, in combat with the wrong people, and the 'wrong' people think that they are in combat with the 'right' people? And so the slithering and evasions continue. Why do men with guns in their hands shout, 'God is great!' and, thus praised, He helps them to irrigate continents with blood spilled from the sale of weapons. Between the rat-a-tat-tat of Kalashnikovs, gunmen smile for the camera, fire in their eyes as if they'd been to a good party. Like boys, they seem to be earnestly at play. Rocks, a pavement, a tank, a cart, a heap of bricks – all are stained with blood. Bit by bit, the camera moves close and then shies away again to avoid the goriest details, and, as always, pity trails behind.

I imagine a time when the whole world was perceived no further than the horizon, and dreamers under the stars saw the universe above and thought that God had pegged down the world like a tent; and before that, when man lived in caves seeking shelter from lightning and floods, and when boulders and fires crushed everything in their path; and even further back when fires under the sea had not yet spewed-up land and blown out caves like glass. Anyone who has stood in a field without shelter when lightning zigzags into the earth can surely see the time before electricity was named and creatures cowered together in clusters, not yet knowing a word for awe.

Instructed in science these days by television, we see cameras looking into volcanoes and fires under the sea and into our bodies, and as we watch we lose the wonder of myths spawned when imagination was alive and child-like, disturbing and frightening, when death was lifted to the realms of metaphysics. 'Death is not real,' the ancients said, 'You will wake up and live again but until you do, here are some pots of food and some tools, and jewels…'

Back in my kitchen, I make myself a refreshing mug of tea with safe water, and having enjoyed every last drop, I go out into a world perfectly adjusted to my needs. I lumber onto a bus and show my free pass, and seated I look out of the window and see people going about their business more or less peaceably; and good though that is, the polling station is the most enduring for me – that is where my gratitude lives on. Someone with a smiling face looks up at me, and then looks down on a list to find my name, and it is ticked off. Then sauntering over to a booth, I make my cross next to my selected candidate, and as I do it a rush of adrenaline goes through me, a sense of history under my feet. Out in the street, I am astonished that people are not breaking into song in celebration of the delicate balance upheld – our civil liberty.

Tea by the Sea

When the invasion of Europe started, one of its aims was to knock out V1 and V2 launching pads sited on the northern coast of France, the shortest distance from England. When that was achieved, England's home front was free from raids. Then, when the battle to liberate Europe from the Nazi scourge continued, I started to read reports of the uneven progress into Germany. When the Rhine was crossed, in and around the areas of Ludwigshafen, my hometown before the war, I was there every step of the way, looking for familiar faces and places in the newsreels and pictures in the papers of dispirited German civilians and soldiers, their arms held up in defeat, when only a short time ago they were raised in praise of the man who had now brought them low.

When the war had long been over, Brighton was awash with students who came to learn English, Germans among them. Walking on the seafront I heard them speak German together. Ever curious, I walked as near to them as I could to snatch what they were saying and what kind of dialect they spoke, drawn to hear more, not just to hear about the price of fares and lodgings. But why after so long did I expect them to alleviate my anger with debates on how their parents and their extended families coped, how and when they knew they'd been duped, the very moment they felt remorse? I longed to know, wishing I could talk about these things with them on the spot.

And then, something like it happened. I was having tea on Brighton seafront. A man about forty years old sat at the next table to me. He was bald on top and what hair he had left fell onto his shoulders. He was smoking a cigarette, exhaling towards the sea. A not-so-down-and-out asked him for a cigarette. 'Sure!' the bald man said expansively, his body leaning forward, the packet of cigarettes open for the man to help himself, and when he had, the bald man clicked open his lighter and put the flame to the cigarette between the not-so-down-and-out's lips.

I had a suspicion that the bald man was German, because the 'r' in 'sure' had that guttural sound a lot of Germans used when speaking English. 'What is your home town in Germany?' I asked. 'München Bayern,' he said directly. 'How long have you been in England?' 'A year or so.' 'I am from Ludwigshafen on the Rhine,' I declared. 'Oh really, and how long have you been in England?' 'Decades and decades,' and then more honestly I added, 'since 1939'. He threw me a sharp look and continued, 'I haven't been home for years, busy travelling the world earning my living on the way in plumbing and on building sites, all sorts of casual work.' 'A lot of people do that these days,' I suggested. 'No, that was not my reason for leaving home.' 'What then, what?' I asked.

'At the end of the war, I was eleven years old. And one day, looking for a toy, I found a shoebox full of photographs, and sorting through them I found one of my father standing on the edge of a pit full of corpses, a gun in his hand. Suddenly I understood the silences between my parents, and my father's drunkenness. As I grew older I knew what that picture meant and what it was about. And I grew silent. When I was sixteen and home from school one day, my father was sitting at our kitchen table, a bottle of brandy in front of him, half full. By suppertime, it was empty: slowly, he slid under the table and died. After his funeral, I left home. I have never been back – not even for my mother's funeral.'

The bald man and I had something in common.

First published in Great Britain by:

Ashgrove Publishing

an imprint of
Hollydata Publishers Ltd
27 John Street
London WC1N 2BX

ISBN 978 185398 174 6

First Edition

Printed and bound in England